Women in Contemporary Politics

Women in Contemporary Politics

Wendy Stokes

Polity

First published in 2005 by Polity Press

Polity Press
65 Bridge Street
Cambridge CB2 1UR, UK.

Polity Press
350 Main Street
Malden, MA 02148, USA

ISBN 0-7456-2498-7
ISBN 0-7456-2499-5 (pb)

A catalogue record for this book is available from the British Library.

Typeset in 10 on 12 pt Times
by SNP Best-set Typesetter Ltd, Hong Kong
Printed and bound in Great Britain by MPG Books Ltd, Bodmin Cornwall

The publisher has used its best endeavours to ensure that the URLs for external websites referred to in this book are correct and active at the time of going to press. However, the publisher has no responsibility for the websites and can make no guarantee that a site will remain live or that the content is or will remain appropriate.

For further information on Polity, visit our website: www.polity.co.uk

CONTENTS

LIST OF TABLES

ACKNOWLEDGEMENTS

Data doesn't hang around on websites waiting to be transferred to the pages of books like this: people go out and collect it. Having done so, they use it to construct and support theories, to write articles and books, and even to add to the sum of available information through websites. This book and I therefore owe a huge debt to all the people, primarily but not exclusively women, who have spent imagination, time and effort collecting and analysing the information about women in politics that is pulled together here. An even larger debt is owed to all the women who have broken paths and stormed bastions in order to achieve their goals, especially those who in so doing have made it a little easier for those who are following them.

One of the articles referred to below describes the difficulties of implementing the 33 per cent reserved seats for women policy in India's panchayats (local government). It describes how one woman, having been elected to a leadership position, found that the chair occupied by her predecessor had been removed: she was to sit on the floor as was the custom for women in her area; she was not to sit on a chair and get above herself. The woman refused to initiate proceedings until the chair was returned and, eventually, in the face of much ill will, she was successful, and the chair was reinstated. The small step of getting to sit on a chair was an achievement of breath-taking significance; each of the small steps described in the following chapters has been bought at great cost, but when they are put together, we can see how far we have come.

One last thing that has emerged as I have been writing this: all the people I have been following, the politicians and the researchers, have worked hard and made sacrifices – but they have also had fun. Women's entry into politics is revolutionary, but as Emma Goldman may have said, 'if I can't dance at it, it's not my revolution!'

The people who read the first draft of this book made valuable suggestions which I hope I have incorporated. Specific thanks are due to Valerie Bryson, Julia Buxton, Sarah Childs, Emma Clarence, Julian Clark, Juliet Landau-Pope, David Miller, Anne Phillips, Vicky Randall, Anne Showstack Sassoon, Debbie Williams, Louise Knight, Jean van Altena, Sarah Dancy and the staff at Polity, and, last but not least, all the members of the Women in Politics Specialist Group. Thanks also to the colleagues, family and friends who have put up with me as I bored for Britain on the finer points of the Ukrainian electoral system!

INTRODUCTION

To include women's concerns, to represent women in the public life of our society, might well lead to a profound redefinition of the nature of public life itself.

Diamond and Hartsock 1975: 721

With some accuracy the twentieth century has been referred to as 'the democratic century'. The notion of popular self-rule, held in contempt for hundreds of years, had become, by the end of the century, the only respectable way of legitimating government. In the course of the century, feudal traditions disappeared, empires dissolved, and newly independent peoples and states emerged, the vast majority of which defined themselves in terms of the popular will. This tidal wave of democracy was driven by a current of civic equality: equality of citizenship regardless of class, caste, religion, language, ethnicity and sex.

The twentieth century witnessed a sustained attack on systems of 'natural' hierarchy, privilege and dominance. Despite resistance and backlash, there is now a global language of equal value and respect, to which we all nod. Extensive lip-service notwithstanding, the issue of equality between men and women remains problematic in ways that no longer pertain (in most of the world) to equality between people from different religious, language or ethnic groups. This is to claim not that equality between such groups has been achieved, but that statements of natural inequality and discriminatory practices are regarded as indisputably wrong by majority opinion (even if they are tolerated). When it comes to men and women, the problem of 'nature' has not been so happily resolved. The 'naturalness' of gender characteristics, particularly those of women, is constantly used to legitimate practices and explain away situations.

If a group was made up of more-or-less equal proportions of two or more ethnic or religious groups, yet the governing body was hugely dominated by people from just one of the groups, this would generally be regarded as a scandal. Yet, when the same thing occurs, and the groups concerned are men and women, not only is there no outcry – in fact, quite the opposite: it is regarded as normal.

Whether we are talking about the government of a nation, the board of directors of a company, the trustees of a charity, the governing body of a university, or the judges of a film festival, the relative absence of women goes largely unremarked.[1] When attention is drawn to such a deficit, the response is along the lines of, either, there were no women with the appropriate training/background/qualifications, or no women put themselves forward. This is what Norris and Lovenduski have referred to as supply/demand-side explanations, and both rely on underlying notions of women's natural characteristics.

The first type of explanation assumes that certain characteristics are required for the job, that these are held only by people with a particular background, and that it is not the fault of those setting the criteria if only men ever seem to acquire that background. The second type of explanation recognizes that fewer women put themselves forward for the job than men, but assumes that this is because women are either uninterested, unable to fit the job into their pre-existing commitments, or unable to see themselves in this particular role. In either case, the resulting situation of unequal representation is seen not as a problem of the job description, or the limited vision of those making the appointments, but as a problem of gender: women either don't fit, or won't make the effort. Moreover, this is not deemed a stumbling block to the legitimacy of the whole project any more than it is regarded as discriminatory on the part of those making the appointments: it is just a natural outcome of natural difference.

The low number of women present on most decision-making bodies in the world is a scandal. It is a scandal now for exactly the same reason that the total exclusion of women from civil rights was deplored in eighteenth-century Europe by Mary Wollstonecraft: if democracy is defined by equal citizenship, then you cannot explain unequal outcomes in terms of 'natural' inequalities. When it comes to citizenship, there is no such thing: either we are all equal, or we don't have a democracy. In so far as we are different from each other – and we are different on a range of measures, including physical ability and amount of daily responsibility for other people – the institutions of democracy should accommodate us, rather than the reverse: because WE are the democracy, not the institutions that have been built to serve us.

This book exists to correct a deficit: the relative absence of discussion of women in politics textbooks. It owes its genesis to the imagination of the editors at Polity, the wisdom of Professor Anne Phillips, and the sloppy methodology of a certain group of writers. Anne Phillips used to run a course on women and politics at London Guildhall University. In the first week she set her students the task of finding in the politics texts that they had been using in their studies so far an example of research that was wrong or misleading because it either omitted all reference to women or assumed that women and men would behave in the same way. As Anne's teaching assistant, I found the textbook *Politics UK*.

Politics UK is in many ways an admirable book: it is clearly written, comprehensive in scope, and accurate in detail. It fails, however, to interrogate any differences in participation or citizenship between men and women. It makes the assumption that we are all equal citizens, and that any differences in outcome are the effect of individual differences between us as people, rather than structural differences in gendered citizenship. Therefore, in the discussion of poverty, it is 'people' who are poor, and the well-documented feminization of poverty is not referred to, let alone shown to be caused by gendered policy-making. The relatively low number of women in Parliament is noted as a fact, but not investigated as a failure of party and parliamentary democracy. Local councillors,

Members of the European Parliament, civil servants and so on are just that: our unsexed representatives.

Two questions arise: Does it matter that the literature overlooks this aspect of representation? And is this representational blip itself of any importance? My answer to both questions is an unequivocal yes. If we are concerned about democracy, an apparent anomaly in the area of representation demands investigation and comment. No taxation without representation was a key demand of the eighteenth century when modern democracy erupted, and arguments ever since have made it plain that representation means more than just being allowed to vote every four or five years: it means the real opportunity to participate actively in policy-making and implementation at all levels. Checking and criticizing the working of our democracies is the job of researchers in the field: we have been keen enough to tabulate the backgrounds of MPs and business people in order to demonstrate their privileged, elite characteristics, and to speculate on what this networking to the exclusion of the less privileged and working classes might mean; equivalent discussions of the exclusion of women have been the monopoly of feminist writers and texts.

Does the relative absence of women matter? Three dimensions in which it might matter spring to mind. First, equal opportunities: current thought about discrimination in employment is that if a significant section of the society is absent from any area, then there is a high probability that discrimination is taking place. While political office is not exactly a job, the same rule can be taken to apply. Second, best value: if significant sectors of the population are not being included in important areas of policy- and decision-making for reasons other than ability, it is possible that we as a community are not being served by the most talented of our citizens. Third, if distinct groups are absent from the political process, it is possible that their interests are not being served, or that their insights are not being included.

The first two of these considerations, equal opportunities and getting the best people, are arguments used generally in the promotion of equal access. The third is perhaps particular to the public sphere. Democratic politics is not like anything else. It is the sphere of complex human relations in which the good of each is balanced against the good of all in a multiplicity of decisions about ends and means. Good decisions depend on good input (as all data analysts know, GIGO: garbage in, garbage out). To make and successfully implement good policies, good information about lives, desires, values, beliefs, aspirations and behaviours is necessary. In order to have this, the whole population has to be involved in the process.

According to a limited view of democracy, the political process can (and should) be professionalized. Professional politicians governed by the rules of their institutions seek information, generate policies, and then put those policies up for the population to accept or reject through voting for one party or another at an election. Citizen input amounts to accepting or rejecting the options on offer. The broader view of democracy demands far higher levels of participation by as much of the citizenry as can bear it, in order both to make good policies and to encourage the development of democratic abilities in the population.

Either way, the quality of the input depends on who is included in the process, and it takes little imagination to see that the narrower the range of types of people, backgrounds and experiences included, the narrower the vision of the policies. In the UK there is an apocryphal story of a Minister for Transport who, when caught in a dispute about cost and quality of public transport in London, asked his secretary to book him a ticket on the Underground. Lack of direct experience can, of course, be compensated for. We are not, however, always aware of the things we *don't* know, especially if the knowledge we lack is linked to a set of experiences deriving from social or economic position.

Which is a long way of saying that we do not know whether it matters if women (or any other social group whose members share distinct characteristics among themselves and not with the wider population) are present or absent from politics. Having rarely had parity between men and women in politics, we cannot know whether it would be any different from what we have now. That being the case, we cannot assume that the present disproportion is not a problem.

This book attempts to plug one gap: the absence of information and discussion of women's political roles from the mainstream literature. In so doing, it aspires to play a small part in plugging the other gap: women's actual absences. By making this discussion part of the mainstream, it just might cause more of us to question what we take for granted and exert pressure for change.

Some Definitions

Feminist political theorists, women's movement activists, and researchers investigating women's lives have had a profound impact on the study of politics. They were instrumental in the extension of the discipline from its traditional focus on parliaments and parties to include more diverse and diffuse phenomena such as social movements and *ad hoc* local campaigns. More specifically, feminist scholarship insisted that 'the political' was an even broader category. Working from a critique of the public/private dichotomy, they argued that the content of the private world (particularly the family, social relationships, and the economy and workplace) was also politicized.[2]

As a result of this reassessment of the extent of politics, many books addressing the issue of women and politics work with a broad canvas, covering the family, work, women's movements, social policy and participation in formal politics. This book breaks with this pattern. The 'politics' of the title is politics narrowly conceived: parliaments and parties. It does this to meet a deficit: the standard texts used on politics courses do not pay enough (if any) attention to women, and the texts that are devoted to women are either very broad in scope, or quite specific (concerned only with women's participation in political parties in one country, for example).[3]

A second critique to emerge from feminist scholarship questions whether it is possible to use the term 'women' to describe a category of people that has any real consistency. After the initial surge of second-wave feminism in the 1960s, women settled down and started to examine themselves, the movements and each other. Fraught tensions and some bitter conflicts were revealed. These included (but were by no means limited to) those between classes, races, ethnicities and women from different parts of the world. Working-class women characterized feminism as middle-class; black women claimed it was essentially white in its concerns; women from less-developed and what were then Communist countries condemned its interests as a function of privilege; lesbians argued that it was heterosexist; mothers that it was matriphobic . . . From the sometimes ugly bickering, a sophisticated position evolved that attempts to encompass both shared and disparate concerns of women.

Having drawn attention to the critique of taking 'women' as a simple category, I now have to admit that this book has a tendency to do just that. I see this book as answering a very specific gap in the literature: as a text that pulls together information and research into the numbers of women in key political locations. Some aspects of differences among women are touched upon by virtue of the different countries and regions described, but I leave the reader to follow up the diversity of women's identities in the extensive, specialized literature that exists.[4]

Finally, something I had hoped to avoid. I am very resistant to pinning down the term 'feminism', but reluctantly admit that some sort of definition might be helpful here. When I was writing my Ph.D., my boyfriend's father used to engage me in intense discussions as to what *exactly* feminism was. In desperation I came up with a form of words anodyne enough to avoid an argument, but radical enough to save face. Over time, I have come to appreciate that hasty definition: feminism is about equality between women and men, to the benefit of both men and women; it is a critique of present inequalities that provides tools for analysis and generates programmes for change. Of course, this is pretty basic. Within feminism there are many different strands, and individual feminists privilege different values and strategies.

Feminism has given rise to more subcategories than any other political theory I can think of. Theorists and practitioners of socialism, conservatism and liberalism don't seem to need to constantly divide themselves up into subgroups, give themselves different names, and devote time and energy to defining their specificity – yet they probably have more internal differences than do feminists! Differentiation in the 1970s into liberal, radical and socialist feminism is well known; since then, more schools of feminism have blossomed, and I sometimes find students writing about a subsection that is little more than the creation of one particular writer. While this emphasis on definition can be annoying, and can lead to trivialization, it indicates just how seriously feminists take getting the detail right.

This book takes a very general approach to feminism: equality matters, getting the analysis of inequality right matters, and getting the right egalitarian mechanisms in place matters. Mary Wollstonecraft was right: domination is bad for both the dominating and the dominated parties. Neither women nor men are undifferentiated groups; the differences between human beings are tremendous. Yet it must be possible to achieve social, political and economic arrangements that permit both difference and equality among human beings without the strait-jacket of rigid gender categories providing order.

Outline

The following chapters take up each of the topics addressed in the usual politics textbooks and approach them from the perspective of women's participation. The book is arranged in six parts. Each part addresses an area of politics: political theory, voting and elections, political parties, parliaments and governments, sub-national politics, and women in international governmental organizations.

The book is based on the United Kingdom and its particular political, electoral and party system. This will be the starting place for the discussion, and not a bad place, since efforts to increase the number of female MPs have been at issue here for some years. While not strictly comparative, the discussion ranges over different countries and systems in order to get a sense of the variety of possibilities. Whenever discussions of women's participation arise, the case of the Nordic countries is introduced: five countries where there are significantly higher proportions of women in the parliaments and governments than elsewhere. These countries form part of the discussion, along with other European countries, the United States of America, Australia, New Zealand, India and other countries.

Part I sets the framework for the rest of the book, discussing the development of women's political activism and feminist engagement with political theory. Women did not suddenly leap into politics in the nineteenth century with fully-fledged demands for enfranchisement. Christine de Pisan was making a feminist case in sixteenth-century France, and women in pre-colonial Nigeria ran a parallel political system to that of men. In eighteenth- and nineteenth-century Europe women were engaged in revolutionary and philosophical movements as well as in local welfare systems, while women were active in Turkey and Egypt in the nineteenth century.

Feminist political thought has generated a comprehensive critique of politics – both the practice and the theory. From the eighteenth century, politics has been criticized for not living up to its own ideals. If all human beings possess reason, how can it be just to exclude women from the exercise of reason? If democracy is about equality, surely it is subverted by sexual inequality? Extensive feminist criticism of politics-as-usual has been accompanied by the creation of new and inclusive ways of constructing such fundamental political concepts as democracy, representation, citizenship, equality and justice. In the twentieth century feminist writers criticized the content of politics for its male bias, and attempted to formulate either a women's agenda or one that was truly gender-comprehensive. Analysts examined the practice of politics and attempted to understand how it excluded women, as well as creating and promoting policies that would increase women's political presence. Here we discuss feminist analyses of democracy and representation, as well as the notion of 'critical mass', and compare the theories to some political practice.

Part II addresses voting and elections. Voting is the most basic of political activities. Women in industrialized countries (with some notable exceptions) had achieved the vote on equal terms with men by the end of the 1920s. Since then, women around the world have been enfranchised as a result of liberation struggles and revolutions. The vote itself varies in value: elections result in major changes in some countries, while in others, such as Burma and Algeria, they are overridden by the ruling group. Women still cannot vote in a few countries, and in many places their votes, like those of the men, count for little. However, the relatively recent phenomenon of the female vote has been the subject of much discussion and research. The enfranchisement of women was dismissed by some, who assumed that they would vote the way that their men told them, and was a cause for concern among others, who feared that women would prove to be a conservative force.

While there may be some evidence of minor occurrences of both these possibilities, of more interest recently has been investigation of the growth of gender gaps. In some times and places women vote differently from men. This has been particularly the case in the USA, as women voted in larger numbers for the Democratic Party; but similar phenomena, cross-cut with patterns of age and class, can sometimes be seen in a range of countries. Differences in voting behaviour can be looked at from two perspectives: that of party loyalty and that of issues. The questions arise whether some parties are more appealing to women, and whether this is connected to a specific women's agenda of issues and policies.

Voting translates into elections. In order to stand in an election, a woman has to become a candidate. In most countries, most of the time, candidature is a function of political parties. One way or another, parties hold the key to who becomes a candidate and, up to a point, who gets elected. Despite enfranchisement, large numbers of women have not figured in elected assemblies until quite recently. Attempts to explain this look at such variables as how long women have had the vote, women's access to education, the economy and professional positions, and cultural factors such as religion and family patterns. While some correlation is found, political factors appear to be much stronger determinants of women's active participation. Such variables as electoral systems, party practices and electoral legislation correlate more strongly than social variables. For many years there was a convenient myth that voters did not vote for women candidates. This has been largely disproved, yet parties in many countries still show a reluctance (in practice) to select women as candidates for seats that they have any chance of winning. Radical measures have been proposed to overcome this, which are discussed next.

Quotas for women are contentious. The arguments for and against quotas are discussed here, before looking at the range of different strategies that fall under the broad heading of 'quotas'. This includes the all-women short lists used by the Labour Party in the United Kingdom for the 1997 general election, as well as the French innovation of parity, and the more usual system of setting aside for women either places on a party list or seats in an assembly. The creation of some sort of quota system is by far the most effective way to improve the balance of men and women in elected assemblies, but it is never without problems.

Part III focuses on political parties, and investigates the specifics of women's partisanship. While women and men vote in more or less equal proportions, that ratio tends to diminish along the road of party involvement. Membership of political parties is a minority characteristic in any population, and one that, despite national and party variations, tends to be slightly more male than female. When we look up the party hierarchy to the officers who run the parties and the people who are selected as candidates for elected office, we note an increasing masculinity, which becomes almost overwhelming at the level of leadership. Here the exceptional example of the Nordic states poses a counter to the norm, while the quota systems being adopted in a surprising number of countries are forcing through changes. Of particular interest here is how parties select candidates for election, and how well women fare in such processes.

The discussion of parties in Part III is broken up into four chapters. The first is a general introduction to political parties and elected systems. This is followed by a discussion of women in political parties in the United Kingdom. The UK is usually thought of as having a two-party system, but this is an over-simplification. The UK comprises England, Scotland, Wales and Northern Ireland. Although there are two dominant parties in England and in the national parliament, the Labour and Conservative parties, there is a third party of increasing relevance, the Liberal Democrats. Perhaps of even greater significance, there are local nationalist parties in Scotland and Wales: the Scottish Nationalist Party and Plaid Cymru. Moreover, Northern Ireland has a completely different set of parties, including Sinn Féin, the Social Democratic and Labour Party (SDLP), the

Ulster Unionist Party, the Democratic Unionist Party, the Alliance, and the Northern Ireland Women's Coalition. The next chapter moves out of the UK and looks at women in the parties of a range of countries, including the Republic of Ireland, the Nordic countries, Russia, the United States and Australia.

Finally, we look at the political oddity of women's parties. There are considerably more women's parties around the world than I had expected to find when I started my research for this book. The Icelandic and Irish parties are familiar ground, but it came as some surprise to discover those in Russia, Belorussia, the Ukraine, Armenia, Lithuania, Kyrgizstan, Slovenia, Serbia, the Netherlands, Greece, Australia, Israel and the Philippines. Although for the most part these are radical, feminist parties (but not radical-feminist), some of the parties take a conservative and traditional approach to women's roles, and it is these which they seek to promote. Present-day women's parties are not trying to get the vote for women, or even basic equalities legislation: these measures are already in place in the countries where women's parties have appeared. Rather, the parties emerge when the political system fails to deliver on its promises with regard to women's participation in elected office and policy-making. The parties appear to be a very specific strategy that is taken up only in certain countries where there is a history of women's autonomous organization.

Part IV is concerned with women's roles and achievements in parliaments and governments. According to United Nations statistics, by the year 2000 only twenty-two countries had ever elected a woman prime minister, and only three countries had done so more than once. Sixteen countries had elected women as president, but only one had done so twice. Meanwhile, the proportion of women in parliaments ranges from about half to none, averaging out at around 10 per cent. In most countries it is not being elected to parliament that matters so much as being elected as part of the governing party, and then being given some sort of cabinet office or committee responsibility. Women make up a relatively small proportion of cabinet members in most countries, and often have low-status portfolios, but this is slowly changing.

Of course, central government is only one political arena, hence the last two parts of the book look at sub-national and supra-national government. Much of politics happens at sub-national level, which is the topic of Part V. The nature of relations between central and local government varies, depending on whether the state in question is unitary or federal. The UK is in the interesting position of being an 'incomplete federation'. Since the devolution of Scotland, Wales and Northern Ireland, it now has regional assemblies with some degree of autonomy in three of its four constituent nations, as well as central government and traditional local government.

Both federal and unitary systems are prone to tensions over jurisdiction between the centre and the periphery. Parties may not operate coherently between the two domains, and the roles of politicians may differ and even clash. In general, women are to be found in higher proportions in local than central government. In the UK there has been a strong tradition of women's participation in local government. This is in part due to pre-enfranchisement, pre-welfare state traditions of female voluntarism, and in part to women's earlier enfranchisement at this level: women could vote and run for office locally some fifty years before they could do the same thing in national elections.

The roles of local representatives are themselves interesting and changing. It is often argued that the issues addressed at local level are of greater direct appeal to women because they are more closely linked to the home. Further, participation in local government is less likely to cause major domestic disruption than going to the capital to serve in central government. It is interesting to note that initiatives to increase women's participation in local government do not run up against as many impediments as those directed at national government. International governmental and non-governmental organizations have been important in the encouragement of women's participation at this level, where it is thought to be an indicator both of democracy and of development. Moreover, local authorities around the world have been co-operating with each other and exchanging ideas since early in the twentieth century.

Part VI moves beyond the nation-state to examine the two largest international governmental organizations (IGOs): the European Union and the United Nations. These organizations have proved themselves to be of considerable importance in promoting sex equality through legislation and international programmes. Policies and agreements deriving from these organizations (and other IGOs) are particularly influential in less developed countries, where adopting policies promoted by IGOs may be part of a strategy to attract aid. However, they are also relevant in more developed countries, where organizations and activists may deploy agreements such as CEDAW (the International Convention for the Elimination of All Forms of Discrimination Against Women) to demand change.

In the countries of the European Union, equalities legislation coming from the centre has overridden local practices and provided a final court of appeal for women and members of other groups who consider themselves unfairly treated by domestic law. Here we assess the presence of women in the European Parliament and the activities of the different sex equality bodies within the EU. Unlike previous chapters, in this part we look at institutions, legislation and policy, since these have international impact. We then move on to the United Nations. The presence of women among delegates to the General Assembly is examined, but, more importantly, this final chapter looks at the evolution of sex equality bodies, policies and conventions in the UN. It looks in particular at CEDAW and the series of international conferences on women that have established new international agendas for sex equality.

PART I

Feminist Political Theory

FEMINIST THEORY AND WOMEN'S POLITICAL ACTIVISM

1

Introduction

This chapter gives the background of developments in feminist political theory which have fed the criticism of women's exclusion from politics and which shape the demands for greater inclusion. It summarizes feminist criticism of the theory and practice of democracy, the creation of alternative conceptions of democracy, and the evolution of a feminist approach to political representation. The theoretical work described here underpins the argument to be found throughout this book: that women's absence is a democratic deficit which requires action.

If it were not for widely held beliefs about democracy and political representation, it would be a lot more difficult to construct the absence of women from politics as a problem than it is now. We cheerfully plagiarize Abraham Lincoln to claim that democracy is government of the people, by the people, for the people – and that this is an unequivocally good thing. More than that, it is the only good thing when it comes to organizing government.

The discussion of women in politics in this book presupposes a rather loose agreement that democracy as self-government is a legitimate goal, and one that we should be continually trying to improve on. It accepts that self-government through representatives is not an easy thing, but a necessary one if we are to have anything like a fair and well-ordered society. It recognizes that self-government of a diverse community entails inclusion of that diversity, however inconvenient that might be.

Theory is our attempt to make sense of the teeming confusion of human experience. We theorize to understand what is going on and, once we have understood, we theorize again to try and find ways to make things better. This chapter is an attempt to understand through political theory why women's absence from politics matters, and why we should do whatever we can to get as many women as men active in politics.

Women, Feminism and Political Theory

Women's political participation is not always – and certainly not only – a feminist concern. Women's access to the vote and membership of political organizations and assemblies can be constructed simply as egalitarian concerns, and there have always been plenty of politically engaged women with little if any notion of feminism. However, with some notable exceptions, interest, research, theory and activism regarding women's participation have been motivated by feminism, rather than by any disinterested conception of equality.

While concern with sex equality and women's rights can be traced back for centuries, and feminism itself can be dated to the seventeenth century (Mitchell 1976), explicit interest in either getting women into political office or theorizing about what it might signify once they were there is relatively recent. Such writers as Mary Astell and Mary Wollstonecraft used current political arguments to claim women's rights to freedom and equality, but even Wollstonecraft did not spend much time thinking about political equality. She died before fulfilling her 'threat' to write a book proposing women's political participation. For a discussion of women as politicians we have little more than Plato's philosopher queens; but, as every feminist critic has pointed out, these androgynous rulers illustrate the problems of including women in politics rather than offer a model (Coole 1988; Okin 1980).

Suffrage movements around the world focused on getting the vote for women. The potential of running for office came with this, and around the world some women made use of this right, but the emphasis was on shaping governments and influencing policy through political parties and voting, rather than on getting women into parliament. However, running through suffrage movements were different currents of belief about women's political natures. While enfranchisement was largely presented as an egalitarian claim, claims were also made on the basis of women's moral natures and the beneficial influence these would have on politics. Some groups went so far as to claim women's moral superiority. According to Sheila Rowbotham, while for many the vote 'became the focus of many hopes of economic and social reform, which required alliances with men', the Women's Social and Political Union (WSPU) 'came increasingly to regard men and women as irreconcilable' (Rowbotham 1992: 168).

The Second World War changed democratic politics irrevocably. After 1945 there could be no turning back from egalitarian, inclusive, redistributive policies. Experience now tells us that democracy is a Pandora's box: once opened, there is no telling what will emerge, and there is no way to cram all the disputatious escapees back in the box. Post-war theorists of democracy presented arguments for democratic bureaucracy with minimal popular participation. Preoccupied with stability and keeping mass mobilization at bay, they posited a peaceful politics of professional competence legitimated by regular elections.[1] This vision of order was rejected by the children of the war. In the 1960s the industrialized world was disrupted by a whole new set of political demands and movements. These new, post-materialist, demands grew out of the conditions of the post-war world, and the movements grew out of a deep dissatisfaction with elite-dominated politics.[2]

Only once adult suffrage had bedded in, and the language of democratic equality had become normalized, did an interest in what women did in politics emerge, albeit via a tortuous route. Twin strands of largely unexamined opinion characterized the nondiscussion of women's politics: on the one hand, women were different from men by virtue of their sex/gender roles, and therefore their interests were not relevant to politics; on the other, their interests and activities were no different from men's, and therefore did not warrant attention. The women's movement of the 1960s and thereafter changed that, even though participation in formal politics arrived rather late on the agenda.

Like other movements of the time, the women's movement was grounded in a rejection of institutional politics. Its targets were the individual consciousness and society. Governments were at best irrelevant, and at worst the enemy. Women's movements in different countries adopted a range of goals and strategies, but, for the most part, these were extra-parliamentary. Government was targeted for policy change, but did not become a target itself until the 1970s. From the 1970s on there developed what might be termed second-wave suffragism, or third-wave feminism: an international, loosely aligned movement to get more women into elected assemblies.

This movement is grounded in both feminism and earlier arguments for political inclusion (Breitenbach and Mackay 2001b: 3). It shares common ground with demands for the inclusion of working-class people and people from different language groups, religions, regions, ethnicities and so on. It is also shaped by the extensive theoretical discussions of both gender and democracy that evolved in the second half of the twentieth century.

Gender and Democracy

Democracy was the great organizing concept of the twentieth century, hence the huge literature and the insistence of politicians from every corner of the political playground that their system was democratic. The most common interpretation of democracy, the one that dominates political practice, is democracy as a way to deliver a legitimate government. The vote we record every few years selects a government and thus amounts to self-government (Schumpeter 1966).

From an alternative point of view, democracy has intrinsic value as well as instrumental function. From this perspective, 'democratic procedures are superior to all other types of decision-making because they offer citizens the right to judge (and to reconsider their judgements about) the quality of these results' (Keane 1988: 26). If we adopt this deeper conception of democracy, it is more than a way of selecting a government. It is an integral part of the daily lives of people who live in a community they want to call democratic (Burnheim 1985; Green 1985: Pateman 1970).

These are two ways of thinking about democracy which actually have very little in common: democracy as choice of how to be governed, and democracy as participation and civic development. Although early formulations of democracy emphasized participation and citizenship, these were overtaken by the more practical application of representation in modern, mass societies. Disillusion with a politics that shared more with the history of elite rule than it did with the promise of democracy led theorists and activists in the second half of the twentieth century to question why it was failing to deliver. This took them back to the parallel history of participatory theory and grass-roots movements: the Greek *polis*, the Roman republic, the Diggers, the Chartists, the Owenites.

The critical take on democracy partnered the social movements of the period: peace, civil rights and anti-racist, women's, green, gay and lesbian, and, more recently, disability and anti-capitalist. While the movements emphasized participation and action, the theorists analysed past and present failures. A fundamental problem of practical democracy is that it continually slices up populations into those who count and those who don't: who is a member and who isn't, who can make use of the benefits of membership and who can't.

Feminist investigations of democracy have been particularly illuminating here, because they brought the private/public dichotomy to the fore. Recognizing the centrality of democracy to twentieth-century politics, feminist political theorists tried to understand why the theory and practice of democracy – which was all about equality and participation – could get along quite nicely with inequality between men and women, and women's exclusion from participation. Feminist reflections on democracy led to investigations of representation, and to difficult questions about the nature of the political interests that are brought into play in democracy. Such conclusions as it has been possible to reach about democracy, political interests and representation have been marshalled into an argument for the inclusion of women in politics on equal terms – and in equal numbers – to men. But more than this, they have led to fundamental questions being asked about the character of the political practices and concepts that have been so taken for granted.[3]

Feminism and democracy

Most feminist critics do not dismiss democracy, but approach it warily, alert to all the ways in which it has been used to consolidate privilege and exclude difference. Consequently, feminists have tended to favour versions of democracy which have a strong participatory component and which are not confined to the political sphere, but take account of the interdependency of the public and the private. When feminist writers support democracy, they do so critically. The hard-line critique would go something like this: the problem of women's second-class citizenship is due not to any weaknesses in the realization of democracy, but to the very nature of democracy itself.[4]

From this perspective, the history of democratic citizenship as a device for excluding those who do not fulfil the criteria of membership is integral to the nature of democracy. Democracy is a means of defining who is and who is not a citizen, and of allocating the rights and duties of citizenship. The criteria of citizenship, and the content of rights and duties, were determined long ago in keeping with the shape of a male life – husband, father, protector – and a male of the property-owning classes at that (Pateman 1988; Mendus 1992; Lister 1997). Little has changed, because little can change. There are 'male' concerns and ways of doing things, which constitute the public domain, where democracy holds sway, and 'female' concerns and modes, which constitute the private part of the world. Like the entwined symbols of yin and yang, the male and female, public and private, domains determine and depend upon each other.

Within this critique it is possible to identify two strands of critical feminist accounts of democracy. According to one, democracy assumed and required a high degree of homogeneity and could not tolerate difference amongst citizens, including distinctions of gender. Thus women could be citizens of a gender-neutral polity as long as their lives conformed to a male pattern; but once issues of care and childbirth intruded, they were excluded from equal membership. The other identified democracy with political goals rooted in individual self-interest, practices built on competition, and conduct reliant on bureaucracy and objectivity. Since these individual characteristics were those ascribed to the male, feminist critiques uncovered a conundrum: democracy was both gender-neutral and inherently male-focused (see Phillips 1999).

In attempting to address this, three possible strategies have emerged. The first presents a politics grounded in connection, inclusion and subjectivity; values usually ascribed to the female and family, or private, domain.[5] The second proposes the political participation of women as a cohesive group with particular interests as a corrective to the false neutrality of masculine politics.[6] The third suggests that gender-neutrality, if generously interpreted, could correct the ways in which democratic citizenship is shaped around norms of male biology. Deborah Rhode argues persuasively for gender-neutral legislation to improve women's equality (Rhode 1989, 1990, 1992). Let us take the example of maternity leave. In the USA it has been customary not to make any allowance for pregnancy in employment and career development, because men do not get pregnant; a generous interpretation of gender-neutrality would provide for everyone to have career breaks for pregnancy, childbirth and caring responsibilities.

The first of these is an interesting, revolutionary, but fairly minority approach. It is a very useful counter to theories of international relations, where the starting point is innate human aggression and the inevitability of conflict; but as a complete theory it runs up against problems (see Dietz 1985 for a good discussion of this). The second approach is also radical, although possibly less so, and less exclusively associated with feminists and the representation of women. It suggests the explicit inclusion of representatives from groups marginalized within the population in order to ensure the inclusion of the interests of such groups. The approach is most commonly associated with Iris Marion Young and Anne Phillips's discussions of Young's work. The third approach given here, that of interpreting gender-neutrality differently, is rather unusual, but has, I think, potential as a way around some of the equality/difference problems.

The difference/equality debate refers to a set of concerns about how to balance the good of women and men that plagued feminist discussions of equality and inclusion for some years. Disagreement arises over what is usually characterized as privileging difference or equality: the inclusion of women and women's interests on an equal footing with men, or the inclusion of women and their interests as different and demanding of specific attention (Bock and James 1992; Phillips 1993).

Feminist critics diverge over equality or difference-based approaches, some favouring gender-neutrality as a route to equality, while others are optimistic about an explicitly sexually differentiated democracy. Anne Phillips suggests that this divergence 'is perhaps best understood as a disagreement about how much difference has to be recognised in order to promote the kind of democracy where citizens can engage on matters of shared importance' (Phillips 1999: 515).

The limits of participation

Reaction against the modern democratic reality of elite rule with popular consent posed increased participation and devolution of power as the preferred alternative. However, there were problems here too. Reliance on participation and devolution can work only if the participants already regard each other as equals. If they are held back by economic and status differences, and if some members are overawed by others, hierarchy and elites re-emerge. This was observed in the women's movement and commented on by Jo Freeman in *The Tyranny of Structurelessness* (1982).

Faith in participatory democracy tends to assume that there is enough shared understanding to permit agreement on shared goals and tolerance of a degree of difference. Moreover, increasing participation even minimally gives rise to problems of organization. While pointing out the real shortcomings of glamorizing participation, Norberto Bobbio suggests that a degree of balance can be achieved through a mixed system, in which certain concerns are resolved through collective decision-making, while strategic areas are dealt with by representatives and experts (Bobbio 1989: 26).

Out of the criticisms of representative democracy, renewed interest in its possibilities has arisen. A modern democracy must somehow combine the insights and civic virtue of participation with the practicality of representation and the expertise of specialists.[7] De Tocqueville's point that democratic liberty might not accomplish all its projects with the skill of an adroit despotism, but that in the end it produces more than any absolute government, still applies.

Gender and Representation

The renewed interest in representative democracy drew attention to two under-analysed aspects of representation: first, the question of what is represented, and second, the question of whether it matters who our representatives are. Discussions of political representation are generally concerned with two goals: the representation of interests and the representation of people. These two often become confused. There is a tendency to blur any distinction, perhaps assuming that they are identical. Interests and people are, in fact, distinct in important ways.

If the inclusion of interests and of people are separated out, some of the problems of contemporary democracy become clearer. While there can be little argument now that the significant interests of different sections of a polity should all be encompassed, the idea that a political assembly might be selected according to anything other than the representation of ideas or policies, by whichever people want to be politicians, is difficult. Yet there is a common assumption that the diversity of a population should, somehow, be 'represented' in a parliament. As a recent study of political recruitment asked, as long as the processes by which people are selected and elected are fair and open, does it matter who ends up representing the rest of us? (Norris and Lovenduski 1995)

Political interests

Traditionally, an interest is connected to a geographical area, a class, a religious group or some other clearly definable demographic. It is assumed that shared interest is known and acknowledged, or can at least be discovered, and that competition of interests forms a reasonable basis for parties, elections and government. Problems with the representation of interests arise when an interest is too dispersed amongst the population or too hard to articulate to be part of a political programme, and particularly when an interest is defined by membership of a marginalized, powerless group.

The tradition of political practice assumes that interests, the groups to which they belong, and their political representation are clearly defined. Yet experience tells us that this is not the case. Once the focus shifts away from the sorts of general interests where differences of opinion can be regarded as matters of 'taste' or 'preference', it moves to issues where opinion is somehow inscribed upon the bearer – where bodies are political, and where identity is implicated in opinion. This is most clearly the case with issues around gender, race, disability or sexuality.

Much of the writing about women and minority groups, and much of the political practice which has been instituted on their behalf, has assumed that they possess a recognizable, agreed-upon set of concerns which constitute an interest.[8] While this raises interesting possibilities, it also gives rise to questions about the nature of groups and the extent of shared interest. All groups are not the same, and although there may be a common ground of marginalization or subordination, the extent of internal cohesion is likely to vary. Native peoples – for example, the native Canadians who feature in Will Kymlicka's work – may possess a higher degree of common interest and internal cohesion than, for example, African Americans, whose shared experiences are cross-cut by class, education and region.[9] Nevertheless, the insight that our interests are not entirely a matter of individual preference, but are, at least in part and for some of us, shaped by group membership, is valuable (I. M. Young 1990; Phillips 1995).

Within groups whose members appear to share common defining characteristics, schisms are likely to occur over the nature of identity, the determination of goals, and the direction of policy most likely to achieve those goals. The closer the political interest is to individual identity, the more likely it is that different opinions will emerge and generate conflict. We can agree to differ and reach compromises over issues outside ourselves, and we can respect other people's points of view when we realize that our own understanding cannot be absolute. However, when we ourselves are the subject of politics, we can believe our understanding and our right to be absolute. Every woman is an expert on being a woman; yet each woman's experience of gender is unique. Thus, within what might appear to be a community of common interest, schisms exist between different and even competing interests. Women differ radically from each other in terms of who they are and what they want, and are often unequal when judged in terms of economic, educational, status and class criteria.

This brings the discussion to the specific issue of the representation of women. It is sometimes taken for granted that women have specific interests that require representation.[10] There are two problems with this: the presumption that one group is associated with an interest to the exclusion of other people, and the belief that women make up a unified group who share an interest. Women certainly share a biological potential for giving birth, but even that commonality is mediated by other differences. Some women have greater control over their fertility than others, and some women can have children while continuing to lead independent lives, while others cannot. Women tend to have less access to economic resources than men, but some women are much better off than other women and some men. Women tend to be vulnerable to male power and violence, but some women are more vulnerable than others. Women are unquestionably linked by shared aspects of sex, gender and experience, but they are also divided by many factors. Emphasis on the way in which some interests derive from group membership is an important counter to the emphasis on individuated interest prominent in liberal politics, but group membership itself is not simple (I. M. Young 1990; Phillips 1995).

The interests possessed by women are usually taken to include issues of maternity, child care, safety, and women's access to employment and pay on equal terms that do not punish them for parenthood (Lister 1995). They may include emphasis on a different approach to politics and the broader society, which is more consensual, less aggressive, more oriented towards problem solving. While there is no doubt that women in general have an investment in these issues, there is a danger to both women and the broader society if women adopt for themselves, *de jure* as well as *de facto*, responsibility for reproduction, nurturing and gender equality as their political identity.

It is fair to say that these issues are the concern of all citizens, although women have a particular perspective on them, because they continue to shoulder their weight disproportionately. If this is the case, the contention that only women can represent women's interests is problematic. If women's interests are constituted as a matrix of issues that are exclusively women's concern, support is given to the misconception that children, women's economic position, and safety are not the responsibility and concern of men as well. Women may be most likely to perceive the need to introduce new issues that particularly concern women, and be able to understand and express the experience of certain issues, but there are pitfalls to discouraging men from engagement in a process of recognizing and promoting such interests. This is a very real dilemma, which women in politics constantly face: only women will raise such issues and work for them, because only women perceive themselves as directly affected by them; but in so doing, they risk perpetuating the belief that these are women's issues alone, and contributing to the political marginalization of both women and the issues (see Mansbridge 1999 for an interesting discussion).

It could therefore be argued that women share not so much a set of political interests, but more a set of perspectives on widely held political interests. This is to draw a distinction between an interest and a perspective. The concept of political interest grows out of the needs, demands or beliefs shared by a body of voters, which shape their political responses across the spectrum and can be translated into a political programme. A political perspective, on the other hand, is less a political programme than a shifting set of priorities which are brought to bear upon particular issues (Stokes 1998).

A perspective, in this respect, constitutes a critique of existing political and social agendas, adding, subtracting and re-focusing items. It has an agenda, but not one that is particularly well suited to form the basis of a political party.

Two points emerge from the foregoing discussion. First, accounts of politics as the competition of interests fail to take account of interests that cannot be translated comfortably into the political programme of a cohesive section of the polity. Second, some political interests are determined less by preference than by identification with, or membership of, a group, particularly a group which is somehow marginalized and lacking in power. When this is the case, the identity of representatives appears to be of particular significance.

Who represents?

The discussion up to this point suggests that the question of who representatives are might be relevant to the content of politics. However, a common criticism of government is that it is 'unrepresentative', meaning that the members are not drawn from across the social spectrum, but all derive from a fairly narrow sector.

The tradition of representation in liberal democracies is grounded in the belief that a representative is able to act on behalf of all the people and interests of the constituency. As the discussion above has suggested, if the content of politics is shaped by the knowledge of participants, and if some areas of knowledge are specific to some groups of people, it is important that representatives are drawn from across the spectrum of the population. In such cases, a more directed strategy for selection might be required than the assumption that if there is equal access to the assembly, then members of all the different, significant sections of the society will naturally find their way there.

An intuitively appealing conception is that of a parliament that is a microcosm of the population. As such, it could act on behalf of the entire population as if it were that population, because all shades of opinion and all the population's varied and competing interests would be present and articulated. The members of such bodies would not be there because of their ambition or because of party strength, but would have been selected on account of their possession of significant characteristics. They could be selected by lot from amongst a number of suitable and willing volunteers, and they could regularly rotate in and out of office (Burnheim 1985). This conception of representation as mirroring is flawed, because it elides interests and bodies, but it has an intuitive appeal.

An approach that shares something of the mirroring function is what Anne Phillips has called a 'politics of presence'. According to this, when an issue is linked very strongly to a particular section of the society, as pregnancy and childbirth are to women, anti-Semitism to Jews, and prejudice and the legacy of colonialism and slavery to people of colour, then members of that section should be present to bring their perspective to bear (Phillips 1991, 1995, 1998). This would ensure that access to all decision-making bodies was open to the population, and would provide suitable procedures to promote the participation of particular groups, including outreach, training and quotas.

The Meaning of Presence

Feminist theory, perhaps more than any other, is intimately connected to political realities. Theory has been driven by activism, and activism has in turn inspired theory. Theoretical interest in participatory democracy reflected and supported women's movements as social movements, outside formal politics. The theoretical shift towards representation paralleled the movement of women informed by feminism into political parties and parliaments – what Alice Brown has called 'third-wave feminism'. This is not to say that all women who attempted to enter politics from the 1970s on were feminists (although they cannot help but have had their approach to life informed by feminism), but just to point out a symmetry, or synergy, between theory and practice.

Attempts to theorize both the importance of women's participation and the obstacles encountered followed. The politics of presence has been very influential, along with arguments grounded in social justice and equality.

Writers have applied Anne Phillips's notion of presence to their studies of women in politics. Marian Sawer, for example, in elaborating arguments for increasing the numbers of women in the Australian Parliament, refers to justice; utility; the symbolic, representation of values, perspectives and experiences; and the representation of interests as different grounds for women's political presence (Sawer 2002). Sarah Childs, in discussing the UK, refers to justice, symbolic, style and substantive arguments (Childs 2004a).

The justice argument is the least controversial. This is the simple claim that women have an equal right alongside men to participate in public life. This is inscribed in Article 25 of the International Covenant on Civil and Political Rights and Article 7 of the Convention on the Elimination of All Forms of Discrimination against Women (CEDAW). As Sawer points out, justice does not rely on women representing women, or on women making a difference in public life. It simply assumes that ability is not the prerogative of one sex, and that the absence of women is a result of discrimination, whether direct or indirect (Sawer 2002: 5).

Symbolic arguments claim that the presence of women in parliament is, on the one hand, important for the status of women generally and, on the other, enhances the legitimacy of parliament (Childs 2004a). Sawer adds to these the more complex notion that the presence of women in parliament provides options with regard to the performance of gender: that being female entails choices other than domesticity and wife/mother identities (Sawer 2002: 6).

What Childs calls the substantive argument captures both of Sawer's representation arguments. This is the most contested, and yet the most interesting to many theorists, of the arguments for women's presence. It links women's physical presence (literally, their embodied experience of gender) to their activities as politicians and their ability to act for women in the community. In this argument, female politicians' experience of being women will incline them to make different choices from men, and to be able to identify and then act on behalf of women and/or women's interests.

The style argument that Childs defines is the contention that women possess a different way of doing things, reflective of sex and gender. These might be traditional, or feminist, conceptions of sex and gender; but, either way, the result is a more consensual and less confrontational approach – what Carol Gilligan (1982) refers to as women's 'different voice'.

Finally, Sawer refers to a utility argument. Here she picks up on something that is common enough, but often overlooked: politicians may seize on the idea of increasing women's presence as a means of pursuing a larger agenda. She points out that the inclusion of 'women can provide a "new look" for parties beset by scandal or associated with harsh economic policies' (Sawer 2002: 6), or can be an attempt to woo women voters, to bolster a failing constituency.

Thus feminist political theory provides a framework within which to argue for the necessity of the presence of women among elected representatives, by unpicking the meaning of 'presence'.

More radical arguments using the framework of maternal thinking and/or eco-feminism have been powerfully influential at the margins. More appealing to people in movement politics than the mainstream, these approaches have none the less raised questions for political analysts, questions revolving around a central challenge: whether women in politics alter priorities and processes.

So, feminist debates around democracy have shifted from a critique of democratic theory and practice, through an analysis of participation, to a reconsideration of representation. The theory and practice of representation have been assessed from feminist perspectives, in order to discover whether having more female representatives would alter politics in women's favour and, if so, how such a process might work. By and large, the jury is still out on this. In the vast majority of countries women's entry into parliament is in its early stages. Those few countries where women are elected in large proportions, however, show some interesting developments.

Critical Mass

It only becomes possible to ask questions about the impact of women on politics – let alone answer them – once there are enough women to pose the possibility of change. But how many is enough? We know that the entry of small numbers of women, the 2–5 per cent common to industrialized countries prior to the 1970s, does not alter politics. For the most part women in such tiny minorities operated just like their male colleagues, setting similar priorities on the basis of party programmes. Although they may have acted as role models, their presence does not appear to have made it any easier for other women to follow them into office.

At what point are there enough women – or enough of any minority group – for their presence to alter the dominant culture? In an influential argument Rosabeth Moss Kanter (1977) defined 'balance' as a ratio between 60:40 and 50:50, and asserted that organizations with a better balance of people would be more tolerant of differences, reduce stress on those who are 'different', reduce pressure to conform, increase capacity to build skills and use the competencies of those who operate at a disadvantage (Thomas 1994: 85). Kanter further argued that as women (or any minority) approached balance, they would be less likely to be perceived as aberrant, and more often able to respond to the environment in an unrestrained manner (Thomas 1994: 88).

Kanter outlined a typology of four different kinds of groups, which became progressively more balanced. The groups were defined as follows: first, the uniform group, in which there is only one significant social group, whose culture dominates the organization; second, the skewed group, in which there is a minority constituting a maximum of 15 per cent of the whole, which is controlled by the dominant group and its culture – here, the minority is relevant only as a token; third, the tilted group, where the minority is between 15 and 40 per cent – here the minority is becoming strong enough to begin to influence the culture of the group; finally, the balanced group with ratios between 60:40 and 50:50, where the culture and interaction of the whole reflect the balanced nature of the group (Childs 2004a; Dahlerup 1988; Lovenduski 2001). Kanter was concerned with business rather than political communities, but her insight has been widely adopted by political analysts trying to pin down mechanisms and defining moments of political change.

Thus, the term 'critical mass' has often been used to describe a point at which the proportion of women in a parliament is large enough to constitute a bloc of influence. At this point, the entry of more women becomes easier; women find it easier to negotiate their daily lives in politics; and the general atmosphere of the parliament is more conducive to women and sex equality. In terms of Kanter's typology, critical mass must be somewhere in the tilting zone – but where, exactly? The notion of critical mass has been taken up enthusiastically by a number of political analysts, including (with reservations) Drude Dahlerup in Sweden and Joni Lovenduski and Pippa Norris in the UK and the USA. It is a very satisfying notion, because it implies a degree of certainty in an otherwise very uncertain field; but the fact of the matter is that we do not know when a tilt will become decisive.

As Sarah Childs points out, critical mass is defined as anywhere between 10 and 35 per cent. The critical mass referred to is simply a count of biological males and females, which does not distinguish between sex and gender, nor take account of how gender identity might vary among women and men. Moreover, it does not take account of the gendered context in which the women representatives operate (Childs 2004a). Furthermore, mass alone cannot be enough. In a plurality system, having 30 per cent of women concentrated in the party that is not in government, or on the back benches of the governing party, does not seem likely to change very much. Similarly, where proportional representation (PR) systems operate, having 30 per cent of women concentrated in parties excluded from the governing coalition, or excluded from office in the governing parties, does not seem particularly promising. So electoral system, party and placement variables must interact with the numbers of women elected in the establishment of influence.

If the exact percentage that constitutes critical mass is difficult to state as a projection, it is no less awkward to claim as an achievement. In order to demonstrate that critical mass has been achieved, it would be necessary to show that influence kicked in at a particular point: that is, when the balance tilted. However, there is a considerable time lag between the entry into politics of an individual or a group of people, and the point at which their influence can be discerned. Policy change takes time, and it is very difficult to separate out the influence of any one factor from everything else surrounding it. Pinning down causality in politics is a difficult trick. So critical mass is, in fact, a very inexplicit concept.

Conclusion

Political theory gives a shape to the deluge of facts available about political life at the same time as it gives direction to political activism. Feminist analysis of democracy helped women to understand why they felt left out of a politics that claimed to be government of the people, by the people, for the people. It gave them the vocabulary and the voice with which to explain that 'the people' did not appear to include them, and then to demand inclusion.

The trajectory of analysis from participation to representation has mapped the path of activism: from the non-hierarchical organizations of the women's movements, to the mobilization around getting women into parliaments. Parallel discussions have considered and predicted what increased numbers of women might mean. Although there are a lot of ideas about, and some indications of what might happen in practice, it has still not been proved whether having more women changes anything, in terms of either agendas or procedures. Apart from anything else, there are a lot of other variables besides raw numbers. Party and electoral systems matter; so do economies and policy priorities of the day.

The following chapters look at the realities of women's numbers and positions in political parties, local and national government, and international governmental organizations. Beneath the descriptions of how women have organized to get into elected office lies the assumption that it matters that they get there. We may not know exactly why it matters – we may have different and even conflicting theories about this – but we are none the less sure that it does.

FURTHER READING

A number of writers have criticized the history of political thought from a feminist perspective. I rather like Susan Okin's version of this. The first writer to attempt a theoretical analysis of political representation was Hana Pitkin. Although her work has not been directly referenced in this chapter, she exerted a profound influence on most of the writers referenced above. Anne Phillips's work on democracy and representation has been enormously important in the development of feminist theory, as have been Jane Mansbridge and Iris Marion Young. Nirmal Puwar has recently published her reflections on feminist theory and making a difference. A rather different way of thinking about women's influence on politics has emerged as an ethic of care. Associated with Sarah Ruddick and Jean Bethke Elshtain, among others, it has also been widely criticized, notably by Mary Dietz.

Dietz, M. 1985: Citizenship with a Feminist Face: The Problem with Maternal Thinking. *Political Theory*, 13(1): 19–37.

Elshtain, J. Bethke 1981: *Public Man, Private Woman: Women in Social and Political Thought*. Oxford: Martin Robertson.

Mansbridge, J. 1999: Should Blacks Represent Blacks and Women Represent Women? A Contingent 'Yes'. *Journal of Politics*, 61(3): 628–58.

Okin, S. M. 1980: *Women in Western Political Thought*. London: Virago.

Phillips, A. 1991: *Engendering Democracy*. Cambridge: Polity.

Phillips, A. 1995: *The Politics of Presence*. Oxford: Oxford University Press.

Pitkin, H. 1972: *The Concept of Representation*. Berkeley: University of California Press.

Puwar, N. 2004: Thinking About Making a Difference. *British Journal of Politics and International Relations*, 6(1): 3–19.

Ruddick, S. 1990: *Maternal Thinking: Towards a Politics of Peace*. London: Women's Press.

Young, I. M. 1990: *Justice and the Politics of Difference*. Princeton: Princeton University Press.

APPLYING THE THEORY

2

Introduction

The previous chapter described three claims that have been made with regard to women's presence in elected assemblies. These are all based on the contention that female politicians' experience of being women will differentiate them from men: first, that they will be inclined to make different choices from men; second, that they will be able to identify and then act on behalf of women and/or women's interests; third, that women possess a different way of doing things, reflective of sex and gender, that will influence their political style. There is overlap between all three claims, and there is also overlap in the following attempt to find evidence to support them. One form of analysis that has been loosely adopted by some researchers is to look at the presence of women in assemblies and their impact through the lens of critical mass. This was discussed in chapter 1, and some of the problems associated with the concept were detailed. In the following discussion we look at the possibilities of applying critical mass in New Zealand, the United States and the United Kingdom.

Initial Problems of Analysis

With regard to the first and second claims (making different choices from men, and acting for women): if women make different choices from men, these are likely to be choices that prioritize issues of particular importance to women (such as abortion and equal pay) – but perhaps not always. As we shall see, female legislators sometimes differ from male legislators over more general issues, particularly the environment and conflict. The third

claim, that of style, is also difficult to unpick: how do we differentiate between supporting different issues and the ways in which they are supported? As we shall see, there is
some evidence, but it is a tricky area.

Part of the difficulty of this analysis is one common to the social sciences: how can we
attribute causality when the variables continually shift and we can only come up with
approximate control situations? We can look at assemblies that have high numbers of
women and compare them to those that have low numbers, look at policies and procedures, and make some claims. However, there are also cultural, economic and generational variables. Are the Nordic countries more egalitarian because there are more women
in parliament, or because there is a broadly egalitarian culture, or because the societies
have relatively egalitarian (and successful) economies, or because the younger generations
of men entering politics are more egalitarian than the older men?

Do Women in Politics Make Different Choices from Men?

Researchers have been interested not just in the raw numbers of women's political presence, but in its content. What do women in parliament do? And how do they see themselves? As discussed in the previous chapter, some theorists have proposed that as
politicians women would tend to focus on different issues: more on caring, peace and
development.

The relative weakness of party discipline in the United States has prompted more
research into the voting patterns of elected representatives than in other countries. In
most countries representatives have little scope for initiative when they vote on legislation, because party discipline overrides all but the most powerful dissent. However, in the
US Congress there is considerable freedom about how to vote, making this an interesting test bed for the investigation of whether male and female representatives behave differently. Research here has indeed established that the sex of elected representatives
influences their legislative priorities and roll call votes in both Congress and State Houses
(Norris and Lovenduski 1995: 211). Barbara Burrell found that female representatives
supported liberal initiatives such as the Civil Rights Act (1964) more than their male colleagues, and that more women than men in Congress supported the Equal Rights Amendment. As early as 1974, research showed that the voting patterns of women in Congress
were significantly different from those of their male counterparts (Burrell 1994: 154).
Between 1972 and 1980 Congresswomen voted in a more liberal direction than men, even
after taking party affiliation into account.

Looking at voting patterns in Congress between 1987 and 1992, Burrell found that
Democrat women were the most liberal group, followed by Democrat men and Republican women, with Republican men tailing behind as the least liberal group. She concluded
that women are a continuing liberal influence on Congress. Although party is the main
indicator of attitude and political division, within parties women form the more liberal
wing (Burrell 1994: 156–9).

Research elsewhere is less detailed, and claims that female representatives have different priorities often rely on the coincidence of new policies and women's success at the
polls. For example, newly elected women in Indian local government have focused on edu-

cation, health, sanitation and alcohol control. Although the first three of these are of general interest, women have prioritized them to a greater extent than men. The last, however, is almost exclusively a female concern.

Similarly, Mavivi Myakayaka-Manzini, a member of the National Assembly of South Africa, makes considerable claims for the women in the Parliament. She argues that the influence of female representatives has led to the establishment of an Office on the Status of Women; government departments have gender focal points that link up with this office. The result has been that 'government departments have issued central policy documents and undertaken a wide range of initiatives that re-prioritize their work, to meet the needs of the entire population, and particularly those of women' (Myakayaka-Manzini 2003). The examples she quotes include the creation of a system of primary health care and the initiation of programmes of sustainable reforestation to benefit rural communities, as well as policies of more specific relevance to women, such as reform of the laws on rape, divorce and domestic violence.

From the limited research available, it would appear that women may take up different positions on policy from men – but we have to bear in mind here that most of the time, for most elected representatives, this simply is not an option because of party discipline. So we are perhaps looking more to the long term and to the potential effects of increased numbers of women on the long run of policy determination. There is more research available that looks at whether women in politics take a special responsibility for women, and whether they initiate and support women-friendly legislation.

Do Women in Politics Act on Behalf of Women?

The second question is whether female representatives consider themselves to be particularly representative of women. Do they take responsibility for representing women, their interests and their perspectives? There is by now a sizeable body of research from around the world that indicates that women have an impact on politics, particularly on policy areas of specific relevance to women. Vallance and Davies (1986) found that women members of the European Parliament played a major role in raising the equality directives on the political agenda in the late 1970s.

A survey conducted for the Inter-Parliamentary Union in 2000 reported that 89 per cent of the 200 women from sixty-five countries included believed that they had a special responsibility to represent the needs and interests of women (Waring, Greenwood and Pintat 2000: 133; Sawer 2002: 8). One woman is quoted as saying: 'I represent women because their needs and interests have been under-represented up to now.' And another: 'those of us women who are in politics should act to consolidate democracy in our countries, fight exclusion, and the sidelining of certain sectors – class and gender' (Waring, Greenwood and Pintat 2000: 136). A common theme was the need to maintain links with women's groups outside parliament in order to share information and support. For example, 'I maintain strong links with the women in my party and in the women's movement. I appoint women to management positions at the ministry. I try not to give the impression that one has to be a superheroine to fill a political position' (Waring, Greenwood and Pintat 2000: 137). Only a minority were offended by the suggestion that they might be seen as representative of their sex: 'I consider the view that women politicians are the representatives of their sex to be profoundly wrong. It turns women politicians into a sort of self-restricted species.' And: 'I represent the needs and interests of the whole population (at least, I try). I think that women's groups, for example, are rather counterproductive' (Waring, Greenwood and Pintat 2000: 134).

In the United Kingdom, Catherine Bochel and Jacqui Briggs undertook small-scale research into female councillors and members of parliament (Bochel and Briggs 2000). Using concepts of women's interests and perspectives generated by earlier writers, they concluded that there is evidence to support the notion of women's perspectives, and that there are women's issues. Bochel and Briggs argue that women politicians do, in fact, possess a range of different views and bring a different perspective to the political arena (Bochel and Briggs 2000: 67).

Also in the UK, Sarah Childs found that female MPs 'identify the articulation of women's concerns as part of their representative function' (Childs 2001: 187). Of the women newly elected to the 1997 Parliament, half of those interviewed argued that their presence would enable the articulation of women's concerns (Childs 2001: 181). Childs suggests that this perception could in turn alter the political agenda, to include women's perspectives on such issues as child care, education, equal opportunities and employment, and that the presence of women would ensure more balanced policies and legislation. Women in the UK Parliament have drawn attention to women's issues on such occasions as Marion Roe's Prohibition of Female Circumcision Act (1985) and Christine McCafferty's attempts to abolish taxation on sanitary products.

Research in the Nordic countries shows that female and male politicians give different priority to policies on child care, welfare support and equal opportunities, based on their dissimilar experiences within the family, welfare state and labour market. More power-fully, Hege Skjeie claims that the political relevance of gender, such as an awareness of differences between women's and men's political interests and the desire of women voters to be represented by women, is an experience common to all the Nordic countries (Skjeie 1992). Christensen argues that this means that male-only and strongly male-dominated organizations and hierarchies within political parties and the political elite have lost their legitimacy, and that in these countries women and gender differences are now integrated into mainstream political culture (Christensen 1999: 84).

Lena Wangerud found that in the Nordic countries,

> legislative behaviour is an area within which an MP's gender is of greater importance than their party affiliation. This is especially clear if we look at contacts between MPs and women's organisations; gender explains 30 per cent of the variance; whereas party affiliation explains only 9 per cent. The finding that 41 per cent of female MPs are in regular contact with women's organisations, compared with just 3 per cent of male MPs, is quite striking. (Wangerud 2000: 143).

She also found that a high proportion of MPs in the region agreed that there were 'con-crete issues on which the position of their party has changed owing to the increased rep-resentation of women' (Wangerud 2000: 145). However, her research did not go into specific policy areas.

Looking specifically at Sweden, Sawer refers to the 1985, 1988 and 1994 *Parliament Studies*, which showed that over 50 per cent of women members of parliament regarded representing the interests and views of women as very important to them personally, as compared with 10 per cent or less of men MPs (Sawer 2002: 8). In Iceland, representatives of the Women's Alliance have made sure that women's issues have featured strongly on the parliamentary agenda. According to Styrkarsdottir, 'issues such as incest, sexual abuse, violence against women, and low pay for women's work have been debated, at times very heatedly, and resulted in new bills and laws' (Styrkarsdottir 1999: 95).

In Russia, the women deputies of 1993 claimed success with their work on legislation, including new family law and alternatives to the draft. They also claimed to have influenced social policy by their definition of social problems and the development of a programme to address these problems. In addition, they pushed for funding of a programme, 'Children of Russia' (Buckley 1997a: 173).

Looking at state legislators in the United States, Sue Thomas found that 57 per cent of female legislators considered representing women to be very important, compared with 33 per cent of male legislators. This translated into women in state government taking greater pride than men in their achievements on behalf of women and children, whereas men took more pride than women in their success on behalf of business (Thomas 1994: 70). Women introduced more bills on children than did men, and in interviews claimed that women's and children's issues took high priority, whereas men placed a higher priority on business, introducing more bills than did women (Thomas 1994: 74–5). Interestingly, women were slightly more successful than men at getting their bills through – especially when the bills related to women, children or families (Thomas 1994: 78).

Similarly, looking at the federal government, Barbara Burrell found that Congresswomen were more supportive of women's issues in the House than were their male colleagues. According to the voting chart compiled by the National Women's Political Caucus, Congresswomen were more likely than men to support such measures as tax relief for day care, flexitime at work, family planning measures, welfare, abortion, minimum wage and gay rights. On a scale of 0–100 women members of Congress were about twelve points more supportive than men in the period 1987–90 (Burrell 1994: 159). The Women's Voting Guide, produced by the Women's Political Action Group, analysed voting on five bills affecting women in 1992, and found that women had an average support score of 90 per cent in comparison with 66 per cent for men (Burrell 1994: 163). Burrell also found that women made feminist speeches on the floor of the House, and sponsored feminist legislation. Burrell concludes that 'Congresswomen's activities in support of women have been shown to be greater than those of Congressmen', and 'a clear connection exists between the election of women to office and pro-woman public policies [. . .] women in national leadership positions today tend to be articulate feminists' (Burrell 1994: 163–73).

In 1977 Congresswomen founded the Congresswomen's Caucus in order to give women an opportunity to discuss issues important to them and to bring their agenda to the attention of high-level cabinet staff. In 1981 this became the Congressional Caucus for Women's Issues (CCWI), and opened its membership to men. At this point it widened its brief to include pressing for the enactment of legislation providing greater opportunities for women in US society and promoting equality between the sexes (Burrell 1994: 164). The Republican Government of George Bush Senior disbanded all Legislative Service Organizations (LSGs), including the women's caucus, as a money-saving initiative. Congresswomen pledged to pursue their agenda, resulting in the creation of the Democratic Women's Members Organization. This established a separate non-profit wing, Women's Policy Inc., that attempted to take over the information services that the women's caucus had provided (Foerstel and Foerstel 1996: 105). To the consternation of the Administration, not only did most female Democrats join the new organization, but so did a number of female Republicans.

At each Congress the CCWI adopted 'a set of legislative priorities. It also has a formal process for endorsing legislation introduced by its members' (Burrell 1994: 165). In 1981 it introduced the Economic Equity Act (EEA), a package of tax, retirement, child care and child support bills designed to secure women's economic rights. This expanded over the years, and by 1992 eighty-nine different measures had been enacted as part of the EEA. The Women's Health Equity Bill was introduced in 1990, as well as the Violence against Women Bill. Elements of these have become law by incorporation into other acts. The CCWI also continued to support the Equal Rights Amendment after its defeat on the floor of the House in 1985. Although this no longer has the high profile it once had, it is introduced in every Congress (Burrell 1994: 169).

While women's interests and women themselves have not been integrated so fully in Canadian politics, Manon Tremblay found that female members of the House of Commons make a difference in politics and represent women better than do male MPs. In debates, women spoke out on women's issues more than twice as often as men. However, from her research into the areas of interest of MPs, the priority given to gender issues, the topics of Private Members Bills, and the topics of legislative debates, she found that although both female and male MPs speak and act in support of women's issues, these issues themselves make up only a small part of government business: 'while women's issues represent a relatively minor field of interest for both women and men in Canada's House of Commons, they occupy a clearer place in the political universe of a larger proportion of female MPs' (Tremblay 1998: 463). Similarly, in Argentina, Htun and Jones found that female deputies introduced more bills concerned with women's rights and children than men did, but by no means all women prioritized these areas. While 33 per cent of them presented one-third or more of their bills in the area of women's rights, and 11 per cent did so with respect to families and children, some 58 per cent of female deputies did not do anything for women's rights, and 61 per cent did nothing for families and children (Htun and Jones 2002: 47).

A study of the Australian Senate, looking at the activities of Senators between 1987 and 1999, found that women members were five times more likely to raise issues of domestic violence and paid parental or maternity leave than their male colleagues – although this was influenced by partisanship: Conservative women were less likely to raise issues than Labor women (Sawer 2002: 9). Party ideology and discipline also emerged as issues for Manon Tremblay in her comparison of federally elected women in Australia and Canada (Tremblay 2003). Tremblay undertook a comparison of the attitudes of female representatives to assess the variables that affected their understanding of political representation and of whether they had a mandate to represent women.

She found that the vast majority of those interviewed in both countries and in all parties understood political representation primarily as representing a given territory – which might be an electorate, a state or even the entire country (Tremblay 2003: 224). Only 25.6 per cent of Australian female MPs and 13.6 per cent of Canadian female MPs spontaneously mentioned representing women. However, when asked directly, 56 per cent of Australian MPs, 88.9 per cent of Australian Senators and 84.1 per cent of Canadian MPs felt that they had a mandate to represent women. Tremblay suggests that party ideology and the number of women elected to a given assembly may have an effect on women's sense of representing women. The women interviewed gave some indications of why they felt limited in their ability to represent women. These were their small number, political rules and the media. Political rules included such things as the parliamentary and party systems, party ideology and discipline, and the ways that networks operate to exclude women. Their concern with the media (print and broadcast) derived from a perception that they were sexist. This was evidenced by their greater interest in the ability of female politicians to balance family and politics than in their policies, and their general scepticism about female competence (Tremblay 2003: 231).

To sum up: there is evidence that elected women can and do believe that they have a particular mandate to represent women. However, the extent to which this is the case is influenced by a range of variables, including numbers, parties, systems and even media pressure. Moreover, the expectation that female parliamentarians will act for women can cause problems. One of the first potential conflicts that the 1997 Labour Government in the United Kingdom had to confront was widespread dislike of a 1997 proposal to cut welfare benefits to lone parents. This was widely perceived as an attack on women (who make up the majority of lone parents). So when only eight of the forty-seven Labour MPs to vote against the proposal were women, this was seen by many as a failure of the new female MPs to support women. This judgement did not take account of the inexperience of the MPs, or their commitment to party policy. Rather, as Bochel and Briggs claim, 'this is an instance where women failed to act decisively on the basis of what some would identify as women's perspectives and issues' (Bochel and Briggs 2000: 66).

Do Women in Politics Possess a Different Style?

Finally, theorists have suggested that women in politics would act differently from men, being more focused on reaching agreement and on collegiate working. It is argued that women in politics have the potential to behave differently from the norm, that some do and that, once there are enough of them, more will. There is a considerable investment in this argument on the part of feminist political scientists (and others) who see too much time-wasting and posturing in the conduct of business in many parliaments: women in a range of parliaments believe that they behave differently from men.

Just under two-thirds of the women Members of Parliament in the United Kingdom interviewed by Sarah Childs argued that women had a different political style. Generally, this was a less combative and more collegiate approach (Childs 2004a: 6). Literally, women adopted a different voice: less likely to shout, to be cutting, to repeat themselves or reiterate what others have said, a point also made by Bochel and Briggs. Female MPs interviewed by both Childs and Bochel and Briggs made reference to being team-players and their community orientation. However, this tendency was cross-cut by party and generation, with older women more likely to adopt male models of behaviour. Bochel and Briggs found that a majority of women politicians in the UK felt that they behaved differently from their male counterparts, and from men in general. The women politicians claimed that they were more willing to co-operate and to negotiate, rather than taking confrontational and adversarial positions. Further, they claimed that women were more interested than men in getting on with representing their constituents, governing, policy-making and legislating, rather than establishing their status (Bochel and Briggs 2000: 67).

In the same vein, women in the Russian Duma claimed that they acted differently from their male colleagues. They emphasized their commitment to hard work, describing themselves as less aggressive, less envious, more progressive, more productive, more painstaking, scrupulous, conscientious, more hard-working, more pragmatic – and opposed to war (Buckley 1997a: 173).

As we might expect, the strongest examples of a different style come from the Nordic countries, where there have been more women in office for longer than elsewhere. The example of the Support Stockings in Sweden shows women both inside and outside the parliament mobilizing to raise awareness of women's issues and to support women politicians without seeking a high public profile or to entrench their organization (Stark 1997). The Icelandic Women's Alliance was also dissolved once it had achieved its goal of getting more women elected (Styrkarsdottir 1999). For people to organize and then to reject offers of political office, and indeed to dissolve the organization once it has done its job, is fairly unusual in the egotistical world of politics.

In the USA, Sue Thomas's research on state legislators suggests that 'female office-holders were more interested in a process that can only be called cooperative rather than competitive [. . .] Women [. . .] were focused on how political processes could be made less zero-sum, less ad hoc, less a fly-by-the-seat-of-the-pants process, less a game of winners and losers, and more a process by which everyone can participate and as many people as possible can emerge with something to praise' (Thomas 1994: 110). She argues that, as legislators, women conform outwardly to the *status quo*, but that 'deeper analysis, however, reveals that they were no more accepting of the ways in which legislators go about their business than were their sisters in the 1970s. Instead, they envisioned an alternative standard in which power and procedure are geared toward and more responsive to their colleagues in the legislature and the constituents to whom they are accountable' (Thomas 1994: 127).

Many female politicians appear to assume for themselves a responsibility for representing women and women's interests. As we have seen, this can translate into supporting different issues from men. Whether this amounts to a different style from that of male politicians is a moot point, despite the claims to difference of a range of female politicians. Political style differs around the world: it reflects the specific politics and culture of each place. Culture, and therefore style, changes generationally: younger politicians, both female and male, may differ from their seniors. Moreover, party and party beliefs will have an effect.

Critical Mass

In the previous chapter we discussed the widely used concept of critical mass: the argument that there is a point at which the proportion of women in an elected body will start to have a decisive effect because there will be enough of them for them to feel confident about acting differently from the norm. We raised the question that a number of political scientists have asked recently: how many women do you need to have before they start to make a difference? The idea that there is a critical mass of women – an identifiable percentage – that, once achieved, will trigger change in favour of women, is a popular one. Unfortunately, it seems to be impossible to define, and is perhaps a mirage. 'Critical mass' suggests that women will start to change parliamentary politics once they achieve a level of representation that is significant, but not as much as 50 per cent. Practice increasingly suggests simply that more is better.

Sue Thomas's research exemplifies the problem. She applied the concept of critical mass in her discussion of women's efficacy in state government in the United States. She compared states with more than 20 per cent of female legislators with those having less than 20 per cent, and found little difference. Although in the first group women gave priority to bills dealing with women, children and the family more often than men, there were no patterns with regard to education, medicine and welfare. Women across the board gave lower priority to business than men, but there were no patterns with regard to crime, the environment, energy or the use of public land, all issues on which a gender gap might have been expected to appear (Thomas 1994).

By contrast, Thomas cites the example of Santa Clara County, California, in the early 1980s, when the mayor of San Jose was a woman and both the San Jose City Council and the Santa Clara County Board of Supervisors had female majorities. Here, the female representatives claimed to feel encouraged to speak out; women on the Board of Supervisors claimed to feel freer to pursue gender issues, and a great deal of legislation focused on women's issues was passed (Thomas 1994: 90). In 1985 Missoula County, Montana, became the first county in the USA to be run by women. The Missoula Board of Supervisors claimed that they worked well together. They settled differences by confronting them head-on, and dealt with problems by investigating them from the ground up and attempting to involve participants in finding solutions (Thomas 1994: 150). Based on these findings, Thomas argues that rather than the vague 20–40 per cent usually claimed to constitute a critical mass, it must take close to parity before an institutional culture can change (Thomas 1994: 99). In the absence of parity, a higher proportion of women does not guarantee the passage of a bill, and a lower percentage makes it very unlikely that female legislators will get a bill of particular relevance to women through, let alone alter legislative priorities (Thomas 1994: 100).

Sandra Grey reached similar conclusions to Thomas from her examination of the New Zealand Parliament in the years from 1975 to 1999, a period in which the numbers of women increased. She argues that the nature of politics will not change significantly until there is a greater proportion of women in the House than discussions of critical mass suggest: closer to parity than 30 per cent. Her argument has two components. On the one hand, Grey notes that as more women entered the New Zealand Parliament women's issues such as child care and parental leave figured more strongly, and women politicians were involved in debating the issues (Grey 2002: 22–3). From 1988, as the number of women grew, the number of politicians claiming to represent women increased, although this did not have a radical impact on parental leave policies. In terms of behaviour, Grey found that female MPs made fewer personal attacks on their colleagues than did the male MPs, and that they interrupted less often in debates.

On the other hand, rather than the presence of women changing parliament into a more polite institution, Grey's research suggests that it has become more aggressive, and that the women have learned the male style (Grey 2002: 24). This may be connected to an apparent increase in hostility towards female MPs, as indicated by the number of derogatory remarks made about the sex of an MP (Grey 2002: 24). Grey concludes that in New Zealand, 'there was evidence of increased feminisation of the political agenda at a time when the gender balance in the House of Representatives rose to almost reach Kantor's "skewed" ration of 15:85 per cent [. . .] When women MPs formed around 20 per cent [. . .] they commented on team spirit [. . .] 29.9 per cent representation in the Parliament from 1996 was insufficient to alter significantly either the parliamentary culture or policy decisions' (Grey 2002: 28).

Case Studies: Northern Ireland and Wales

Consideration of two of the new devolved assemblies in the UK (prior to the 2003 elections) offers some illumination of the impact of increased numbers of women. In the Northern Ireland Assembly women constituted some 13 per cent. Gender is not high on the political agenda in Northern Ireland and, despite the best efforts of the Northern Ireland Women's Coalition and women in the assembly, this does not seem to be changing much. Margaret Ward describes the insulting behaviour of (male) Assembly Members towards their female colleagues, and the failure to consider gender equity when establishing such new initiatives as the Policing Board (50 per cent Catholic, 50 per cent non-Catholic, but no consideration of gender). The same trend is apparent in the Northern Ireland Human Rights Commission, where new appointments are on the basis of religious community and balance, with gender disregarded (M. Ward 2002: 8).

Women assembly members were rarely selected to be present on official visits or in official deputations, where their presence would improve their credibility as representatives (M. Ward 2002: 11). There was no effort to raise the profile of the female members, or to highlight their participation on the Enterprise, Trade and Investment Committee. There were no women on the Agriculture, Personnel and Finance or Regional Development Committees, although there were five women on Health. There was no equalities committee.

Wales, on the other hand, had one of the highest proportions of women in the world in its assembly, at 41.7 per cent. As a result of the equality duty included in the Government of Wales Act, the legislature assumed responsibility for the introduction of family-friendly hours and the adoption of gender-neutral official titles (Chaney 2002: 4). The Assembly's Equality Committee adopted a wide-ranging approach to equality in the community, not only for women, ethnic minorities and disabled people, but also for groups defined by language, sexuality, age and faith, as well as gypsy-travellers (Chaney 2002: 6). The committee worked on the equalities responsibilities of the government as employer, the gender pay gap, equality in public appointments, reforms in the National Health Service and Welsh local government, economic development and the policy process. Chaney concludes that although equality is not a high priority for assembly members beyond a small, dedicated group, 'leading women AMs, supported by the Equalities Committee, have used the formal structural links between the Assembly and the public sector bodies that come under the legislature's remit to promote extensive equality reforms in the public sector' (Chaney 2002: 12).

Conclusion

Applying the theory is not easy. There have only been enough women in enough places for a fairly short time, and research funding is hard to come by. Further, it is difficult to pick one's way through the evidence while separating out different strands of the theory. More work is being done and will emerge in the next few years: it is emerging even as this book is being written. What we have so far suggests quite strongly that there are both gender and generational effects occurring among elected representatives. There is some evidence that women (some women, in some places, some of the time) make different choices from men in politics, consciously act for women, and adopt a different political style. However, this is complicated by party variables – and the simple fact that younger men, newer to politics, may have an outlook informed by feminism. On the other hand, the idea that there is an identifiable moment when women achieve a critical mass, defined by quantity, and are enabled to act differently from their male colleagues, is looking a bit shaky. In terms of the number of women, simply, more is better; but being able to exert a different kind of influence is not just a matter of numbers. The positions of the women – in majority or minority parties, in government or opposition – matter. So do the political perspectives of elected women – and men!

FURTHER READING

This is an area that a number of researchers are investigating at the moment, but research is in its early days, since women have only recently been elected to office in large enough numbers to make the research telling. Of the writers referred to here, Childs, Grey, Sawer, Thomas and Tremblay most directly address the problem of applying theory to practice. Joni Lovenduski and Pippa Norris have recently published an article applying the ideas of presence to the UK.

Childs, S. 2004a: A Feminized Style of Politics? Women MPs in the House of Commons. *British Journal of Politics and International Relations*, 6 (1): 3–19.

Grey, S. 2002: Does Size Matter? Critical Mass and New Zealand's Women MPs. *Parliamentary Affairs*, 55 (1): 19–29.

Lovenduski, J. and Norris, P. 2003b: Westminster Women: The Politics of Presence. *Political Studies*, 51 (1): 84–102.

Mackay, F. 2004: Gender and Political Representation in the UK: The State of the Discipline. *British Journal of Politics and International Relations*, 6 (1): 99–120.

Sawer, M. 2002: The Representation of Women in Australia: Meaning and Make-Believe. *Parliamentary Affairs*, 55 (1): 5–18.

Thomas, S. 1994: *How Women Legislate*. Oxford: Oxford University Press.

Tremblay, M. 1998: Do Female MPs Substantively Represent Women? A Study of Legislative Behaviour in Canada's 35th Parliament. *Canadian Journal of Political Science*, 31 (3): 435–65.

Wangerud, L. 2000: Representing Women. In P. Esaiasson and K. Heidar (eds), *Beyond Westminster and Congress: The Nordic Experience*. Columbus: Ohio State University Press.

PART II

Voting and Elections

VOTING AND ELECTIONS: BACKGROUND INFORMATION

3

Introduction

This part of *Women in Contemporary Politics* addresses the two most basic elements of democratic politics: voting and elections. Around the world women were excluded from both of these until quite recently, so it comes as no surprise to find that both the practice of voting and elections, and the research done on them, have been constructed in ways that reflect the interests and opportunities of men rather than women. The following chapters examine both what we know about women's behaviour with regard to voting and elections, and also the research that has been undertaken. Very little research was done on the specifics of women's political behaviour until feminist researchers started asking whether women did anything differently from men. In order to open up the topics of voting and elections and quotas, this chapter will give some background information.

Voting

Voting: the most routine of political acts for many people, so much taken for granted that vast numbers of people entitled to vote don't bother. Only when a group of previously disenfranchised people get the vote, or when an election touches a nerve, do we pay attention to just how important this small act is. When the black population of South Africa got the vote in 1994, people queued for days to exercise their democratic right; when the French Presidential election threatened to legitimate a far Right contender in 2002, people took to the streets to raise awareness, turn-out increased, and Le Pen, the National Front candidate, was marginalized; around the world there are women who place their vote as much in homage to the people who fought for their right to do so as in support for a particular policy or party.

People's participation in governing themselves has varied tremendously between times and places. However, it is fair to say that for most of the people, for most of the time, government has been something inflicted on the majority by a tiny minority. In industrializing countries the franchise was slowly extended to most men, but women, who were somehow excluded from the category of 'people', had to fight for inclusion. By the start of the twenty-first century women had achieved the vote in all but a few countries. For the first women to get the vote, this was a result of the suffrage movement that grew up in many countries at the end of the nineteenth century; in other countries the vote came as an effect of colonialism, de-colonization or revolution. What women do with their votes was initially of little interest. It has become more interesting to analysts, however, as it has become clear that women may not always vote in the same ways as the men around them, and that the female vote might be something for political parties to court.

Global Extension of the Franchise to Women

The franchise was extended to women in waves. The first group of countries to give women the vote were the more developed, industrializing countries where arguments about civil rights were quite advanced. Women had achieved the vote in most industrialized countries by the end of the 1920s, although there were some interesting exceptions. New Zealand enfranchised women in 1893, Australia in 1902, and Norway in 1913. The United States of America passed the Nineteenth Amendment, which entitled women to vote, in 1920, and Britain admitted women to the franchise in stages. The Representation of the People Act of 1918 admitted all women over thirty who were on the local government register, or who were married to men on the register. Then in 1928 the Equal Franchise Act enabled women to vote on the same terms as men. However, France did not extend the vote to women until 1946, and Liechtenstein managed to continue to exclude women until 1984 (Burns, Lehman, Schlozman and Verba 2001: 1; Rowbotham 1997: 69–90).

In Africa the franchise was extended to women in some colonized countries at the same time as women got the vote in the colonizing nation. For example, the francophone countries Senegal, Togo, Liberia, Cameroon, Niger and the Seychelles all extended the franchise in the 1940s. Other African states gave the vote to women on gaining independence. Between 1952 and 1989 some forty or so African states enfranchised women. In South Africa white women got the vote in 1930, coloured and Indian women in 1984, and black women, along with black men, in 1994.

Among Asian countries, Mongolian women got the vote in 1924, those in Sri Lanka in 1931, in Thailand and the Maldives in 1932, in Burma (Myanmar) in 1935, in the Philippines in 1937, in Japan in 1945, in China in 1949 and in Bangladesh in 1972. In the Pacific region the vote came fairly late, with women of Samoa entering the franchise in 1990. Arab countries were also late to enfranchise women. Women in Djibouti got the vote in 1946, in Syria in 1953, in Egypt in 1956, in Tunisia in 1958, in Mauritania in 1961, in Algeria in 1962, in Morocco in 1963, in Libya in 1964, in South Yemen in 1967, in

North Yemen in 1970, in Jordan in 1974, and in Iraq in 1980. In a few Arab countries – Saudi Arabia, Qatar, Oman and the United Arab Emirates – neither men nor women can vote, and women are excluded from the franchise in Kuwait (IPU 1995: 8; Rose 2000: 345).

Women Getting Elected

The votes that we cast are, of course, the raw material that an election converts into a parliament and a government. Around the world women have been largely absent from elected parliaments and governments until very recently. This is not to say that they have been absent from politics: there have been some magnificent hostesses, queens and leaders who have turned governments and defined periods of history, and there have been myriad workers behind the scenes; but until recently there have been few women elected. Despite access to the franchise in the early years of the twentieth century, access to parliament in significant numbers has been slow in coming: for the most part a very late twentieth-century achievement.

Awareness that the relative absence of women constituted a democratic deficit and warranted attention arose at different times in different countries. Denmark was remarkable in making women's participation in politics an issue immediately after the Second World War. Initially this was marked by a change to the Succession of the Throne Act, enabling women to succeed, as Queen Margrethe did some time later in 1972. Between 1945 and 1970 the proportion of women in the Folkeling, the Danish Parliament, rose from 5.4 to 11.8 per cent, and then to 23 per cent in the 1980s (Flanz 1983: 118). Denmark now has one of the highest proportions of women in parliament in the world, at 38 per cent (IPU website: June 2004). Just for comparison, in the United Kingdom 2.7 per cent of members of parliament were women in 1951, and this did not get above 5 per cent until 1987, when it reached 6.7 per cent (Norris and Lovenduski 1995: 103). Even in 2004 it is only 17.9 per cent. What was then West Germany elected 7 per cent women in 1949, rising to 10 per cent in 1983 (Kolinsky 1993: 136). Germany now has 32.2 per cent women in its Lower House and 24.6 in its Upper (IPU website: June 2004).

Early achievement of high numbers of women elected to parliament is largely confined to the Nordic countries. Norway elected 9.3 per cent women to the Storting (Parliament) in 1969, increasing this to 16.1 per cent in 1975. In 1981 Gro Harlem Brundtland was elected as the first female Prime Minister. Sweden elected 14 per cent women in 1971, and 23 per cent in 1977. At the time of writing, Sweden has the second highest proportion of women in parliament in the world at 45.3 per cent (IPU website: June 2004). A total absence of women is largely confined to Arab states, such as the United Arab Emirates and Kuwait, where women are formally excluded from public life, and countries in the Pacific region where late enfranchisement may be having an effect: the Federal States of Micronesia, Nauru, Paulau, the Solomon Islands, Tonga and Tuvalu (IPU website: June 2004).

While many less developed countries have very low numbers of women (Bangladesh has 2 per cent, Swaziland 3.1 per cent, Morocco 0.6 per cent), others, such as Mozambique, 30 per cent, Namibia, 25 per cent, and the Philippines, 17.8 per cent, are

Table 3.1 Women in parliaments: countries with the highest and lowest percentage

Rank	Country	Elections	Lower House % women	Upper House % women
1	Rwanda	September 2003	48.8	–
2	Sweden	September 2002	45.3	–
3	Denmark	November 2001	38.0	–
4	Finland	March 2003	37.5	–
5	Netherlands	January 2003	36.7	32.0
6	Norway	September 2001	36.4	–
7	Cuba	January 2003	36.0	–
7	Spain	March 2004	36.0	23.2
8	Belgium	May 2003	35.3	31.0
9	Costa Rica	February 2002	35.1	–
10	Argentina	October 2001	34.0	33.3
⋮	⋮	⋮	⋮	⋮
111	Haiti	May 2000	3.6	25.9
112	Belize	March 2003	3.3	23.1
113	Marshall Islands	November 2003	3.0	–
114	Egypt	November 2000	2.4	–
115	Lebanon	August 2000	2.3	–
116	Bangladesh	October 2001	2.0	–
117	Vanuatu	May 2002	1.9	–
118	Niger	November 1999	1.2	–
119	Papua New Guinea	June 2002	0.9	–
120	Yemen	April 2003	0.3	–
121	Bahrain	October 2002	0.0	15.0

Source: IPU website: 11 June 2004

doing rather well, and in 2003 Rwanda elected 48.8 per cent, and became the country with the highest proportion of women in its parliament (IPU website: 30 Sept. 2003). Similarly, in some of the more economically developed countries there are high proportions of women, as described above, while in others the proportions are average or below: France has 12.2 per cent, Italy 11.5, the Russian Federation 7.6, and Japan 7.3 (IPU website: 30 Sept. 2003) (see table 3.1).

Electoral Systems

Many different factors come into play when trying to explain differences in the representation of women. These have been extensively researched and debated. The major contenders are: political factors (how long since women got the vote, the nature of the party, and parliamentary and electoral systems), socio-economic factors (women's legal rights, access to education and employment, and family patterns) and cultural factors (religion and gender traditions).

When we talk about who gets elected, attention is immediately drawn to how people get elected: how electoral systems operate and how they are manipulated by political parties. The big differences are between electoral systems based on some form of proportional representation (PR) and multi-member constituencies, and those that use a simple plurality, more commonly called first-past-the-post (FPP), and single-member constituencies. The details of electoral systems can be found in any number of texts dealing with the mechanisms of politics. For the purposes of this book a basic understanding is required, so a much simplified description of the main points follows.

The legitimacy of a parliament as a decision-making body depends on whether it is considered to be representative of the interests of the population. In democracies this derives from a relationship between people and members of parliament grounded in accountability, responsiveness and responsibility. The relationship between people and their representatives is established and maintained through elections. So it is important that an election demonstrates the existence of a relationship. This is achieved through a conjunction of party and geography.

In most countries elections and representation revolve around geographically defined constituencies: representatives thus represent the people living in a particular geographical area. But how this is articulated varies. Some countries, such as the UK, are divided up into constituencies represented by one elected member. Other countries have constituencies that have more than one representative. Rarely, the entire country may be considered as a constituency (Israel), and all representatives represent the whole.

Generally speaking, where there are single-member constituencies, elections are contested by a number of candidates from different parties putting themselves forward. In each constituency the candidate who gets more votes than any other (simple plurality) wins; in the country, the party that gets more seats than any other wins the election and gets to form a government.

Where there are multi-member constituencies and proportional representation, on the other hand, the election is contested by parties who each put forward a number of candidates. The seats are allocated to parties proportionally, in accordance with the proportion of the votes they have won. In this system there may well be no outright winner of an election at national level, and a government is more likely to be formed from a coalition of parties joining together to produce a majority of members of parliament.

There are a large number of different ways of operating proportional representation, and some electoral systems use a mixture of both PR and FPP (the Scottish and Welsh regional assemblies in the UK do this). One important characteristic that needs to be clarified is the use of party lists. Most systems of PR use a party list. This means that at election each party, in each constituency, presents a list of its candidates for the seats. These lists can be 'closed' or 'open'.

A closed list is one where the party has decided on the ordering of candidates on the list and the voter votes for the party; an open list is one where the voter can choose which candidates on the list to vote for (and may be able to split their vote across parties). With a closed list, as a party accumulates votes, so candidates win seats in the order of the list – so the first few positions on the list are the most secure. With an open list, candidates accumulate votes individually. While an open list is sometimes described as the most democratic, a closed list offers a party the opportunity to manipulate the nature of its representation, sometimes to democratic effect.

Research suggests that achieving elected office is rather easier for women (and minorities) in systems where there are multi-member constituencies and/or proportional representation (as compared with first-past-the-post). Easier, but not guaranteed. As we shall see, although political variables are the most significant for women's selection and election, culture exerts an influence: hence the anomaly of Japan, where proportional representation and very low numbers of women in parliament coexist.

Conclusion

The particularities of voting practices and electoral systems have far-reaching effects for women, which are detailed in the following chapters. The institutional aspects of political science can easily be dismissed as we get excited about issues and causes – but, as this discussion shows, institutions and institutional reform matter!

FURTHER READING

There is a huge and ever-expanding literature on political institutions, a lot of which does not pay much attention to the positions and roles of women. Andrew Heywood is a very accessible writer and his book *Politics* covers the basic structures well. The Inter-Parliamentary Union is a wonderful resource for everything to do with parliaments and elections, and its website has sections on women and a bibliography, <www.ipu.org>. Its publications are excellent, although the survey of women in parliaments is now nearly ten years old.

Heywood, A. 2004: *Politics*. London: Palgrave Macmillan.
Inter-Parliamentary Union (IPU) 1995: *Women in Parliaments 1945–1995*, Reports and Documents 23. Geneva: IPU.
Inter-Parliamentary Union (IPU) 1997: *Men and Women in Politics: Democracy Still in the Making*. Geneva: IPU.
(Both of the IPU books are obtainable through the IPU website <www.ipu.org>.)

GETTING AND USING THE VOTE

4

Introduction

This chapter is concerned with voting. It looks first at how women's enfranchisement was achieved, starting with the example of Britain and then making comparisons with a number of other countries, including the Nordic countries, Russia, the United States and New Zealand. From there it moves on to discuss interpretations of women's politicization and of how women have used their votes. It focuses in particular on the notion of gender gap and the contention that women are more conservative than men. We conclude with some examples of how political parties have attempted to attract women's votes.

In order to get the vote, women (and men) around the world used a range of arguments, from equality and justice to pleas based on women's particular moral qualities. Resisters were similarly creative.

Achieving the Franchise

Rose divides women's enfranchisement into three phases. The first phase is development, the period in which women organized for political and social rights. Phase two is the achievement of legal enfranchisement, usually towards the end of wars, *coups* or revolutions, or on gaining national independence. Third is the implementation phase (Rose 2000: 345). This section looks at the first and second phase in developed countries, starting with the United Kingdom.

Demands to extend the franchise to include women were current in industrializing countries from the second half of the nineteenth century: the events usually deemed significant are the Seneca Falls Convention in the USA in 1848 and John Stuart Mill's speech to the House of Commons in Britain in 1867. We are going to look at Britain in some detail here before going on to summarize the suffrage movements in some other countries, because although Britain was not the first country to enfranchise women, 'for decades the English Women's Rights movement provided a model to other European equal rights movements' (Anderson and Zinsser 1990: 357).

In Britain women gradually became more equal to men in the second half of the nineteenth century. By the start of the twentieth century they had achieved a lot: they could become poor law officers and factory inspectors, they could vote in municipal and county elections if they met the property requirement, and they could become mayors – but they could not vote in national elections (Anderson and Zinsser 1990: 362). At this point the onward movement of equalization got stuck, and it got stuck not just in Britain, but elsewhere, because the men who were its allies, the liberals, socialists and radicals, feared that the women's vote, if achieved, would go not to themselves but to conservative parties (Anderson and Zinsser 1990: 362). In both Catholic and Protestant countries women were thought to be more religious, and thus more conservative. Conservative parties did not support the vote for women, considering it to be disruptive of the natural order; none the less, intelligent men assumed that women in possession of the vote would use it in support of parties that would deny it to them.

Enfranchisement

Britain

Not surprisingly, the stakes were upped at the turn of the century when, as Sheila Rowbotham claims, 'a new century demanded a new woman and she duly arrived' (Rowbotham 1997: 7). Up until this point the women's suffrage movement had been largely a matter of constitutional claims based on reason and justice: with the creation of the Women's Social and Political Union (WSPU) by Emmeline Pankhurst in 1903, the shock troops arrived. The constitutional side of the movement, comprising such organizations as Millicent Fawcett's National Union of Women's Suffrage Societies (NUWSS), kept up the pressure, but it was the WSPU that set the pace. Despite representing only a minority of those active in the cause of suffrage, the WSPU sought publicity and dramatically raised the profile of the cause.

Thus the first division to arise within the suffrage movement was over strategy: constitutional demands on the one hand and radical activism on the other. While the constitutionalist path was slow, the alternative was high-risk. It led to imprisonment and to being pilloried, as well as praised, in the press.

The WSPU was itself a combustible organization. The creation of Emmeline Pankhurst, it remained in thrall to the charismatic and authoritarian leadership of her and her daughters Christabel and Sylvia. In 1907 Theresa Billington split off to form the Women's Freedom League, and in 1913 Sylvia Pankhurst herself was expelled from the WSPU and moved to the East London Federation of Suffragettes (Rowbotham 1997:

14). Two divisions emerge here. The first was over leadership, a common enough cause of division in campaigning organizations, but particularly prescient in the world of feminist organization, where strong characters have continued to exist in tension with ideals of equality and non-hierarchical organization. The second was over goals. The WSPU, as led by Emmeline and Christabel Pankhurst, focused on women, increasingly regarding men as the enemy. Socialists like Sylvia Pankhurst, on the other hand, considered women's rights to be inseparable from labour issues.

The First World War created more tensions within the movement. The WSPU supported the war, while Sylvia Pankhurst and other socialist suffragists did not, and the NUWSS was divided. There was an international women's peace movement, and women from the suffrage movement supported war resisters (Rowbotham 1997: 67). Thus there was another split, which links to present-day debates, as to whether women have a particular affinity to peace and non-violence.

There were as well, of course, women's movements that opposed suffrage. Notably the Primrose League, the Conservative women's organization which argued that women would lose their special influence if they gained the franchise (Rowbotham 1997: 17). This is paralleled in the present by women of the Christian Right in the USA, and any number of figures claiming that women have been made unhappy by liberation, that all the ills of the world derive from sex equality, and that women should therefore surrender themselves to raising children and baking in order to save both themselves and society.

The suffrage movement gave rise to divisions across the political spectrum. Socialists disagreed about whether they should be backing equal suffrage or adult suffrage. The Liberal leadership rejected the demands of the Women's Liberal Federation. In Ireland supporters of Home Rule and suffrage were faced with a dilemma when the government offered them Home Rule in return for supporting the government in opposing women's suffrage (Rowbotham 1997: 14).

Women in Britain eventually achieved the vote after the First World War, largely as a result of the miners' union putting pressure on the Labour Party. Despite the flamboyant campaign tactics, which included women chaining themselves to the railings in Downing Street, imprisonment and hunger strikes, the arguments deployed were largely those that Mary Wollstonecraft and John Stuart Mill would have recognized: the equality of human beings to have a right to self-determination, on the one hand, and the value of women's 'special' qualities to the political sphere, on the other. Equal rights feminism was powerful, but for many, the vote was one step down a path to greater social and economic equality. Across Europe equal rights and socialist feminists differed in tactics as well as arguments.

The Nordic countries

The suffrage movement in Britain was particularly explosive and prone to fission. Movements in other countries shared the basic arguments, but most followed the more constitutional route. No discussion of women in politics is complete without consideration of the Nordic countries which have broken new ground time after time in the inclusion of women. In each of the five countries women's emancipation followed a different course as a result of the country's particular position in the nineteenth century. Finland, which

Table 4.1 Enfranchisement of women in the Nordic countries

Country	Year
Finland	1906
Norway	1913
Denmark	1915
Sweden	1919
Iceland	1920

Source: IPU website

had been a Swedish dominion for many years, became an autonomous grand duchy under the Russian tsar in 1809, and remained so until becoming independent at the time of the Russian Revolution in 1917. Norway, which had been under Danish rule, became independent in 1814, but rapidly surrendered its independence for union with Sweden, which lasted until 1905. Both countries were self-governing, but with restricted sovereignty. Iceland was subject to Denmark until 1918, when it was recognized as a sovereign state, although it remained in union with Denmark until 1944. Thus, only Sweden and Denmark were independent states at the end of the nineteenth century, when women's emancipation became an issue.

In each of these countries male emancipation took a different route, with Norway the first to achieve anything like adult male enfranchisement. In 1814 all male farmers were enfranchised, thereby giving the vote to 45 per cent of all men over the age of twenty-five. This was followed by universal male suffrage in 1898. While Denmark achieved universal male suffrage in 1901, Sweden, Finland and Iceland achieved full adult male suffrage at the same time as women's suffrage. In Finland this was in 1906, as a result of the first Russian Revolution, whereas in Sweden it took until 1919, and in Iceland until 1920 (Raaum 1999: 30).

Danish women were the first to create an organization to fight for women's rights, in 1871. This was followed by a suffrage organization in 1889. In Sweden, Norway and Finland, women's rights organizations were founded in 1884, followed by the founding of a women's suffrage organization in Norway the next year. After Finland's remarkable achievement of an adult franchise in 1906, Norway and Denmark followed in 1913 and 1915 respectively, with Sweden and Iceland trailing (see table 4.1). The demands for women's suffrage in all five countries were bound up with the particular political circumstances of each: independence, dominance and revolution, as well as urbanization and the creation of modern political parties and assemblies.

Russia

A different route to enfranchisement is apparent in Russia, where women gained equal legal and political rights with men as a result of the February Revolution of 1917 (Anderson and Zinsser 1999: 393). Two streams of feminism had been active in Russia: equal rights feminism, focused on the plight of women, and socialist feminism, which placed the situation of women within the larger socialist struggle against poverty and for equality. Women were active during the Revolution, both in the leadership of the Bol-shevik Party and in the army (Clements 1997). After the Revolution women were side-lined. Alexandra Kollontai was the only woman in Lenin's government, where, from 1920, she headed the Zhendotdel, the Soviet Women's Organization (Clements 1997: 204). The Zhendotdel spearheaded a range of developments in legislation and social policy; however, the Soviet Union was at war, and there were few resources for radical change. The Zhendotdel was dissolved in 1930 as Stalin's economic and ideological approaches started to bite. The party never rejected its original conception that women should be fully equal participants in society, but in the 1930s it adopted as well the notion that women should also find fulfilment in taking care of their families. Women were to be cit-izens, workers, housekeepers, wives and mothers. They were to serve their families and the nation (Clements 1997: 275). We shall see in the following chapters the problems that arise when women are allowed access to politics, but without any corresponding change in society as a whole.

The United States of America

Demands for the vote for women in the United States actually pre-date the country's exis-tence. In 1647 landowner Margaret Brent of Maryland demanded the right to two votes in the colonial assembly: one for herself and one on behalf of Lord Baltimore, whose power of attorney she held. She was refused (Conway 2000: 74). A century later, at the time of the formation of the USA and the creation of the Declaration of Independence, Abigail Adams wrote to her husband, John Adams, one of the founders, asking him to 'Remember the Ladies'. However, despite having possessed the vote for a short time in New Jersey, only to lose it in 1807, women in the USA were not able to vote until 1920.

The campaign in the USA grew out of the anti-slavery movement, influenced by the same equal rights literature. Women in the anti-slavery movement became politicized about their own position when they found themselves excluded from the World Anti-Slavery Convention in 1840 because they were women (Ford 2002: 38). The Seneca Falls women's rights convention of 1848, prompted by this exclusion, is usually noted as a key moment in the movement for women's rights and enfranchisement. The Declaration of Sentiments and Resolutions, which was to serve as a rallying point for women's rights in the USA, drafted by Elizabeth Cady Stanton, was ratified by the convention.

The women's suffrage movement in the USA was both energized and complicated by the anti-slavery movement of the time and by the Civil War. The American Equal Rights Association (AERA) was founded in 1866 to campaign for the vote on behalf of black and white women and black men. The organization became caught up in a struggle between those who argued that black male suffrage should come first and those whose priority was women's emancipation (Ford 2002: 40). The AERA was dissolved, and two organizations for women's suffrage emerged from the wreckage in 1869: the National Woman Suffrage Association (NWSA) led by Elizabeth Cady Stanton and Susan B. Anthony, which favoured universal suffrage, and the more conservative American Woman Suffrage Association (AWSA) formed by Lucy Stone, Henry Blackwell and Julia Ward Howe. The two movements later reunited, in 1890, as the National American Woman Suffrage Association (NAWSA) (Barber and Natason).

Tensions in the movement were exacerbated by the enfranchisement of black men in 1870, with NWSA refusing to work for the ratification of the amendment and insisting on universal enfranchisement. Another powerful lobby entered the arena in 1874, when the Women's Christian Temperance Union (WCTU) was formed. This added the appeal of morality to that of equality: its argument was that enfranchised women should use their votes to prohibit the sale of alcohol.

Between 1869 and 1874 the NWSA adopted a more confrontational approach. In Missouri, Virginia and Francis Minor reinterpreted the Fourteenth Amendment to include women in the franchise. This strategy was taken up by other activists, and in 1872 a number of women, including Susan B. Anthony and Virginia Minor, attempted to vote. This resulted in high-profile arrests and trials, which in Minor's case went to the Supreme Court (Ford 2002: 43).

The Woman Suffrage Amendment was introduced into Congress in 1878. In the years until its ratification women organized, campaigned and educated themselves. The original leadership of NAWSA aged, and a younger group of suffragists emerged, including Alice Paul and Lucy Burns, who were influenced by the direct action strategies of the WSPU. A suffrage parade in March 1913 became violent, and conflict arose within the NAWSA. Paul broke away and formed the Congressional Union (CU).

As in Europe, the First World War caused suffragists to reconsider their priorities. The CU became the National Women's Party (NWP) and, ignoring the war, continued to press for women's enfranchisement. NWP activists courted controversy. Picketers and marchers were imprisoned and undertook hunger strikes (Ford 2002: 49). In the meantime, the NAWSA pursued a more constitutional route. Under the leadership of Carrie Chapman Catt, it targeted individual states, pressing them to pass state constitutional amendments.

The inclusion of women in the franchise of individual states eased the acceptance of women's national suffrage: by 1918 women had been enfranchised in fifteen states (Conway 2000: 75). Nationally, Theodore Roosevelt's Progressive (BullMoose/Republican) Party adopted women's suffrage in 1912. Meanwhile, the movement had been recognized by the formation of an anti-suffrage organization, a coalition of conservatives, Catholics, capitalists and liquor producers: the National Association Opposed to Woman Suffrage.

The Nineteenth Amendment to the US Constitution, extending the franchise to women, was proposed in 1919 and ratified in 1920. NAWSA closed up shop, but some of its members went on to form the League of Women Voters. In 1923 the National Women's Party, continuing the struggle, proposed the Equal Rights Amendment, which has still not been ratified (Ford 2002: 55; Barber and Natason).

New Zealand

Both the British and the US campaigns influenced that in New Zealand. Women in New Zealand were, however, the first in the world to achieve the vote, in 1893. The New Zealand suffrage movement was influenced, on the one hand, by the equal rights approach of Mary Wollstonecraft and John Stuart Mill and, on the other, by the American-based Women's Christian Temperance Union – thus it had both an equality and a moral stance (Atkinson 2003: 85). Women's suffrage was initially debated in parliament by prominent male politicians who were influenced by female activists. The issue of women's suffrage was an extension of the debates around manhood and Maori suffrage, and between 1874 and 1893 women's suffrage was repeatedly proposed in a series of debates and bills.

Women were included in the local franchise by 1876, and a campaign for full female suffrage gathered momentum outside parliament in the 1880s. The campaign was initially driven by the New Zealand branches of the Temperance Union, which organized a petition of 9,000 signatures in 1891, followed by another 19,700 in 1892 – the largest presented to the parliament at that point. The prominence of the petition led to the creation of non-temperance Women's Franchise Groups. The liquor trade joined with conservatives to oppose women's suffrage, but the force of the pro-suffrage franchise petitioning – now augmented by public rallies – was too powerful to ignore, and the bill eventually passed, including the right to stand for office and encompassing Maori women (Atkinson 2003: 93).

Although relatively peaceful, the New Zealand campaign used highly public mobilization as well as harnessing the efforts of key political actors. The dual focus on equality and morality illuminates an ambivalence about women in public life that persists until today.

India

India is an example of enfranchisement as an effect of both colonialism and liberation. Under colonial rule, the Women's India Association was founded in 1917, very much on the lines of the British suffrage movement, and largely in response to similar movements in the West. Then in 1919 the Government of India Act empowered provincial legislatures to remove the sex barrier, at their discretion (Ramchander and Lakshmi 1993: 7). This permissive legislation achieved the vote for a limited number of women, while far more benefited from the 1935 Government of India Act that incorporated all women over the age of twenty-one who were literate property-owners or the wives of property-owners. However, it was only after independence in 1947 that women gained access to the franchise on equal terms with men.

One way or another, in the course of the twentieth century most women in the world became enfranchised. Political analysts, however, took little interest in what this might mean, and political parties paid little attention to what this might require of them.

Research into Women's Political Participation

As Marianne Githens has noted, prior to the 1960s very little research was done on women and politics, and that which was undertaken relied on 'prevailing assumptions about women's political behaviour [. . .] largely drawn from conventional wisdom rather than from empirically tested hypotheses' (Githens 1983: 472).

It has generally been assumed that women participate in politics less than men, are less interested and less well informed. This is generally accounted for by any variation or combination of the following:

- women have less time and energy for politics than men because of domestic responsibilities;
- as children and adults women are socialized into roles incompatible with political interest and activism;
- this is compounded by the influence of patriarchal family life;
- women have less access than men to socio-economic resources;
- and, finally, discrimination.

Such research as was undertaken into women's political interest and participation tended to affirm assumptions rather than interrogate them. Extensive research in the USA between 1959 and 1979 found sex-related differences in knowledge about political parties and in political ambition. Researchers linked this to gender-role socialization. However, Githens is critical of both the research and the conclusions. She queries whether the survey questions administered were appropriate to establishing political knowledge, and whether the researchers decided too easily that socialization alone could account for the differences they discovered. She points out that other research conducted since 1971 has found little difference (Githens 1983: 475–6).

Among the many research projects criticized for failing to take account of women is Almond and Verba's magisterial account of *The Civic Culture* (Goot and Reid 1984: 123). However, Sidney Verba collaborated in a recent work that seeks to make good the forty-year-old omission. This sizeable research project sought to explain differential political participation in the USA in terms of differences in domestic and labour market positions and experiences. While the researchers found that there were overall differences between women and men in terms of political interest, political information, amount of political discussion, sensitivity to political cues, exposure to the media, and a sense of political efficacy, differences were not always what they had expected.

They found that 'although there is a long list of issues on which men and women might be expected to have different opinions, their actual preferences reflect these expectations very imperfectly, if at all' (Burns, Lehman, Schlozman and Verba 2001: 31). Men and women differed little over abortion, but there were long-standing differences of opinion on a range of issues involving violence, and a more recent difference over government welfare programmes.

What is particularly interesting is how the researchers account for these differences. In among the familiar explanations entailing socialization, socio-economic factors, and domestic responsibility, we find the claim that 'a powerful factor in explaining the gender difference in these orientations is the gender composition of the political environment [. . .] when women appear on the political scene in visible and powerful positions, the political involvement of women citizens increases significantly' (Burns, Lehman, Schlozman and Verba 2001: 353).

Of course, simply claiming this does not really clarify things. Rather, it leaves open the question of how those visible and powerful women managed to break through. Is it that women in general are politicized by these remarkable and successful women (the role-model effect)? Or has there been a change a priori that encouraged the politicization of women in general and permitted a few to break the political mould? At least this research lifts some of the burden from women themselves and opens up the possibility that it might not be the women who are passive but rather a system that locks them out. Perhaps in having a lower estimate of their political efficacy than men did, women were not showing a lack of political nous, but rather a realistic assessment of modern democratic politics!

All this leaves unanswered at least one question: is it that women are less interested and active, or are researchers asking the wrong questions? Delli Carpini and Keeter investigated political knowledge in the USA and found that there were measurable differences between men's and women's knowledge of national politics and government that persisted (although diminished) when social and economic variables were taken into account. There was no difference, however, when it came to knowledge of local politics, and less difference over issues of particular relevance to women (Delli Carpini and Keeter 2000). This gives some support to the argument that women are interested in different things from men, and are knowledgeable about those. As the authors point out, knowledge matters. Women are voting in greater numbers than men in the USA, so it matters that their votes are informed; and if people want to change things, they have to understand what it is they are trying to change (we should remember that this is US research and may not be universally applicable).

With regard to participation, Susan Welch found that 'women as a whole participate as much as men once structural and situational factors are considered [. . .] women participate in the aggregate less than men not because of some belief that they hold about the role of women in politics, but largely because they are less likely to be found in those categories of people who participate in politics: the employed and highly educated in particular.' (Welch 1977: 727–8). Which is to say that if the primary determinants of political engagement are a good job, decent pay, economic security, a good education and a fair amount of free time, and if fewer women possess these than men, it is not sex *per se* that is causing any differences, but instead the sexism that locks more women than men into disadvantageous social and economic positions.

More recent research undertaken in the UK for the Electoral Commission by Norris, Lovenduski and Campbell found an activism gap that varied according to social status and resources. They found a smaller gap in better-off households and among graduates, and the largest gap among those with the lowest levels of education. Married women were less likely to participate than married men, the difference being greatest where there were children living at home. Activism varied with age, but men were found to be more active than women at all ages. Along with age, ethnicity had an effect: although no activism gap was found between ethnic minority and other men, minority women were less active than other women.

As in the US research, the UK project found that women had 'a weaker sense of their own ability to make a political difference than men and are less interested in politics' (Electoral Commission 2004: 2). One finding – much repeated in the media in the days after publication of the report – was that

> the presence of women as representatives increases women's activism. In seats where a woman MP was elected in 2001 women's turnout was 4% higher than men's. Women were also less interested in the election campaign and less likely to say they would volunteer to work for a candidate or party in seats with a male MP. Women were far more likely to agree that 'government benefits people like me' in constituencies with a female MP (49% compared to 38%). Where a man represented the seat, this gap reversed. (Electoral Commission 2004: 2)

Similarly, asking the right questions was key for Inglehart and Norris. From extensive international research, they conclude that although across societies women are slightly less politically active than men, that difference will likely diminish with time, as the younger cohorts succeed the older (Inglehart and Norris 2003: 126). In addition, the activism difference varies across countries, with agrarian societies showing larger gaps in political interest and activism than post-industrial societies.

It is further argued that not only are researchers looking at the wrong things, they are often looking in the wrong places. One of the important corrections that feminism has made to political science is its insistence that politics happens in a wide range of places outside parliaments and parties (as demonstrated in the essays in Githens et al. 1994). Once we look at local politics and pressure groups, *ad hoc* political movements and street-level campaigning, as well as the workers behind the scenes in political parties, we find much higher levels of female activism (for example, Parry, Moyser and Day (1991) identified this in the UK; Delli Carpini and Keeter (2000) found that women had higher levels of local than national political knowledge in the USA).

The research funded by the Electoral Commission in the UK (2004) found that the type of activity was key in identifying differences in participation between men and women. While no difference was found in voter turn-out, women were equally or more likely than men

> to participate in cause-oriented activities such as signing petitions or boycotting products. Yet in relation to other activities such as participating in demonstrations or protesting illegally, there are no gender differences. Men are significantly more active than women in campaign politics across all activities such as party membership, party donations and contacting politicians. Men are also generally more involved in civic-orientated activities such as belonging to voluntary associations, hobby, consumer or professional groups and sports or social clubs. (Electoral Commission 2004: 2)

Reinforcing this, Inglehart and Norris found in their international comparison that the gap in activism they identified between men and women 'varies substantially by the type of organisation. Men tend to dominate some organisations, such as sports clubs and professional associations, while women predominate as members of religious, health-related and social welfare groups' (Inglehart and Norris 2003: 126).

When considering the sorts of things that women might participate in that would show up only in carefully designed research, the example of the Support Stockings in Sweden, as described by A. Stark, is instructive. After the 1991 elections the proportion of women in elected office fell for the first time since 1919, from 38 to 33 per cent of representatives. This was largely an effect of the Greens losing their seats and a new conservative party, New Democracy, making gains. The Support Stockings formed as a network to support women already engaged in politics (Stark 1997: 229). They operated informally and secretly, relying on pre-existing extensive networks of women in the public and private sectors, trades unions and politics, researchers, pensioners and activists (Stark 1997: 231). As policies emerged from the new government that would disadvantage women, the Support Stockings mobilized. They wrote articles and letters, made phone calls, gave lectures, used networks, contacted politicians, and gradually raised awareness and inserted new items into the political agenda. Quite quickly other groups emerged, and women's organizations within political parties took note.

There was pressure on the Support Stockings to form a women's list (party). A poll in 1993 showed that 40 per cent of voters would consider voting for a women's list headed by a key Support Stocking (Stark 1997: 235). However, the pressure was resisted by the Support Stockings – although the perceived threat of a new party encouraged existing parties to include more women on their lists for the next election. The goal of the Support Stockings was to achieve a real political shift – and this was more likely to happen if a number of parties changed their policies, rather than one new party entering parliament (Stark 1997: 240). The strategy was successful. At the next election more women than ever were elected, and the new government declared that it would make gender a top priority.

The political activism of the women in this example is targeted, sophisticated and effective. However, it would not necessarily show up in any standard survey of political participation that looked at parties and parliaments in isolation from grass-roots networks. This may, in part, account for assumptions that have been made about women's political participation in the absence of good information. The sort of research recently undertaken by Inglehart and Norris, and by Norris, Lovenduski and Campbell for the Electoral Commission, is going a long way to correct this deficit.

Gender Gap

There is a long-standing, little-examined assumption that women are politically more conservative than men. This has been backed up by voting statistics which show women tending to vote for more conservative parties in slightly larger proportions than men at least some of the time. Recently, this contention has come in for intensive investigation. Questions arise about the demographics of the population, the nature of the parties and policies, and whether voting alone is enough of an indicator from which to make sweeping judgements about opinions.

Voting behaviour is an area of research to which huge amounts of energy and resources have been dedicated. Why people vote, how they vote, what influences their vote – all of these questions have been extensively analysed. As we have seen, one of the most profound misgivings about giving women the vote was what they might do with it. If they simply voted as their menfolk instructed them, it would make no difference; if they voted more conservatively than men (as was predicted by some, on the basis of women's religiosity, connection to the home, and investment in the *status quo*) it could tilt the balance in favour of conservative parties; and if they formed women's parties, voting as a block favouring certain policies and issues (paralleling class politics), it could disrupt entire political systems. Once it became clear that women voted on party lines, just like men, interest in their interests diminished (Levy 2001: 186).

A general assumption that the voting preferences of men and women from the same socio-economic groups were largely undifferentiated persisted into the 1970s. Data showed that women tended to vote in slightly higher proportions for more conservative parties, but this seems to have been regarded as only to be expected, rather than deserving of investigation. In 1975 Goot and Reid wrote, 'it may come as something of a surprise to find on turning to the academic literature, that the political behaviour of this half of the electorate has been the object of little in the way of questioning or systematic research' (Goot and Reid 1984: 122). In their article, 'Women: If Not Apolitical, Then

Conservative', they expose, first, how little had been written directly about women and, second, how mainstream researchers failed to pay attention to the women included in their data. One researcher quoted had dropped all the women from his survey because 'a claimed interest in politics is largely concentrated among men' (Goot and Reid 1984: 123). Goot and Reid were on the whole puzzled by their finding that, despite research which showed women in the UK voting for the Labour Party in equal or even greater numbers than men at particular times, women were still characterized as Conservative-voting and conservative. Their puzzlement was compounded by reports from the USA, Belgium and Australia detailing elections where women supported left or socialist parties more than men.

Although voting statistics from a range of countries in the post-war period showed a tendency for women to vote in slightly higher proportions than men for more conservative parties, more recently there have been some reversals. The term 'gender dealignment' was coined in the 1980s to describe the discovery of minimal sex differences in voting behaviour and party preference, while in the USA the term 'gender gap' was used to describe a phenomenon that emerged in the Reagan years of greater proportions of women voting for the Democratic Party than men, and more men than women voting Republican (Inglehart and Norris 2003: 75–100). But what are these statistics telling us? Is it enough to look at accumulated numbers and make judgements about whole populations? And what about the terms 'gender dealignment' and 'gender gap'? Is it meaningful to refer simply to these large groups of men and women, or do we need to break down the numbers rather more carefully?

Taking the UK as an example, voting analysis is usually done in terms of class, traditionally an array of five economic groups, since class is considered to be the most important variable in UK politics. However, when it came to differences between men and women, these were often assessed on raw statistics without factoring in such variables as class, race, religion, age or language, which might otherwise be regarded as significant in voting behaviour.

Exhaustive analysis undertaken by Pippa Norris and others has demonstrated that quite different things emerge once you get the variables right. Using British election surveys compiled since 1964 and the Eurobarometer, she reaches two conclusions: first, that, 'Rather than a simple "generation-gap" we argue that it is more useful to talk about a "gender-generation gap" [. . .] Older women remain more conservative than older men [. . .] nevertheless, younger women are more left-wing than their male counterparts' (Norris 1996b: 333; also Inglehart and Norris 2003).

Norris found that in the period researched in the UK, women were initially more Conservative than men in their voting. This gap diminished in the 1980s, reappeared in 1992, but reversed by generation: in the eighteen to twenty-four age-group, 53 per cent of women voted Labour, compared to 33 per cent of men, a 20 per cent gap; in the older age-group there was an 18 per cent gap going the other way. Once established, this pattern has held for most subsequent elections (Norris 1996b: 336).

Second, looking across the range of countries covered by the Eurobarometer, Norris found regional differences. Taking Europe as a whole, Norris found that in 1983 younger women positioned themselves slightly to the left, and older women slightly to the right, of men in the same age-group. In 1994 this trend was even more marked (Norris 1996b: 339). However, she concludes that her research 'suggests considerable variation cross-nationally in the gender gap, with women more right-wing than men in Britain, Australia,

Luxembourg and Italy while women are more left-wing in Germany, Spain, Portugal and the USA' (Norris 1996b: 333). Finally, 'The results suggest that the conventional wisdom about women's greater conservatism across Europe is no longer valid' (Norris 1996b: 340).

In their comparative study of eleven European nations, De Vaus and McAllister pick up the debate around women's relative conservatism and move the argument on:

> The view that women are more conservative than men can also be criticised as focusing too narrowly on voting behaviour and ignoring various aspects of sociopolitical behaviour where females appear less conservative than males. For example, women are more opposed to war, the use of force, nuclear energy and nuclear weapons, and generally more favourable to welfare programmes and environmentalism. (De Vaus and McAllister 1989: 242)

Further research undertaken by Inglehart and Norris led the writers to conclude that women held more 'left-leaning' values than men in most countries – a reversal of their positions up until the 1980s. Like De Vaus and McAllister, the writers explain this in terms of the different 'value orientations' of men and women, particularly with respect to 'postmaterialism, the role of government, and gender equality'. Differences are defined by generation; therefore, 'if this finding reflects a generational change, as seems likely, rather than a life-cycle effect, it implies that in the long term, as younger voters gradually replace older generations, the shift toward left-leaning values among women should become stronger in affluent nations' (Inglehart and Norris 2003: 99–100). Thus, both generation and region, as well as the content of values, need to be taken into account when discussing whether women differ from men in political orientation.

Just to demonstrate that voting behaviour is a continually shifting target, in the most recent data the UK appears to have reversed slightly. According to a MORI poll taken in August 2003, men and women supported Labour to the same extent, 41 per cent, while the Conservative Party drew more support from men than women, 31 as against 29 per cent, and fewer men than women supported the Liberal Democrats, 21 as compared to 22 per cent (Turquet 2003a, b).

Acknowledging the existence of gender gaps is one thing, explaining them another. As Studlar, McAllister and Hayes point out, explanations for differences between women and men still tend to follow the same pattern: differing early socialization, gender inequalities in socio-economic achievement, the constraints experienced by women in different social/economic and political situations, and gender differences in political characteristics (Studlar, McAllister and Hayes 1998). Their research, which compared the USA, the UK and Australia, indicates that the explanation of gender gaps varies from one country to another. They concluded that in the UK and Australia structural factors, such as occupational experiences as well as family commitments, explained the gender gap, whereas in the USA it was due primarily to political orientations.

So, to sum up, women's voting behaviour is not consistently different from that of men, although it differs from that of men often enough to be of interest. Women are not consistently either more radical or more conservative than men (and it should be noted that the very terms 'radical' and 'conservative' are themselves problematic: was it entirely fair to characterize voting for Margaret Thatcher as conservative when her government's policies were the most radical of a generation? Was it conservative or radical to vote for neo-liberal policies in post-socialist countries?). If voting surveys are sensitive enough to use accurate sex, gender and policy variables, we shall be able to trace differences, but experience so far suggests that we may be surprised by what we find.

Political Parties and Women's Votes

While political analysts were failing to examine differences between the voting behaviour of men and women, political parties were failing to target women's votes. So strong were assumptions about the dominance of other cleavages, such as class, that variations within those groups were not considered. Moreover, parties were confident about their own constituencies.

Political parties in industrial countries sustained three major shocks in the late twentieth century. First, in the 1960s, with the growth of social movements and single-issue groups, people – particularly but not exclusively the young – created alternative channels for their political energy. Second, the 1980s saw the growth of new parties (Green, Right, Nationalist and, in at least two instances, Women's). Third, with economic change those parties that had been reliant on strongly defined constituencies, such as unionized labour in heavy industry, started to lose those constituencies. These factors, in conjunction with growing political apathy and/or cynicism forced political parties to attempt to rejuvenate their roots.

At around the same time, whereas formerly women had concentrated their political activism outside formal politics, now they started to focus on parliaments and parties. This coincided with issues raised by women at grass-roots level, such as domestic violence, rape, child care, and the distribution of taxes and benefits, gradually filtering up into formal politics. As a result, parties began to court women's votes.

A pamphlet from the 1980s published by the Institute of Workers' Control in London presents what was then a fairly novel argument: that the Labour Party should attempt to salvage its electoral position by recruiting women from outside the working class (Eldergill 1984: 6). The writer claims: 'Clearly women have a gender interest in socialism since their political subservience is rooted in their social and economic position [. . .] If Labour is to make gender an issue, and use it to complement the class orientation of its vote, then to be credible and successful will mean substantial reform within the party' (Eldergill 1984: 6–7). The writer goes on to argue that both the party and the unions should change their practices in order to make themselves accessible to women. During the 1980s the Women's Action Committee was set up within the Labour Party, both to improve women's participation in party structures and to push the party towards paying attention to women's interests, and thus their votes (although the last of these was not the specific concern of the WAC). Eldergill took issue with the leadership of the party to claim that 'women's organisation and women's rights are seen to be the fourth greatest topic of concern to affiliated groups in 1983 [. . .] Neil Kinnock ignores these at his peril when he makes glib comments on television about WAC's Anne Petifor not being in any sense representative of constituency opinion' (Eldergill 1984: 16).

In the 1990s, as it looked increasingly unelectable and embarked on radical change, the Labour Party began to take this seriously. It committed itself to a women's minister and ministry for women, should it come to office. To the despair of feminists in the party, this was announced in a glossy brochure, fronted by a photograph of a 30-ish white woman in a suit, wearing a wedding ring.

Conclusion

From the vantage point of the early twenty-first century, we can see that women around the world have the vote on equal terms with men, and that they use that vote in similar proportions. Their voting behaviour is cross-cut by similar class, regional, ethnic and religious variables to that of men, and is, therefore, similarly complex.

Women may vote differently from their male counterparts at particular times and places – sometimes more conservatively, sometimes more radically. Research into voting behaviour needs to take greater account of this and to pay more attention to underlying determining factors, such as concern for the environment, welfare and war. Parties target women's votes, but not all parties and not all of the time. There are major debates about the differences and similarities of the political interests of men and women, but political parties tend to trail behind the rest of society in addressing these.

FURTHER READING

The suffrage movement has attracted large numbers of writers from both historical and political perspectives. In addition to texts cited above, both Richard Evans and Olive Banks are of interest, since they provide international perspectives. Pippa Norris has written extensively on women's voting behaviour, and Rosie Campbell has recently undertaken research into how British women's voting decisions are made.

Banks, O. 1986: *Faces of Feminism*. Oxford: Basil Blackwell.

Campbell, R. 2004: Gender, Ideology and Issue Preference: Is There Such a Thing as a Political Women's Interest in Britain? *British Journal of Politics and International Relations*, 6 (1): 20–44.

Evans, R. 1977: *The Feminists*. London: Croom Helm.

Inglehart, M. L. 1981: Political Interest in West European Women. *Comparative Political Studies*, 14 (3): 299–326.

Inglehart, R. and Norris, P. 2003: *Rising Tide: Gender Equality and Cultural Change Around the World*. Cambridge: Cambridge University Press.

Norris, P. 1996a: Gender Realignment in Comparative Perspective. In M. Simms (ed.), *The Paradox of Parties*, St Leonards: Allen and Unwin, pp. 109–29.

Norris, P. 1996b: Mobilising the 'Women's Vote': The Gender-Generation Gap in Voting Behaviour. *Parliamentary Affairs*, 49 (2): 333–42.

Norris, P. (ed.) 1998: *Elections and Voting Behaviour*. Aldershot: Dartmouth.

Norris, P. 2001: *Britain Votes 2001*. Oxford: Oxford University Press.

WOMEN AND ELECTIONS

5

Introduction

This chapter examines the issues and research surrounding the election of women to national assemblies. First, the disputed claim that electorates won't vote for women: this has been used as an excuse for the failure of parties to promote female candidates, although there is little evidence that it exists. Second, we consider the barriers impeding women's election. And third, we discuss the ways of overcoming these impediments that have been proposed and executed. The discussion of solutions in this chapter looks at strategies other than quotas; quotas themselves are the subject of chapter 6.

Research into Voting for Women

In order to get elected, women first have to become candidates, and then they have to win enough votes to take their place in the parliament. Misgivings about women's ability to win votes have served as a reason (or excuse) for not selecting them as candidates; so we shall start there.

Contrary to popular belief, electorates show little evidence of sex discrimination when they come to vote: 'Repeated studies of gender and voting behaviour indicate that the absence of women in electoral office is not the result of voting in general elections but is attributable to party nomination practices' (Economic Commission for Europe 2000: 170). People may allocate their votes on the basis of party, policy or prejudice, but the sex of the candidate is seldom considered relevant. The research that Norris and Lovenduski undertook into candidates for the 1992 election in the United Kingdom looked into voter discrimination. They concluded that 'it is the lack of women inheritors and strong challengers, not voter discrimination, that is responsible for the under-representation of women in the Commons' (Norris and Lovenduski 1995: 234). In general, voters want a party rather than a person to win an election. Loyalty may accrue to a particular MP over time, but this again tends to transcend sex.

The definition of some terms will be useful before proceeding here. An 'incumbent' is someone who has been elected to an office (say, Labour Member of Parliament for Hastings) and is holding that office at the time of the upcoming election. A 'challenger' is someone from another party (say, Conservative or Liberal Democrat) standing for election to that office. An 'inheritor' is someone who is clearly marked out as successor to a retiring incumbent (such as the selected Labour candidate standing for election in Hastings when the incumbent Labour MP is retiring). Other important concepts are those of 'safe' and 'marginal' seats. A safe seat is one that a particular party has won at previous elections with big majorities; a marginal seat is one that is held with a small majority and that has swung between different parties in the past. These are sometimes called 'winnable' seats. Another important term is 'turnover' – the proportion or number of seats that become vacant in an election period, or the rate at which new members are able to enter the Parliament.

These terms, and the situations to which they apply, matter when it comes to changing the elected personnel, as we shall see below.

The United Kingdom

In the aftermath of the Labour Party's landslide win in the 1997 General Election in the United Kingdom, Studlar and McAllister analysed the impact on voting behaviour of the all-women short lists, a quota system that the Labour Party had put to limited use. They found that:

> First, women did less well than men in every party in terms of votes, notably Labour (receiving 3.3 per cent fewer votes than men). But most of this was attributable to the fact that fewer of the women who stood were incumbents. Indeed, among challengers, Labour women actually did better than men in the votes they received, by 1.4 per cent. Second, voters did not discriminate to any extent between men and women candidates, with the slight exception of Labour where the women as a whole did less well than their male counterparts. Finally, within the Labour party, candidates from the women-only shortlists did substantially better in attracting votes than their male counterparts as well as compared to women candidates who were nominated on open shortlists. They also achieved a larger vote increase in their favour. (Studlar and McAllister 1998: 81)

So, it would appear that voters in the UK are not much concerned about the sex of a candidate. Moreover, having been selected for candidacy through a pro-active strategy did not, in this instance, disadvantage women – rather, the reverse!

The United States of America

The United States is in a sense the polar opposite of the UK: whereas in the UK voters are almost entirely directed by party loyalty and may well not know the name of the person they are voting for, voters in the USA are encouraged to consider the individual and the policies, rather than the party. Analysing voting for House of Representatives candidates between 1968 and 1992, Barbara Burrell found that the differences between men and women were negligible, concluding that sex counted for less than 1 per cent of the variation (Burrell 1994: 141). Extending the analysis to 1994 and 1996, Richard Fox found that there was very little difference in the vote totals of men and women candidates, and that in two of the categories he analysed (women running for open seats in 1994 and female challengers in 1996), women had an advantage over men (Fox 2000: 233).

If Americans are happy to vote for a woman, we are still left with the question of why there are so few (in terms of international comparisons) elected. Analysing US voting patterns, Adell Cook points out that although many more men than women win elections in the USA, this is not due to voter bias, but to the fact that most candidates and incumbents are men. She adds:

> [t]his does not mean that no voters are biased. Survey data shows that as many as one in five of voters agree that women are less well-suited to politics than men [. . .] In almost all cases, those voters who display a gender preference also consider other factors in making their vote decisions [. . .] thus, although the sex of the candidate is a factor, incumbency, partisanship, and ideology drive most vote decisions. (Adell Cook 1998: 71)

This research from the UK and the USA strongly suggests that (at least in these two countries) voters are not discouraged by female candidates, and that analysts should look elsewhere for explanations of women's relatively low presence in politics.

Barriers to Women's Election

Candidate selection procedures

Once the relative absence of women from elected office came to be seen as a problem, both researchers and activists debated causes and solutions. Interestingly, this was not considered to be a problem until the 1970s. On the one hand, it was assumed that, given legal equality, in time, women would filter into parliament just as they would filter into the professions; on the other, the doctrine of liberal democratic representation assumed that being a representative transcended personal qualities, and that anyone could (and should) represent everyone.

Women's movements, like other social movements of the 1960s and 1970s, were initially dismissive of formal politics. However, as women became more conspicuous in other areas of society, and as women's movements moved on, the booted-and-suited appearance of our assemblies and the thwarted ambitions of those women who *did* want to get elected advanced a new agenda. Getting women elected became a goal for the first time. This entailed analysis of both the processes and the potential candidates, as well as measures to remedy the situation.

In the search for understanding why there are relatively few women elected to the majority of parliaments, analysis from around the world comes down firmly on the side of political factors: party procedures for the selection of candidates, along with incumbency and the single-member district simple plurality electoral system, seem to discourage the selection of women. Structural factors, such as the rate of turnover of seats, the quantity of seats that a party wins, and the number of seats in a constituency, seem to influence the chances of women getting elected. While social, economic and family variables may disadvantage women, these do not actually stop women coming forward (although they probably ensure that fewer women come forward than would like to in a perfect world).

The major barrier to women's election is the resistance of parties to select women as candidates for winnable seats (in first-past-the-post systems) or to select women and place them on lists in positions that make it likely that they will be elected (PR list systems) (Norris and Lovenduski 1995). Women also face barriers in terms of their socio-economic positions, which discourage them from coming forward in equal (or greater) numbers than men. Women around the world earn less money than men, possess less wealth and have less free time. They are less likely to have the sort of professional and community experience that is considered (rightly or wrongly) to be appropriate to a politician, and less likely to have access to the sorts of contacts and networks that provide support to prospective politicians (for example, professional, business, trade union and masonic networks) (Inglehart and Norris 2003: 29–48). Moreover, they may be actively prohibited from involvement outside the home by family and community power structures (see Inglehart and Norris 2003 for a good discussion of the role of culture). All of these are connected to women's traditional roles in the family and the community, and are strong disincentives to getting involved in politics. Women *do* get involved in politics, however, but often at more local, informal levels. That being the case, the question arises of whether there is something about formal national politics (apart from the selection system) that discourages women.

Again, countries and systems vary, but it is argued that in general the organization of national politics has not been conducive to women's participation. The distance from home of the seat of government, working hours that do not permit family responsibility, lack of supportive facilities for members who are carers, attitudes and practices that tend to exclude women (or anyone else who does not conform to a particular stereotype of the politician) . . . all of these have been cited as reasons why women do not appear to be as enthusiastic about going into national politics as men. There is certainly some truth in these, but all can be dealt with – or changed – and women do deal with them, and change does take place, albeit not as many or as much as we might like.

A quantity of research, conducted internationally, has analysed the variables related to women's political participation. From a comprehensive summary of the research, Kenworthy and Malami conclude that 'political factors clearly play a central role in determining the degree of gender inequality in political representation. We find strong support for the effect of the electoral system structure. Party list/multi-member district systems are more conducive to the election of women to national legislatures than are candidate-centred/single-member district systems' (Kenworthy and Malami 1999: 251).

They further conclude that the timing of women's suffrage – how long since women have achieved the vote and the right to run for office – is related to women's political representation: the longer women have possessed the vote, the more women are to be found in elected offices. Rather surprisingly, socio-economic factors are less significant. Only women's share of professional occupations is consistently associated with the proportion of women's parliamentary seats. Neither women's overall participation in the labour market, their level of educational attainment in the society, the number of national women's organizations, nor the general level of economic development of the country appear to have a direct effect. On the other hand, Kenworthy and Malami's analysis confirms expectations about the relevance of cultural attitudes: nations in which religions emphasizing traditional roles for women dominate tend to have fewer women in parliament.

By pulling together research and data from around the world, Kenworthy and Malami are able to point to patterns at an international level. The relevance of political factors to women's political representation in developed countries has been accepted for some time; this analysis extends the relevance to less developed countries, and then indicates the universal significance of the timing of women's suffrage and cultural attitudes.

Specific analyses of Argentina and Costa Rica support these findings. In addition, the experience of these countries suggests that the type of list system used matters. Closed lists, in which the party determines the order of candidates, produce more elected women than open lists from which voters select candidates. These analyses confirm that the size of the constituency matters, larger constituencies being more favourable to women's election than smaller ones, and add that the size of a party's vote matters: the larger the vote, the more opportunity there is for women to share in it (Matland and Taylor 1997; M. Jones 1998).

Discrimination

While not overstating the case, we should not dismiss overt discrimination against women in selection processes. Research undertaken for the Fawcett Society in the UK, funded by Nuffield and conducted through focus groups and interviews, asserts strongly, and contrary to some earlier studies that discrimination does take place. With regard to the Conservative Party, the Fawcett Society claims:

> Our research found that in some cases discrimination manifests itself in the form of overt sexual harassment. More often, women are treated differently to men in the candidate selection process. Women are asked questions about issues such as child-care, which male candidates are not. Old-fashioned views of 'a woman's place' among selection panel members often undermine the possibility of a fair selection process. As a result of these outdated views, the Conservative Party is losing high quality female candidates. (Fawcett Society 2003a)

Conservative MP Theresa Gorman bore witness to the attitudes within the party when she told G. E. Maguire that selection committee chairs would comment on female candidates' appearance: her own high heels and that others were too fat, too small, or even too glamorous (Maguire 1998: 197).

Similarly, research into the Labour Party found that 'overt discrimination and sexual harassment during the selection process are significant factors in the failure of women to get selected to safe/winnable Labour Party seats' and that 'Equal Opportunities in the selection process are not fully understood. Women continue to be assessed differently than men' (Fawcett Society 2003b).

With regard to the Liberal Democrats too, the Fawcett Society found that 'forms of covert discrimination are widespread and are a significant factor in the failure of women to get selected'. Further, good equal opportunities practices were not regularly followed in selection processes, so female candidates were asked different questions from male candidates (Fawcett Society 2003c; see also Lovenduski 2004 for further analysis of the discrimination data).

Evidence of discrimination can be found around the world. For example, although there is disagreement among US analysts, at least one school of thought argues that discrimination occurs in the form of gender stereotyping (see the discussion in Fox 2000 and Ford 2002); researchers in India found widespread discrimination inhibiting the success of quotas (Desai 1997); and in Russia there seems to be broad agreement that discrimination takes place (Kochkina 2001).

Case Studies

The first three case studies discussed here are the United Kingdom, the United States and Canada, anglophone countries where first-past-the-post is the dominant electoral system. These are followed by a discussion of New Zealand, which adopted a version of proportional representation fairly recently and remains somewhat undecided about it; Russia, which operates a form of proportional representation; and Japan, which also operates a form of PR.

Parties which build expectations of candidates on gendered assumptions fail women. They do this either by not putting them forward as election candidates, or by ensuring that they will lose. As critics of the UK Labour Party have pointed out, 'the members of selection conferences are as subject to conditioning as everyone else and the myth of women's unsuitability for public office, together with the newer one that they are vote losers, makes it difficult for all but the most outstanding to succeed' (Watson and Anand 1984: 14).

The United Kingdom

Norris and Lovenduski cite the absence of inheritors and strong challengers in order to explain the relatively small numbers of women elected in the United Kingdom. The absence of inheritors today is a result of the absence of strong challengers yesterday. Norris and Lovenduski investigated the lack of strong female candidates in terms of the supply of women candidates, and parties' demand for women candidates. They discovered differences between the practices of the major political parties; however, their research clearly demonstrated the problems of both supply and demand. They concluded that the main obstacle to women's candidature in the United Kingdom was the conservatism (and covert sexism) of selection committees (Norris and Lovenduski 1995).

Each country and electoral system has its own unique characteristics. In the United Kingdom the dominance of two parties that control all but a tiny number of seats in single-member constituencies via a first-past-the-post electoral system, has telling effects. Although all seats are up for grabs at a general election, relatively few actually change hands. First, most seats are fought by the people who actually hold them (incumbents). Second, incumbents are returned more often than not. This means that the party holding a seat will not be looking for a new candidate, and the candidate for the party challenging the seat is unlikely to win. A small number of seats are marginal: held by one party with such a small majority of votes that the other party is likely to take it. These are the seats that decide elections. This means that there is relatively little turnover of Members of Parliament and that parties tend to focus on a relatively small number of seats and candidates at each general election. With general elections held about every four years, and some 95 per cent of seats held by men in the 1970s, it was painfully clear that, even with good will, it would be a long time before there was a significant number of Labour women in Parliament (see Matland and Studlar 2004 for a discussion of the importance of turnover).

In the 1980s the UK Labour Party was locked out of office by the success of the Conservative Party and demographics: its key constituency of workers in heavy industry was fast diminishing as heavy industry disappeared and the UK restructured itself as a service economy. The Labour Party was strongly recommended to direct itself towards an alternative constituency: women. However, this was not intended to be a purely cynical recommendation, since '[i]f Labour is to make gender an issue, and use it to complement the class orientation of its vote, then to be credible and successful will mean substantial reform within the party' (Eldergill 1984: 7). Reforms would include positive discrimination, child care for elected officers and Members of Parliament, a recruiting drive, and education to encourage women and challenge men's sexism (Watson and Anand 1984: 14). The Labour Party introduced a positive measure to ensure the selection of a greater number of female candidates than ever before for the 1997 general election: all-women short lists for half of the vacant safe seats. This was a remarkably successful, although short-lived, initiative, achieving the selection of thirty-five women candidates before being terminated in response to a sex discrimination decision in a tribunal brought by two male Labour Party members (see Studlar and McAllister 1998).

In 2004 the Conservative Party is in a position similar to that of Labour in the 1980s. Although the party has always had over 50 per cent female membership, and its grassroots mobilization relies on women in the constituencies, women do not figure strongly in the party hierarchy or in Parliament (Maguire 1998). Like Labour, the Conservative Party realizes that it needs more women, both as party officers and as candidates, but it is even less willing to take strong measures to achieve it. In a recent pamphlet Fiona Buxton gives four reasons for increasing the number of female candidates: to achieve a better intuitive understanding of the electorate, to represent women's interests more credibly and effectively, to access a broader and deeper pool of talent, and to create a visible symbol of the party's commitment to equality (Buxton 2001: 6). She goes on to analyse the problems in the party: there are few female members who are under the age of forty-five and likely to want to be candidates; when women do apply, there is no evidence of discrimination in selecting candidates for the approved list, but there is a degree of discrimination by local constituencies in selecting candidates from the list (Buxton 2001: 6).

Canada

Thus, in the UK the obstacles are single-member constituencies, the first-past-the-post electoral system, incumbency, and the independence of constituency parties when it comes to selecting candidates. Similarly in Canada, Gidengil claims that 'the numerical underrepresentation of women seems to reflect biases in the recruitment and nomination process rather than discrimination on the part of voters. Local party control over recruitment is cited as a critical barrier to women's access to elected office. Women are much less likely than men to be candidates, and female candidates are less likely to win than male candidates because they are more likely to be nominated to un-winnable seats' (Gidengil 1996: 23). However, Canada benefits from an unusually high rate of turnover, which increases opportunities for new candidates, including women. Like Gidengil, Heather MacIvor also identifies the tradition of local patronage and the weak central control of parties as a problem for the selection of women, while drawing attention to some supply-side issues. Women in Canada face the problems of women everywhere: family responsibilities and relatively limited resources; but she argues that the nature of Canadian politics might be particularly off-putting, since it is characterized by intense partisanship and aggressive posturing (MacIvor 2003: 32).

The United States of America

According to Fox, there is disagreement among researchers in the USA about whether sex discrimination exists in the electoral process, with one group claiming that women are in fact on an equal footing with men (Fox 2000: 230). This group of researchers argues that there are no significant differences between women and men in terms of winning percentages, vote totals and fund-raising receipts; thus the only problem is the shortage of women coming forward (Burrell 1998; Selzer, Newman and Leighton 1997; Chaney and Sinclair 1994, quoted in Fox 2000: 230). On the other hand, Fox details another group of researchers who claim that gendered stereotypes and expectations persist throughout the electoral system and that these disadvantage women (Conover and Gray 1983; Fox 1997; Kahn 1996; Huddy and Terkildsen 1993a and 1993b, quoted in Fox 2000: 230).

There appear to be several issues of particular relevance to women standing for election (Ford 2002: 106–22). Perception of electability is one shared with much of the rest of the world. Research indicates that women are as electable as men, once they are candidates, but false perceptions may be a factor in women choosing not to stand. It is a fact that fewer women run than men. Georgia Duerst-Lahti analysed the obstacles facing women in the USA and identified 'pipeline' as one of the major impediments to their selection and election. This is the process of preparing and running for office. Since fewer women than men enter politics at the lower levels, as a result of having less access to financial and other forms of support, there are fewer women trained and experienced to run for the more senior posts (Duerst-Lahti 1998: 18–20).

In the United States political parties have far less control over the selection of candidates than in the UK and other European countries. Although parties endorse candidates and can provide finance, candidates can put themselves forward on party tickets and provide their own finance. Parties are none the less important gatekeepers and providers of funds. There is no agreement among researchers as to whether parties discriminate in the selection of candidates. David Niven's 1998 research suggests that gender bias was present, and this links with broader findings about the influence of stereotypes and the media (Ford 2002: 111, 117).

Recent research conducted by the Women's Leadership Fund and reported in the *Christian Science Monitor* suggests that media coverage of women candidates in the USA may contribute to their difficulties (Feldman 2003). The study claims that media coverage of women candidates for executive office focuses less on their positions on political issues, and more on their personal characteristics, than the coverage of male candidates does. So readers know more about what men intend to do if they get into office than they do about women's intentions, although they know more about the women's appearances and families. This emphasis might suggest to readers that the men are more qualified than the women. While this is not proved to influence voting, it is suggestive.

Pressure to raise money is a powerful factor for the individual in US politics, not usually experienced in Europe. It is generally believed that women have more difficulty raising money than men because of their social positioning; however, Burrell's research (1998) suggests that women raise nearly as much money as men. The impact of specific funds (Political Action Committees, or PACs) for women has been important here. Women contribute to funds in order to provide resources for female candidates, but do women vote for women? In the USA, as in the UK, research is indicating a preference for female candidates among female voters (Selzer, Newman and Leighton 1997). Women tended to vote Democrat more than men (gender gap), but the gender gap grew when the candidate was a woman, and in several cases reversed when the Republican candidate was a woman (Ford 2002: 117).

Finally, aspects of the electoral system have effects on women. Incumbency is a powerful obstacle to women, since incumbents usually hold their seats at subsequent elections, and there are very few women incumbents. When women are incumbents, they in fact do slightly better than men at retaining their seats (Duerst-Lahti 1998: 18–20). However, there are moves to introduce term limits at state level. Where these have been implemented, the majority of legislators affected have been men, and women have benefited, although the results have been mixed (Thompson and Moncrief 1993; Caress 1999; Ford 2002: 119). Additionally, although the USA practises first-past-the-post, like the UK, at local level it has both single-member and multi-member constituencies. As in the UK, women and minorities tend to do better where there are multi-member constituencies (Ford 2002: 121).

New Zealand

Having changed its electoral system from first-past-the-post to mixed-member proportional (MMP) in 1996, and confirmed it in 2001, New Zealand is a good test case for the effects of an electoral system on women's political presence. In the three elections since the change of system, the numbers of women elected initially increased, only to decrease slightly at the 2002 election. The number of minority representatives has increased, and

Table 5.1 Women elected to Parliament in New Zealand

Year of election	Percentage
1993	21.2
1996	29.2
1999	30.8
2002	29.17

Source: IPU website

the number of parties increased prior to 2002, when it decreased again, along with voter turn-out (Boston et al. 2000; McLeay 2003).

First-past-the-post disadvantages women; however, New Zealand managed to elect a greater proportion of women under this system than did other countries (McLeay 2000: 212). McLeay accounts for the growing number of women elected in the 1980s and 1990s in terms of party politics. Women active in the women's movement and single-issue politics moved into the Labour Party in the 1970s. There, 'they encouraged women to become candidates and urged the organisation to select them' (McLeay 2000: 212). The National Party responded to this by selecting a few women for winnable seats. Once MMP was introduced, the inclusion of women gained a new impetus.

Under MMP each voter has two votes. Half of the seats in the House of Representatives are filled through party lists, and half by single-member constituencies. McLeay argues that the existence of party lists spurred parties to demonstrate their feminist credentials by producing gender-balanced lists. Further, the new parties that entered Parliament under this system produced more elected women because there was no incumbency problem for them to negotiate. In addition, some of the new small parties had explicitly feminist agendas. As a result, there was a leap in the number of women MPs in 1996 from 21.2 to 29.2 per cent. This increased again, to 30.8 per cent, at the 1999 election. However, in the 2002 election the number of women decreased to 29.17 per cent (see table 5.1).

In the 1996 and 1999 elections more women entered Parliament through the party lists than the single-member seats. At this point McLeay suggested that the nature of the system, combined with the nature of the parties, may have been delivering a new form of glass ceiling, as the parties relied on the party lists to return female MPs while leaving the obstacle course of local selection processes and incumbency to dominate the single-member seats. The Labour Party tried to address this and encouraged the selection of women for single-member seats: twenty-three women stood in the 1999 election. The National Party, on the other hand, is not addressing the problem, and the four seats from which two female and two male MPs retired before the 1999 election were all fought and won by men in 1999 (McLeay 2000).

In 2002 women's relative success in list seats reversed, and they won more single-member seats. McLeay attributes this to parties: 'the domination of political party over voter choice has ensured that parties are the gatekeepers for electoral success' (McLeay 2003: 302). The more left-wing Green Party, Labour and ACT are the most woman-friendly of the parties, all returning over 35 per cent female MPs in 2002; other parties returned a smaller proportion. For Labour, male incumbency is a problem; moreover, the two MPs retiring in 2002 were both replaced by men. McLeay comments: 'the experience of Labour shows that even when a party is ideologically in favour of women's representation, and there is a reasonably adequate supply of women candidates (28 out of 65), incumbency and electoral mechanics can work against women's equal representation' (McLeay 2003: 300). The Greens were far more successful, in large part because they did not have to work around incumbency.

The parties of the centre and the right both selected and returned far fewer women – significant for the overall numbers of women in an election that resulted in a centre coalition government. Both the conservative New Zealand First Party and the centrist United Future returned no women in electoral seats, and placed women in disadvantageous positions on their lists, resulting in 7 and 13 per cent respectively (McLeay 2003). It is not clear whether the scarcity of women selected by parties of the centre and the right is due to prejudice or a lack of candidates (McLeay 2003: 299). With regard to the National Party, on the other hand, there is evidence of a sufficient supply of women candidates, but 'women rarely gain nomination by National for winnable electorates and do not gain many high National list places' (McLeay 2003: 300). In 2002 four National women lost their seats because they were placed low on the list.

Russia

The number of women in elected office in Russia has diminished radically since 1990, after the abolition of the quota system in national elections that had operated during the Soviet period. Salmenniemi argues that during the period of *perestroika*, as the Soviet Union crumbled, women queued for food, while men established the ground rules for the future. As a result, although there are many women active in politics locally and in informal activities, and although women vote in larger numbers than men, they are excluded from formal politics and government (Salmenniemi 2003). Unusually, proportional representation has not promoted women's representation in Russia. To the contrary, in an electoral system that has both PR list and single-member seats, women are more successful in the single-member election (with the exception of Women of Russia in 1993) (Moser 2003). There are more female candidates for list seats, but they are less successful than the women nominated for single-member seats. This appears to be a function of the power that parties have to define constituencies and to position candidates on lists. Moser concludes that, 'left to their own devices as individual candidates in SMDs [single-member districts], women perform remarkably well. Because PR tier nominations are party-controlled, and parties routinely place most of their women in unwinnable spots on the PR list, women usually do not do well in PR elections' (Moser 2003: 162).

In the run-up to the 2003 election, women did not figure strongly among selected candidates: only Yabloko had a quota for women. The Communist Party and the Union of Right Forces had only two women candidates in the first ten positions on their party lists. Yabloko had two candidates, but not among the first ten; United Russia, President Putin's party, had no female candidates in its federal party list. It is no great surprise, therefore, that, according to Hesli et al., among Russian feminists, 'there is a distrust of the state and its apparatus that runs deep in virtually all women activists' (Hesli et al. 2001: 70).

The emergence of the Women of Russia party and its initial electoral success went some way to getting women into the Duma, but most commentators seem to agree that male politicians and the political parties obstruct women's entry at all levels. A comment made about post-Communist countries in general adds to this: 'In many countries an outright majority of women believe that men make better leaders. In others, the proportion is sufficiently sizable that it poses a significant electoral barrier. Clearly, there is currently little unorganized demand for electing more women to legislatures in east and central Europe' (Wilcox, Stark and Thomas 2003: 60).

Japan

Since 2000, Japan has operated a mixed electoral system with 300 representatives returned from single-member constituencies, elected by simple majority, and 180 seats filled through allocation based on the parties' share of the national vote in eleven large multi-member districts (IPU website). Japan regularly elects one of the smallest proportions of women in any stable democracy. It is easy to assume that this is due to a conservative and traditional culture in which women are defined by family roles. However, research into the influence of political variables here is instructive, and supports the claim that these are universally the most important determinants of women's electoral success, or otherwise.

In its first post-war election, over 8 per cent of those elected to the Diet were women – more than in the UK, the USA, Australia, New Zealand, France and most other industrialized countries. However, this rapidly fell, and has rarely exceeded 3 per cent subsequently (Darcy and Nixon 1997). Women's poor political performance is usually accounted for by Japanese culture. Japanese women are limited in their social roles, and economically lag considerably behind men. However, the electoral and party systems, and other political variables, should not be dismissed.

Darcy and Nixon point out that the 1946 election, in which women won more seats than before or since, operated in a way never again repeated. First, there were no incumbents, as a result of a purge of pre-war politicians. Second, the election used multi-member constituencies in which electors had more than one vote. Moreover, for that election alone there was only one House. In subsequent elections, electors have had only one vote; multi-member constituencies became instead two-member constituencies, incumbency began to kick in, and the left-wing parties decreased in importance. According to Darcy and Nixon, 'After 1946, rather than building on electoral features that had encouraged the election of women, the political system revoked such features. Certainly none of these reversals were taken with the intent of reducing the number of women elected. That was merely a side effect. Absent, of course, was the political purpose of electing more women' (Darcy and Nixon 1997: 7).

From 1946 Japan used a system of multi-member constituencies, with voters exercising one vote. This appears to have operated with the same disadvantages for women as first-past-the-post. Political change in Japan should have meant that the 1993 election signalled change for women in politics. New parties had emerged in response to widespread dissatisfaction with the discredited old politics and parties. There were seventy female candidates running in 43 per cent of the constituencies; women were prominent in party advertising and posters, and received considerable media attention. Moreover, women had done well in elections to the Upper House and in a recent local election (Darcy and Nixon

1997: 8). In the event, only 2.7 per cent of those elected to the Lower House in 1993 were women. This was largely an effect of women running for parties that did not win, and in seats where their parties lost. Thus it came down to women being put forward for unwinnable seats.

The 1996 election saw an increase in the numbers of women both as candidates, to 153, and as elected members, to 23. The increase in the number of women continued in the 2000 election, fought under the revised electoral system: 202 women ran for office (14.4 per cent of candidates) and 35 were elected (7.3 per cent of the total seats). In the Social Democratic Party, led by a woman, Takako Doi, ten of the nineteen representatives elected were women (52.9 per cent) (*Women's International Network News* 2000). The political system had not changed radically, but politicians had become aware of social change in gender relations and roles and sought female candidates – what came to be called 'the Madonna Effect'.

Japanese women experience the undoubted disadvantage of a culture in which they are strongly discouraged from public activity. The Japanese word for wife means 'Mrs-in-the-back-of-the-house', and there are legal incentives to encourage married women to quit full-time jobs (*Women's International Network News* 1997). None the less, political and party variables are important here, as in other countries, as the comparison of the 1946 and subsequent elections shows.

Solutions

While deploring the low numbers of elected women is common practice, agreeing on what, if anything, should be done about it is not. In 1997 the Fawcett Society sent a questionnaire to all 120 of the women Members of Parliament in the United Kingdom in an effort to ascertain their opinions about which measures should be taken to improve this situation. The 120 included a number of women who had benefited from the Labour Party's short-lived all-women short list initiative. While only 3 per cent of respondents thought that no action should be taken, support for positive measures was varied, as shown in table 5.2. Strongest support was for the least controversial measure, party training schemes for women: 98 per cent of respondents approved of this. Least support was for changing parliamentary hours to nine to five (only 35 per cent approved) and introducing a proportional voting system for election (45 per cent). All-women short lists and better child care facilities were strongly supported (71 per cent and 77 per cent); a three-day parliamentary week and financial support for women were quite strongly supported (62 per cent and 60 per cent) (Stephenson 2001: 6).

While these responses show unequivocal support for the existence of positive measures, they show rather less than might be expected from people who have witnessed years of women failing to get elected, and the remarkable effects of a one-off initiative to improve their chances. Conservative and Labour women had different attitudes to the proposals for increasing the number of women in Parliament: the majority of Conservatives disapproved of all the proposals except for candidate training by parties.

The survey indicates some of the problems of even thinking about introducing positive measures, particularly partisan or ideological differences. The reluctance of women

Table 5.2 Support among female MPs in the UK for measures to increase the number of women elected

Measure	Approve strongly (%)	Approve (%)	Disapprove (%)	Disapprove strongly (%)	Not stated (%)
Party training programmes for women	76	22	0	1	1
All-women short lists	33	38	13	13	3
Better child care facilities in Parliament	36	41	10	4	9
Changing parliamentary hours to 9-5	14	21	27	24	14
Three-day parliamentary week	35	27	22	6	10
Financial support for women candidates	15	45	27	5	8
Introducing PR voting system for elections	21	24	18	26	11
No action	3	0	12	37	48

Source: Stephenson 2001

on the Right to support positive measures reflects the general finding that there are more women elected where leftist parties dominate.

The most straightforward and uncontroversial form of positive action is simply for parties and governments to claim that they would like more women to come forward. Rather like a business proclaiming itself an Equal Opportunities Employer, this gesture of good will is sometimes assumed to be adequate, and, having made it, the beneficiaries of the *status quo* sit back and wait for change to happen.

If the research discussed above is accurate, it strongly suggests that measures to increase women's participation that do not address the nature of the political system and/or deeply entrenched cultural values will not achieve very much! This is pretty much borne out by the experience of countries where years of waiting for the effects of political access to feed through, and of witnessing the empty rhetoric of politicians and parties, has been translated into demands for radical positive action and positive discrimination.

In the UK, radical action (short of positive discrimination) has tended to come from outside parties. The strategy of raising funds to assist women candidates, Emily's List (Early Money Is Like Yeast), was created in the USA and adopted in other countries. By providing money for women to campaign, and support to enable them to do so, Emily's List attempted to help women around one of the obstacles to participation: their relative lack of resources. The 300 Group is a UK initiative, founded as a campaigning group to raise awareness and get more women into Parliament (300 members of parliament would constitute approximately one-half). It provides a network for women, as well as training courses and seminars.

The Conservative Party limits itself to encouraging women to stand. In the 1980s, when Emma Nicholson was vice-chair for women of the party, she instituted high-flyers' conferences. These were annual, high-profile conferences to which successful women were invited. These women, not necessarily party members, were then encouraged to partici-pate in the party. Having lost two elections, three leaders and much of their credibility as the opposition party, the Conservative Party since 2001 has been vocal in its recognition of the need for female candidates. While he was leader, Iain Duncan-Smith made at least one speech to this effect; Caroline Spelman MP has a special responsibility for this; and Fiona Buxton has written a pamphlet for the Bow Group laying out the options. These, however, do not include much by the way of active assistance for women.

Buxton acknowledges the problems: the pool of prospective candidates is small, since there are few women members under forty-five; there is discrimination by local constituencies when they come to select candidates from the recommended list. Her solu-tions range from creating structures to encourage younger women to join the party, through creating policies that appeal to women, to training, mentoring and outreach, as well as monitoring selection procedures to eliminate discrimination. The party has reformed the first stage of its selection process, selection to the approved list. The party has identified the key skills necessary for an MP and assesses applicants on the basis of such skills. It is finding that men and women perform equally well. But there has been little or no reform of the second stage of selection, which takes place in local party associations.

In the UK, positive action on the part of parties and government has been limited by interpretation of the Sex Discrimination Act, which outlaws all differentiation of treat-ment on the basis of sex (this was amended in 2002 to make an exception for political parties). By the late 1980s, the absence of women had become a key theme, 'practically every week, in every political party, people are saying, both at internal meetings and in public, they hope far more women will stand for elected office and especially for Parlia-ment' (Abdela 1989: 30). But it was not an issue that parties seemed to know how to address beyond exhortation, prior to the 1997 and 1999 elections discussed in the fol-lowing chapter. Campaigns for electoral reform have included in their arguments the claim that first-past-the-post militates against women and members of minorities, and that change to a system of proportional representation would result in a more representative assembly, but no party has retained its commitment to PR once it has formed a govern-ment (although the 1997 Labour Government has instituted a limited form of PR in the new regional assemblies, the system of Additional Members).

In the USA, finance represents a major obstacle that is relatively easy to address (although a lot harder to solve). Both the Republican and the Democratic parties promote women's candidature through recruitment, training and campaign funding. Women's financial donations to parties are increasingly important and sought after. The Women's Leadership Forum (WLF) of the Democratic National Committee raises money for women and engages them in grass-roots activities. Founded in 1993, it has twenty state and regional chapters, and claims a membership of over 6,000. The DNC also sponsors a Women's Vote Center, which encourages women in the USA to vote for the Democra-tic Party.

Funding is clearly a central issue for women wanting to enter politics in the USA – hence the creation of Emily's List, which funds Democratic women preparing and running for office. It has 68,000 members and raised $9 million in the run-up to the 1999–2000 election round. It is the largest PAC in the country. The Wish-List raises money for pro-choice Republican women running for elected office. The Women's Senate Network,

Women on the Road to the Senate, and Women LEAD all raise money from women, for women (see Ford 2002 for details of funding organizations).

At the more general level of raising awareness, there is a range of organizations, such as the National Women's Political Caucus, which aims to increase women's participation through training and recruitment; the National Federation of Republican Women, which disseminates republican values and encourages women voters; and the League of Women Voters of the USA, which is a non-partisan organization that seeks to inform and encourage women. However, although individual women match individual men when it comes to funding, the differences in the raw numbers of women and men running for office suggests that these measures are failing to convince women that they will be able to match the funding that men can achieve through their business and patronage networks. Although there is disagreement, it is argued that the tradition of independence from parties, and of individual fund raising disadvantages women.

Conclusion

While women are less equipped than their male counterparts to stand for office in terms of time, money, skills and contacts, they do put themselves forward. They do so even when such cultural considerations as family norms and religion discourage them. However, the structures of politics prove resistant to their efforts. Electoral systems are of particular importance, as Matland and Studlar demonstrate in their comparison of Canada and Norway (Matland and Studlar 1996). Practices within parties, especially at the local level, tend to exclude women from candidacy unless strong measures are taken. The supportive measures described above help individuals, but do not necessarily change structures. The quota systems discussed in the next chapter go further and achieve real change very quickly.

FURTHER READING

Joni Lovenduski, along with Pippa Norris, Vicky Randall and, more recently, Rosie Campbell and Sarah Childs, has comprehensively researched women's political participation in the UK. Her most recent book, *Feminising Politics*, includes an illuminating account of what happens when women run for office. Fiona Mackay specializes in Scottish politics, and in *Love and Politics* examines elections to the Scottish Parliament. Lynne Ford's textbook gives a good summary of the issues in the USA, while the chapters in Thomas and Wilcox are more focused. Manon Tremblay's article is illuminating about the impact of the electoral system and party variables on the political representation of women in Australia and Canada, the chapters in Simms are excellent on Australia, as are those in Boston et al. on New Zealand.

Boston, J., Church, S., Levine, S., McLeay, E. and Roberts, N. 2003: *New Zealand Votes: The General Election of 2002*. Wellington: Victoria University Press.

Buckley, M. 1997b: *Post-Soviet Women: From the Baltic to Central Asia*. Cambridge: Cambridge University Press.

Ford, L. E. 2002: *Women and Politics: The Pursuit of Equality*. Boston: Houghton Mifflin.

Lovenduski, J. 2004: *Feminising Politics*. Cambridge: Polity.

Mackay, F. 2001: *Love and Politics*. London: Continuum.

Poonacha, V. (ed). 1997: *Women, Empowerment and Political Parties*. Research Centre for Women's Studies, SNDT Women's University.

Simms, M. (ed). 1996: *The Paradox of Politics*. St Leonards: Allen and Unwin.

Thomas, S. and Wilcox, C. 1998: *Women and Elective Office: Past, Present and Future*. Oxford: Oxford University Press.

Tremblay, M. 2003: Women's Representational Role in Australia and Canada: The Impact of Political Context. *Australian Journal of Political Science*, 38 (2): 215–38.

QUOTAS FOR WOMEN IN PARTIES AND PARLIAMENTS

6

Introduction

In politics a quota is a number or proportion of seats or places on a list that has been set aside for members of a particular group of people. Quotas are operated for members of religious, language and ethnic groups, as well as for women. A quota system can operate at party or governmental level, voluntarily or by statute. With regard to quotas for women, Drude Dahlerup explains that

> the core idea behind this system is to recruit women into political positions and to ensure that women are not isolated in political life. Previous notions of having reserved seats for only one or for a very few women, representing a vague and all-embracing category of 'woman', are no longer considered sufficient. Today, quota systems aim at ensuring that women constitute at least a 'critical minority' of 30 or 40 per cent. Quotas may be applied as a temporary measure, that is to say, until the barriers for women's entry into politics are removed. (Dahlerup 1998: 92)

This chapter looks first at the rationale behind quotas, before moving on to specific examples. The first two examples given are not strictly quotas (a percentage of seats or positions on a list), but are systems appropriate to the electoral system or culture of a particular country. These are the all-women short lists and twinning of constituency strategies adopted in the UK, and the parity initiative adopted in France. From these we move on to the more orthodox party quotas used in a range of countries, before looking at the issue of reserved seats for women in India.

The Arguments For and Against Quotas

In a surprisingly large number of countries the relative absence of women has been taken so seriously by either parties or government that positive action has been adopted. The soft option is to encourage women to run for office and to include both training and pleas for women to come forward in party programmes. The tougher route is to make some sort of quota system part of either a party's election strategy or a government's constitution.[1] The second route is frequently controversial. None the less, quotas of one sort or another have been put in place in a remarkable number of countries: not only the well-known case of Norway, but also a number of South American, Asian and African countries.

Political parties in Norway have operated quotas since the 1970s, and in Germany since the 1980s, but it was in the 1990s that they became popular more widely. Quotas are operated voluntarily by at least some parties in France, Israel, Mexico, Nicaragua, Paraguay, Spain and South Africa. National laws have been introduced making quotas applicable to all parties in Argentina, Belgium, Bolivia, Brazil, Ecuador, Italy (later revoked) and Peru. They have also been considered in Colombia, Costa Rica, the Dominican Republic, India, Panama and Venezuela (M. Jones 1998; Russell 2000b).

How these have been achieved varies according to the particular electoral and party system of a country. A long-standing method has been to set aside, or reserve, a number of seats for women. India does this in local government, and parties often practise this internally in elections to their national executive committees and other bodies. However, in parliaments it is more common to find quotas operating at the level of candidates for office rather than set-aside seats. Quotas are easiest to achieve in systems where proportional representation operates using a list of candidates. In such a case candidate lists can be used to include women. The best case is when a closed list is 'zipped' so that women and men alternate on the list. However, electoral systems where open lists and even first-past-the-post are used have been manipulated by parties to achieve higher level of female candidature (Russell 2000b).

According to the Inter-Parliamentary Union, by 1995 some eighty-four parties in thirty-six nations had enacted parliamentary quotas (quoted in Caul 2001). By 2003 quotas were, or had been, used in seventy-five countries (<www.idea.int/quota>). Quotas work. Where there are quotas, there are more women in elected office. They have their limitations. As Htun and Jones point out in their discussion of quotas in Latin America, unless either the good will of a party or legislation ensures that women are placed in electable positions on lists, parties can subvert the intention of quotas by placing female candidates in positions that guarantee that they will not be elected. In addition, the size of an electoral district and of a party's share in the vote can limit the number of seats available to women (Htun and Jones 2002).

Moreover, quotas are acceptable only when the relative absence of women from politics is agreed to be a democratic deficit that requires redress through positive action. On the whole, anglophone liberal democracies are very uncomfortable with quotas, construing them as an undemocratic measure granting unfair advantage, rather than a way of addressing undemocratic distribution of advantage. In Gidengil's Canadian research, only 26 per cent of men and 36 per cent of women interviewed regarded the relatively small number of women in the House of Commons as a serious problem. Following on from this, 32 per cent of men and 45 per cent of women favoured quotas requiring the parties to choose as many women as men candidates (Gidengil 1996: 28). She concludes that although there were interesting differences between men and women, the fact of the matter was that, even among women, quotas failed to receive majority support. 'Overall, only two in five of those surveyed favoured requiring political parties to offer gender-balanced slates. Building support for quotas will require an understanding of the factors that enhance, or depress, commitment to equitable representation' (Gidengil 1996: 29). Many other countries around the world are, however, relatively comfortable with the idea. These include countries in Europe, Africa, Asia and Latin America.

Drude Dahlerup has researched and written about quotas extensively. Listing the pros and cons she claims the following:

Against quotas   According to Dahlerup, the reasons usually given for opposition to quotas are as follows. Quotas are against the principle of equal opportunity for all, since women are given preference. They are therefore undemocratic, since they prevent voters from electing their representatives. Quotas prevent the best-qualified people from getting elected, since they imply that politicians are elected because of their sex, not because of their ability: the more qualified (but male) candidates are pushed aside. Finally, introducing quotas creates significant conflict within the party organization (Dahlerup 1998: 94).

In favour of quotas   In order to make the argument for quotas, Dahlerup starts by questioning the assumption that what we already have is democratic. She points out that intervening in the selection process is not necessarily undemocratic, since the process is rather less perfect than it is claimed to be. Since she assumes that women have a right to equal representation, her main contention is that a quota is not discriminatory; rather, it is a way of compensating for the barriers that prevent women from getting their fair share of seats. This scarcely disrupts voters' selection of representatives, since this is done by parties anyway. Nor does it impede the selection of qualified candidates; instead, it prevents political parties from continually reproducing the *status quo* and failing to appreciate the range of qualifications that women possess just because they are not the same as men's. This is vital, since women's experiences are as necessary to political life as those of men, because election in democratic politics is about the representation of citizens and their interests, not the employment of experts. Having a quota ensures that there will be more than one woman on any committee or in any assembly, thus reducing the stress often experienced by a lone token woman, and enabling them to work productively. Quotas may cause conflict to start with, but this does die down, and it is worth it (Dahlerup 1998: 95).

On the whole, Dahlerup's arguments for quotas answer the arguments against. Opposition to quotas is based on the assumption that the *status quo* is democratic and does not discriminate. Dahlerup's arguments start from the position that this is mistaken: our practices are undemocratic and biased in favour of men, and this needs to be corrected. She contends that

quotas for women represent a shift from one concept of equality to another. The classic liberal notion of equality was a notion of 'equal opportunity' or 'competitive equality'. Removing the formal barriers, for example, giving women voting rights, was considered sufficient. The rest was up to individual women. Following strong feminist pressure in the last few decades, a second concept of equality is gaining increasing relevance and support: the notion of 'equality of result'. The argument is that real equality of opportunity does not exist just because formal barriers are removed. Direct discrimination, as well as a complex pattern of hidden barriers, prevents women from getting their share of political influence. Quotas and other forms of positive measures are thus a means towards equality of result. The argument is based on the experience that equality as a goal cannot be reached by formal equal treatment as a means. If barriers exist, it is argued, compensatory measures must be introduced as a means to reach equality of result. (Dahlerup 1998: 95)

In order to discover patterns in the adoption of quotas, Caul undertook research into the political parties of eleven different countries. From her analysis she found that in order to understand the increased adoption of quotas, 'both an external party-system-level influence and internal party characteristics are important [. . .] At the party-system level, the presence of a prototype quota policy makes it more likely that a party will adopt gender quotas. Further, both a greater number of women on a party's highest decision-making body and leftist values within a party significantly increase the chances that a party will adopt quotas sooner' (Caul 2001: 1226). Further, Caul adopts the notion of applying a 'contagion' effect to the creation of quotas, whereby once one party has introduced a quota, others may follow. This is attributed to competition between parties to demonstrate support for women's issues and thereby compete for women's votes. Matland and Studlar (1996) previously applied the idea of 'contagion' in their study of Norway and Canada.

Case Studies

The first examples given here are the approaches adopted by the United Kingdom and France, which are not particularly representative of quota systems adopted elsewhere. Only the Labour Party has adopted anything like a quota in the UK. The party had to be creative, since the UK does not use proportional representation, thereby ruling out the most obvious form of quota: setting aside places on the party list for female candidates. Two attempts at using quotas have been made: the adoption of all-women short lists for the 1997 general election, and of twinning for elections to the new regional assemblies set up in 1999. France, on the other hand, has adopted the goal of parity (equal numbers of male and female representatives) without making explicit how this should be achieved. Other countries have experimented with using quotas in party lists in various ways, some examples of which follow.

The United Kingdom

The United Kingdom is something of a special case because forms of quotas have been introduced into what is predominantly a single-member, simple plurality system. The UK has undergone considerable constitutional change in recent years, and the introduction of all-women short lists by the Labour Party prior to the 1997 election was the first step. Having been elected (with more female MPs than ever before) the 1997 Labour Government embarked on a programme of constitutional change that included creating devolved regional assemblies in Scotland, Wales, Northern Ireland and London. The electoral system for the new assemblies introduced a move away from first-past-the-post, by shifting to the Additional Member system – the weakest form of proportional representation. In this system most of the members are elected from single-member constituencies on a simple plurality vote; however, a number of top-up seats are allocated to parties according to their proportion of the vote. This permits parties a degree of flexibility in assigning candidates to the top-up seats.

The 1997 general election   According to Abdela, the Labour Party in the 1987 general election fielded all-women short lists in a number of constituencies, and 'made a conscious choice to select women for a number of their winnable and Labour-held seats' (Abdela 1989: 31). At the same election Liberal Democrats were obliged to field a minimum of two women and two men on each of their constituency short lists, while the Conservatives did not practise any sort of direct action and instead relied on their high-flyers' conferences to recruit more women candidates. However, Labour did not win the 1987 election, and only 6.3 per cent of MPs elected were women.

In preparation for the 1997 general election, the Labour Party formalized a system of all-women short lists in winnable seats. At the 1993 annual party conference it was agreed that there would be all-women short lists in half of the party's eighty most favourable seats at the next general election. These were either Labour seats occupied by a retiring MP or winnable target marginal seats. The decisions as to which constituencies would run women-only lists were to be made by regional consultation, with the last resort option of the National Executive Committee (NEC) imposing an all-women short list (Studlar and McAllister 1998: 75). This would ensure that women candidates would stand at the general election for at least half of Labour's winnable seats.

The decision was controversial, but thirty-five women were selected in this way before two men from the Leeds Labour Party objected and took the party to an industrial tribunal, claiming sex discrimination. The case was decided in their favour, and all-women short lists were discontinued in January 1996 (Studlar and McAllister 1998: 73). The decision was open to dispute, since the 'job' of an MP is not generally regarded as being the same as the regular forms of employment that fall within the remit of such tribunals. However, the Labour Party did not dispute the decision. On the other hand, constituencies that had selected using the all-women lists did not re-select, and three other constituencies voluntarily chose their candidate from all-women short lists (Studlar and McAllister 1998: 76). The end result was that Labour fielded a considerably higher number of women in the 1997 election than ever before. This in turn translated into more women being elected to Parliament than ever before.

The Scottish Parliament   Interpretation of the Sex Discrimination Act, which had blocked the use of all-women short lists in the 1997 general election in the United Kingdom, continued to be an issue when new elected assemblies with radical agendas were created in Scotland and Wales in 1999.

The Scottish Parliament and the Welsh Assembly are unusual institutions: completely new political spaces created within a successful democracy in a time of peace. As such, their creators were able to use the experience and information available to them to generate a political assembly that benefited from the mistakes of the past, and was shaped to achieve their aspirations. One of those aspirations (at least on the part of a significant minority) was gender equity in representation.

Mobilization for gender equality among elected representatives started well before the Scottish Parliament came into being. The demand for 50 : 50 representation was so strongly pronounced that Tom Nairn claimed that it became symbolic of Scotland's radical, new nationalism: 'the first legislature of modern times fully to acknowledge the equality of genders and build an authentic constitution around that act of liberation' (Nairn 2001: 195). Alice Brown describes the process whereby this happened: 'the mobilisation of women in Scotland [. . .] provides an example of a form of coalition and agenda building politics which has proved one of the most successful strategies for women's advancement' (Brown 2001c: 197). In short: in order to achieve your demands, get them incorporated as symbolic and central to something else that a lot of people are committed to achieving!

Long before the Scottish Parliament was instituted, Scottish women were preparing for it. The Scottish Convention of Women was formed in 1977 as a result of the United Nations Women's Year of 1975. One of its goals was to raise issues of women's representation in the progress towards a Scottish Parliament. It had membership from trades unions, local groups including the Women's Guild, and individuals. The Convention continued to exist throughout the years and participated in the Scottish Constitutional Convention, the organization established to determine the nature of the new Parliament. In 1989 the Scottish Constitutional Convention announced that 'submissions received by the Women's Issues Group were unanimous on the need to ensure that the low level of women's representation in Scottish politics was not continued into a Scottish Parliament' (Levy 2001: 183–6). There were, however, disputes about how this was to be achieved.

The Final Report of the Scottish Constitutional Convention in 1995 included an electoral contract, brokered by women in both parties and the Women's Co-ordination Group. This was a commitment to achieving an equal number of men and women in the first Parliament. The parties were committed to selecting and fielding equal numbers of men and women, ensuring that they were fairly distributed, using the Additional Member system, and ensuring that the size of the Parliament was large enough to facilitate democratic government (Mackay 2001: 40). All of these measures would help to ensure that a significant number of women got elected as well as selected.

The electoral system decided upon for the new Parliament introduced elements of proportionality through the Additional Member seats, along with modern working practices and family-friendly policies: elements which we have seen are regarded as desirable by women, and have proved to be conducive to high levels of women's participation.

All parties except for the Conservatives offered training to potential women candidates. Parties introduced more professional selection procedures, including, in the Labour Party, model job descriptions and person specifications as well as self-nomination. These innovations were of great importance in avoiding the trap common to selection committees of selecting a new candidate on the basis of a close likeness to the previous candidates.

Job descriptions and person specifications force selectors to think about what the 'job' of representative entails, and what personal qualities it calls for. A widespread criticism of selection committees has been that they continue to select candidates on the basis of eighteenth- or nineteenth-century notions of what it is to be a representative. For example, they look for skills in oratory, rather than the ability to co-operate on committees; an aptitude for business rather than the interpersonal skills required for constituency advocacy, and so on. More professional selection procedures mean that the selectors take account of these and work with the requirements rather than their intuitions about suitable people. These procedures, deriving from standard equal opportunities practices, should make it more likely that women and other non-stereotypical applicants are seriously considered as candidates. Allowing self-nomination got around the problem of organized local interests, such as trades unions, monopolizing the applications for selection, and enabled people without links to the traditional organizations to put themselves forward.

The Labour Party in Scotland established a selection board including independent advisers. Criteria-led selection procedures were undertaken to draw up a panel of candidates from which local constituency parties would make their selections (Mackay 2001: 41). The Scottish National Party (SNP) also allowed self-nomination and drew up a final approved list of potential candidates over a selection weekend. The Liberal Democrats encouraged their constituency parties to field equal numbers of women and men, and the Conservatives drew up an approved list of candidates. However, only the Labour Party adopted a specific mechanism designed to produce gender balance. This was 'pairing', or 'twinning', whereby neighbouring constituencies were paired for the purpose of selection, with members in two constituencies voting together to select a woman and a man as candidates for the two seats (Mackay 2001: 41).

The Liberal Democrats planned balanced short lists of two men and two women for each seat, with a zipping mechanism to redress any imbalance at constituency level, but the policy was defeated at their 1998 conference on the grounds that it could be open to legal challenge. In fairness, the Liberal Democrats did try, without success, to get legislation to support pro-active measures in party selection, and backed the Sex Discrimination (Election Candidates) Bill a few years later (more of that below).

The end result was that the first Scottish Parliament was elected in 1999 with 36.4 per cent women, almost equalling the very highest-achieving national parliaments. The Labour Party very nearly achieved the goal of equality, with 48.2 per cent women. According to Alice Brown, 'there was a general agreement that the twinning mechanism introduced by the Labour party had been essential – "if things had been left to take their course it would have been just jobs for the boys" – as had the long women's movement campaign and that women in and outside the political parties had worked together' (Brown 2001b: 252).

In the second election to the Scottish Parliament in May 2003 the achievement was sustained, with the election of 39.5 per cent female MSPs. Women constitute over half of Labour's Parliamentary Labour Party in the Scottish Parliament, a slight increase on the last election. The number of Liberal Democrat women remained the same, while the Conservative Party increased its number of women representatives from three to four. The percentage of women representing the Scottish Nationalist Party increased to 46, and there are also women representing the Scottish Socialists and the Green Party.

The Welsh Assembly   In the preparation for the creation of the Welsh Assembly, equality was added to the agenda by the intervention of women experienced in the women's movement. A draft Democracy Declaration was issued by the Parliament for Wales Campaign in 1994. This document contained an equality clause, inserted under pressure from Jane Hutt, director of Chwarae Teg (Fair Play), and Val Feld, director of the Equal Opportunities Commission in Wales, both of whom would go on to be elected as Assembly Members. The equalities clause stated that 'a future Welsh Parliament will ensure, from the start, that there is gender balance in its elected representatives, and will ensure that its procedures will enable women, men and minority groups to participate to the fullest extent' (Chaney 2002: 4).

As in Scotland, equality came to be regarded as key to the devolution campaign. An increased commitment to achieving equality was made and included in the Government of Wales Act: '[to] make appropriate arrangements with a view to securing that its functions are exercised with due regard to the principle that there should be equality of opportunity for all people' (Chaney 2002: 4). According to Chaney, this equality duty is unique in its non-prescriptive phrasing and consequent all-embracing scope. It applies to all the Assembly's functions and to all people.

In the elections to the Welsh Assembly the Labour Party adopted a twinning method like that used in Scotland, and the Liberal Democrats used balanced short lists in the constituencies. Plaid Cymru used the Additional Member lists to attempt to partially correct under-representation of women in constituencies by selecting a woman to head up each of the five regional lists. The results were even more beneficial to women than in Scotland, with women elected to 38.3 per cent of seats in the Assembly. This included 53.6 per cent of Labour Party representatives and 50 per cent of the Liberal Democrats. However, the Conservatives returned no women and nine men; and Plaid Cymru six women and eleven men (Mackay 2001: 42; Russell 2000a: 43).

Like Scotland, Wales went to the polls again in May 2003. The result of this election was even more remarkable: thirty women were elected, an increase of five, which gave the Welsh Assembly a startling 50 per cent of female members. This makes it the only national parliament in the world to have equal representation of men and women (although it is a national parliament in only a limited sense, and not counted as such by the Inter-Parliamentary Union). Of the Labour Party Assembly Members (AMs) 63 per cent are women – again an unprecedented proportion. The Liberal Democrats and Plaid Cymru both returned 50 per cent women, and the Conservative Party improved its showing with 18 per cent.

The Northern Ireland Legislative Assembly   A new assembly was created in Northern Ireland at the same time as those in Scotland and Wales, but no quota systems have been used in either of the two elections held there. Neither Labour, the Conservative Party nor the Liberal Democrats organize in Northern Ireland, so nothing that these parties had been doing elsewhere carried over. The Northern Ireland Women's Coalition was formed in response to women's absence from Northern Irish politics, and succeeded in getting two women elected to the assembly. The only other party actively to promote women's participation was Sinn Féin, with the result that it returned the next highest proportion of women, 27.8 per cent. The Alliance returned 16.7 per cent, the SDLP 12.6, the Ulster Unionists 7.1, and the Democratic Unionists 5 per cent. There were fifteen women returned in all, 12.9 per cent. While this was a high proportion of women for Northern Ireland, it was a very poor showing in comparison with the other new assemblies.

Table 6.1 Women elected to the European Parliament from the
UK in 1999 as percentage of each party's MEPs

Party	Number of women	% of MEPs
Labour	11	38
Conservative	3	8
Liberal Democrat	5	50
Other	3	–
Total	22	25

Sources: Fawcett Society 2003a,b,c

Representation in the European Parliament Elections to the European Parliament are
conducted using proportional representation: closed party lists for multi-member constituencies. This resulted in an increase in the number of women elected to twenty-two
(out of eighty-seven seats) in 2001, making 25 per cent of the total. Of these twenty-two,
eleven were Labour (38 per cent of Labour's MEPs), three were Conservative (8 per cent
of their MEPs), five were Liberal Democrat (50 per cent), and two were Green (100 per
cent) (Fawcett Society website) (see table 6.1). As the 2004 election approached, the
Labour Party was fielding just short of 50 per cent female candidates, the Liberal Democrats about 40 per cent, but the Conservatives only about 24 per cent (political party websites). This resulted in a return of 24.4 per cent female MEPs. Of the seventy-eight seats
which the UK was allocated in the 2004 Parliament, nineteen went to women: seven
Labour, six Liberal Democrat, three Green, two Conservative and one Sinn Féin.

The Sex Discrimination (Election Candidates) Act 2002 As the 2001 General Election
approached, it became apparent that without any positive action to promote women candidates, the number of women in Parliament was likely to fall. The Fawcett Society, along
with other groups and individuals, mobilized to clarify the legality of party measures to
secure women candidates. When the number of female MPs did indeed fall in 2001, pressure on government increased.

In 2002 the government of the United Kingdom passed the Sex Discrimination (Election Candidates) Act. This finally answered the industrial tribunal decision on all-women
short lists and the Liberal Democrats' doubts about manipulating their short lists and
Additional Member lists in Scotland and Wales. The legislation is permissive rather than
prescriptive. It allows political parties choice in their selection methods, while excepting
them from the Sex Discrimination Act, but does not define what (if anything) they should
do. The French parity legislation, by contrast, is prescriptive, in that it regulates the proportion of women candidates and requires zipped lists. The UK legislation, moreover,
has a 'sunset' clause: it will expire at the end of 2015 unless a statutory instrument
is passed to ensure its continuation. This is in the expectation that by 2015 equality of
representation will have been achieved (Childs 2002a: 2).

The Labour Party has pledged to make use of the legislation to reintroduce all-women
short lists for the next general election. Of the other major parties, the Liberal Democrats voted against introducing any sort of positive measures at their 2001 conference and

may have difficulty turning this around; the Conservative Party does not appear to have a policy beyond exhortation and a wish list of one-third of winnable seats to be contested by female candidates. Without any means of the central party organization enforcing the selection of women, it is hard to see how the highly autonomous constituency parties will meet this goal.

France and parity

France has also adopted a highly individual approach, doubtless more suited to French political culture than the straightforward practice of party quotas taken by such countries as Norway and described below.

The parity movement in France started as positive action and resulted in a form of quota. The movement has its roots in a conference on women and decision-making in the European Union, held in Athens in 1992. At this conference women representatives, including Edith Cresson and Simone Weil from France, signed a declaration, known as the Athens Charter, describing a strategy designed to bring about a balanced participation of men and women in political decision-making by means of a parity democracy. A parity democracy would be one in which there were equal numbers of women and men in elected office. This was taken up in France the following year, when a campaigning group took out an advertisement in *Le Monde* to publicize 'The Manifesto of the 577 for a Parity-Democracy'. This demanded that a law should be passed to ensure that as many women as men held elected offices in France (Haase-Dubosc 1999). Opinion polls over the next few years showed remarkable levels of support for parity, 86 per cent by 1996, and political parties picked up on it by the mid-1990s (see Jenson and Valiente's (2003) article for an interesting discussion of the parity movement).

The French system of democracy includes a large number of parties and several different electoral systems, including both FPP and PR. Elections to the European Parliament use a closed party list system in which voters choose parties and parties choose candidates. At the 1994 European election, six French parties submitted lists that reached or nearly reached parity between men and women (Haase-Dubosc 1999). As a result, the French returned 29.9 per cent women to the European Parliament, 4 per cent above the European total.

During the 1995 French Presidential campaign, candidates were asked to state their positions on parity. All except for Jean-Marie Le Pen (Fronte Nationale) said it was a desirable goal. Despite setbacks over the next few years, parity became increasingly accepted as a democratic goal. In the 1997 elections for the National Assembly, national leaders of the Left parties decided that significant proportions of women should be run. There was local opposition, but this none the less translated into 'a lot of women candidates on the left. The most important change was among the socialist candidates, not exactly parity, but 30% of women nevertheless' (Jenson and Valiente 2003: 74–83; Montane 2000: 3).

Parity was passed into law in 1999. This was achieved by an amendment to Article 3 of the Constitution, enabling the National Assembly to determine laws to encourage equal access to elected office for women and men. New electoral legislation in 2000 regulated the proportion of women candidates at all levels, including the European

Table 6.2 Women elected in France

Level of government	Year	% women
Local government	2001	48
Assembly	2002	12.2
Senate	2001	10.9
European Parliament	1999	42.5

Source: IPU website

Union, although presidential elections and some local elections are excepted (Bird 2003: 14). Gender-balanced party lists have been required since March 2001, and lists for the European Parliament and the national Senate must be zipped. Unbalanced lists result in fines (Russell 2000b: 19). The local elections of 2001 resulted in an increase in the number of women holding municipal office from 22 to 48 per cent (see table 6.2). In the same year, elections to the Senate returned only 10.9 per cent female members, as a result of 'opposition from Senators and machinations by them' (Jenson and Valiente 2003: 70). The 2002 election to the Lower House, however, resulted in a rather better 12.2 per cent (IPU, 30 October 2003; Lovenduski 2004).

While the implementation of parity has been resisted – both by individuals who want to retain their seats and by parties that can afford to forfeit some of their funding – its application has been uneven. As Karen Bird points out, in the 2001 local elections it applied to only 2,624 of more than 36,500 municipalities. Further, it did not apply to the selection of mayors or of their cabinets (Bird 2003: 14). Bird concludes that the parity law was effective in bringing women into politics, where it applied, but that political leaders showed themselves to be unlikely to cede power to newcomers unless required to do so by law (Bird 2003: 15).

Party quotas (or not) in the Nordic countries

The Nordic countries (Norway, Sweden, Denmark, Finland and Iceland) provide the key example of party quotas and, in the case of Norway, what they can achieve. The five countries are not, however, identical and have taken somewhat different approaches, with Iceland avoiding quotas altogether.[2]

With reference to Norway, Hege Skjeie writes: 'gender quotas are not simply the result of a sudden recognition by party leaderships that women indeed constitute half the population. Nor are they merely a question of party tactics. Gender quotas are also an end product of a line of political arguments that have forcefully maintained that gender constitutes an important category that needs to be fully represented' (Skjeie 1991: 236). The electoral system in Norway is one of proportional representation in multi-member districts. The multi-party system includes Social Democratic, Labour Socialist, Conservative, Progress, Centre and Christian People's parties. Between 1975 and the early 1990s several parties introduced 'formal quota regulations which specify the composition of party-controlled political posts. Minimum quotas specifying a 40/60 percentage balance were first introduced on the left by the Socialist Left party in 1975, then adopted also by the Labour party in 1981/3. In 1989 the Centre party followed suit' (Skjeie 1993: 235–6; see also Matland and Studlar 1996).

In Norway, quotas have supported a political system and culture that was clearly predisposed towards encouraging women's participation. As a result,

> [n]o Norwegian cabinet since May 1986 has included less than 40 per cent women. By May 1991, half the major political parties had elected a woman as leader. And a male journalist about to organise a debate on recent developments in the negotiations on European economic cooperation might well discover that, if he wants to include the most important political actors, he himself would be the only man on the panel. (Skjeie 1993: 231)

There is a tendency to talk about the Nordic countries as a group, as if there were no differences between them. While it is true that their differences from each other pale in comparison to their difference from the rest of the world (with respect to gender equality), their differences are none the less important, as the recent collection of essays, *Equal Democracies? Gender and Politics in the Nordic Countries*, edited by Christina Bergqvist et al. (1999) has detailed. With regard to quotas we tend to generalize from the Norwegian experience, and overlook the fact that Iceland and Finland do not operate quotas, only one party in Sweden has a quota, Denmark ceased to use quotas in 1996, and Iceland uses separate women's lists and the Women's Alliance party.[3] The use of quotas is not consistent. As Christensen points out, 'It gives pause for thought that, as the Swedish and Finnish social democracies are in the process of introducing gender quotas for the first time, the practice is being voted out by their Danish sister party after having been in use for about fifteen years' (Christensen 1999: 81). Differences in the acceptability and usefulness of quotas seem to derive from differences in electoral systems and political culture. For example, the Finnish electoral system is based on a personal ballot. There, voting specifically for a woman has been important, and women's political organizations have focused on 'Vote for a Woman' campaigns (Christensen 1999: 81). In Sweden, although formal quotas are very recent, the informal principle of Varannan Damernas, 'Every Other Seat a Woman's Seat', has been in effect since the 1980s (Christensen 1999: 82). Iceland, on the other hand, rediscovered the practice of separate women's lists in 1982, generating the parliamentary Women's Alliance party in 1983 (Styrkarsdottir 1999: 91).

Other examples of party quotas

Germany is an example of a country where political parties adopted quotas of women candidates for election. Eva Kolinsky writes of Germany: '[t]he focus on quotas has considerably extended the chances for women to play an active role in political parties and to rise through office holding and candidacies to parliamentary seats and leadership positions' (Kolinsky 1993: 134). In what was then West Germany, the emergence of the Green Party in the 1980s presented a challenge to the existing parties when it pledged to ensure equal access to party posts and parliamentary seats for men and women (Kolinsky 1993: 131). This translated into a 50 per cent women's quota added to the party's statutes in 1985, and 57 per cent of the Green Party elected to the Bundestag in 1987.

Following the example of the Greens (and chasing the same youth vote), the Social Democratic Party (SPD) incorporated a women's quota into party statutes in 1988 (Kolinsky 1993: 130). This was the achievement of ten years of activism by women in the SPD, which had included a separate election campaign in 1976. It was agreed that by 1994 women should hold no less than 40 per cent of all party offices, and that by 1998 the quota should be applied to party lists and parliamentary representation (Kolinsky 1993: 130). According to Kolinsky, the newly introduced quotas made a visible impact on the 1990 Bundestag elections, in that more women than ever before were nominated to favourable positions. This resulted in an overall increase of women's membership from 15 per cent in 1987 to 20 per cent in 1990. For the SPD this was the far greater increase from 16 to 27 per cent (Kolinsky 1993: 136). The proportion of women now stands at 32.2 per cent (IPU, 30 October 2003).

After unification, the Party of Democratic Socialism (PDS) introduced a 50 per cent quota combined with a zipping mechanism, and has met or even exceeded its targets in elections (European database: women in decision-making. Country Report Germany). Following suit, the Christian Democratic Party introduced a requirement for 30 per cent representation of women in party functions and election lists, but this is not yet being met.

Although there is an impetus to include women, it is often done carelessly by parties other than the SPD, PDS and the Greens: 'in the CDU, CSU, and FDP women tend to cluster at the bottom of the lists. By contrast the SPD and Greens have linked the nomination of women to the order of places and enforced a more even gender distribution on their lists.' (Kolinsky 1993:142). Influenced by the Beijing Platform for Action, government is developing strategies to secure women's equal participation in all forms of decision-making, including political participation.

Across Europe quotas have been experimented with. In Belgium political parties have been obliged to employ a minimum quota of 25 per cent women on all party lists since 1994 (Russell 2000:19), while in the Netherlands one party, Labour, introduced a 25 per cent quota for all party boards and candidate lists in 1977 (Leijenaar 1998: 99). Italy, on the other hand, introduced a law in 1993 that required parties to zip their lists, which was repealed in 1995 (Russell 2000:20). The Spanish Socialist Party introduced a quota of 25 per cent minimum women in 1988, and all other parties introduced quotas in the 1990s.

The Israeli Labor Party and Meretz operate quotas for women on their lists for election to the Knesset. Labor increased its quota from 10 to 25 per cent for the last election. However, rather than 'zipping' its list (alternating male and female candidates – the most pro-active option) it manipulates the placement of women on the list. For example, reserving three places in the first ten, three in the second ten and so on. Since there are also quotas for other groups, such as immigrants, women are sometimes 'double-reserved' with one place on the list accounting for two quota reservations. Meretz has a quota of 30 per cent and has decided to reserve four places in the first twelve of the list for women, with one in the first five. It does not allow double-reserving, so women standing as immigrants or Arabs are in addition to the women's quota. Likud does not operate a quota, but manipulates its list to push some women up if they do not get enough votes to qualify. So if no woman is included in the top ten of the party's vote-winners, the woman with the highest number of votes is pushed up into the tenth place. Despite strong egalitarian trends in Israel, counter trends of religious conservatism tend to impede the progress of women into the Knesset, with the result that only 15 per cent of the representatives elected in 2003 were women (*Ha'aretz*, English edition, 18 December 2003).

Party quotas have been adopted in a number of Latin American countries. Argentina was one of the first countries in the world to use a gender quota to increase women's political participation when the Peronist Party did so for congressional elections in the 1950s. This resulted in women making up 15 per cent of the national Chamber of Deputies in 1952, and 22 per cent in 1955 (M. Jones 1998). Use of quotas was then suspended for some forty years, reappearing in 1991. In 1991 Argentina introduced a law that required parties running in national elections to include a minimum of 30 per cent of female candidates on closed party lists in all the country's twenty-four multi-member electoral districts, and to place these women in electable positions on the lists (Gray 2003). Party lists that did not meet these requirements were to be rejected (M. Jones 1998). This was very successful in getting more women elected.

Between 1983 and 1991 only 4 per cent of the Deputies elected were, on average, women. At the 1993 election, the first since the new legislation, 21 per cent of the Deputies elected were women. This increased to 28 per cent in 1995, and fell to 27 per cent in 1997 and 26.5 in 1999: it is one of the higher proportions of women in the world, although the downward trajectory gives pause for thought.

Argentina is a federal state with twenty-three provinces, each of which has its own constitution and electoral system. Twenty-one of these adopted gender quotas, as did many of the local electoral bodies in the City of Buenos Aires Council. Cordoba increased its quota to 50 per cent (Htun and Jones 2002). There is considerable variation between the provinces: some are unicameral and some bicameral, they have different schedules for re-election, and they operate different sorts of party list. Nevertheless, the effect of quotas was to increase the numbers of women, although the degree of the increase varied according to the type of list used (M. Jones 1998; Craske 1999: 70–7). Further, a law was passed in 2000 applying a 30 per cent quota to the candidate list for elections to the Senate (Gray 2003). Htun and Jones argue that quotas have been successful in Argentina because of the use of closed lists, rules that determine the placement of women in electable slots on the lists, the large size of electoral districts, and good faith! – factors which do not apply in all countries seeking to increase the numbers of women elected through the introduction of quotas (Htun and Jones 2002).

India and its neighbours

Like the UK, India is struggling to facilitate the election of women in a first-past-the-post electoral system. Like Israel and Northern Ireland, difficulties are compounded by conservative religious parties. The issue of quotas ('reservations') is hotly contested in India – although it is not new, and reserved seats already exist for scheduled castes and tribes. In 1974 the Committee on the Status of Women in India recommended statutory reservations of 30 per cent for women at local level, and called on the parties to adopt positive measures to ensure that significant numbers of women stood as electoral candidates. When the 30 per cent reservation at local government level (Panchayat and Zilla Panishad) was passed into law via constitutional amendment in 1993, it led to calls for similar reservations in state assemblies and the national Parliament. This was formalized as the 81st Amendment, but attempts made to pass it into law have failed, giving rise to ongoing bitter disputes (Rai 2000: 157–62).

The majority of male MPs seem to believe that introducing a 33 per cent reservation for women, in addition to the seats reserved already for scheduled castes and tribes, would severely restrict the number of seats available to them. In an attempt to break the impasse has come a recent suggestion from Shivraj Patil, Deputy Leader of the Congress Party in the Lok Sabha (Lower House). The suggestion is that the bill can only be passed if one-third of all parliamentary seats become double-member constituencies. This would mean that 182 seats in Parliament would be represented by two MPs with one vote between them, one of whom would be a woman. While this has met with the approval of the senior ranks of the Bharatiya Janata Party (BJP), women's activists do not support it, regarding it as just another delaying tactic. The Election Commission has put forward an alternative plan for political parties to nominate 33 per cent women candidates, but politicians are not particularly supportive of this (Arora 2003). The return of the Congress Party to government in 2004 may result in change.

A number of the countries neighbouring India use quotas to varying effect. Pakistan operates a party quota system for local elections, introduced by the military government of General Pervez Musharraf. The quotas became operative in 2001, as local elections took place throughout the year, across the country. Gender is an important issue in Pakistan, where there are constant calls for the introduction of sharia law, which is widely considered to disadvantage women, where honour killings of women are not uncommon, and where poverty and conflict have gendered effects. There is an obvious tension in the notion of democratization under a military regime, but as a representative of the Aurat Foundation, an advocacy group for women's rights, stated, 'either we could ignore these elections, or we could support them. We supported them because no government in future would be able to turn around and say that there aren't any women out there to contest' (Bokhari 2001: 7). Bangladesh reserves thirty seats for women in the national parliament and one-third of seats in local government; while in Nepal the Constitution and electoral law demand that 5 per cent of the candidates of each political party or organization must be women. However, according to Dahlerup, most female candidates in Nepal are placed in constituencies where they are unlikely to be elected (Dahlerup 1998: 97).

Conclusion

From the research it is abundantly clear that quotas work: where there is a quota, more women get elected. Moreover, women who are elected via a quota system do not appear to be regarded as tokens. It would appear that both national-cultural and party-political differences play a part in whether quotas are adopted. From her analysis of the use of quotas in European Union countries, Pippa Norris concludes that left-wing socialist parties are more inclined to adopt them than centrist and right-wing parties (Norris 1997b). This is supported by Christensen's analysis of the Nordic countries, where she finds that 'it is the social democratic and the non-dogmatic left-wing parties that have especially practised gender quotas' (Christensen 1999: 83).

FURTHER READING

Drude Dahlerup's work on quotas is of great importance, and is cited by most writers in the field. This has been taken up most recently by Joni Lovenduski in her 2004 book, *Feminising Politics*, which has a particularly useful section on parity in France as well as details of Lovenduski's research into the discrimination that takes place in candidate selection in the UK. The Jenson and Valiente chapter is good on parity and makes interesting comparisons with Spain. Meg Russell and Judith Squires have both written useful articles on quotas – Russell's promoted the change of law in the UK to permit all-women short lists and other such measures. For more on Argentina and other Latin American countries, Nikki Craske's book is very readable.

Craske, N. 1999: *Women and Politics in Latin America*. Cambridge: Polity.

Dahlerup, D. 1998: Using Quotas to Increase Women's Political Participation. In A. Karam (ed.), *Women in Parliament: Beyond Numbers*, Stockholm: International Institute for Democracy and Electoral Assistance (IDEA), pp. 91–106.

Gray, T. 2003: Electoral Gender Quotas: Lessons from Argentina and Chile. *Bulletin of Latin American Research*, 22(1): 52–78.

Jenson, J. and Valiente, C. 2003: Comparing Two Movements for Gender Parity. In L. Banaszak, K. Beckwith, and D. Rucht (eds), *Women's Movements Facing the Reconfigured State*. Cambridge: Cambridge University Press, pp. 69–93.

Lovenduski, J. 2004: *Feminising Politics*. Cambridge: Polity.

Russell, M. 2000b: *Women's Representation in UK Politics: What Can be Done within the Law?* London: The Constitution Unit, University College.

Squires, J. 1996: Quotas for Women: Fair Representation? In *Parliamentary Affairs*, 49(1): 71–88.

PART III

Women and Political Parties

POLITICAL PARTIES: BACKGROUND INFORMATION

7

Introduction

This part of the book moves on from voting and elections to the next levels of political participation: party activism and parliamentary candidacy. In order to open up the topics covered, this chapter will give some background to the issues discussed in the following three chapters.

Membership of Political Parties

Women were active in political parties long before they could officially vote or run for office. The best-selling biography of Georgiana, duchess of Devonshire in the eighteenth century, describes her both getting the vote out in her father's and husband's constituencies and running a political salon in which she arranged meetings between politicians and led policy discussions. She was a particularly charismatic figure, but by no means alone. A century or so later, the Conservative Party would never have got anywhere without the mobilization of the Primrose League – an association of Conservative women who ran the party at the grass roots, while opposing giving the vote to women.

Only a small section of any population belongs to a political party: there is a difference between identification with a party and actually belonging to it. Belonging to a party at a minimum entails paying a fee; it can also entail attending meetings, fund raising, chairing, electioneering and maybe, eventually, running for office.

Grass-roots membership is often overlooked in discussions of political parties, yet it is this membership that sustains a party, particularly when it is out of office and at election times. Parties do not always analyse their membership numbers, and they certainly do not always make those numbers available to the outside world. Interestingly, the major European and international data banks do not hold information on the breakdown of membership of political parties by sex. The Inter-Parliamentary Union undertook a large survey of parliaments and political parties in 1995, in which the breakdown of a number of parties around the world was revealed.

Women's membership of parties turned out to be slightly lower than that of men (with exceptions). It varies by country and party, but only in a few of the given instances did women's membership equal or exceed that of men (for a discussion of women's political activism, see Inglehart and Norris 2003). The proportion of women appears to be higher in the more left or environmentalist parties, with the exception of the Conservative Party in the UK, which has a strong tradition of women's grass-roots activism. Included among the countries that revealed their data are the following:

Cuba: women constitute 25 per cent of the Communist Party.
Finland: women constitute between 30 and 40 per cent of the membership of political parties.
Iceland: women constitute 34 per cent of the People's Alliance.
Republic of Ireland: women constitute 38 per cent of the Labour Party, 40 per cent of the Workers Party, and 50 per cent of the Progressive Democrats.
Japan: women constitute 6.6 per cent of the Japan Democratic Socialist Party, 35.9 per cent of the Liberal Democrats, and 45 per cent of Komeito.
New Zealand: women constitute 50 per cent of the Labour Party, 33 per cent of New Labour, and 30 per cent of the Greens.
Sweden: women constitute 40 per cent of the Social Democratic Party and 51 per cent of both the Greens and the Liberals.
UK: women constitute over 50 per cent of the Conservative Party, 40 per cent of the Labour Party, 50 per cent of the Liberal Democrats, Plaid Cymru and the Greens.
USA: the parties do not keep centralized statistics; however, according to opinion polls, 34 per cent of women identify as Republican, 41 per cent as Democrat, 21 per cent as independent, and 2 per cent with other parties (IPU 1992: 66–8).

Activism in Political Parties

While women show comparable levels of grass-roots activism to men, their presence tends to diminish as we trace a path up through party hierarchies. The pyramid effect becomes even more pronounced once we look at the candidates that parties put forward for election, the people who are elected to parliaments, and then the people who form governments; but there are exceptions to this general rule. For example, as we have seen in previous chapters, the Nordic countries have achieved remarkable levels of female candidacy, election and participation in government. In exceptional circumstances, women attempt to address this democratic deficit by forming a women's party.

In the twentieth century, political parties became more formal organizations than they had been before – indeed, in some countries political parties scarcely existed before then.

In most of the world, parties are now recognized membership organizations, governed by legislation that regulates how they raise and spend money. Within party organizations are intricate structures for managing relations between the grass-roots membership, the politicians and the party bureaucrats. The elected politicians are the front line, but behind them are ranks of policy-makers, fund-raisers and election managers.

A political party is an organization of people sharing political beliefs or ideology and focused on getting into parliament and government. Typically, the party will have grown out of an identifiable section of the population: perhaps a class, a religious community, a language group or a regional/ethnic group. As a party it will have salaried officers as well as subscription-paying members, and it will have an organizational structure. Structures represent fund raising, policy-making and electioneering functions. These may be performed by separate or combined offices. Typically there will be local branches and a national executive.

Within a party there are various ways that decision-making can take place. Generally, the more radical the party, the more democratic and devolved its decision-making; the more conservative, the more likely it is that decisions will be made by the leadership. All the political parties in the UK, and many of those in other countries, have an annual national conference or convention at which policies are made. Party members, party members of parliament and party bureaucrats attend the conference to make policy. If interest groups have a role in a party – as trades unions have done in the British Labour and Australian Labor parties – then representatives of these may also have a voice. In a radical party, policies are proposed by the membership and agreed by the leadership; in a conservative party, the reverse tends to be the rule.

Political parties are organizations. They have business premises, employees, employee benefits, wages and hierarchies, as well as a large voluntary sector attached. Internal party organization takes a range of forms, so there is a range of different jobs in different parties. It is important to note who holds these posts, since post-holders and bureaucrats within party structures influence policy and shape the ethos of a party.

Party and Electoral Systems

It is through political parties that a large part of political mobilization takes place. In most countries parties monopolize elections and form governments. There are few political systems in the world that do not operate on the basis of parties, and few representatives that get into an elected assembly, let alone a government, without a party affiliation. Parties and party systems vary tremendously, none the less.

The biggest difference is in the number of parties: one, two or multi-party systems.[1] This is related to the electoral system and influences the way in which candidates for election are selected and the way in which elected members are treated. Electoral systems operate according to some variety of proportional representation (PR) or first-past-the-post (FPP), also referred to as majoritarian, simple plurality or single-member constituency. As we have seen, this has implications for female candidates. Other factors that have been demonstrated to be relevant to the numbers of female candidates and representatives include the size of constituencies, whether these are single- or multi-member, and the size of the winning party's majority. In each case, the bigger the size or number, the more conducive it seems to be to the election of women.

Most states making any claim to democracy operate a competitive system in which two or more parties compete for elected seats and the opportunity to form a government. Parties therefore compete for resources in order to mount and win an election campaign. Resources include both party members and money.

The relationship between members, money and the party again varies a lot, depending on the type of party and the regulations surrounding parties and elections established by the government in any country. For example, there may be limitations on campaign fund raising, limitations on the money that a candidate can spend, restrictions on advertising, and so on. Parties have memberships, but they may also have affiliations to interest groups to which they may owe some sort of loyalty. The most clear example is probably the link often found between socialist/labour parties and trades unions. Trades unions may make financial donations to a party and may have a formal role in policy determination, as in the British Labour Party. In the United Kingdom, trades unions also fund researchers and individual Members of Parliament. They may in this way have input to candidate selection. Businesses often donate funds to political parties and, where it is permissible, may fund individual candidates. Thus business interests may influence candidate choice. There are also parties closely tied to religious or ethnic groups in particular communities, which thus limit their membership and constituency.

Women and Political Parties

Parties grow up around a shared interest. Class has been a significant determinant of party formation, as have region, language, religion and ethnicity. Sex has rarely formed the basis of a political party, although a surprising number of women's parties have emerged around the world, including those in Iceland, Russia and Northern Ireland. Women's demands have more often resulted in the formation of pressure groups outside formal politics, and the creation of women's organizations within political parties, than actual parties. Women's parties tend to emerge only in particular sets of circumstances: conflict, change and intransigence on the part of power-holders.

Political parties have sometimes responded to women's demands as threats, and have sometimes sought women's participation. On the whole, the men who dominate political parties have been very slow to accept that women might have different political interests from men, that women's interests might be political; and that women might be political actors on a par with men. This is changing.

Conclusion

In most countries political parties are the key entry points to politics. In order to under-stand – and change – women's participation in politics, it is important to understand how parties operate. Women comprise a significant proportion of political party membership around the world. Moreover, in many countries they are very active in grass-roots mobilization. In Britain the Conservative Party is sustained by the organizational skills of its women, and anecdotal evidence suggests that this is increasingly the case for Labour too. However, contributing a hefty proportion of the membership and hours dedicated to service does not guarantee women a share of the decision-making positions in parties. Parties may have become aware of a need to attract women's votes; they may have created woman-focused policies in order to do so; but, as we shall see, they have been much slower (for the most part) in opening up their internal structures to women.

FURTHER READING

Most mainstream books on political parties do not pay a lot of attention to women. I picked up a new edited volume recently and found three references to women in the index – one of which did not actually exist when I turned to the page! Andrew Heywood's text is a good discussion of the basics of party organization. Paul Webb's book goes into greater depth while remaining accessible. The volume edited by Joni Lovenduski and Pippa Norris contains chapters about women in the parties of particular countries.

Heywood, A. 2004: *Politics*. London: Palgrave Macmillan.
Lovenduski, J. and Norris, P. (eds) 1993a: *Gender and Party Politics*. London: Sage Publications.
Webb, P. 2002: *Political Parties in Advanced Industrial Democracies*. Oxford: Oxford University Press.

WOMEN IN POLITICAL PARTIES IN THE UNITED KINGDOM

8

Introduction

This chapter looks at women's roles in political parties in the United Kingdom. It starts with a discussion of the main parties that organize at Westminster: Labour, the Conservatives, and the Liberal Democrats, examining policies and practices for the inclusion of women, both in the party organizations and as candidates for election. It then moves on to the regional assemblies, where it looks at the behaviour of both the dominant parties and the parties that organize regionally, such as the Scottish Nationalist Party (SNP), Plaid Cymru, Sinn Fein and the Ulster Unionists.

National Party Organization in the United Kingdom

Margaret Thatcher is the only woman ever to lead a mainstream UK political party, the Conservative Party, although Margaret Beckett was Deputy Leader of the Labour Party for a time (out of office). In the heyday of the UK Green Party in the 1980s, it had a collective leadership, the most high-profile member of which was a woman, Sara Parkin. Parties in the UK vary considerably in their policies with regard to women's participation, as the following discussion shows.

The Labour Party

The Labour Party has traditionally included women's organizations in its structure. Women's Sections were established at constituency level from 1918, and in 1999 these were replaced by Women's Forums. The first women Labour MPs were elected in 1923: Margaret Bondfield and Susan Lawrence. Bondfield went on to become the first woman minister, as Minister of Labour in 1929, while Lawrence became the first woman to chair the Labour National Executive Committee (NEC).

Within the organization of the Labour Party there are a National Women's Officer and local women's organizers; however, the party's attitude to women has always been somewhat ambivalent. Its links with the old trades unions, established in heavy industry, and the unions' commitment to retaining a 'family wage', accompanied by a lack of interest in unionizing and protecting working women, cast something of a shadow until the 1970s. The comment of David Blunkett, then Labour leader of Sheffield Council, that he opposed the creation of a Women's Committee because it would draw energy away from the class struggle, more or less sums up the problem.

The loss of the 1979 general election to Margaret Thatcher's renewed Conservative Party propelled the Labour Party into debate over how to both counter the Conservative Government and make itself electable.[1] Labour's power base in the manual working class had shrunk, and was likely to continue to do so because the old industries were shrinking and the profile of the working population was changing. Labour politicians in pursuit of a constituency started to look at marginalized groups in the community and to think in terms of using them to build a coalition of opposition. According to Loretta Loach, at this point 'a unique set of relations existed between old guard socialists, young revolutionaries and militant feminists' (Loach 1985a: 18).

One result was the establishment of the Women's Action Committee (WAC) within the Labour Party, to 'achieve for women what the democratic reforms had achieved for the rank and file' (Loach 1985a: 19). The first meeting of WAC in 1980 was attended by several hundred women, and in 1981 it started putting resolutions to the national conference. These were primarily concerned with the principle of autonomy and power within the party: according to Loach, the WAC wanted to recover the power that women within the Labour Party had before the First World War (and before women got the vote) when there was a semi-autonomous women's organization with its own newspaper. At the same time as the WAC was established, local Labour constituency parties were revitalizing the long-established mechanism of women's sections. According to Jan Parker, there were 1,200 of these by the end of 1981, which led to the invigoration of the Labour Women's Conference that year by 'new members who were younger, more radical, unashamedly feminist' (J. Parker 1981: 31).

The WAC spearheaded change in the Labour Party, against considerable (if passive) resistance. Ann Petifor, a founder of the WAC, spoke out bitterly about the resistance of Labour men to change, a complaint echoed in Sarah Perrigo's description of the internal politics of the Leeds Labour Party in the 1970s and 1980s (Loach 1985a, 1985b; Perrigo 1986). However, change slowly took place. The principle of quotas was first agreed in the Labour Party at the annual conference in 1989. According to Judith Squires,

the reasons for the decisions were widely perceived to include: the lack of any real progress in terms of women's representation at any level of the party; the experience of socialist parties in other countries, which had used quotas to increase the number of women in their own organisations; post election research in 1977 indicating that a key problem was women's perception of Labour as a male dominated party; the belief that creating more positions of power and responsibility for women within the party at all levels would not only be more equitable but might bring significant electoral rewards. (Squires 1996: 71–2)

After the 1989 annual Labour Party conference there was a period of consultation. The 1990 conference endorsed a far-reaching programme of quotas. It adopted a 40 per cent quota for the National Executive Committee, constituency Labour parties, branch officers and delegations. It adopted the target of 50 per cent for the Parliamentary Labour Party (elected Members of Parliament) within ten years or three general elections. The following year, the 1991 conference voted for rule changes concerning all levels of the party. In 1993, the conference endorsed rule changes implementing quotas for the Conference Arrangements Committee, National Constitutional Committee, Regional Councils and the European Constituency Labour Party. It was further decided to set a target of 50 per cent women candidates for the next general election in all seats where a Labour MP was retiring, and in 50 per cent of the most winnable seats (Squires 1996: 72).

For the selection of candidates to fight the 1997 election, Labour introduced all-women short lists, to be used in half of all winnable seats becoming vacant. This was both radical and successful in getting more women selected. Response to the short lists was passionate, and not all of it was positive. Both men and women were concerned that the affirmative measure would result in the selection and election of women who were tokens. It was also felt by some that it was an unfair and undemocratic move, since men who had been working in a constituency for some time and felt entitled to at least apply for candidacy would be excluded. Since then, legislation has been passed that makes such measures legal, the 2002 Sex Discrimination (Election Candidates) Act, and Labour has pledged to reintroduce all-women short lists for the 2005 general election.

In 1999 the party reorganized. Instead of Women's Sections, local Labour constituency parties are encouraged to have a women's officer and to establish Women's Forums. At constituency level a Women's Forum can elect two delegates to the General Committee and to the Local Government Committee, send motions to the General Committee, nominate individuals as constituency officers, and nominate candidates and representatives. As such, a Women's Forum is part of the grass-roots (voluntary) organization of local parties. It is still unclear how effective these are.

So, in terms of its national organization, the Labour Party has mechanisms in place for women to organize and press women's issues. There are places set aside for women at all levels of the organization; women are active in the party, and have achieved significant positions, from Susan Lawrence to Harriet Harman.

The Conservative Party

The Conservative Party has always been kept afloat by the women of its grass-roots organization. It has a very high female membership of over 50 per cent, yet in 1992 (the last time it won a general election) only 6 per cent of the Parliamentary Conservative Party (Members of Parliament) were women. As Lovenduski et al. note, 'in the Conservative Party, far more time was spent discussing how to win women's votes than involving women in the party organisation' (Lovenduski, Norris and Burns 1994: 617).

The women of the Conservative Party organized early on with the creation of the Primrose League in Wales in 1883, and in Scotland in 1884, which gave the Tories the machinery of a modern mass party. By 1885 several thousand women were involved in canvassing, preparing electoral registers, and distributing propaganda. In 1885 the Ladies Grand Council of the Conservative Party was instituted.

When the party was reorganized in 1918 just prior to women's suffrage, there were already substantial organized groups of Conservative women. In 1928, when women achieved the vote on the same terms as men, the Central Women's Advisory Committee was formally recognized, and women's branches employing women's organizers were steadily established. An annual Women's Conference was organized, and Women's Committees were created at constituency level, which fed into the Conservative Women's National Committee. Women were, and continue to be, essential to the organization of the Conservative Party, but their roles were primarily behind the scenes.

Under the leadership of Iain Duncan-Smith in 2002, the party appointed a woman as chair for the first time. However, it was still the case that, 'at present, the Conservative Party has a larger proportion of women members than Labour, but comparatively few at a senior level [. . .] many traditional elements of the party organisation have a strong masculine ethos' (Buxton 2001: 6). In 2001, most leading party figures were men. The highest forum for organization and management of the party, the Party Board, had twelve men and four women; of the four vice-chairs of the party, only one was a woman; the committee that selects candidates and manages the approved list had only one woman among its ten members; the Policy Forum Council that manages the policy ideas that come from the constituency associations had three women among its twelve members; and only two of the seven Central Office Directors, the people who administer the party, were women (Buxton 2001: 15). Women held more offices at constituency level, but it was obvious that the more significant the office, the fewer women held it. In Parliament 8.4 per cent of Conservative MPs were women; women constituted 8.7 per cent of the Shadow Cabinet; and 7.4 per cent of Front Bench speakers (Buxton 2001: 16).

The Conservative Party has fielded fewer women than Labour at every general election since 1918. Despite frequent pressure to put forward more female candidates, party activists and elected members alike seem to find the idea of women running for election rather odd (Lovenduski, Norris and Burns 1994: 626).

The process for the selection of candidates is generally regarded to favour men. Prospective candidates apply to the party and, if their application and references are acceptable, attend a weekend selection board. The selection board includes scrutiny by an area agent, Central Office, and party activists. Once approved, candidates appear on a list and are available for selection by local constituency parties. This in turn entails application, short-listing and interview. In the 1990s women made up 17.3 per cent of the approved list, 7.6 per cent of candidates, and 4.5 per cent of elected MPs (Lovenduski, Norris and Burns 1994: 628–9). Emma Nicholson's account of her own trials on the road to selection are illuminating, and support the findings of Lovenduski et al. that both the criteria and the specifications are gendered (Nicholson 1996: 53–7).

In 1983, Emma Nicholson, an energetic party worker and prospective candidate, was invited to take up the voluntary post of Vice-Chair for Women. In this position she raised the profile of women in the party and at the women's conference, as well as raising women's issues as policy areas. She organized the first high-flyers' conferences to which women from both within and without the party were invited, in order to promote the party's appeal to women, and from which new women candidates emerged. Yet Nicholson herself had difficulty getting selected for a seat, encountered sexism in Conservative

Party Central Office, and eventually left the party with her gendered experiences playing a part in her decision. In the 1990s Lady Seccombe was the Vice President for Women, and she again attempted to increase the number of women candidates.

All of this was to little effect. In January 2004, Laura Touquet, Policy Officer of the Fawcett Society, wrote to the *Independent* newspaper:

> The problem with the Conservative Party's candidate selection process is that it is not a meritocratic system, it is a discriminatory system. Research by the Fawcett Society shows that prospective women candidates are frequently discriminated against in the candidate selection process. As a result, women make up less than 10% of Conservative MPs. A prospective Conservative candidate that Fawcett interviewed was asked, 'if you got the seat and were in Westminster during the week, what would your husband do for sex?' It is not only unfair, it is an enormous waste of talent. Domestic and international evidence clearly shows that the only way to eliminate this kind of discrimination is to use positive mechanisms, such as all-women shortlists and twinning. (Fawcett Society website)

Given the obstacles faced by women in the Conservative Party, it is quite remarkable that it should have been the first (and so far only) major UK party to select a female leader. As party leader and Prime Minister, Margaret Thatcher was very successful. First, she led the party to success at the polls, then she kept it in government for some eleven years. During that time the party was strong, radical and influential. As discussed earlier, she did not encourage other women politicians and, although some of them, such as Edwina Currie, continued to admire her, others, like Emma Nicholson, became disenchanted. Thatcher operated very much as the men around her did, and was respected for so doing. Nothing that has been said so far about women's agendas, issues and different ways of doing things would have cut any ice with her.

Among Conservative MPs during the Thatcher years were a range of strong women holding office, including Angela Rumbold, Gillian Shephard and Virginia Bottomley; however, none of them ever made it into the cabinet. With John Major as leader and Prime Minister from 1991 to 1997, two women were appointed to the cabinet, but the party took few other steps forward in encouraging women as candidates and MPs (Abdela 1989; McDougall 1998; Nicholson 1996).

The party would like to see female candidates in half of its winnable seats at the next election, but this desire is accompanied by an apparent lack of policies to promote the participation of women either in the party organization or as candidates. The party has reformed the initial stage of the selection process to make it more hospitable to women. Selection for the approved list now takes place on the basis of the key skills identified as necessary for an MP.

In her pamphlet analysing the problem, Fiona Buxton recommends changes to the party structure to create more groups appealing to young women in order to increase membership; development of woman-friendly policies; training of local selection committees; training, outreach and mentoring of prospective female candidates; and monitoring of selection procedures to eliminate discrimination (Buxton 2001: 6). She points to the women's groups, established in particular areas, that bring together a cross-section of women of different ages and professions, providing opportunities for professional and social networking, as a source of future candidates (Buxton 2001: 18).

Under the leadership of Michael Howard, the party does not appear to place women's representation high on its list of priorities. No new initiatives have been created in the party, and in May 2004 there were only two women among the twelve key shadow ministers. Twenty-six of the 151 shadow positions were held by women, but this only amounts to twenty-one women, since four of them hold more than one position (Conservative Party website). The party has started selection for the 2005 election. Out of 132 target seats, twenty-seven women, 20 per cent of the total, have been selected – an improvement on the 16 per cent selected for the 2001 election, but still inadequate even by the party's own standards (Turquet 2003a). According to a press release, the Conservative Party has selected more men named Philip for their top twenty target seats than women (Fawcett Press website, 25 February 2004).

The Liberal Democrats

The Liberal Democratic Party, like its forerunners the Liberal Party and the Social Democrats, has considerable appeal for women because of its straightforward equal rights approach, unencumbered by considerations of either class or tradition. Unfortunately, that same egalitarianism ties the party in knots when it comes to addressing gender inequality. Its liberalism makes it unable to institute positive steps to eradicate inequality. Hence, at local level the Liberal Democrats were more opposed to Women's Committees than the Conservatives, and, generally, they do not support quotas or other forms of positive action (Stokes 1998). The most they have been able to do is to recommend that each candidate short list should include at least one man and one woman.

There is, however, a Women's Liberal Federation which makes proposals and exerts pressure on the party. The party is organized through a system of internal committees. In 2003 six of the fifteen members elected to the Federal Executive Committee were women, two of the sixteen elected to the Federal Policy Committee were women, six of the twelve elected to the Federal Conference Committee, and three of the eight elected to the ELDR Council delegation. But no women were elected to the International Relations Committee (e-mail from Debbie Enver, WLD Administrative Support Officer).

In a 1993 Consultation Paper, *Women*, the party states its commitment to equality between men and women in education, the workplace and the family, as well as with regard to taxation and welfare benefits, health care and the law. With regard to women's participation in politics as representatives, the paper asks questions, but does not answer them. It states the party's opposition to the Labour plan for a Ministry for Women, but asks whether this has damaged the party's standing with women voters (Liberal Democrats 1993: 23). It describes local authority Women's Units favourably, and asks whether the party should reconsider its opposition to Women's Committees (a bit late in the day this, since Women's Committees were disappearing rapidly by 1993). Finally, having restated the party's belief that the introduction of proportional representation (a long-standing Liberal and Liberal Democrat policy) would be beneficial for women, the paper asks whether the party should consider promoting the introduction of quotas for women alongside PR (Liberal Democrats 1993: 24).

A policy paper produced some two years later, *Equal Citizens*, discusses reform of the political system. It suggests the creation of a new Ministry of Justice, which would ensure (among other things) that one-third of all appointees to public bodies would be women (Liberal Democrats 1995: 32). The paper argues that all public sector posts should be adequately advertised and recruited using equal opportunities procedures, including gender-balanced short lists. It recommends the demystification of public life, including the content of public posts, as well as training and mentoring programmes. The comment on public life refers to the opacity of present processes for appointment to a wide range of public bodies, which amounts to a power of patronage operated by prime minister and government.

With regard to procedure within the party, the paper recommends a constitutional guarantee that women will make up one-third of those elected to party committees and short lists for Westminster elections. The shortage of women in Parliament is again connected to the electoral system, and the paper recommends electoral reform, plus state funding for parties and the promotion of women within the Liberal Democrat Party (Liberal Democrats 1995: 33).

The Liberal Democrats have started selection for candidates for the 2005 election. For seventy-eight of its key target seats and the three seats where Liberal Democrat incumbents are retiring, the party has selected 35 per cent female candidates. However, only four of the top twenty seats will be fought by women, and only one of the three seats that is becoming empty because of retirement has selected a woman (Turquet 2003b).

Despite its confusion over how, exactly, to get more women elected while remaining true to liberal principles, the party has included a number of strong women in prominent roles, such as Shirley Williams and Emma Nicholson, and does consistently focus on policy areas of concern to women. In the past ten years it has published policy documents on child abuse and protection (1990), education (1990, 1991), care in the community (1990), personal social services (1993), prostitution (1993, 1994), sustainable economy (1993), consumer rights (1993), genetic engineering (1993), retirement (1993), disability (1993, 1994), crime and safer neighbourhoods (1993), nursery education and care (1994), health care and the National Health Service (1994), transport policy (1994) and community politics (1994).

Other parties

The Green Party, by contrast, was overtly feminist and egalitarian in its approach from the outset, and is the only UK party to have had early success in putting forward fair numbers of female candidates (although not in getting them elected). Having a woman, Sara Parkin, in the collective leadership of the 1980s was symbolic of its general ethos. Although it has never returned a Green MP to Westminster, the UK Green Party does have Members of the European Parliament, members of regional assemblies, and local councillors, among whom women feature quite strongly.

The UK does not have a far right political party of equivalent strength and legitimacy to the National Front in France, but it does have the small British National Party (BNP). Until very recently this was of little account and dubious legitimacy. It is still very much a minority party, despite its high profile of late and its grand ambitions. In the 2002 local elections the BNP, for only the second time, returned a small number of local councillors; these were augmented in the 2003 elections. In 2002 some 20 per cent of the BNP candidates were women, and one of the four councillors to gain a seat was a woman. The party has no declared policy with regard to women, although women feature on its website. It did, however, respond to an enquiry about equality with the following:

> I don't know what is meant by a 'gender equality policy' – I don't even know what 'equality' means (except in the sense that 2 + 2 = 4). The problem is that even if there is equality of opportunity this will be undermined by the phoney, politically correct quest for equality of outcome. eg you can adjust the starting blocks at the beginning of a race but how do you prevent the best runners from winning whilst the race is in progress? To suggest that women and men are indistinguishable (which I gather is the cornerstone of the abysmal feminist (or feminazi) movement) is a lie. Each has a different role, so perhaps it's best the women, and more importantly, young girls, are encouraged to follow their maternal instincts and leave the grind of politics to the beasts. (Received from pressoffice@bnp.org.uk, 11 December 2003)

The statement goes rather against the attempts of the BNP to establish itself as a sophisticated, modern party of the Right, and rather calls into question the position of its female activists, candidates and elected representatives. It shows a remarkable lack of savvy about equalities philosophy, debate and law, while marking a departure from the history of the British far Right. In the early twentieth century, the British Union of Fascists was unusual for its relatively liberal position with regard to women and the involvement of women who had been active in the suffrage movement in its organization.

Parties in Regional Assemblies in the United Kingdom

Scotland

Political parties in Scotland have been interested in women since the beginning of the twentieth century, but largely in terms of securing their votes. The nature of party competition ensured that 'the few women who were successful in obtaining Parliamentary seats did not see themselves as campaigners for the advancement of women, and they resisted attempts by others to label them as "women MPs" who were in Parliament to raise issues of importance to women. The Scottish women MPs rarely declared their support for, and were rarely prepared to take up what are traditionally defined as, women's issues at Westminster' (Brown, McCrone and Paterson 1998: 172).

Political parties in Scotland are not separate from those in the rest of Britain: there is one Labour Party, one Conservative Party and one Liberal Democrat Party. Nevertheless, there are some differences in organization: for example, in 1993 the Scottish Labour Women's Caucus was formed to campaign for greater representation of women at all levels of the party. Despite party unity, the nature of constituency parties may vary, and Scotland, of course, has its own party in the Scottish Nationalists. The Scottish National Party (SNP) has a Women's Forum, membership of which is open to all. It returns an annual report to the National Committee or Conference and can submit resolutions, nominations and amendments.

In 1997 Scotland returned twelve women to Westminster, 16.6 per cent of the total and less than the UK average of 18.2 per cent. Nine of these were from the Labour Party, one was Liberal Democrat, and two were Scottish Nationalists (Brown, McCrone and Paterson 1998: 175). At local government level women's representation has been somewhat higher, reaching over 22 per cent in the 1990s.

In order to explain this poor performance, Brown et al. looked to a 1994 interview survey of women political activists in the main political parties in Scotland. Barriers given included the distance of the Westminster Parliament from home in Scotland; women's roles in the family, and factors within political parties. Interestingly, some women acknowledged that 'family responsibilities is too "easy" an explanation for the low representation of women and avoids analysing potentially more contentious reasons such as discrimination against women' (Brown, McCrone and Paterson 1998: 179).

Women from different parties varied in their opinion of the extent to which discrimination took place during selection, but there was general agreement that it occurred. Women in the Scottish Liberal Democrats and the Scottish National Party did not identify any particular selection problems in their own parties, but thought that they did exist in the Scottish Conservative and Labour parties. Some of the women interviewed from the Conservative Party thought that discrimination took place in selection because of the attitudes of selectors, both men and women. Women in the Scottish Labour Party argued that female prospective candidates faced considerable difficulty in getting selected, partly because of Labour's success in Scottish politics.

Labour returns a very high proportion of Scottish MPs to Westminster: fifty-six of the seventy-two seats in 1997. With overwhelming dominance and a high rate of incumbency, the party has little need to institute new mechanisms for pursuing votes. All-women short lists were used, and dropped, by the party in Scotland, as in the rest of Britain (Brown, McCrone and Paterson 1998: 180). The women interviewed from the Labour Party gave specific examples of strong women candidates having been excluded from short lists, and 'for them it was clearly an issue of power and the refusal of many men to share power with women in the party' (Brown, McCrone and Paterson 1998: 181).

The creation of the new Scottish Parliament, and the implementation of (limited) proportional representation for regional elections, has pushed the parties in Scotland to adopt more positive policies towards women – strongly encouraged by powerful organization on the part of women. These have included zipped lists for the Additional Member seats and twinning of Labour constituencies to ensure one male and one female candidate. However, none of the parties adopted positive measures to secure women's election at the 2001 general election to Westminster. As a result, 21.9 per cent of the candidates were women, and 15.3 per cent of the elected MPs (eleven women out of seventy-two total). This is lower than the proportion of women in the Scottish Parliament, and lower than the overall proportion of women at Westminster. The second election to the Scottish Parliament returned an even higher proportion of women, underlining the odd discrepancy between national and regional politics.

Wales

Wales has elected only seven women to Westminster since women's enfranchisement in 1918. In 1997 – the breakthrough election for women at Westminster – the Labour Party held 85 per cent of the Welsh seats, thirty-four out of the forty Welsh constituencies, yet only four of the MPs were women, and three of these were from all-women short lists. Plaid Cymru (the Welsh Nationalist Party) returned no women MPs to Westminster; nor did the Liberal Democrats. This makes the achievement of 50 per cent women in the new Welsh Assembly not far short of miraculous.

Edwards and McAllister (2002) cast a quizzical eye over this achievement, in the light of the Welsh parties' hitherto obliviousness to women. The Labour Party has an established women's framework, but has never placed high priority on it. From 1918 to 1999 the Labour Party has encouraged separate constituency-based women's sections, but in Wales these were branch-based and therefore smaller and with less authority. Each ward could have a Women's Section – if it wanted it. In 1999 the party reorganized, abolishing the sections and creating constituency-based forums. Delegates from the forums meet annually at the All-Wales Women's Forum.

Since its establishment in 1925, Plaid Cymru has had an official women's section. This was initially a fund-raising body, but in the early 1980s, influenced by the women's movement, it developed an equalities agenda. It pushed for equal representation, and developed a training and education role (Edwards and McAllister 2002: 160). Many of the leading women in the party have come through the women's section. From 1981 five women representatives sat on the National Executive Committee for a trial period of five years. At the end of this the experiment was deemed a success by the party and terminated. Unsurprisingly, the role of the women's section declined in the following years. In 1993, as the movement towards devolution gained momentum, the party established an internal Gender Balance Commission, and recommended that 50 per cent of candidates for the Welsh Assembly should be women.

In the preparations for elections to the Welsh Assembly, the Welsh parties were influenced by the equality strategies of the Scottish parties. This resulted in the remarkable achievement of selecting, and then getting elected, a very high percentage of women: 38.3 per cent of the seats went to women in 1999 and 50 per cent in 2003. Given the history of the parties in Wales, there is a question mark over the extent to which the equality strategies adopted were sincere or instrumental, but the results are proving interesting. It is thought-provoking that, despite the internationally astounding result achieved at the elections to the Welsh Assembly in 1999 and 2003, accounts given of the campaign in Wales for the 2001 general election fail to mention women at all (Jones and Trystan 2001). Further, as selection for the next general election gets under way, and the Labour Party reinstitutes all-women short lists in the light of the 2002 Act, a Welsh constituency, Blaenau Gwent, has been the first to object (McSmith 2003).

Northern Ireland

As stated above, the Conservative, Labour and Liberal Democrat parties do not organize in Northern Ireland. The SDLP is the nearest equivalent to Labour, the Unionist parties ally themselves with the Conservatives, and the Alliance is allied to the Liberal Democrats. As writers repeatedly point out, sectarian conflict dominates all political discourse in Northern Ireland. Division and struggle for equality between Unionists and Nationalists leave no space to debate or develop policy around gender equality. Party politics itself is victim to cynicism and apathy.

In 1996 only 1.6 per cent of women and 2.1 per cent of men belonged to a political party. However, 60 per cent of the membership of the Democratic Unionists (DU) were women; 50 per cent of the Alliance Party of Northern Ireland (APNI); 42 per cent of the Ulster Unionists (UU); 47 per cent of the Social Democratic and Labour Party (SDLP); and 33 per cent of Sinn Féin (Wilford and Galligan 2000: 170). Both the APNI and the SDLP have been chaired by women, but only the Unionist Party of Northern Ireland has been led by a woman – and that was only very briefly.

In the 1997 general election no women were returned to Westminster from Northern Ireland. Despite the first elected woman to Westminster having been a Sinn Fein representative (who did not take up her seat), Northern Ireland has returned only six women in its entire existence – three of them in 2001.

There are several Unionist parties, none of which is known for its interest in women's issues or for promoting women. Rachel Ward (2002) refers to women in Unionist politics as 'invisible'. The parties are opposed to preferential treatment. At the time of writing Ward found only thirty-nine female Unionist local councillors in Northern Ireland, from five different parties, and three female Unionist members of the new Legislative Assembly, from two parties.

In its 1998 manifesto the Ulster Democratic Party stated that 'women should play a larger role in the social, political, and cultural development of Ulster' (M. Ward 2002: 175). The UDP supports equal pay, subsidies for workplace nurseries, flexible working hours, training and education for women, support for single mothers, paid care leave and family planning – but not, apparently female UDP representatives, since there are no UDP councillors or Members of the Legislative Assembly (MLAs).

The Parliamentary Unionist Party has a Women's Commission, which was developing policies for women to include addressing under-representation and abortion when Ward did her research (R. Ward 2002: 176). At the 1998 conference of the Ulster Unionist Party there was a proposal to adopt a positive strategy for recruiting women candidates.

The Ulster Unionist Party (UUP) has the Ulster Women's Unionist Council, but this is governed by the Ulster Unionist Council, which in 1995 comprised only 15 per cent women. At the same time there were 22 per cent female constituency officers in the party (Wilford and Galligan 2000: 170).

The centrist Alliance (APNI) is organized through twenty-three local associations. In 1995 six of these were chaired by women, and ten had female secretaries and treasurers. The policy-making body of the party, its executive, comprised one-third women, including the vice-chair of the party (R. Ward 2002: 170).

On the republican wing, the SDLP has six women on its Executive of fifteen. This includes the Chair of the Women's Group. In 1995 it established quotas of 40 per cent for the National Executive, and set aside two places for women on its new General Council.

Sinn Féin is organized in nine departments, six of which are headed by women. It operates a 40 per cent gender quota for the National Executive, and claimed in its 1997 manifesto that 'women in Ireland suffer from systematic and institutionalised sexual discrimination', which it proposed to eliminate (Wilford and Galligan 2000: 179).

Political parties in Northern Ireland have lagged far behind those in other parts of Europe in taking account of gender as a factor in voting and policy-making. Perhaps party leaders have not needed to pay attention in the way that their equivalents in other countries have, because sectarianism has guaranteed and delivered their vote. However, with the peace process under way, the new Legislative Assembly in place, and an emerging will to push sectarianism aside, women are staking their claims. Hence the success of the Northern Ireland Women's Coalition (NIWC).

Conclusion

It would appear that the only UK parties that have clear, effective policies for getting women into elected office are Labour, the Greens and Sinn Féin. These same parties have internal mechanisms for the representation of women and women's interests within the party organizations.

The Conservative Party is an oddity, in that it has high female membership, well-established women's organizations, yet relatively few women in either party positions or elected office. Perhaps this reflects a traditionalism within Conservatism about gender roles and the broader society that has continued despite the onslaught of Thatcherite neo-liberalism. Broadly, the position of women within parties reflects party ideology: the more radical, the more women, and vice versa. But we should make no simple assumptions about how easy it is for women in the more radical parties, or how much women like their situation in the more conservative ones.

FURTHER READING

A considerable literature is growing up around women's participation in UK political parties. This has been driven, at least in part, by the impetus to create the new regional assemblies, and by the space that opened up in the Labour Party. Alice Brown, Fiona Mackay and Esther Breitenbach have written extensively on Scotland, while Yvonne Galligan and Rick Wilford have taken on Ireland. Joni Lovenduski has been in pursuit of the Labour Party for years, and is now joined by Sarah Childs. More research is undertaken and more writing accomplished analysing Labour and the Liberal Democrats than the Conservatives. This perhaps reflects the interests of researchers and writers, but it makes Maguire's book on Conservative women all the more important. The Centre for Advancement of Women in Politics at Queen's University, Belfast runs a website that details numbers of women in UK politics: <www.qub.ac.uk/cawp/>.

Brown, A., Donoghy, T. B., Mackay, F. and Meehan, E. 2002: Women and Constitutional Change in Scotland and Northern Ireland. *Parliamentary Affairs*, 55(1): 71–84.
Childs, S. 2004b: *New Labour's Women MPs: Women Representing Women*. London: Routledge.
Galligan, Y. and Wilford, R. 1999a: Gender and Party Politics in the Republic of Ireland. In Y. Galligan, R. Ward and R. Wilford (eds), *Contesting Politics*, Oxford: Westview Press, pp. 149–68.

Galligan, Y. and Wilford, R. 1999b: Women's Political Representation in Ireland. In Y. Galligan, R. Ward and R. Wilford (eds), *Contesting Politics*, Oxford: Westview Press, pp. 130–48.

Lovenduski, J. 2004: *Feminising Politics*. Cambridge: Polity.

Mackay, F. 2001: *Love and Politics*. London: Continuum.

Maguire, G. E. 1998: *Conservative Women: A History of Women and the Conservative Party*, 1874–1997. Basingstoke: Macmillan.

POLITICAL PARTIES OUTSIDE THE UNITED KINGDOM

9

Introduction

This chapter discusses the position of women in the political parties of a range of different countries. Political parties and party systems are shaped by the history of a country, its culture and its electoral system. None of these exists in a vacuum. The existence of multiple parties tends to reflect multiple political cleavages in the society, which in turn result from distinct cultural differences. The roles of women within political parties reflect all of these.

The Republic of Ireland

From the creation of the Republic of Ireland in 1922, until the resurgence of the women's movement in the 1970s, little is recorded about Irish women's political activities. This was a period of nation-building and consolidation, and traditional assumptions about women's roles dominated, despite women's participation in the struggle for independence. From the early 1970s the influence of the women's movement and of the European Union began to tell. In 1972 the Commission on the Status of Women undertook the first research into the role and status of women. Women at this time made up 25 per cent of political party membership, but held no positions of influence in party or politics (Galligan and Wilford 1999a: 152).

Irish politics is dominated by two parties, Fianna Fáil and Fine Gael, both inheritors of the traditions of the nationalist movement which fought for and achieved independence in 1922. From 1977 these both started to woo women voters (Galligan and Wilford 1999a: 153).

Fianna Fáil

Fianna Fáil formed twenty-one of the thirty-five governments between 1922 and 1997. Although women had been prominent in the nationalist movement, post-independence the party was traditional and patriarchal in its approach to gender. In 1977 the party put forward only ten female candidates for the general election. In 1981 a Women's Consultative Committee was created comprising women parliamentarians and female members of the party executive. This was reorganized in 1985 as the National Women's Committee, and again in 1996 as the Fianna Fáil National Women's Forum. Its goal was to increase women's membership of the party, encourage the participation and representation of women in party structures, and to influence party policy: women's membership increased to 35 per cent. This initiative was accompanied in 1986 by a Women's Conference and the creation of the post of Women's Co-ordinator at constituency level (Galligan and Wilford 1999a: 155). In 1997 women made up 18 per cent of the National Executive of the party and 24 per cent of constituency office-holders. In the election of that year there were fourteen women candidates, 12.3 per cent, and a successful woman candidate for President, Mary McAleese. McAleese is still President in 2004, and in the 2002 election Fianna Fáil returned six female TDs (Teachta Dála, members of parliament).

Fianna Fáil opposes quotas for women and instead favours a positive action programme to 'facilitate women's promotion to senior positions within the party organisation and as public representatives' (Galligan and Wilford 1999a: 155). Recent policy shifts have made the party slightly more favourable to tackling women's problems, such as pay inequality and sexual harassment.

Fine Gael

The other major party, Fine Gael, shares Fianna Fáil's origins and approach to gender. In the 1980s it targeted women's electoral support and modernized its organization. A number of well-known feminist activists were associated with the party, and it opened its senior positions to women. At this point the National Executive comprised 28 per cent women, and 44 per cent of constituency office holders were women (Galligan and Wilford 1999a: 158). A Fine Gael Women's Group was created, and a positive action programme proposed in 1997, although quotas are not supported by the party. The positive action programme included the appointment of a full-time women's officer and a strategy of affirmative action to get more women involved in party decision-making (Galligan and Wilford, 1999a: 159). There are no reserved seats on the National Executive Committee, but by the late 1990s, 33 per cent of the members were women. The party nominated a woman, Mary Banotti, for the 1997 Presidential election. The 2002 election returned three Fine Gael women to the Dáil.

The Irish Labour Party

In 1971 the national Women's Committee of the Irish Labour Party attempted to introduce a feminist perspective to the party, but this was not recognized until 1979. In 1981 the party agreed to reserve two seats on the National Executive for women, and in 1985 a gender quota of 25 per cent was introduced for candidates to local elections (Galligan and Wilford 1999a: 161). In 1989 a Gender Quota Committee was established, which resulted in the institution of 20 per cent quotas for all decision-making bodies within the party and for electoral politics in 1991 (Galligan and Wilford 1999a: 162). This was accompanied by a commitment to increase the quota to 40 per cent. In 1990 Mary Robinson was nominated successfully for the Presidential election, and Adi Roche was nominated in 1997. In government from 1992, Labour introduced a policy of 40 per cent women on state boards. At the 2002 election Labour returned six female TDs.

Other political parties in the Republic of Ireland

The minority parties are more actively engaged in promoting women – a cynic might say that they can afford to be, since they are unlikely ever to have to put their policies into practice in power. The Progressive Democrats were founded in 1985 out of Fianna Fáil and have 5 per cent of electoral support. The party was co-founded by a woman, Mary Harney, and, although ideologically conservative, it has a high level of female activism. Of the office-holders at constituency level 30 per cent are women; and there is a similar percentage on the National Executive (Galligan and Wilford 1999a: 160). In 2002 four female TDs were elected from the Progressive Democrats. The Green Party, created in 1991, has 41.6 per cent women on its co-ordinating committee and a 40 per cent quota for all bodies and candidates, but no women were elected to the Dáil in 2002. Neither Sinn Féin nor the Socialists returned any female TDs. The newest party, the Democratic Left, created in 1992, is committed to affirmative action, and has a 40 per cent quota for the National Executive, candidates, and all local party bodies.

On the one hand, the Republic of Ireland is a traditional society in which the Catholic Church continues to exert a strong influence; on the other, it is a highly successful part of the European Union with a booming economy. Both facets are reflected in the political parties as they struggle to deal with change. One peculiarity is that the position of President has come to be seen as a woman's job, with most of the parties proposing female candidates. In 1997 Fianna Fáil proposed Mary McAleese; Fine Gael, Mary Banotti; Labour, Adi Roche; and Dana Rosemary Scallon stood as an independent, with a lone male, Derek Nally, also independent.

The Nordic Countries

As in much of the rest of Europe, women only began to become integrated into political parties in the 1970s. At the start of the 1970s women made up around 35 per cent of the membership of political parties in the Nordic countries; by the end of the 1980s, membership of men and women was about equal in Denmark and Norway, while it remained at about one-third women in Finland and Sweden (Christensen 1999: 69). In these countries there is a well-established tradition of separate women's sections within political parties. This is in keeping with the highly organized nature of Nordic societies, and of the women of these societies. National councils for women have existed in all the Nordic countries, which functioned as umbrella organizations for a range of women's organizations, with the purpose of influencing public authorities by representing women's interests (Christensen 1999: 73).

In a detailed examination of women's membership and access to power in Scandinavian political parties (Denmark, Finland, Norway and Sweden), Jan Sundberg claims that both women's membership of political parties and the number of issues raised at party congresses by female activists have increased since the 1960s. In attempting to find the heart of party power structures, Sundberg points to the party executives that meet more regularly than the councils or congresses (Sundberg 1995: 96). 'The party executive is the most important unit concerning power and influence in the organisation' (Sundberg 1995: 101).

Sundberg found that there were fewer women on the executives than in the parties as a whole, but that this varied by party and country. By the end of the 1980s women comprised 36 per cent of party executives in Denmark, 39 per cent in Finland, 47 per cent in Norway, and 47 per cent in Sweden (Sundberg 1995: 97–8). In international terms these numbers are a considerable achievement for women. The big change came in the Norwegian Labour Party in the early 1970s, when the proportion of women in the executive doubled within five years. In Denmark and Sweden the change came in the late 1970s, and in Finland some ten years later. As a result, socialist parties in all four countries have a high proportion of women in executive positions.

The liberal parties in Denmark and Finland have increased their inclusion of women, although their share was still under 30 per cent at the end of the 1980s. In the liberal parties of Norway and Sweden women comprised around half of the executive bodies. In the centre (agrarian) parties of Denmark and Finland, men dominate the executive, whereas the equivalent parties in Norway and Sweden have let in significant numbers of women. This just leaves the conservative parties. Those of Denmark and Finland remain male-dominated, while those of Norway and Sweden broke with tradition in the 1970s and 1980s to include a significant proportion of women.

While all of these countries figure highly in any international comparison, Norway and Sweden stand out for their achievement of sex equality in parties, as in government. In Norway this might be attributed to the quota policy adopted by all but one conservative party, but in Sweden quotas have been used by only one party. While mobilization within parties has been considered important in these two countries, according to Sundberg, 'Danish female party members put less emphasis on winning influence through the executive than on other non-traditional channels like grass-roots movements and protests' (Sundberg 1995: 100). This is not confined to Denmark, as exemplified by the Swedish Support Stocking initiative and the women's strikes organized in Iceland (Stark 1997; Dominelli and Jonsdottir 1988). On the other hand, Finnish parties have a much more authoritative culture, which seems to disadvantage women. Iceland is rather different from the other four Nordic countries, because of its organization of a women's party.

France

French politics is dominated by five political parties operating both locally and nationally: the Parti Communiste Français (PCF), the Parti Socialiste (PS), the Union pour la Democratie Française (UDF), the Rassemblement pour la République (RPR), and the Front National (FN).

Women's presence in the Executive and Legislature of the National Assembly made little progress between the 1970s and the advent of the parity movement, described in chapter 6. This is at least in part due to the reluctance of parties to advance women both in party office and as electoral candidates.

Although accounts of the membership of French parties are notoriously unreliable, it is generally agreed that the French join political parties in smaller numbers than people in other European countries (Appleton and Mazur 1993: 101). In 1985 the RPR claimed that 43 per cent of its membership were women, the PS claimed 21 per cent, and the PCF 36 per cent.

Parti Socialiste

In the 1970s feminists within the PS demanded a quota for women at all levels of party structures to reflect the proportion of women in the party. The party agreed to a quota of 10 per cent in 1973, which was subsequently raised to 15, 20 and then 30 per cent. However, quotas were not respected at either local or national level, and no oversight mechanism was established (Appleton and Mazur 1993: 103). In 1990, women held 18.5 per cent of the places on the National Executive and 21.4 per cent of the positions in the party's National Legislature. In addition, one of the fourteen National Secretaries was a woman, although her area of responsibility was women's rights. Of the 100 local federations that make up the party, only seven were headed up by female First Secretaries (Appleton and Mazur 1993: 102). These numbers show only a small advance on the previous ten years. Appleton and Mazur claim that 'out of all the parties in France it has been the PS that has devoted the most attention to women's rights issues on its campaign platform. However, support for women's rights issues such as day care, equal employment for women and state-funded abortion was a result of the combination of the party's interest (and especially that of François Mitterrand) in attracting the shifting women's vote, and the pressure from PS feminists' (Appleton and Mazur 1993: 106). The commitment of the party did not extend to overturning the power balance in its own ranks.

Rassemblement pour la Republique

The RPR is the Gaullist party. In 1965 President and party leader de Gaulle created the Centre Feminin d'Études et d'Information (CFEI) as a parallel organization to the political party to educate and mobilize women to become Gaullist voters. However, Gaullist women saw it as a move to marginalize women and remove internal threats from women members to change the party's policies on women (Appleton and Mazur 1993: 107). The group has become more political over time, promoting women's rights, supporting women candidates, and taking part in the party's national congress. An active women's section within the party has existed since the 1980s, but this struggles against the party's 'long-standing apathy toward gender issues' (Appleton and Mazur 1993: 108).

The RPR does not have formal quotas for women in internal offices. Like many conservative and liberal parties, it takes the position that increased representation of women within the party will occur naturally in parallel with women's changing roles in society. In 1985, 5 per cent of the National Secretariat were women, and 7.1 per cent of the Executive Bureau, while the party Legislature was 11.1 per cent women. In 1990, 25 per cent of the Assistant General Secretaries (two in number) were women, and 24 per cent of the Secretaries; however, most of these had responsibility for traditionally female sectors (Appleton and Mazur 1993: 107).

All parties committed themselves, in principle, to support of the 2000 parity law. In practice, especially at national level, implementation of parity has been gently resisted. Karen Bird points out that the sitting members of the national assembly were most reluctant to give up their seats at the behest of a party bound to nominate equal numbers of male and female candidates. Although parties that fail to nominate a gender balance of candidates are liable to lose part of their public subsidy, they remain eligible to fight the election. This proved effective in ensuring that small parties nominated a balance of men and women, but did not achieve the goal of forcing larger parties to do the same. Moreover, parties only have to field an equal number of men and women; the law has nothing to say about where they should be fielded. So if women are placed as candidates for unwinnable seats, the law has been obeyed, although nothing will have changed (Bird 2003: 13).

Germany

Women's political participation in Germany has been complicated, first by National Socialism and then by partition into East (Communist) and West Germany until 1990. Prior to this, there had been strong women's movements in Germany, both socialist and conservative, which sponsored women's education. During partition, the West followed a similar path to other liberal democracies, while the East gave the appearance of providing considerable gender equality. However, with unification it became apparent that the civic equality guaranteed to women had been undermined by inequalities in the domestic and economic spheres (Kolinsky 1993: 114).

None the less, women in East Germany had been active in politics both locally and nationally, and they continued their activism in transitional politics through the Independent Women's Movement. Unfortunately, their concerns and issues were considered secondary by the male politicians who set the agenda (Rueschemeyer 2003). Arguably, women in the East have suffered disproportionately from the end of communism and the withdrawal of state-provided child care along with a range of other benefits and guarantees. East German women engaged in transitional politics did not necessarily have a women's agenda. The interests and concerns of women from the East and the West differed both before and after unification, resulting in differences over priorities.

Voter turn-out had been high in West Germany, although slightly lower among men than women. Post-unification, the turn-out rate has dropped, especially among younger voters. On the other hand, party membership has grown, as has the proportion of female members. The party system altered slightly after unification, and different voting patterns have emerged in the East and the West. After unification the West German parties built organizations in the East of Germany modelled on their own, except for the Greens. The East German party has its own name, although the two are generally grouped together in analyses as Alliance 90/Green. In addition, the Party of Democratic Socialism (PDS) emerged as a predominantly East German party, alongside the West German Christian Democrats and Christian Social Union (CDU/CSU), Social Democrats (SPD), and Free Democrats (FDP).

Looking at the internal organization of parties, the SPD and CDU established women's sections within the parties in the early twentieth century. In the SPD this mutated into a powerful pressure group arguing for women's equality in the party. The CDU women's organization, by contrast, was kept separate, as was that in the CSU. The FDP never created a women's organization and claimed to offer women equality within the party. Its obvious failure to achieve this led to the creation of an external women's organization in 1990 (Kolinsky 1993: 129).

Social Democratic Party

Although the SPD had traditionally segregated women in its organization, it set aside a minimum number of seats for women on the Party Executive. This was finally overturned in 1994, when it was agreed that women should hold no less than 40 per cent of all party offices – a radical measure that the party expects to abolish in 2013, by which time equality should be established. As a result, by 1990 the proportion of women on the Party Executive had increased to 36 per cent from 6 per cent in 1977; the proportion on the Presidium of the party to 38 from 8; the Party Council to 37 from 6; and Congress delegates to 42 from around 6.

Christian Democratic Union

The CDU concentrated on policy change rather than women's participation in party structure, adapting its policies to take account of women's changing roles. It did not introduce quotas for internal offices, but did pass a recommendation that women should be represented in party structures to reflect their membership. As a result, little has changed, although prominent women have been recruited into the political leadership over the heads of party workers. This led to the contradiction that although there were women in cabinet posts, no career track for women was established (Kolinsky 1993: 132). In 1991,

21 per cent of the Party Executive were women, 18 per cent of the Presidium, and 17 per cent of Congress delegates.

Free Democratic Party

The FDP also supported the idea of increasing women's representation without taking steps to achieve it. From 1987 it has been producing annual reports on women's participation in party offices and placing a new emphasis on including women in the party leadership. Although a frequent junior partner in government coalitions, the FDP is a small party. As a result, women's representation varies according to local circumstances. Like the CDU and the CSU, the FDP has offered political office to women who have not gone through a long period of service to the party. In 1991 the Party Executive included 18 per cent women, the Presidium 31 per cent, Congress delegates 21 per cent, and members of the Party Committee 8 per cent.

Green Party

The Green Party broke the mould of German politics and pushed the other parties to improve their equalities practices. From its inception, the Green Party was committed to gender equality in party offices and candidates; this was written into Party statutes as a 50 per cent quota in 1985. Women have subsequently held at least half of all party posts, candidacies and parliamentary seats (Kolinsky 1993: 131). Moreover, they are not confined to traditional women's policy areas.

Women have achieved party leadership in both West Germany and unified Germany: the West German Green Party had one of the best-known party leaders of the 1980s in joint-leader Petra Kelly. Since then Claudia Roth has led the party in conjunction with Fritz Kuhn. The Party of Democratic Socialism has been led by Gabi Zimmer, and Angela Merkel leads the CDU.

Russia

The Constitution and the law oblige political parties to observe the principle of equal rights and opportunities in the formation of party lists in elections and in their organizational structures. However, party leaderships appear to routinely ignore their obligation. Salmenniemi (2003) argues that they are breaking the law, and suggests that women's organizations take legal action against them.

The United States of America

The political and party system of the United States is unique, surprisingly. Surprisingly, because neither the citizens of the USA nor many of the citizens of countries affected by US culture and international relations realize just how unusual it is. The overwhelming dominance of two political parties, which are none the less unified by neither organization nor ideology; the independence from party discipline, policy and finance of people who choose to run (and be elected) under party banners; the choice of candidates by voters (who may or may not be party members or even supporters) rather than by parties; a cabinet of appointed rather than elected Presidential advisers; and a complex web of federal, state and local political layers – all these factors, and others, make US politics unlike that of most other countries, and especially unlike the highly disciplined party democracies of the European countries with which it is usually classed.

In the party democracies discussed so far, political parties, party discipline and the habits of generations of party activists have often presented barriers to women. Yet the absence of party organization and centralized control has not been noticeably to the advantage of women in the USA. Although parties may nominate and approve candidates, candidates for election are actually selected by voters through a system of Primaries. The process of selection is governed by state rules rather than parties themselves, and the rules allow for outsiders to run on a party label. Candidates often recruit themselves or are put forward by groups other than parties. Theoretically, this could be to women's advantage, since party customs have tended to work against women in the countries we have looked at so far. But in her investigation of women in US politics, Burrell concludes that the entrepreneurial style of primary-nomination and candidate-oriented election campaigns seem to discriminate against women (Burrell 1994: 83).

Both of the major parties, Republican and Democrat, have long histories of women's organizations. At federal level, the Republican National Women's Executive was founded in 1918, and the Republican Women's Advisory Council of One Hundred in 1919. In 1929 the Republican Party voted to appoint seven women to the National Executive Committee in the future, and in 1924 to select one man and one woman from each state for the NEC. This was duplicated at state level by eighteen states. From 1932 the Democratic Party included women on all Democratic Party Convention standing committees. In the 1970s the party adopted Presidential nomination reforms to include such minority groups as women and young people in each state's delegation in proportion to their presence in the population. It also ruled that there should be equal representation of men and women at the National Convention (Burrell 1994: 86). In 1974 the party sponsored a Campaign Conference for Democratic Women aimed at electing more women to office that was attended by 1,200 women.

Both parties have established units to aid women candidates, and the Democrats have the Eleanor Roosevelt Fund, which supports women running for state and local office (Burrell 1994: 95). In the 1990s the Democrats put on special training sessions for women candidates, and the Democratic Women's Council, an official party organization for the recruitment and support of women candidates, was established. This organization provides support for female candidates once they have been nominated by the party. In the 1970s the Republican Party decided that each state should endeavour to have equal representation of men and women at its National Convention. In the 1980s it established the Women's Congressional Council to raise money for female candidates for the House of Representatives, and in the 1990s created the National Federation of Republican Women. This is an autonomous, financially independent affiliate of the Republican National Committee, which runs candidate seminars and campaign management schools for women activists.

Women have held leadership positions in the national organization of both parties, including the Political Director of the Democratic National Committee and the Chair of the Republican National Committee. In 1991 five of the Democratic state party chairs were women, and seven of the Republican chairs. Democratic women were executive directors of the party in seventeen states, and Republican women in eight states. According to Burrell, 'women have served as spokespersons for their party. They have directed congressional campaign committees, managed a presidential campaign, and chaired the National Committees of both parties' (Burrell 1994: 88).

It seems fair to say that the parties are doing their best for women. Since they do not control nomination and selection, their major avenue of support is financial – but the amount of financial aid they can offer is limited by the Federal Election Campaign Act. Between 1980 and 1990 the Republican Party gave a larger average amount to their female candidates than to their male; the Democrats did the same in four out of six elections (Burrell 1994: 96–7). As Burrell comments: 'those individuals who wish to seek public office are free to compete for the support of the general public. The party organisations contain no monopoly over the recruitment of candidates nor over selection of nominees. The major parties are used by the candidates. However, the parties do attempt to recruit candidates, offer training programmes for potential candidates, and provide a substantial base for their nominees for national office' (Burrell 1994: 98–9). Unfortunately, this commitment is outweighed by the far greater power and resources of other groups to fund and promote candidates.

Thus women in the USA are disadvantaged by a political system that has too little independence from the economy. Women's relative disadvantage in the economy and labour market carries over into a political system where money and business networks count. None the less, Burrell and others argue that women are not disadvantaged as candidates in comparison with similarly placed men (Burrell 1998; see Fox 2000 for a discussion of the arguments). It is a tricky argument. On the one hand, if you look at male and female candidates, they appear to be similarly positioned. On the other, there are fewer female candidates, and you have to ask why this is, and whether some form of discrimination (indirect or direct) has kicked in at an earlier stage, ensuring that only a certain type of person (whether male or female) gets to be a candidate (Adell Cook 1998; see also Lovenduski and Norris's (1993) discussions of supply and demand in the UK).

Canada

Canada's political parties all took an unusual approach to women's emancipation in 1920. Instead of incorporating women into the parties, they set up women's auxiliary organizations, separate from the main parties. These auxiliary parties did not have an autonomous existence, but served to support and service the main party (MacIvor 1996: 255). The auxiliary parties persisted into the second half of the twentieth century. In 1969 the Women's Liberal Federation was amalgamated into the main party, but the Progressive Conservative Party of Canada (PCP) did not recommend abolition of the women's organization until 1995; in 1981 it merely changed its name from the Women's Association to the Women's Federation (MacIvor 1996: 256). The New Democratic Party (NDP) has never had a separate women's organization, but when it became concerned about its small number of women members, it created the Participation of Women Committee, in 1969. All three of these parties provide special funds for female candidates (MacIvor 1996: 257). In 1983 the NDP ruled that 50 per cent of places on the National Executive Committee and all other party committees should be occupied by women, while the Liberal leader has the power to appoint female candidates over the heads of local associations (MacIvor 1996: 260).

Perhaps as a legacy of the separate organizations, in all parties the higher the level, or the more competitive the post, the fewer women are to be found (Baskevin 1991: 61). Women are under-represented in decision-making positions at constituency, provincial and federal levels of party organization, including the election of delegates to party conferences and of members to the party executives (MacIvor 1996: 258). There have been female party leaders: Audrey McLaughlin was leader of the federal NDP in 1989, and Kim Campbell leader of the Progressive Conservatives in 1993, as well as a number of female party leaders at provincial level (MacIvor 1996: 259). But Baskevin found that far more women held the post of constituency party secretary than were to be found as local presidents, treasurers or chief financial officers. She argued that 'large numbers of Canadian women continue to fulfil primarily secretarial functions in local party executives' (Baskevin 1991: 62). Commenting on the women who became party leaders, MacIvor points out that 'the extraordinary achievement of these women should not be underestimated in any way, however, we cannot overlook the fact that most of them won the leadership of dispirited, uncompetitive parties over a field of uninspiring male candidates' (MacIvor 1996: 259).

In the face of pressure from women's groups both inside and outside formal politics, the resistance to women is diminishing. A window of opportunity appeared in 1992, when the electorate was thoroughly disillusioned with politics, and making women more prominent in the parties was a way of presenting a fresh image. The next year the proportion of female candidates for election had increased to 21.7 per cent. This was facilitated by the shift of selection away from closed local groups and towards a more open nomination process; but, according to MacIvor, adverse opinions of women's suitability for office still dominate (MacIvor 1996: 262).

Australia

It is telling that three very serious books on Australian politics published in the 1990s do not mention women in the context of political parties – except for one sentence on women's voting behaviour. Similarly, in a collection of articles about politics in Australia and New Zealand published in 1999, only two of the twenty-five articles were written by women, and none of them were about women – this despite the international interest in the Australian femocrat phenomenon (the creation of an equalities bureaucracy staffed by women experienced in feminism, for which see S. Watson (ed.), *Playing the State* (London: Verso 1990), especially Hester Eisenstein's chapter, 'Femocrats, Official Feminism and the Uses of Power') and the remarkable success of women in New Zealand! Thankfully, Marian Simms (1996) has edited a volume of essays on Australian politics that does analyse women's roles within the parties.

Australian politics, especially those of the Australian Labor Party (ALP), are characterized by 'mateship'. Mateship, the unifying strength of the union movement that was absorbed by the Australian Labor Party and mythologized as uniquely Australian egalitarianism, is criticized for being, in fact, racist, sexist, ethnocentric, conformist and oppressive (Huntley 2000: 7). This masculine culture has made it difficult for women to find their way in the one major political party that ought – according to its egalitarian ideology – to be their natural home. In the 1990s the ALP, as well as adopting the new structures described below, promoted a number of high-profile women: 'golden girls' such as Cheryl Kernot (former leader of the Australian Democrats), Carmen Lawrence and Mary Delahunty (a former ABC television presenter). These have tended to suffer from being 'caught within a bizarre ethical spiral that deems them to be, at once, too good and not good enough for politics' (Else-Mitchell 2000: 12).

The acknowledgement that political structures need to change in order to take account of women and women's interests owes much to the strength of the Australian women's movement. The major women's organizations formed a coalition, Women into Politics, in order to put pressure on political parties to act for women's representation. In 1994 Women into Politics submitted to all the major political parties the claim that women's under-representation at all levels of political life frustrated Australian women and constituted a failure of democracy. Moreover, Women into Politics claimed that it was within the power of the major political parties to do something about it (Broad and Kirner 1996: 79).

Australian Labor Party

The Australian Labor Party (ALP) initially had separate women's organizations within its structure. From 1981 it adopted affirmative action principles to increase the representation of women in the party and in parliament. However, by 1994 it was apparent that the principles had not achieved much. At its 1994 annual conference the ALP adopted a new set of national rules, which included affirmative action within the party: some of this was formalization at national level of what already existed; some of it was new. The new rules included the requirement that one-third of all elected positions within the party should be held by women; delegations to state and territory party conferences must include at least one-third women (this to include delegations from unions, unless the union itself was less than one-third women, in which case the proportions of delegates should be representative); and candidate selection should ensure that a minimum of 35 per cent of public offices were held by women. The conference adopted further measures in order to enable the national party to enforce the policies at local levels (Broad and Kirner 1996: 80).

The insistence that union delegations must include fair proportions of women is highly significant. The ALP, like the British Labour Party, but unlike other Australian parties, includes trades unions in its decision-making. The introduction of quotas and targets generally moved Australian politics on to a new level. The adoption of the 35 per cent rule was the result of a campaign by women in the ALP to achieve the adoption of a national 50 per cent rule by 2000. Broad and Kirner argue that 35 per cent is clearly achievable, and that the party should regard this as a starting point and move on to 50 per cent once it is achieved. According to these writers, the ALP is aware that there are plenty of capable women who want to be in politics, but who have been excluded by the 'male dominated concept of merit' that has characterized selection processes in the party: 'as one delegate to the ALP National Conference puts it, it's a bit like testing people for pre-selection according to how far they can kick a football or how well they sing base baritone' (Broad and Kirner 1996: 82).

National Party of Australia

The National Party of Australia is the main conservative party. Like many conservative parties, it has had individual women in conspicuous offices without achieving high representation for women in general – either in party office or elected office. Again like many conservative parties, its emphasis is on encouragement, exhortation and training, rather than quotas, reservations and enabling measures. According to Gardiner and Ferguson, the grass roots of the party are opposed to quotas, but may look favourably on targets. The writers claim that this is supported by the party leadership (Gardiner and Ferguson 1996: 89). There is an awareness that the party disadvantages women in selection, and moves are afoot to get women selected for winnable seats.

Australian Liberal Party

According to Chris McDiven, there have been reserved places in the Australian Liberal Party since the party's creation – and this is in keeping with liberal philosophy. The Federal Women's Committee was established at the inaugural Federal Executive of the party in 1945, and was immediately incorporated into the federal constitution as a recognized part of the party (McDiven 1996: 95). The Women's Committee mobilized around policy, elections and women's progress. That a female vice-president of the party should be elected as early as 1949 says something about its success. Writing in 1996, McDiven describes the constitution of the federal party as ruling that one of the annually elected vice-presidents must be a woman, that the President of the Women's Section in each state division should sit on the Federal Council, that the President of the federal Women's Committee should have a seat on the Federal Executive and on the Advisory Committee on Policy, and at every level of organization from branch to state executive there should be both a male and a female vice-president.

However, women are not noticeably successful in the Liberal Party beyond the reserved positions. Apart from the representative of the Women's Committee and the female vice-president, there was at the time McDiven was writing only one woman elected to the Federal Executive – making three out of sixteen seats. McDiven records tremendous variation in the presence of women in the state party organizations, with Victoria having close to equal representation and Queensland doing very poorly (McDiven 1996: 96). Like other Liberal parties, that in Australia does not support electoral quotas, and is reliant on training programmes and encouragement to bring women forward for both party office and selection for election. McDiven organized the Liberal Women's Forum Program, which acted both to change attitudes and to recruit, train and support women candidates. This may be one of the reasons for the increasing number of Liberal Members of Parliament in Australia.

The introduction of quotas into the ALP has made a considerable difference to the number of Labor women elected to the federal assembly. The proportion of women elected from New South Wales to the House of Representatives increased from zero in 1980 to 22.73 per cent in 1998, while in Victoria the increase was from 5.88 per cent in 1980 to 21.05 per cent in 1998. Australia's women are caught in a cultural contradiction: on the one hand, the culture of equality and meritocracy gives them an advantage, but on the other, the culture of 'mateship' marginalizes them. Changes are taking place, but not without considerable effort and bitterness.

New Zealand

Unlike Australia, New Zealand operates a system of proportional representation for elections: mixed-member proportional (MMP). After two elections this was reviewed in 2001 by Parliament, and retained, unchanged. From being the most clearly developed example of the Westminster model of a one-party government, delivered through single-member constituencies, New Zealand has transformed itself into a multi-party system that delivers coalition governments. In so doing, it initially achieved both higher turn-outs and an increased number of parties, although these diminished at the 2002 election.

Having been the first country to give women the vote in 1893, the first woman Prime Minister was appointed in 1997, Jenny Shipley. New Zealand achieved another first in 1999 when it became the first democracy in which voters had to choose between two women (leaders of the major parties) for Prime Minister: Jenny Shipley and Helen Clark. In the same election the Green Party was co-led by a woman, Jeannette Fitzsimmons; and the leader of the ACT lost his seat to a woman. Labour, the Greens and ACT are the parties most accommodating to women; parties of the centre and right are characterized by a 'blokeishness' not conducive to the inclusion of women (McLeay 2003: 299).

Labour and the Greens are the most pro-active with regard to women. ACT is accommodating but resists pro-active measures. In a promotional pamphlet published in 2000, *Values not Politics*, it made no mention of gender equality or issues. Helen Clark, Labour leader, on the other hand, 'has a clear model for the future of the Labour party in a PR environment. She wants her party to emulate the Norwegian Labour Party, and she is an admirer of Gro Harlem Brundtland, Norway's first and very successful female PM' (Boston et al. 1996: 55).

Conclusion

Women are active as voters and as the foot-soldiers of political parties, but their participation in the decision-making of parties is more limited. Women's access to influential positions within political parties is constrained in similar ways to their access to elected office. It would appear that effective change at the top – election of women to parliaments – can be achieved only through action at the bottom – the participation of parties at local level. National parliaments and parties can make statements of intent – they can even legislate – but without the support of local party activists, little will be achieved. The hierarchies of local parties are resistant to change, but not immovable, as some of the examples presented here show.

FURTHER READING

Lovenduski and Norris's book is invaluable for pulling together chapters on women in political parties in different countries. Bergqvist et al.'s volume looks at the Nordic countries more broadly, but there is plenty in it about parties. The Beckwith and Jenson and Valiente chapters are both good on France, and Beckwith is useful on the UK and the USA, while Jenson and Valiente look at Canada. Simms's collection is excellent on Australia, Poonacha's on India, and Craske's commentary on Latin America is very readable. The chapters in Tolleson-Rinehart and Josephson are good on different aspects of the USA and, those in Tremblay and Trimble on Canada.

Beckwith, K. 2003: The Gendering Ways of States: Women's Representation and State Reconfiguration in France, Great Britain and the United States. In L. Banaszak, K. Beckwith and D. Rucht (eds), *Women's Movements Facing the Reconfigured State*, Cambridge: Cambridge University Press, pp. 169–202.
Bergqvist, C. et al. (eds) 1999: *Equal Democracies? Gender and Politics in the Nordic Countries*. Oslo: Scandinavian University Press.
Craske, N. 1999: *Women and Politics in Latin America*. Cambridge: Polity.
Jenson, J. and Valiente, C. 2003: Comparing Two Movements for Gender Parity. In L. Banaszak, K. Beckwith and D. Rucht (eds), *Women's Movements Facing the Reconfigured State*, Cambridge: Cambridge University Press, pp. 69–93.
Lovenduski, J. and Norris, P. (eds) 1993a: *Gender and Party Politics*. London: Sage Publications.
Poonacha, V. (ed.) 1997b: *Women, Empowerment and Political Parties*. Research Centre for Women's Studies, SNDT Women's University.
Simms, M. (ed.) 1996: *The Paradox of Parties*. St Leonards: Allen and Unwin.

Tolleson-Rinehart, S. and Josephson, J. J. (eds) 2000: *Gender and American Politics: Women, Men and the Political Process*. Armonk, NY: M. E. Sharpe.

Tremblay, M. and Trimble, L. 2003: *Women and Electoral Politics in Canada*. Toronto: Oxford University Press.

WOMEN'S PARTIES

10

Introduction

This chapter addresses the very particular phenomenon of women's parties. Initially I assumed that women's parties would be no more than a curious little postscript to this book, but it quickly became apparent that they were more than this. First, there are more of them than I had expected. Although there is no English-language text devoted to them, a surprising number of women's parties can be found through pretty basic research. Second, they are more widespread than I had thought and can be found in most parts of the world. Third, they are indicative of very particular failures in political systems. This chapter focuses on the women's parties in Northern Ireland, Iceland and Russia, while also taking into account those in Australia, the Ukraine, Armenia, Cambodia and the Philippines.

Women's Parties Defined

Women's parties are exceptional. As we have seen, women in politics tend to see themselves as serving party interests before those of women, and parties have grown up around significant interests in a political community, among which gender does not usually figure. It is generally argued that although women may share a core of interests at a particular time and place, these are not enough to constitute the basis of a political party, because women will also have other interests that are not shared, and that are captured by a range of other parties. None the less, women's parties have emerged in surprising numbers.

A range of countries have had experience of women's parties in the past. For example, there was the National Women's Party in the United States early in the twentieth century; Eva Peron started a women's party in Argentina in 1949; and there was a women's party in Spain in the 1930s. At present, women's parties appear to be particularly likely to emerge either in countries undergoing major change, or where there is a tradition of separate women's culture in politics. One of the best-known women's parties is the Women's Alliance in Iceland. The creation of this was in keeping with a tradition of women's separate political organization dating from the early twentieth century. Women's parties in Russia and former Soviet states appear to be reflective of both a tradition of separate women's organizations and the changes (and conflict) taking place in the region. The parties in Northern Ireland, Israel and the former Yugoslav states Slovenia and Serbia appear to be symptomatic of the conflict in these regions. There are also women's parties in the Netherlands, Australia, the Philippines and Greece.

Women's parties have in common the goal of achieving better political representation of women, both by getting more women into elected office and by getting issues important to women on to the political agenda. They are also associated with the pursuit of peace across sectarian divides, most obviously in the case of the Northern Ireland and Israeli parties. Despite (at least in some cases) announcing full political programmes, it is questionable whether women's parties are likely to sustain a real political existence if the goal of getting a significant number of women into elected office is achieved. The example of the Women's Alliance in Iceland is illuminating on this point (see below).

Northern Ireland Women's Coalition

A women's movement emerged in Northern Ireland in the 1970s, parallel with that in the Republic of Ireland and elsewhere. The issues pursued by the women's movement in Northern Ireland reflected those in other countries, with the added impetus of inequality with the rest of the UK with respect to abortion (when abortion became legal in Great Britain, it remained against the law in Northern Ireland). The movement was dominated and fragmented by almost thirty years of conflict. But it none the less followed similar patterns to women's movements elsewhere, and then it founded a women's party. The Northern Ireland Women's Coalition (NIWC) was founded in 1996 to continue the work that women had been doing, developing and maintaining contact across the fissures in the society, and to field candidates in local and national elections.

In the 1996 local elections the NIWC candidate for the Down District Council, Ann Carr, was elected. Two years later, when the first elections to the new Northern Ireland Assembly took place, the NIWC fielded six candidates, two of whom were elected: Jane Morrice to represent North Down and Monica McWilliams to represent South Belfast. The NIWC won 0.4 per cent of the vote in the 2001 general election in 2001, but no candidate was elected. The Northern Ireland Legislative Assembly was suspended in 2000, and later dissolved. Elections were held for a second time in November 2003. The NIWC fielded seven candidates, but the two incumbents, Monica McWilliams and Jane Morrice, lost their seats, and no others were won. Despite setbacks, the party is still active.

The Coalition was created against the backdrop of women's virtual exclusion from mainstream politics, with the goal of inserting women, women's issues and women's perspectives on mainstream issues into the politics and government of Northern Ireland. The women of the NIWC have met with considerable hostility, but are determined to hold their own. In a press release on 6 December 2003 the Women's Coalition stated:

> Thousands of people in Northern Ireland registered their support for the Women's Coalition in this election. The views of these people, and others whose voices are excluded or silent in political debate, need to be heard and promoted. Our role as a cross-community, non-sectarian, progressive party is vital and will continue in the future [. . .] As one of the authors of the [Good Friday] Agreement, the Women's Coalition will not walk away from it. The vision of a peaceful, shared, equal Northern Ireland is as relevant and badly-needed now as it was when the party was formed in 1996 [. . .] This election result is an obstacle, yet we will not be deflected from our goals. (NIWC)

Icelandic Women's Alliance

The existence of separate women's lists in Iceland, which approximate to political parties, goes back to the beginning of the twentieth century, prior to women having the vote. In 1908 women's associations in Reykjavik campaigned on a separate electoral list. Women's lists contested elections in Reykjavik and two other towns until 1921, and in 1922 the first female member of the Icelandic parliament was elected from a women's list (Styrkarsdottir 1999: 88; Dominelli and Jonsdottir 1988).

The Icelandic women's movement was very active in the 1970s, often adopting unconventional methods and attracting international attention, such as the women's strike in 1975. Women's lists re-emerged at this time as a protest against the failure of the mainstream to incorporate women, and against prevailing social conditions (Styrkarsdottir 1999: 89). Women's lists were put up at the 1982 local elections in Reykjavik and Akureyri. In Reykjavik the women's list won 11 per cent of the votes and two seats on the city council (just over 10 per cent); in Akureyri, the women's list won 17 per cent of the vote and two seats on the city council (just over 20 per cent). Between 1982 and 1994 women's lists have been put up in seven of Iceland's municipalities – the percentage here is variable, since the number of municipalities has dropped from 202 in 1982 to 171 in 1994. While the lists have had varying success, they have underpinned the increased representation of women in Icelandic politics, not least because the established parties perceived the lists as a threat to which they responded by promoting more women.

In 1983 a national women's list, the parliamentary Women's Alliance (Kvennalistinn), was formed. That year women's lists ran in three of the eight constituencies in Iceland, winning 5.5 per cent of the votes and three parliamentary seats (5 per cent). In the next three elections women's lists ran in every constituency, winning both votes and seats, and scaring the other parties into putting up more women. The percentage of women elected has risen from 5 in 1971 to 34.9 in 1999, even though the Women's Alliance had, at most, six seats (10 per cent) and did not contest the 1999 election (Styrkarsdottir 1999: 91).

In 1994 the Reykjavik women's list joined with three other parties to form the Reykjavik list in order to defeat the ruling Independence Party. It succeeded and implemented many of the policies that the women's list had been promoting, particularly with regard to day care. Thus, in 1994 the women's list achieved its initial goal of women's inclusion and ceased to exist as an independent entity. Since then, women have comprised at least half of the city councillors, and a woman has become mayor.

The Women's Alliance continued to adhere to its grass-roots origins and social movement ethos. Its ideology was grounded in the belief that a distinct women's culture exists and that it should be understood and respected alongside the masculine culture. The Alliance had no leader, and the parliamentary group elected a leader for one year at a time. There was no central leadership, but a national congress which decided the political manifesto. As Dominelli and Jonsdottir's research in Reykjavik has shown, the combination of political office and social movement method is not an easy one to negotiate, and can cause conflict and bitterness, with both sides feeling let down or even betrayed.

In 1998 no women's lists were run at local elections; instead, women who had been involved with the lists formed umbrella parties with the Social Democrats and the People's Alliance. At the 1999 general election the Women's Alliance, the Social Democrats and the People's Alliance formed a new party, the United Alliance, and won seventeen seats, nine of which went to women (Styrkarsdottir 1999: 95). The Women's Alliance had done its job: there were many more women in Parliament and local government; the political agenda had expanded to take on women's issues; and many more women had become politically active.

Women of Russia and Women's Parties in the Former Soviet Republics

Women of Russia

A surprising number of women's parties have emerged in Russia and the former Soviet republics. During the Communist period there were separate women's political organizations and quotas. Whether or not these offered any real opportunities for political influence is debatable; none the less, women in the region were accustomed to the existence of women's organizations and, presumably, continue to find this an appropriate way to organize. Women of Russia is a movement rather than a party, but it nevertheless contests elections and constituted itself as a faction within the Duma (lower house) between 1993 and 1999.

There are also women's parties in (at least) Belorussia, the Ukraine, Armenia, Lithuania and Kyrgizstan. John Ishiyama analysed women's parties in Eastern Europe and the former Soviet Union in 2003 in an attempt to discover why they emerged, and why they were successful, in some countries but not others (Ishiyama 2003). He concluded that they were more likely to appear in countries where the electoral system placed a strong emphasis on the personal characteristics of individual candidates. He also found a correlation between the appearance of a women's party and the existence of a powerful presidency (Ishiyama 2003: 302).

As we saw in the discussion of women in Russian politics in chapter 9, women are close to invisible in Russian political life. A complaint repeated frequently in the literature is that 'today the basic rights of women to participate in political life are being violated' (Sillaste 1995). Russian social, economic and political life continues to undergo radical change in the post-Soviet era. Perhaps for many people, men and women, the social and the economic take precedence over the political – although it is also argued that while women were dealing with the day-to-day emergencies of transition, men were organizing politics to suit themselves (Salmenniemi 2003).

During the Soviet period women had been represented by the Soviet Women's Committee. After liberalization, this became the Union of Women of Russia in the independent Russian Federation. This reorganized body joined with the Association of Women Entrepreneurs, the Alliance of Women of Russia, and Women of the Naval Fleet to form the Women of Russia movement, which was registered as a political organization with the Ministry of Justice of the Russian Federation on 11 October 1993 (Buckley 1997a: 158). The goal of the new movement was to defend the interests of women in the campaign for elections to the Federal Assembly.

The movement had to collect 100,000 signatures from across several regions of Russia before it could qualify to put candidates up for election. The involvement of the Union of Women of Russia, and the existence of a network of women's councils (*zhensovety*) facilitated this, and the signatures were achieved in about a week. Women of Russia entered the election as one of thirteen parties. The election to the state Duma (Lower House) was organized in two parts: half of the seats were allocated through a system of proportional representation, via party lists, and half via single-member seats. In the 1993 general election, Women of Russia fielded thirty-six candidates for the PR list seats and won 8.1 per cent of the vote, the fourth largest, and twenty-one seats. It won a further two seats in single-member constituencies, bringing the total to twenty-three (Buckley 1997a: 162). Overall, women won 13.5 per cent of seats in the Duma.

Women's attitudes towards the new organization were complex. According to Sillaste, 45 per cent of a group of women interviewed in Moscow agreed that women's organizations should run a separate election campaign from other parties, while 29 per cent thought this was inadvisable, and 17 per cent thought it mistaken. Nevertheless, 28 per cent of young Moscow women interviewed in another survey intended to vote for the Women of Russia candidate. Sillaste claims that Russian women are, on the one hand, mistrustful of political leaders, but on the other, doubtful of whether women possess leadership characteristics.

Both the former chair of the Soviet Women's Committee, Alevatina Fedulova, and Women of Russia's most prominent activist and chair, Ekaterina Lakhova, were elected to the Duma. Lakhova declared the organization's goal: 'all parties are dominated by men. Male politics is dirty. We want to make it cleaner' (Buckley 1997b: 161). The policies of the organization were centrist, favouring economic reform and new market relations, but also arguing that social protection was required in housing, education and health care. The loss of the social guarantees of the Soviet era had created problems, especially for women, in terms of poverty and unemployment, which needed to be addressed by government: women constituted 70 per cent of the unemployed (Buckley 1997a: 164). Women of Russia also emphasized law and order, and opposed violence and pornography.

The party's support came overwhelmingly from women: 82 per cent of its vote. Of these, 19 per cent were aged between 19 and 29, and 37 per cent between 30 and 44; 22 per cent had received higher education, 30 per cent were workers, 27 per cent employees, 13 per cent engineering or technical workers, 3 per cent peasants, 8 per cent intellectuals, 1 per cent bureaucrats, 1 per cent business people, 1 per cent military, and 16 per cent pensioners (Buckley 1997b: 164).

Women of Russia confidently entered eighty candidates in the next election in 1995. Despite their previous success, they were largely unsuccessful this time. The party won 4.6 per cent of the vote, failed to cross the 5 per cent threshold, and was not allocated any seats (although it had achieved more than 5 per cent in some areas). It did, however, retain its two single-member seats.

What went wrong? Women of Russia had limited funds to run a campaign, and was able to buy very little television time. According to Buckley, the 'campaign also fought amid the frequent hurling of patriarchal insults against women's participation in politics' (Buckley 1997a: 175). The other parties fielded a few more female candidates, but the end result was fewer women in the Duma, 10.2 per cent.

In 1999 Women of Russia ran again. This time they won only 2.04 per cent of the vote, and no seats. Two other electoral organizations with women's issue platforms ran: Tatyana Roschina's Russian Party in Defence of Women, which achieved 0.81 per cent of the vote, and Ella Pamfilova's For Civil Dignity, which won 0.6 per cent. All the major parties included women on their lists and as contenders for single-member seats. Thirteen women were elected from the party lists, and nineteen in single-member seats. The proportion of women in the Duma dropped to 7.6 per cent (Hesli et al. 2001: 68–70).

The party did not participate in the 2003 election, and Lakhova ran as a candidate on the United Russia party list, the party to which Women of Russia now gives its support. Fedulova claims that United Russia has promised that it will help women to advance in parliament (Salmenniemi 2003). The general consensus among political analysts appears to be that Russian politics (and male politicians) discourages women's participation, and this is compounded by the feminization of unemployment and poverty. The widespread cynicism about politics and politicians has been reinforced by the manipulation of parties in the 2003 election to strengthen the power of the elite around the President.

Elsewhere in post-Communist states

As in Russia, during the Soviet period quotas for women operated in the Ukraine, ensuring that one-half of the seats in local councils and one-third of the seats in Ukraine's Supreme Soviet were occupied by women. After independence the proportion of women initially declined to 2.9 per cent, and then increased to 4.6 and 8 per cent in 1998. Five of the 130 registered political parties in the Ukraine are women's parties. In 1998 the All Ukrainian Party of Women's Initiatives (founded by Valentina Datsenko in 1997) fielded twenty-seven candidates in the national election, twenty-two of whom were women. It won 0.6 per cent of the proportional representation list vote (Ishiyama 2003: 281). The party, however, was scarcely radical. It saw women primarily as mothers with responsibilities for care of the family, and did not address any of the issues faced by women as a group (Birch 2003: 145).

Writing prior to the 2002 election, Birch argued that women were becoming more evident in politics, largely because in each of the three main parties a small group of women had risen to prominence. She concluded that women had not been successful when they had promoted explicitly female causes (Birch 2003: 149). The 2002 election appears to support at least part of her contention. In 2002 a new party, Women of the Future (registered in 2001), displaced the All Ukrainian Party of Women's Initiatives and fought the election. It did not achieve any seats. Only two women's parties had registered for the election: the All Ukrainian Party of Women's Initiatives and Women of the Future, and the All Ukrainian Party was disqualified from the election at the last minute.

Writing for *Ukraine Weekly* and *RFE/RL Newsline*, Taras Kuzio claimed that there was a government strategy to ensure that only one women's party ran in the 2002 election, and that Women of the Future was created as a vehicle for governmental interests. Women of the Future claimed 320,000 members in 500 branches. It was led and financed by people with powerful links to Soviet era and present-day elites, including Liudmyla Kuchma, wife of the President. These links may account for how it achieved a high profile and remarkable popularity very quickly. Taras Kuzio argues that these links ensured the new party popularity and success denied to the other women's parties that lacked similar resources.

The party courted popularity by distributing food free of charge in some areas of the Ukraine and organizing concerts in towns and villages. Yet Kuzio argues that it did not have an ideological position of any sort: its popularity was not because of its defence of women's rights, but simply due to its distribution of goods. Kuzio claims that the creation of Women of the Future was a fairly cynical move to attract the women's vote away from other, more radical, women's parties. Women of the Future was expected to ally itself with the pro-Presidential faction in the parliament and to follow a conservative line with regard to women. This argument would seem to be supported by the annulment of the registration for the election of the Women's Initiatives Party (Kuzio: 2002a). In the election of March 2002, only twenty-four women were elected, constituting 5.3 per cent of the parliament. Of these none were from the women's party.

Nadzeya, founded in Belarus in 1994, has not won any seats in the parliament. Neither have either of the Bulgarian women's parties: the Democratic Women's Union (1993) and the Party of Bulgarian Women (1995), nor the Georgian Women's Party (1995). The Shamiram Women's Party in Armenia (1995) has been more successful. It won 16.9 per cent of the vote and twelve seats in 1995, although this fell to 0.6 per cent of the vote and no seats in 1999. In Moldova the Association of Women won 2.8 per cent of the vote in 1994, although no seats; the Women's Party of Lithuania (1995) was in fifteenth place among the parties competing in the election of 1986, with 3.9 per cent of the vote, and won one seat; the Democratic Party of Women of Kyrgyzstan (1994) won 12.38 per cent of the vote in 2000, and came in third place (Ishiyama 2003: 280).

Women's autonomous organization in parties appears to have stalled in the countries of the former Soviet Union and other post-Communist countries – with the possible exception of Bulgaria (Kostadinova 2003). Although the countries are different, there seems to be a trend towards the consolidation of elites around a president, that operates through networks to which women have limited access.

Other Women's Parties

A number of women's parties have been founded around the world very recently. As a trend, this echoes the wave of creation of Green parties that started a few years earlier. However, the women's parties do not seem to share the common ground and communication networks that characterized the Green movement. Rather, the women's parties are very much grounded in local experience and are responding to local circumstances, although many (but not all) share a loosely feminist approach.

The Australian Women's Party (AWP) was founded in 2002 in response to the failure of the Australian Labor Party (ALP) to fulfil its commitment to allocate female candidates to 35 per cent of winnable seats by 2002. The new party was created by people with long histories in the labour and women's movements, most of whom were disaffected ALP members. Its primary goal is to achieve a change to the constitution to guarantee equal male and female representation in the federal parliament. Beyond this, the party takes broadly Left positions on the key issues in Australian politics: indigenous peoples, industrial relations, social security, the environment, immigration, fertility control, housing, transport, community and domestic violence, child care and human rights. The creation of the party exposes a split within the ALP and loss of the support of feminists throughout the society which it had been guaranteed in the past. If the party is at all successful, it poses a threat to the ALP, which has suffered from a number of splits, leaving its claims to radicalism severely challenged (Greenleft; Australian Women's Party website).

Women in Mindanao in the Philippines founded the Gabriela Women's Party in 2003, a party list offshoot of the Gabriela Women's Coalition, which is an alliance of women's organizations in the region. The new party appears to be on the more radical wing of politics, favouring social, political and economic change and promoting women's issues, as well as wanting to get more women into politics. Party publicity emphasizes women's high rate of voter turn-out in comparison with their low numbers in elected office, and points out that only women from privileged backgrounds and elite families have been able to run for office (Mindanews 2003).

The Cambodian Women's Party is another small, radical party in a less developed country that is undergoing social, economic and political change. Founded in 1998, the party takes a strong position on women's rights and development issues. Unusually, the Cambodian party includes male candidates for election, although they are on the bottom half of the list (Phomphipak and Henk).

Women's lists have contested a number of national elections in Israel. Their only success was in the first Knesset, when WIZO (Women's International Zionist Organization for Improved Israeli Society) returned one female member. Since then, women's lists have contested four general elections, including that in 1999. The Pnina Rosenblum Party registered for the 1999 election. Led by the eponymous member of the Knesset, this was a women's party focused on increasing women's representation. There are also a number of women's peace organizations that are closely linked to political parties. Women's politics is very powerful in Israel; however, women's parties are impeded by cross-cutting cleavages of ethnicity and religion even more than in other countries.

While many women's parties take radical and feminist positions, others are more conservative in their goals. The platform of the Hellenic Women's Political Party of Greece, for example, emphasizes women's family roles as mothers, housekeepers and managers of the household budget. It appears to link women's participation in parliament to their traditional roles and to the preservation of the nation (Hellenic Women's Political Party 1998).

There is a strong connection between feminist politics and environmentalism, which may have some mileage in the future – as implied in the platform of the Australian Women's Party, where the environment figures alongside more woman-specific goals. Green parties around the world have integrated a feminist agenda into their political programmes. They have, for the most part, grown up alongside each other, and share both programmes and practices. The philosophy and organization of both radical women's parties and Green parties draw heavily on the model of social movements, which prescribes collectivity, equality and informality, rather than hierarchy. When Green parties achieve office, they often compromise on at least some of their goals and practices, but the inclusion of women is well established. In 1997 the Green parties of Germany and France entered formal, national politics. In Germany, Andrea Fischer was given the Health portfolio, and in France Dominique Voynet became Environment Minister. In 1999 two Belgian Green parties won a share in government: Isabelle Durant of the French-speaking Ecolo party and Magda Aelvoet of the Dutch-speaking Agalev both became government ministers.

Conclusion

From the examples discussed here we can see that women's parties do not share much common ground with mainstream European-style political parties. The majority of them are minority parties with narrow platforms, more like pressure groups than parties. Like the Green parties that sprang up around the world at around the same time, they suffer from the problem of having a key political theme that is easily and frequently taken over by other – better resourced and more established – political parties.

Women's parties do not have a fixed place on the Left–Right political spectrum: while many are to the Left, such as the Australian, Icelandic and Northern Ireland parties, others are to the Right, including the Women of the Future in the Ukraine and the Hellenic Women of Greece. The most successful of the radical parties have emerged in response to a particular situation that can be characterized as follows. Women have achieved formal equality, the political system recognizes women's rights, and the parties pay lip-service to the equal inclusion of women; however, in the real world not much is changing. Women with political aspirations are frustrated, and women with egalitarian social vision become angry. The frustration and anger find expression in the creation of a political party when a particular event triggers it. In Northern Ireland it was the establishment of the Legislative Assembly and the Good Friday Agreement; in Australia the failure of the ALP to meet its quota policy and the marginalization of particular women; in Russia and Iceland the realization that women could not break into the *status quo*, despite the apparent promise that it was possible to do so. Individual women may be important in galvanizing the movement, as the examples of Russia and Australia have suggested.

Women's parties find a place more easily in multi-party systems where there is a history of minority – and even of women's – mobilization. Hence the proliferation of women's parties in post-Communist countries. The plight of women's parties in the Ukraine is disturbing, but this is more a function of politics in countries of the former Soviet Union than a failure of women's parties *per se*. Recent elections in both Russia and the Ukraine have been characterized by the appearance of new parties that are simply instruments of the ruling elite.

FURTHER READING

The Northern Ireland Women's Coalition has been detailed in the broader literature of Northern Irish politics, particularly the work of Yvonne Galligan and Rick Wilford. Discussion of the Icelandic Women's List features in much of the Nordic literature, including *Equal Democracies?* and an interesting, if rather old, article by Dominelli and Jonsdottir. Mary Buckley has documented Women of Russia, and an article by John Ishiyama discusses a number of women's parties in post-Communist countries. Several of the chapters in Matland and Montgomery are informative about women's parties in post-Communist countries.

Bergqvist, C. et al. (eds) 1999: *Equal Democracies? Gender and Politics in the Nordic Countries.* Oslo: Scandinavian University Press.

Brown, A., Donoghy, T. B., Mackay, F. and Meehan, E. 2002: Women and Constitutional Change in Scotland and Northern Ireland. *Parliamentary Affairs*, 55 (1): 71–84.

Buckley, M. 1997a: Adaptation of the Soviet Women's Committee: Deputies' Voices from 'Women of Russia'. In M. Buckley (ed.), *Post-Soviet Women: From the Baltic to Central Asia*, Cambridge: Cambridge University Press, pp. 157–85.

Dominelli, L. and Jonsdottir, G. 1988: Feminist Political Organisation in Iceland: Some Reflections on the Experience of Kwenna Frambothid. *Feminist Review*, 28: 36–60.

Ishiyama, J. 2003: Women's Parties in Post-Communist Politics. *East European Politics*, 17 (2): 266–304.

Matland, R. E. and Montgomery, K. (eds) 2003: *Women's Access to Political Power in Post-Communist Europe.* Oxford: Oxford University Press.

PART IV

Parliaments and Governments

MEMBERS AND MINISTERS

11

Introduction

Part IV moves on up the political hierarchy. Part II looked at voting and elections; Part III at parties. Now we move on to parliaments and governments – cabinets in particular. We have only recently been getting enough information to be able to make some generalizations about what women do once in parliament, because only recently have there been enough women, who have spent enough time as legislators, for us to be able to study them as groups rather than individuals. This chapter presents a general discussion of women in parliaments and cabinets and the other two chapters in this section move on to look at specific examples and issues.

Women in Parliaments

Women populate the grass roots of parties, diligently raising funds with dinners, garden fetes and pub quizzes. As we look up the party hierarchy in almost all countries, we find fewer and fewer women. It is a curious anomaly that a woman can be leader of a political party that has few other elected women or women in party positions and take little account of women in her government's policies. In India, Indira Gandhi led the Congress Party in such circumstances, just as Benazir Bhutto in Pakistan led the Pakistan Peoples Party (PPP). These were both women whose tenure of office had more to do with their family connections than their political acuity or the systems in which they were active (although it is fair to say that family connections are important for male politicians too). Margaret Thatcher gained office on exactly the same terms as a man; however, she led the Conservative Party in the United Kingdom at a time when there were very few women in parliament and her party had no consciously pro-women agenda. Similarly, Michele Alliot-Marie was briefly leader of the right-wing French Rassemblement pour la République Party (RPR).

In representative democracies the main point of organized politics is to form a government in order to implement policy: party mobilization, policy creation and elections are all to this end. In multi-party systems characterized by proportional representation, getting into parliament may well be enough to achieve a voice in the direction of policy. However, in two-party and/or first-past-the-post systems, only being elected as part of the governing party offers such access – offers, but does not guarantee, it. In the UK, only membership of government – the inner core of the governing party in parliament – guarantees influence. In the United States of America, it is membership – or, better still, occupying the chair – of an important committee that matters. These are positions reliant on seniority and/or patronage.

Whether this focusing of power on a small group of people is seen simply as efficient modern democracy or as a travesty of democracy depends rather on the view of democracy adopted. It is relevant to women seeking to participate in politics, however, because it both narrows the goal and moves that goal further away. In order to be effective in politics in the UK, and in other increasingly centralized systems, getting elected (itself difficult and time-consuming) merely gets you through the door of the parliament. Influence is still a long way in the distance. Influence requires being in the governing party, getting on to important committees, being appointed to office in an important department, and becoming a key member of the cabinet – that is, getting appointed to one of a relatively small number of positions in the face of the claims of a large number of other elected members, who have been collecting brownie points in the party and parliament for years.

Getting elected is an essential starting point, but it may prove to be just that. Women entering politics and their supporters can be disappointed when getting elected is followed by . . . not much. It is variously argued that party and parliamentary traditions militate against any sort of change: that there is a 'career path' for elected members that entails serving time on the dull but worthy committees before getting advancement, that the men's club atmosphere of politics closes women out, and that institutional sexism operates to hold women back. While this would appear to be true in many countries, it is not a universal or necessary truth, as the examples of the Nordic countries show.

Whenever we talk about the political representation of women, we have to be careful to distinguish between two rather different issues: first, women getting into parliament and executive office, and second, the controversial claim that having women in elected office should somehow make a difference to the nature of politics, as we saw in chapter 2.

Women in Governments

Merely getting elected has proved to be difficult. The proportions of women in elected national assemblies varies enormously – from zero in some Arab countries to almost half in the Nordic countries, averaging out at between 10 and 12 per cent. Getting beyond this, from the legislature to the executive, has been even more variable. According to United Nations statistics, by the year 2000 only twenty-two countries had at any time elected a woman Prime Minister, and only Bangladesh, New Zealand and Sri Lanka had elected two women to that position. Sixteen countries had elected women as Presidents, but only the Republic of Ireland had repeated the experiment. The longest-standing female office-holder is Vigdis Finnbogadottir, who was President of Iceland for sixteen years, from 1980 to 1996. Sri Lanka stands out for having had both a woman as Prime Minister and a woman as President from 1994, while Sweden is notable for its 50:50 practice with regard to cabinet appointments, and Norway for having over 40 per cent women in the cabinet since 1988 (Social Statistics and Indicators 2000: 170).

The proportions of women in parliaments range from nearly half to none, averaging around 15 per cent in 2003 (IPU, 30 October 2003). While the Nordic countries regularly top the list, and Arab states tail it, there is considerable variation in between. Women's inclusion in cabinets is similarly varied. In parliamentary systems the cabinet is the heart of government. It is the link between the legislature and the executive; it is a parliamentary committee with enormous power. It is, however, a somewhat illusive institution. In most countries the size of the cabinet and the qualifications for membership are not fixed (Spain is an exception here, with the number of ministers defined by law, as is the USA, where the federal cabinet is made up of unelected presidential appointees). Rebecca Howard Davis describes cabinets as consisting of concentric circles arranged around the Prime Minister. The inner circle consists of the ministers for finance and foreign affairs, the next circle of senior ministers holding full voting privileges, and an outer rim of associates, secretaries of state and junior ministers (Davis 1997: 12).

In general, the size of governments and cabinets has grown in the post-war period, and the proportion of women has increased. Cabinets vary in their internal working on a scale of hierarchical/egalitarian. Single-party cabinets tend to be more hierarchical – that in the UK is a good example – and coalition cabinets more egalitarian – for example, the Finnish cabinet. Davis surveyed fifteen European cabinets in 1992, and found that the proportion and number of women cabinet ministers had grown since 1968 – except in Portugal. There were, however, differences between regions. The numbers in the Nordic countries had grown most, and in southern Europe least. While there was near parity between men and women in the Nordic countries, southern European cabinets had 5 per cent or fewer women (Davis 1997: 15). She concludes that while cultural and political factors are of importance, individual political actors can shape situations. For example, in the UK in the 1960s and 1970s, when there were very few women in parliament, Barbara Castle was a regular and high-profile member of Labour cabinets. She first held the Overseas Development portfolio, then Education and Productivity, then Health and Social Security.

In attempting to explain both the increase in numbers and the differences, Davis argues that the number of women in a cabinet reflects the numbers in a parliament. Although ideologically more left parties are generally credited with including more women, this does not stand out in her research, and the absolute number of women in a parliament is a better indicator of the number of women in a cabinet than the political orientation of the governing party (Davis 1997: 70). She concludes that 'political parties are likely to appoint women to the government only when their opponents are also likely to do so' (Davis 1997: 70).

Looking at what women did in cabinets, Davis found that roughly 40 per cent of women's portfolios were in 'soft' areas: education, health, social welfare, culture, family and consumer affairs – areas not generally included in the inner cabinet (Davis 1997: 16). In the years covered by her research, no woman ever held a portfolio for economic affairs, defence, relations with parliament, equipment or the budget. She points out that 'women have held office in only half the functional areas in which there are cabinet-level positions' (Davis 1997: 16). This could be explained by the committees that women are on prior to achieving ministerial office, and it is certainly the case that there are more women on family, social affairs, health and education committees than on finance and defence. The question is whether women choose to work in these areas, or are channelled into stereotypical roles.

In the years since Davis investigated cabinets, there have been some changes. Since then, the UK cabinet has included more women in more varied positions, including Trade and Industry and Northern Ireland, and female cabinet ministers in the Nordic countries have moved into some of the 'harder' policy areas. However, there is a conundrum here. If (as some research suggests) female politicians have different interests and a different approach to politics from men, and if they see themselves as representative of women, could it be that women and men will choose different political trajectories? Just to complicate the issue, some research suggests that younger generations of male politicians are more like their female counterparts than their older male colleagues; so perhaps the political spectrum could start to shift towards an emphasis on more traditionally female areas.

The second question – whether it makes a difference having women in elected office – is much more difficult to tease out. As discussed in Part I, there has been an assumption that the presence of women in parliaments matters not just on equal opportunity terms, but also on the grounds of including a range of interests not otherwise accessible, and (perhaps) in the expectation that the nature of political process will be changed by becoming more feminized.

Conclusion

Politicians and media commentators accustomed to the *status quo* have lost no opportunity to draw attention to both the newly arrived women and any pro-active policies that have assisted them. Old-school politicians have challenged and jeered at women, while journalists have focused on their appearances and families in ways that would be unthinkable with regard to their male colleagues. At the same time, the press has very high expectations of elected women: they should be as tough as the men, yet should represent women's interests (even though they were not explicitly elected to do so). They should work the hours, deal with the conditions, yet be glamorous and good wives and mothers.

It should come as no surprise that in the circumstances some women back away, while some others become embittered. Female representatives, however, do appear to want to take up the challenge of both doing the job and representing women. Of course, both personal and party variables come into play here. Research suggests that at least some elected women think that they have an obligation to represent women, and would lay some claim to changing the nature of politics. Research into what goes on in parliaments suggests that elected women do, sometimes, vote differently in the House from men (although there are also age and party variables), and that the presence of larger numbers of women in a legislature may have an effect on policy-making.

FURTHER READING

For general reading on the roles of parliaments and governments, a general text like that of Heywood is an easy way in. For more specific reading, the book by Rebecca Howard Davis referred to here is an important source of information and analysis of women in office. Sarah Childs has looked at women in the Labour Government of the UK, Borrelli at women in the US Cabinet, and for a first-hand account of being a Prime Minister, try Margaret Thatcher's diaries!

Borrelli, M. 2000: Gender, Politics and Change in the United States Cabinet: The Madeleine Korbel Albright and Janet Reno Appointments. In S. Tolleson-Rinehart and J. J. Josephson (eds), *Gender and American Politics: Women, Men and the Political Process*, Armonk, NY: M. E. Sharpe, pp. 185–204.

Childs, S. 2004: *New Labour's Women MPs: Women Representing Women*. London: Routledge.

Davis, R. H. 1997: *Women and Power in Parliamentary Democracies*. Lincoln and London: University of Nebraska Press.

Heywood, A. 2004: *Politics*. London: Palgrave Macmillan.

Thatcher, M. 1995: *The Downing Street Years*. London: Harper Collins.

WOMEN IN ELECTED ASSEMBLIES IN THE UNITED KINGDOM

12

Introduction

This chapter takes up the issue of women in parliaments, governments and cabinets, focusing on the United Kingdom. Since the UK devolved some of its centralized power from the parliament at Westminster to the regional assemblies in Scotland, Wales, Northern Ireland and London in 1999, there are now five places to look (although the Greater London Authority (GLA) has little power, and the Northern Ireland Legislative Assembly has met for only a small part of its existence). If women were slow to make it into the UK parliament, they were even slower at getting into the cabinet. The slowness was compounded by the dominance of the least pro-active party, the Conservatives, during the period in the late twentieth century when women around the world were entering politics in increasing numbers. Since the Tories lost their grip on power in 1997, the numbers of women have gone up perceptibly, and all parties have taken note.

Prior to the 1987 general election in the United Kingdom, there had been very few women in Parliament, let alone high office. There had rarely been more than one woman in the cabinet at a time (and often no women at all). There were very significant individual women in Labour governments of the mid-twentieth century – Jennie Lee and Barbara Castle stand out – but it is only since the start of the 1980s that there have been enough women, with enough standing, to make a mark. Since the Conservative Party was in office from 1979 to 1997, it was only Conservative women who had any chance of achieving office, although during that period Labour women were included in shadow cabinets.

Table 12.1 Percentage of women in the UK Parliament

Year of election	Percentage of women MPs
1979	3
1983	3.5
1987	6.3
1992	9.2
1997	18.2
2001	17.9

Source: Fawcett Society website; IPU website

The Conservative Party in Parliament

Margaret Thatcher is remarkable for having become Prime Minister on exactly the same terms as a man: no positive action, no electoral fixes, no quotas. Nor was she part of a political dynasty (although her father had been a town councillor and mayor). She is also remarkable for being one of the few politicians after whom a period and a political approach is named: the Thatcher era and Thatcherism, along with Thatcher's Children, are likely to be with us for some time yet. She is, however, not at all remarkable for her feminism. Thatcher was a radical Conservative politician. Thatcherism contained a hefty dose of liberalism and, as such, operated in terms of individuals and individual freedoms, not people as members of groups: not classes, not ethnicities, not sexes. This approach appealed to many women. Recognition for individual achievement without regard for class, race or sex is desirable. However, critics point out that denying the existence of discrimination and structures that tend to exclude, inhibits change. Moreover, it causes individuals to blame themselves when they fail, rather than attempting to change the things around them that helped them to fail.

Despite the masculinity of her achievement, Margaret Thatcher did not lack a certain sex appeal: many of the male politicians who surrounded her have described her femininity in their biographies (Maguire 1998: 185). Thatcher exploited her sex in her dealings with the men in the cabinet and the party, about whom she had few illusions. She wrote in her memoir, 'my experience is that a number of the men I have dealt with in politics demonstrate precisely those characteristics which they attribute to women – vanity and an inability to make tough decisions' (Thatcher 1995: 129). In her speeches to the public, she often drew attention to her sex by making reference to running a family budget or cooking for the family (Maguire 1998: 188). However, as Maguire points out, it would be a mistake to confuse Thatcher's femininity with feminism (Maguire 1998: 188).

During the first half of the Conservative period in office the proportion of women in parliament did not get above 5 per cent. At the 1987 election this rose to 6.3 per cent and then to 9.2 per cent in 1992 (see table 12.1). Looking at the Conservative party itself, the proportion of female Tory MPs rose from 3.3 per cent in 1983 to 6.0 per cent in 1992. Out of office, the proportion of women in the Parliamentary Conservative Party continued to rise slowly to 7.8 per cent in 1997 and 8.4 per cent in 2001 (Squires and Wickham-Jones 2001: 51).

A number of women had high-profile political careers during the Conservative governments. Edwina Currie, who famously claimed, 'I'm not a woman, I'm a Conservative', was made a Parliamentary Under-Secretary at the Department of Health (a ministerial post) in 1986, having first been elected to Parliament in 1983 (Maguire 1998: 195). Her short but colourful ministerial career ended in 1988, when she resigned after having created a scandal by claiming that most of the egg production in the UK was contaminated with salmonella. Given the food horrors that have dogged the UK since then, she can now be regarded as merely prescient, but at the time there was an uproar. Journalist Polly Toynbee attributed Currie's treatment at the hands of both the Press and other MPs to her sex: 'A lot of the abuse she gets is because she is a woman [. . .] A lot of the things she says are very straightforward [. . .] It doesn't seem to me that she often says anything that is seriously wrong. It's something to do with the way she says it and who she is that gets up people's noses' (Abdela 1989: 2). Explaining Currie's fall from grace, a Conservative colleague, Lynda Chalker, said: 'I do actually think it was partly the campaign certain male-dominated groups ran against her' (Abdela 1989: 3).

Chalker herself was a skilled politician who, by many accounts, should have been a Cabinet Minister. During her time as Prime Minister (1979–90) Margaret Thatcher only once, briefly, appointed another woman to the cabinet, Baroness Young. Chalker held office in the departments of Health and Social Services, Transport, and the Foreign Office, but was never a Cabinet Minister. Angela Rumbold, Gillian Shephard and Virginia Bottomley were also successful Conservative politicians who held ministerial office, but never cabinet rank under Thatcher.

When John Major became Prime Minister in 1990, he had no qualms about appointing an all-male cabinet, although times had changed enough for this to be noted by the Press and parliamentarians alike. Major included two women in the cabinet in 1992: Gillian Shephard at Employment and Virginia Bottomley at the Department of Health, constituting about 8 per cent. Major again broke new (Conservative) ground in 1996 when Jacqui Lait became the first woman Conservative Whip in the Commons – and the seventh woman in his government. The Conservative governments included a Minister for Women, but this was a low-profile portfolio, held by a minister with other responsibilities – who was usually a man. After the 1992 election, party chair Norman Fowler made the first high-profile Conservative statement about increasing women's presence in the House when he announced that there should be at least 100 female candidates selected for the next general election (Maguire 1998: 190).

The Labour Party in Parliament

The Labour Party that came to power in 1997 and formed the first Blair government had learned a lot of lessons. Blair named five women to his first cabinet: Harriet Harman, Secretary for Social Security; Marjorie Mowlam, Northern Ireland Secretary; Margaret Beckett, President of the Board of Trade; Clare Short, Secretary for International Development; and Ann Taylor, President of the Council and Leader of the House (Seldon 2001). The new parliament had an unprecedented number of female MPs, 120, forming 18.2 per cent of the total. This was a breakthrough not only for parliament, but also for

Labour. In the preceding years the party had a higher percentage of women in the Commons than other parties, but it was not high. In 1983 it was 4.8 per cent, increasing to 9.2 in 1987, 13.7 in 1992, and 24.7 in 1997. This was to fall to 23.1 per cent in 2001 (Squires and Wickham-Jones 2001: 51).

Labour had made an election manifesto commitment to creating a Ministry for Women. On election it kept its promise, but in a less than whole-hearted fashion. Harriet Harman was given responsibility for this, along with Social Security, and Joan Ruddock was made a junior minister, but without pay. Harman then had to weather the first storm of the Labour Government when a change in welfare benefits to single parents was widely perceived as a cut in support for women. This gave rise to condemnation in the media of the newly elected Labour women, and the first hints of a back-bench revolt.

The Press had already prepared the ground for an assault on the new Labour women when it announced that these were 'Blair's Babes'. This had been accompanied by an unfortunate photograph of the Prime Minister as the sole suited man surrounded by colourfully dressed, smiling female MPs: a sultan with his harem. The name stuck, and served as a focus for a stream of articles questioning the decisions, abilities and suitability of the new women MPs. As Lucy Ward was to write three years after the event, 'the media's verdict on Blair's Babes en masse is largely of disappointment and dissatisfaction' (L. Ward 2000: 24). A new epithet was coined when Helen Brinton MP argued in an interview that it was the job of a back-bencher to follow the leadership line loyally. Henceforth the women MPs were to be referred to as 'Stepford Wives' (L. Ward 2000: 26).

In office, Labour appointed more women to government posts than had ever been done before. Cabinet and other ministerial posts change hands fairly often, but just prior to the 2001 election nearly a third of ministerial positions were held by women. This included six of the twenty-two cabinet posts and a further twenty-two non-cabinet posts of minister or under-secretary. Women also made up 10 per cent of the whips and around a third of parliamentary private secretaries. In the cabinet, Margaret Beckett held the post of President of the Council and Leader of the House of Commons; Ann Taylor was Chief Whip and Parliamentary Secretary to the Treasury; Mo Mowlam was Minister for the Cabinet Office; Clare Short, Secretary of State for International Development; Baroness Jay, Leader of the Lords and Minister for Women; and Helen Lidell, Secretary of State for Scotland (Squires and Wickham-Jones 2001: 53).

After the great success in getting women into parliament in the 1997 election, there was concern that in the absence of positive action numbers might dip when the UK went to the polls again in 2001. When this suspicion proved correct, and the number of women MPs dropped to 17.9 per cent overall and 23.1 per cent of the Parliamentary Labour Party, it became apparent that intervention was necessary to enable parties to compel selection of women candidates, as Labour had done in 1997 through all-women short lists. MPs, activists and pressure groups combined to push for legislation to facilitate affirmative action. This resulted in the Sex Discrimination (Electoral Candidates) Act in 2002, which excludes political parties from the Sex Discrimination Act, for the purposes of promoting women, until 2015 (Childs 2002b).

The 2001 general election was followed by a cabinet re-shuffle. This resulted in seven women having cabinet portfolios, making 30.4 per cent of the cabinet female. These were Patricia Hewitt at Trade and Industry; Tessa Jowell at Culture, Media and Sports; Estelle Morris at Education and Skills; Margaret Beckett at Environment and Rural Affairs;

Helen Lidell, who continued from the previous parliament as Secretary of State for Scotland; Clare Short continuing at International Development; and Hilary Armstrong as Chief Whip (Squires and Wickham-Jones 2001: 53). Patricia Hewitt and Sally Morgan, both of whom held other posts, became the Ministers for Women. Twenty-three women were appointed to non-cabinet ministerial posts (Squires and Wickham-Jones 2001: 54).

Importantly, the 2001 election and re-shuffle saw women moving into ministries where they would have responsibility for government spending, such as Morris at Education, and key areas of policy, such as Hewitt at the DTI. Labour has maintained an unprecedented number of women in office. In particular, Mo Mowlam during her time as Secretary for Northern Ireland, Margaret Beckett and Patricia Hewitt at the Department of Trade and Industry, and Harriet Harman as the Solicitor-General, diverge from the model of female ministers in so-called soft ministries (although soft ministries like Health and Education are, of course, high-spending ministries).

By the end of 2003 the number of women in cabinet had been reduced to five. Beckett, Hewitt, Jowell and Armstrong were still in place; Clare Short and Estelle Morris had resigned, and Baroness Amos had been moved in as Leader of the House of Lords and President of the Council. There were, however, some twenty-nine women in non-cabinet government posts, including Harriet Harman as Solicitor-General, Lynda Clark as Advocate-General for Scotland, and Dawn Primarolo as Paymaster-General.

There have been some high-profile conflicts. Clare Short publicly disagreed with the government over drugs and defence policies, and finally resigned from cabinet over the Iraq War; Mowlam was less than graceful when replaced at the Northern Ireland Office; and Morris's resignation from Education gave rise to a lot of questions about government policy and practice. Morris subsequently returned to government – although not to cabinet – as Minister of State for the Arts. Women on Labour's back-benches have not all been satisfied with their roles. It is interesting that Joan Ruddock, while remaining an MP, has reverted to her previous engagement in single-issue, extra-parliamentary politics, and taken up the welfare of women in Afghanistan, creating an organization to raise funds and lobby on their behalf.

Scotland

Scottish constituencies returned women MPs to the House of Commons at a rate of about 7 per cent from when they first became eligible for election in 1918. This increased to 16.7 per cent in 1997, in line with the general increase in numbers of women. Of these twelve women, nine were Labour, one was a Liberal Democrat, and two were Scottish Nationalists. The number fell to eleven in 2001, reflecting the general picture, ten from Labour and one Scottish Nationalist (Squires and Wickham-Jones 2001: 54).

After the first election that created the new Scottish Parliament in 1999, women comprised 37.2 per cent of the new assembly. Having demanded the new assembly and campaigned for the first election under the 50:50 banner, the Scots achieved a good result in cabinet as well as parliament. Of the eleven members of cabinet, three were initially women, 27 per cent of the total: Sarah Boyack, Transport and the Environment; Susan Deacon, Health; and Wendy Alexander with the Committees and Equal Opportunities

Table 12.2 Women in the Scottish Parliament

	1999 (%)	2003 (%)
Parliament	37.2	39.5
Cabinet	27.0	–
Committees	38.0	–

Source: Fawcett Society website

portfolio. After the sudden death of First Minister Donald Dewar, cabinet was re-shuffled to include Jackie Baillie, taking the Social Justice portfolio, and making 33 per cent (Squires and Wickham-Jones 2001: 56). There were also women in non-cabinet ministerial posts, and 20 per cent of deputy ministers were women.

Of the 135 committee positions on seventeen committees 38 per cent were occupied by women, although only four of these (Health and Community Care, Justice II, Equal Opportunities, and Public Petitions) had a majority of women. Only three women convened committees, although there were ten female deputy-conveners (Busby and McLeod 2002: 37–8).

The second election in 2003 returned 39.5 per cent women to the Scottish Parliament. Again, three women were included in the eleven-member cabinet: Margaret Curran as Minister for the Communities; Cathy Jamieson as Minister for Justice; and Patricia Ferguson as Minister for Parliamentary Business. There was also one Deputy Cabinet Minister, Mary Mulligan at Communities, and Elish Angiolini was appointed Solicitor-General. Six of the committees were now convened by women: both the Justice committees, Health, Environment, Subordinate Legislation, and Equal Opportunities. Moreover, the Conveners' Group, at which the conveners of all the committees meet to discuss business, was convened by a woman, Trish Godman (Scottish parliament website). The increased percentage of women in the parliament is reflected in the increased number of committee conveners and the retention of three women in the cabinet, although the proportion of women in these positions does not quite reflect their proportion in the assembly.

The new parliament gives a real priority to equal opportunities, both in its own operation and in appointments to public bodies. According to Wendy Alexander, the minister responsible for Equal Opportunities in the 1999 Parliament, and her deputy, Jackie Baillie, the intention was to lay down long-term foundations while dealing with immediate priorities (Alexander 2000: 83). The new assembly is creating equalities policies in order to entrench the 50:50 vision in society as well as parliament. As long-term strategies, an Equality Unit has been established, and a Scottish Equalities Strategy (SES) defined. The SES requires all Executive Bills to be accompanied by a statement of potential impact on equal opportunities (an approach adopted from local authority equal opportunities practice, promoted by Equalities Committees and Units since the 1980s). Immediate priorities include addressing domestic violence (Edinburgh pioneered the zero-tolerance campaign raising awareness and combating domestic violence in the 1990s). An Anti-Domestic Abuse Fund has been established, and some fifty projects across Scotland are being supported (Alexander 2000: 85).

With regard to its own approach to employment, the parliament has adopted the goal of increasing the number of employees from previously under-represented groups, especially at senior levels. Quotas have been set for the civil service, with the intention of achieving 30 per cent women by 2005 from a base of 20.6 per cent in 2000. In 1998, 47 per cent of public appointees were women, although only 22 per cent of such bodies were chaired by women, and many of the appointments were to children's panels (Busby and McLeod 2002: 40).

Wales

Welsh electoral politics has not been particularly friendly towards women. In the years between women's emancipation in 1918 and 1997, Wales returned only four female MPs to the Westminster parliament. After the landslide 1997 election, the Labour Party held thirty-four of the forty Welsh seats, 85 per cent, yet only four Welsh MPs were women. Three of these had been selected from Labour's all-women short lists. Plaid Cymru and the Liberal Democrats returned no female MPs, and the Conservative Party did not win any Welsh seats. This constituted 10 per cent of the Welsh seats at Westminster. The proportion remained the same at the 2001 election.

This changed radically at the election to the new Welsh Assembly, largely as a result of pressure from women's organizations. Despite the startling results of the elections in 1999 and 2003, which achieved 50 per cent representation of women in the assembly, and the steps taken by the assembly since then, a question mark still hangs over the parties' commitment to gender equality, since the numbers of women elected to Westminster do not appear to be changing (Edwards and McAllister 2002).

As a result of the pro-women measures adopted in the elections to the Welsh Assembly, Wales has one of the highest proportions of females representatives in the world, at 41.7 per cent in 1999 and 50 per cent in 2003 (Chaney 2002: 5) (see table 12.3). In 1999 twenty-five of the sixty assembly members were women: while the majority were Labour, this included six of the twenty-eight representatives of Plaid Cymru and three of the six Liberal Democrats. Women formed a majority of five of the nine members of the assembly's cabinet.

After the 2003 election, five of the nine cabinet positions were again occupied by women: Sue Essex as Minister for Finance, Local Government and Public Services; Karen Sinclair as Minister for Business; Edwina Hart as Minister for Social Justice and Regeneration; Jane Hutt as Minister for Health and Social Security; and Jane Davidson as Minister for Education and Lifelong Learning. Among the senior civil servants executing the business of the new assembly, the representation of women is less remarkable. Four of the eighteen civil servants on the Executive Board are women, with responsibil-

Table 12.3 Women in the Welsh Assembly

	1999 (%)	2003 (%)
Assembly	41.7	50
Cabinet	54.0	54

Source: Fawcett Society website

ities for Health, Social Security, and Research and Development (Welsh Assembly website).

The assembly has a cross-party, eleven-member, Standing Equality Committee which has overseen a raft of reforms initiated in the short time the assembly has existed. Areas covered include the government's behaviour as an employer, the gender pay gap, gender equality in public appointments, equality reforms in the National Health Service and in Welsh local government, economic development, and the policy process. Contract compliance is mooted as a means to enable local authorities to influence the employment practices of contractors that want to win public contracts (Chaney 2002: 6).

Northern Ireland

At the 1997 election to Westminster, Northern Ireland did not return one female MP. In fact, from the time the province came into existence until the 2001 general election, it had only ever returned three women. This increased to six in 2001, when three women were elected to Westminster from Northern Ireland: one Sinn Féin, one Ulster Unionist, and one Democratic Unionist. It could be argued that this unusual increase was prompted by the activism of the Northern Ireland Women's Coalition, as well as the more egalitarian approach of Sinn Féin. From 1920 to 1972 Northern Ireland had its own devolved assembly at Stormont. During those years only twenty female candidates ran for office, and nine were elected (Brown et al. 2002: 77).

The constitution of the UK was amended in 1999 to include the re-establishment of an assembly in Northern Ireland at the same time as the creation of new assemblies in Scotland and Wales. This is, however, a rather different political undertaking on account of the conflict within Northern Ireland and between groups in Northern Ireland and the UK government, and the previous existence of a Northern Ireland parliament at Stormont. Despite the existence of a women's movement in parallel with movements elsewhere, gender issues and sex equality have been subordinated to other issues and equalities. Equality between women and men is overshadowed by equality between Catholics and Protestants. The exclusivity of Northern Ireland politics is magnified by a system in which the hidden exercise of power serves to maintain the existence of opposing communities. Such organizations as the Orange Order, Opus Dei and the Ancient Order of Hibernians serve both to privilege religious affiliation and to exclude women (M. Ward 2002: 6).

In the 1999 election to the assembly, the Unionist parties did not adopt any positive strategies for women, and those adopted by Nationalists 'did not extend to their recruitment or selection procedures' (Brown et al. 2002: 79). With the exception of Sinn Féin, the proportion of women elected was less than the proportion of women running, meaning that women were kept out of winnable seats. None the less, in the 1999 assembly women's political representation was greater than it had been before in any of the elected bodies. Fourteen women, 12.9 per cent, were elected to the Northern Ireland Assembly (see table 12.4), considerably more than in Northern Ireland local government, Northern Ireland representatives to the Westminster parliament, or women elected to the previous Northern Ireland Assembly (M. Ward 2002: 4).

Table 12.4 Women in the Northern Ireland Assembly

	1999 (%)
Assembly	12.9
Committees	15.5

Source: Fawcett Society website

Breaking this down by party, the Ulster Unionists returned 7.1 per cent women; the Social Democratic and Labour Party, 12.5 per cent; the Democratic Unionists, 5 per cent; Sinn Féin, 27.8 per cent; the Alliance, 16.7 per cent; the Northern Ireland Women's Coalition, 100 per cent; and the other parties, no women. In total there were fifteen women in the Assembly (fourteen initially elected plus one who was co-opted as a replacement for John Hume, who resigned). Two women were appointed as ministers: Brid Rogers of the SDLP and Baibre de Brun of Sinn Féin. Women held seventeen of the 110 places on committees, 15.5 per cent, and three deputy committee chairs (no chairs) (Brown et al. 2002: 80). More women ran for office than had done so before, 16.5 per cent. In addition, three women were elected to Westminster in 2001. Mainstream parties in Northern Ireland did not institute any pro-active mechanisms for the election of women. Women's activism in the peace movement and the involvement of the Northern Ireland Women's Coalition nevertheless had an impact on women's inclusion.

The Northern Ireland Legislative Assembly was suspended in 2000, and again in 2002, before being dissolved in April of 2003 as a result of tensions between Unionists and Republicans. Northern Ireland therefore did not accompany Scotland and Wales to the polls in May 2003. An election was held instead in November 2003, but the assembly remained suspended. An increased total of twenty of the seats in the suspended assembly went to women: two Alliance, eight Sinn Féin, five SDLP, two Democratic Unionist, and three Ulster Unionists. The Northern Ireland Women's Coalition ran seven candidates, including two incumbents in the election, none of whom won, although the party is determined to continue to campaign. Thus the majority of women are (or will be, when the Assembly sits) on the opposition, Republican benches.

This election signalled a political shift, the effects of which can still only be guessed at. Where the previous assembly had been dominated by the more moderate of the Republican and Unionist parties, the SDLP and the Ulster Unionists, the 2003 elections heralded breakthroughs for the more radical Sinn Féin and Democratic Unionists. For women this means that there will be even less space for consideration of gender equality as divisions between Unionists and Republicans intensify.

The greater number of women in the Northern Ireland Assembly than in any other political body in Northern Ireland was not well received by all the representatives. According to Margaret Ward, in the early days of the Peace Talks other (male) delegates mooed when representatives of the Northern Ireland Women's Coalition started to speak (M. Ward 2002: 6). In the assembly, female members were subjected to name-calling along the lines of 'cross-dressers', 'drag queens' and 'political hermaphrodites' (M. Ward 2002: 5). Ward argues that women face considerable barriers in what is in many ways still a traditional society. Discrimination against women in Northern Ireland goes unremarked, while issues of inequality and discrimination between Catholics and Protestants dominate all political discourse. This was, after all, a part of the UK that was excluded from the legal provision of abortion through the National Health Service in 1968.

The failure to consider gender equality alongside parity of the religious communities is apparent in political appointments and priorities. Gender equality is not an issue in the establishment of new bodies, such as the Policing Board. However, women do make up 38 per cent of the Civic Forum, and a Northern Ireland Equality Commission has been established.

Conclusion

Women have made sudden inroads into the UK parliaments and are filtering into the cabinets. At Westminster the numbers in parliament are not yet approaching what might be called 'critical mass', although the proportion of women in cabinet exceeds that in the House of Commons. Women have surpassed the threshold of critical mass in the Scottish and Welsh regional assemblies. As Davis suggests, the proportion of women in Cabinet does tend to reflect the proportion of women in the parliament, and arguably both of these reflect the will of the political parties involved. We can see that once the media pick up the issue of women in parliament, politicians have to respond. The media attention may not always be pleasant, but it has meant that such politicians as Mowlam, Short, Harman, Beckett and Hewitt have a high public profile, which their colleagues have to take into account. Once there are more women in parliament, they start to move into more serious cabinet positions, and media attention starts to shift away from their sex and towards their policies.

FURTHER READING

Biographies and autobiographies are an excellent way to get a feel for political life – and politicians do like to write them! Try Hugo Young on Margaret Thatcher, Thatcher's own memoir, and Emma Nicholson's account of the Thatcher years. For Labour governments, have a look at Barbara Castle's account of early parliaments and Mo Mowlam's dissection of the Blair governments. For a more rigorous and less personalized version, have a look at Sarah Childs's book on Labour women, Maguire on Conservatives, and Lovenduski and Norris on women at Westminster.

Centre for the Advancement of Women in Politics website: <www.qub.ac.uk/cawp/>
Childs, S. 2004a: A Feminized Style of Politics? Women MPs in the House of Commons. *British Journal of Politics and International Relations*, 6(1): 3–19.
Lovenduski, J. and Norris, P. 2003: Westminster Women: The Politics of Presence. *Political Studies*, 51(1): 84–102.
Maguire, G. E. 1998: *Conservative Women: A History of Women and the Conservative Party, 1874–1997*. Basingstoke: Macmillan.

Mowlam, M. 2003: *Momentum: The Struggle for Peace, Politics and the People*. London: Coronet.

Nicholson, E. 1996: *Secret Society: Inside and Outside the Conservative Party*. London: Indigo.

Perkins, A. 2004: *The Authorised Biography of Barbara Castle*. London: Pan.

Thatcher, M. 1995: *The Downing Street Years*. London: HarperCollins.

Young, H. 1993: *One of Us*. London: Pan.

WOMEN IN ELECTED ASSEMBLIES OUTSIDE THE UNITED KINGDOM

13

Introduction

This chapter moves out from the United Kingdom to look at parliaments and cabinets around the world. Here we see the effects of party and electoral systems on the numbers of women elected, and some of the problems encountered by women once elected. Cabinets show considerable variation in the numbers of women included and which posts they hold – although broadly bearing out Davis's thesis that the numbers reflect those in a parliament as a whole.

The Republic of Ireland

In 1997 Mary McAleese was elected to the presidency of the Republic of Ireland, where she remains in 2004: the second female president of a country otherwise resistant to the election of women. The 1997 general election, held in the same year as the ground-breaking UK election, returned twenty women Members of Parliament (TDs) to the Irish Dail. This comprised 12 per cent of the total, and represented a decrease of 3 per cent on the previous parliament, just when other countries were increasing the proportion of their female representatives. Between 1922, when the state of the Republic of Ireland came into being, and 1972 there was an average of four women, or 3 per cent in the parliament, and sixty-one individuals were elected in total. In 1997 there was a record number of female candidates, of whom thirty-eight (39.5 per cent) stood as independents or minor-party candidates. Of the major parties, Fianna Fáil selected fourteen women, Fine Gael selected fifteen, Labour twelve, the Progressive Democrats thirteen, the Democratic Left four. Women constituted 20 per cent of the candidates for the five major parties at the election, but only 12 per cent of the elected members (Galligan and Wilford 1999b: 131).

After the 2002 election the parliament included twenty-two women, or 13.3 per cent – a small increase. Six of these came from each of Fianna Fáil and Labour, four from the Progressive Democrats, three independents, three from Fine Gael, and none from Sinn Féin, the Socialist Party or the Greens (Irish Government website: <www.ireachtas.ie>). Only seven women have held cabinet office in the Republic, all of these appointed since 1979 (Galligan and Wilford 1999b: 133). In 1997, 20 per cent of the cabinet were women, and the leader of the Progressive Democrats, Mary Harney, was Deputy Prime Minister. Mary Harney continued as Deputy Prime Minister in 2002, with one other woman in the cabinet, Mary Coughlan at Social Security and Family Affairs.

Why are there still so few women elected in Ireland? The description above suggests one simple explanation: most of the women who run for office do so either on the tickets of unelectable parties, or for electable parties but in unwinnable seats. Women candidates are still believed to be vote losers, and the political parties that act as gatekeepers are reluctant to select women. Moreover, the single transferable vote (STV) system used is the least proportional of the proportional representation systems so far invented. Galligan and Wilford refer to 'a complex interaction of individual, situational and structural variables that have the aggregate effect of making the public realm a near-male monopoly' (Galligan and Wilford 1999b: 145). They also refer to the persistence of patriarchy, which is augmented by the active involvement of the Catholic Church, although the influence of the European Union is weakening the grip of tradition.

The Nordic Countries

The most recent elections in the Nordic countries show the individual states continuing to elect high proportions of women (table 13.1). All have unicameral parliaments. In 2001 Denmark elected 38 per cent women, and Norway 36.4 per cent; Sweden elected 45.3 per cent women in 2002; and in 2003 Finland elected 37.5 per cent, and Iceland 30.2 per cent (Inter-Parliamentary Union website).

After the general election of 1973, women in Norway secured 20 per cent of the seats in the cabinet, and in 1981 elected the first Nordic woman Prime Minister, Gro Harlem

Table 13.1 Women elected in the Nordic countries

Country	Year	% Women
Denmark	2001	38
Norway	2001	36.4
Sweden	2002	45.3
Finland	2003	37.5
Iceland	2003	30.2

Source: IPU website

Brundtland. In 1986 Brundtland's 'women's government' was appointed with eight women in the eighteen-person cabinet. The Gender Equality Act passed in 1988 required the authorities to ensure a representation of at least 40 per cent of both sexes on all non-elected public boards, councils and committees, including cabinet. As a result, the proportion of women in government has never fallen below 42 per cent (Raaum 1999: 36). In recent elections the electorate has been presented with three alternative candidates for Prime Minister: all women.

Sweden crossed the threshold of 20 per cent women in the cabinet in 1976, Denmark in 1981, and Finland in 1987. By 1998, 38 per cent of cabinet ministers in Denmark were women, 28 per cent in Finland, 47 per cent in Norway, and 50 per cent in Sweden. In Iceland, however, only 10 per cent of the cabinet was female. Both Norway and Finland have elected female Prime Ministers, but only Iceland has elected a female President (Raaum 1999: 32).

The differences reflect differences in the history of political mobilization, political institutions and culture. The Nordic countries developed political parties much later than other European countries. Denmark first formed political parties in the 1870s; Sweden, Norway and Finland did so ten years later; and Iceland formed parties only after 1916. Women's political mobilization followed the wider mobilization into political parties. Danish women were the first to found a feminist organization dedicated to achieving women's rights in 1871. This was followed in 1889 by an organization to fight for women's suffrage. Women's rights organizations were founded in Sweden, Norway and Finland in 1884, and Norway created a society for women's suffrage in 1885 (Raaum 1999: 33).

Women in Iceland organized prior to the creation of political parties. They were running for office in local elections on separate women's lists as early as 1908, and in the general elections of 1922 and 1926 (Raaum 1999: 33). Universal suffrage was achieved in the Nordic countries between 1906 and 1919, and the election of the first women to parliament between 1907 and 1921. Finland is remarkable here in electing over 10 per cent female representatives in 1907 (Raaum 1999: 32).

While Sweden has consistently returned high proportions of women to parliament, there was a dip in the numbers in Norway in 1997. This is attributed to the success of the far-right Progress Party, which had very few women among its candidates. Numbers in Denmark stagnated at around 34 per cent for some years. This reflected the relatively low level of party political organization among women, the absence of specifically feminist organizations, and the lack of equal status measures, such as quotas (Raaum 1999: 37). The proportion increased at the 1997 election. Women in Finland and Iceland (especially the latter) have done less well than those in Sweden and Norway. According to Raaum, the Icelandic situation was historically an effect of structural, cultural and political factors, but is now largely the result of the electoral and party system.

France

As discussed in chapter 6, in 1999 France introduced the policy of parity to counter the low number of women in politics. France has a Catholic history and enfranchised women comparatively late, in 1944. Both these factors tend to correlate with low political participation rates for women. Yet, France is an advanced, industrialized democracy in which women have access to education and the economy on a par with men. Moreover, there is public provision of child care and good maternity benefits. While political parties compete with each other for policies to appeal to the woman voter, they have not been similarly eager to promote the woman candidate.

France has a bicameral assembly; members of both chambers are elected, as is the President. In 1980, 4 per cent of the members of the National Assembly were women, and 2.3 per cent of the Senate. In 1978 there were six women among the forty-one members of the government; in 1980 there were only three, one of whom was the Minister of Women's Condition. Despite the creation of a State Secretariat for Women's Condition in 1974, important legislation on sex discrimination, divorce and family law, rape and abortion, as well as the presence of a number of high-profile women in politics, progress was slow. Women's socio-economic position accounts for some of this, but political variables are important.

Candidates in France are elected by a single vote rather than a party list, and for a long time elected officials were able to hold more than one post. For example, Prime Minister Alain Juppe was also mayor of Bordeaux, president of metropolitan Bordeaux, and leader of the RPR. Since deputies tend to hold on to office for decades, this left little opportunity for new candidates of either sex to gain entry. As one RPR minister said, 'It's been tough to increase the number of women candidates, because we have so many incumbents who are men. They have been loyal, so we can't just tell them they can't run' (*Christian Science Monitor* 1997: 1).

In 1991 Edith Cresson became the first woman Prime Minister in France; however, her tenure was short and ugly. By 1993 the percentage of women in the National Assembly had only increased to six, even though women had accounted for 20 per cent of the candidates (*Women's International Network News* 1994a: 65). Both the Left and the Right made attempts to increase women's participation – or at least visibility. By 1995 the Jospin Cabinet included nearly one-third women, and there were thirty-seven Socialist women in the National Assembly. In the same year Michele Alliot-Marie became leader of the Rassemblement pour la République (RPR) Gaullist party. As *The Economist* noted, this appointment gave more hope to French women in politics than to the battered Gaullists (*Economist*, 1999).

In 1995 right-wing Alain Juppe was named Prime Minister of France by newly elected President Chirac. The first Juppe government included twelve women in the cabinet. The Press heralded these women as the Juppettes (which means short skirts), and they were rapidly removed from Cabinet in a reorganization only a few months after the election (Jenson and Valiente 2003). At this point the Socialist Party agreed that 30 per cent of their candidates for the next election would be women. A record 1,448 women campaigned for the 1997 election, resulting in the highest number of women ever elected, sixty-three, constituting nearly 11 per cent of the National Assembly. Prime Minister Jospin named eight women cabinet ministers, including three in top positions. One was the post regarded as second only to the Prime Minister, Minister of Labour, Martine Aubry. Continuing with the tradition of trivializing attempts to include more women in politics, the media referred to Jospin's pledge to introduce parity legislation as 'chabadabada', a play on the theme song from the iconic film 'Un Homme et une Femme' ('A Man and a Woman').

In 2000, 10.9 per cent of the Lower House and 5.6 of the Upper House were women, but 34.4 per cent of government posts were held by women (Simon-Peirano 2000). As of the 2002 election, there are 12.2 per cent women in the Lower House, 10.9 in the Upper House; but not one of the key government committees is chaired by a woman (IPU website; French Government website).

Germany

Germany uses a mixed system of election to the federal parliament (Bundestag), with PR seats and single-member districts. Each voter has two votes. The post-unification elections have seen the parties and the electorates in what were West and East Germany adjusting, but differences between the two regions persist. More female MPs are returned from the East than the West – 36.5 as opposed to 29.0 per cent in 1998. This is largely due to the relative strengths of the different parties in the different areas, particularly of the Alliance 90/Green Party in the East (Brzinski 2003: 67). Strong parties get women elected into electoral seats, others rely on list seats. Women tend to have more success with electoral seats in the East than in the West.

The 2004 Cabinet is made up from the SPD and Alliance 90/Greens. There are six women members in the fourteen-strong cabinet. Ulla Schmidt is the SPD Minister for Health and Social Security; Renate Schmidt is the SPD Minister for Family Affairs, Senior Citizens, Women and Youth; Heidemarie Wieczorek-Zeul is the SPD Minister for Economic Co-operation and Development; Renate Kunast is the Alliance 90/Greens Minister of Consumer Protection, Food and Agriculture; Brigitte Zypries is the SPD Minister of Justice; and Edelgard Bulmahn is the SPD Minister of Education and Research. All of these have long histories in their party organizations and in state-level elected positions.

Russia

The proportion of women in the present Russian parliament, at 7.6 per cent in the Lower House, is dramatically less than that in the Supreme Soviet of the USSR prior to 1990. The same is broadly true of all the central-eastern European former Socialist countries (with the exception of Bulgaria, where 26.3 per cent of the MPs elected in 2001 were women, and there was a female Deputy Prime Minister (Kostadinova 2003)). Prior to liberalization, in 1984, women made up 33 per cent of the Supreme Soviet; whereas after liberalization, in 1997, they constituted 10.5 per cent of the State Duma (Lower House) and only 0.5 per cent of the Federation Council of the Russian Federation (Upper House). This has subsequently decreased to 7.6 per cent in the Lower House, although the percentage of women in the Upper House has increased to 3.4 (IPU website).

While the representation of women is a significant and real political issue in many countries around the world, it does not appear to figure in either academic or political debate in Russia. Elena Kochkina argues that women are hardly present at all at the highest levels of Russian federal and regional government. Numbers fell steadily at both regional and federal level after 1989, although there was considerable regional variation: from no women at all in four regional legislatures, to over 20 per cent in nine (Kochkina 2001). At local levels the proportion of women fell from 50 per cent in 1985 to 9 per cent in 1997. Analysis is complicated by serial change to the electoral systems.

Although numbers of women have been dropping steadily since 1990, the election of 1993 suggested an alternative. A women's party, Women of Russia, mobilized for the 1993 election, achieving 8.1 per cent of the vote and twenty-three seats in the Duma, as well as having one of their number, Fedulova, elected to Deputy Chair of the Duma. The women elected came from professional backgrounds: nine teachers, six health care workers, four entrepreneurs, three lawyers and one actress. They were aged between thirty-two and fifty-four.

The new female deputies were involved in extensive committee work, by no means all in traditionally female areas. The committees women sat on included Security; Budgetary Planning of Security; Budget, Taxes, Banks and Finance; Legislation and Legal Reform; Economic Policy; Geopolitics; and Economic Security. A woman chaired the committee for women, family and youth; another chaired the commission on refugees and needy migrants. One committee had a woman Deputy Chair, and ten subcommittees were chaired by women (Buckley 1997a: 168–70). However, the following elections were less kind to Women of Russia, and women in general. In 1995 Women of Russia achieved 4.5 per cent of the vote, thus failing to reach the 5 per cent threshold for entry into the Duma party lists. There were only two women among the seventy-four top officials of the federal executive; only one of the thirty-five cabinet members was a woman; and the Presidium, the most important government body at the time, had no women at all. Overall, women made up 1.4 per cent of top officials in the ministries and cabinet (Kochkina 2001). By 1997 this had improved to 4 per cent.

In early 2003 the First Deputy Chair and one of the Deputy Chairs of the Duma were women, and women chaired three committees: the Committee on Women, Family and Youth; the Committee on Problems in the North and Far East; and the Committee on Ethics. It must be said that these are not very important committees, and tend to deal with issues associated with women's traditional roles; they are not, therefore, positions sought by male deputies. By March 2004 there were no women in President Putin's cabinet. Kochkina asserts that 'this situation reflects government policy, which was and is directed toward maintaining male dominance of decision making at the highest levels' (Kochkina 2001: 50). Women's relative exclusion from politics is accounted for by both socio-economic and political factors. The political factors include gender bias in the compilation of electoral lists, due to the processes of selection of candidates by parties, inadequate monitoring of campaign finances, unequal access to the media, and the use of traditional sex stereotypes against female candidates. Kochkina also cites the failure of Russian electoral law to regulate financial contributions, allocation of campaign financing, and the nature of media campaigning.

Kochkina is not optimistic about the possibility of adopting any of the mechanisms used in other countries, or their efficacy in Russia. She concludes: 'I am deeply convinced that the main barrier Russian women face in their attempt to secure political appointments is not the type of electoral system but the Russian style of government, in which most top appointments depend on the president and his entourage' (2001: 54). The 2003 general election, which consolidated the position of President Putin, has been criticized for processes that have strengthened the *status quo*.

The Curious Case of the USA

No clearer example of the effects of an electoral and party system on women's participation exists than the USA. An advanced democracy, in which women won the vote relatively early, where women have access to education alongside men, do well in the professions, and earn no smaller percentage of the male wage than anywhere else – the country, indeed, where the women's movements of the nineteenth and twentieth centuries kicked off – elects no larger proportion of women than Andorra, and a smaller proportion than its neighbour, Mexico.

The USA is a federal state with a bicameral national congress. Members of both chambers and the President are elected. As of the 2002 election, there were 14.3 per cent women in the House of Representatives and 13.0 per cent in the Senate, compared with 22.6 and 15.6 in Mexico (IPU website, 21 September 2004). This made the USA joint 59th in the international league table, alongside Andorra. There have been some important women in key political positions in recent federal governments, but this does not signify what it might in many other countries, since the cabinet is appointed by the President from outside the elected assembly. Thus, Janet Reno, Madeleine Korbel Albright, Condoleezza Rice and other high-profile figures were not elected, but appointed.

The first woman appointed to the cabinet was Frances Perkins, as Secretary for Labor in 1933. Since then twenty-eight women have served in the cabinet, making up 5.6 per cent of the total 497 people to have held cabinet positions (<www.gendergap.com>). Madeleine Korbel Albright held the highest position when she was appointed Secretary of State for Foreign Affairs by President Clinton in 1996. Borrelli argues that presidents encounter sex-specific problems when attempting to appoint women to cabinet posts. For example, opponents campaigned against the unmarried Janet Reno as a lesbian, which she countered with an alternative stereotype, by calling herself 'an old maid who prefers men' (Borrelli 2000: 196). The women appointed to the cabinet tend to share the characteristics of men so appointed: to be in their mid-fifties, white, married and with an elite education. The women appointees tend to have been mentored and supported in their careers by a man, and to be generalists – although Albright is an exception to this (Borrelli 2000: 196).

Since Carter, every President has appointed one or two women to the cabinet. Clinton appointed more women to cabinet positions than before, four in each term, although he ran into difficulties with appointments that tended to underline the obstacles that women address when attempting to participate in public life. George W. Bush has also appointed women to significant posts, although at the end of 2003 only three of the twenty-one members of the cabinet were women: Anne M. Veneman at Agriculture, Gale Norton at the Department of the Interior, and Elaine Chao at Labor. Two other women held high-level posts: Condoleezza Rice as National Security Adviser in the Executive Office of the President and Christine Todd Whitman at the Environmental Protection Agency (US Government website <www.firstgov.gov>).

The specificities of the US party and electoral system appear to disadvantage women. Parties may nominate candidates for office, who may run on a party ticket, but candidature results from the primary process in which voters select the party candidate. Potential candidates can run under the name of a party without that party having sanctioned them. Candidates generate their own funding and their own support base, and there are problems of pipeline and incumbency (although the move to introduce term limits may change this). Moreover, the elections are run on a single-member, simple plurality basis, which is generally agreed to disadvantage women and minority candidates (some local elections have multi-member constituencies, and women and members of minorities tend to do better in these). None the less, those women who do run for office have a good chance of winning. Fox writes that 'women are more successfully competing in House races than at any time in history. There are few differences between men and women candidates in terms of the major indicators of electoral success' (Fox 2000: 252). On the other hand, he found considerable regional differences in the election of women, and argues that gender stereotypes and an electoral environment in which 'many women candidates report a credibility problem' pose strong, although subtle, obstacles to women (Fox 1997: 25).

Congress itself is dominated by systems of seniority, which present a problem for newcomers, and networks, which present a problem for outsiders. The numbers of women in Congress, as in other areas of public office in the USA, increased in the 1990s; indeed, 1992 is referred to as the Year of the Woman, when 108 women were nominated for seats in the House of Representatives, and eleven for the Senate. More women were elected than ever before, including the first black, female Senator. However, the numbers did not increase here as much as they did in other comparable countries. Moreover, the increased numbers did not of themselves entail increased power and influence for congresswomen. As Foerstel and Foerstel write, 'though women came to the House and Senate in unprecedented numbers during the 1990s, their power within Congress has grown only minimally. One factor in women's slow ascension to congressional power has been their meagre representation in the committee structure, within which all major business on Capitol Hill is accomplished' (Foerstel and Foerstel 1996: 91).

This cannot be accounted for simply by women's relatively small numbers. In 1993 women comprised 14 per cent of House Democrats, yet occupied only 4 per cent of committee and subcommittee chairs. At the same time, Blacks made up 14 per cent of House Democrats and held 14 per cent of the chairs, and Hispanics comprised 6 per cent of House Democrats and 5 per cent of the chairs. It is argued that this is because 'the obstacles that today's congressional women face in winning prime committee assignments have roots that run deep into the male-dominated culture on Capitol Hill' (Foerstel and Foerstel 1996: 94).

Canada

Canadian politics has been resistant to women until quite recently. However, this resistance is diminishing under pressure from women's groups both inside and outside parliament. The changing political landscape has also been an influence, and, as in other countries, including more women has been seen as a way to re-engage with disillusioned voters (MacIvor 1996: 259).

Canada has a bicameral parliament. Government is led by the Prime Minister, and the country is in the odd position of having the British monarch as head of state. In 1993 Canada elected an unprecedented fifty-three women to the House of Commons, 18 per cent, two-thirds of whom were Liberals (Tremblay 1998: 445). The same year Canada had its first woman Prime Minister, Kim Campbell, albeit only for six months. There has also been a female leader of a major opposition party, Audrey McLaughlin, and a Deputy Prime Minister, Sheila Copps.

The 1993 election was ground-breaking because, prior to this, there had been only seventy women ever elected since enfranchisement in 1921. The first woman cabinet member was appointed in 1957, and stayed until 1963. Another woman was then appointed to the cabinet in 1963. When Member of Parliament Pauline Jewett asked Prime Minister Pearson if she could serve in his cabinet in 1965, he responded that there was already a woman in the cabinet and he did not think that she wanted to be replaced (MacIvor 1996: 283). During the 1970s Prime Minister Trudeau included three women in the cabinet, but by 1995 this had increased only to five out of the twenty-four senior cabinet ministers. Although this constituted a higher proportion of women in the cabinet than in the House, they did not have important portfolios (MacIvor 1996: 284). MacIvor argues that the low ranking of women in the cabinet results from male seniority, since junior ministers do not belong to the inner cabinet or have a final say in government policy.

The Liberal women of 1993 constituted the Women's Caucus, an official Liberal caucus where issues of the day were discussed from a woman's perspective (Tremblay 1998: 446). Tremblay suggests that the caucus both exerted pressure on the Liberal Party in parliament, encouraged Liberal MPs to adopt strong positions on women's issues, and enabled female representatives from other parties to take up similar positions so that the Liberals did not monopolize the representation of women.

As of the 2000 election, there were 20.6 per cent women in the Lower House and 32.4 in the Upper. The cabinet of thirty-four members included eleven women (just under 33 per cent), while three of the non-cabinet Secretaries of State were women (25 per cent). These included Claudette Bradshaw as Minister of Labour, Albina Guarnieri as Associate Minister of National Defence, and Anne A. McLellan as Deputy Prime Minister and Minister of Public Safety and Emergency Preparedness. Only one of the nine government committees is chaired by a woman: Anne A. McLellan at Operations and Public Health (Canadian Government website).

Despite considerable improvement in the numbers and position of women in the Canadian Parliament, there are still some real obstacles. MacIvor points to the overt aggression that takes place in the chamber: 'Any Canadian who watches the television news has seen clips of Question Period in the House of Commons. Every so often, those clips show a confrontation between a male Cabinet Minister and a female opposition MP. All too often the man is using sexist or demeaning language in an attempt to silence the woman' (MacIvor 1996: 289). On one occasion John Crosbie MP referred to Sheila Copps MP (one-time Deputy Prime Minister) as a 'slut'.

Australia

Australia is a federal state with bicameral parliaments at state and federal levels. Government is headed by a prime minister. Like Canada, it is in the odd position of having the British monarch as head of state. Strategies adopted by Australian political parties, particularly quotas in the Labor Party, have gone some way to increasing the numbers of women in parliament and government. Australia is in the slightly unusual position of having a larger proportion of women in government than in the House (Moon and Fountain 1997). In 1993, 9.5 per cent of members of the Lower House were women; this grew to 15.5 per cent in 1996. In 2001 there were 25.3 per cent women elected to the Lower House, and 28.9 per cent were elected to the Upper House in 1998. The percentage of women at ministerial level was consistently slightly higher; for example, in 1992, 14 per cent of MPs were women, but 20.4 per cent of ministers. By 1997 there had been twenty-seven female ministers, most of them since 1970. Moon and Fountain attribute this largely to the predominance of Labor (ALP) governments, which are more pro-active than those of other parties at promoting women. Even so, they found that female ministers tended to have 'soft' portfolios, while the 'hard' portfolios were almost always held by male ministers.

With the Liberal Party in office, only two of the seventeen members of the cabinet were women at the end of 2003: Kay Patterson at Family and Community Services, who also has responsibility for the Status of Women; and Amanda Vanstone at Immigration, Multicultural, and Indigenous Affairs, who also has responsibility for Reconciliation. There are also two women with non-cabinet ministerial posts, and five female Parliamentary Secretaries. On the other hand, the shadow (Labor) cabinet has a female Deputy Leader in Jenny Macklin, and seven other women with shadow portfolios (Australian Parliament website). None the less, the Australian Labor Party is considered to have failed to meet its commitment to equality, and an Australian Women's Party has been founded.

New Zealand

New Zealand has a bicameral parliament. Government is led by a prime minister, while the British monarch is head of state. New Zealand was, of course, the first country in which women achieved the right to vote on equal terms with men, and the first country in the British Empire to award a bachelor's degree to a woman. In 1997 it achieved the feat of having female leaders of both the main political parties, when Jenny Shipley replaced Jim Bolger as Prime Minister, mid-term. She had previously held the posts of Minister of Social Welfare and Transport Minister (Cohen 1997).

In 1993 voters in New Zealand decided to change the electoral system from first-past-the-post to a form of proportional representation. Mixed-member proportional (MMP) was the system selected. This seems to have resulted in there being more political parties, a more diverse parliament, and coalition government. Coalitions of the centre right, centre left, and in 2002 of the centre have emerged. However, voter disillusion, which this measure sought to address, was still in evidence, and there was some evidence that voters would like to revert to the original system, although Parliament decided to keep MMP, unchanged, in 2001. The change has proved beneficial to women: the number of women MPs increased from 21.2 to 29.2 per cent in 1996, and 30.8 per cent in 1999, although it fell to 28.3 per cent in 2002.

The first female cabinet minister in New Zealand was Hilda Ross, from 1954. Since 1984 women in the cabinet have had responsibility for the police, finance, employment, disarmament, arms control and labour portfolios, as well as heading the Ministry for Women's Affairs (McLeay 1995: 146). In 2000 Silvia Cartwright was appointed Governor-General; at the same time, the Labour Prime Minister was a woman, Helen Clark; as was the Chief Justice, Sian Elias; the Attorney-General, Margaret Wilson; the mayor of Auckland (the largest city), Christine Fletcher; and the leader of the opposition National Party, former Prime Minister Jenny Shipley (Cohen 2000). Prior to the 2002 election, in June 2001, there were seven women in the cabinet.

Labour won the 2002 election, and formed a governing coalition with the Progressive Coalition (already in partnership with United Future). The number of women elected fell for the first time in twenty years, although the number of Maori MPs increased. The fall in the number of women is attributed to male domination of the party lists of conservative New Zealand First and centrist United Future and male incumbency in Labour seats. Helen Clark is still Prime Minister, and there are five other women in the cabinet (of which there are twenty-seven members), including Attorney-General Margaret Wilson. It is noticeable that the traditional 'hard' portfolios, including Finance, Economic Development, Foreign Affairs and Internal Affairs, are held by men, while women hold Health, Environment and Consumer Affairs (New Zealand Government website).

Japan

In 1994, despite disappointing election results for women, there were women serving at the top tiers of all three branches of government: Executive, Legislature and Judiciary (*Women's International Network News* 1994b). Takao Doi, leader of the Social Democratic Party, had been elected Speaker of the Lower House; there were three women in the cabinet: Ryoko Akamatsu from the Ministry of Labour, Wakako Hironaka from the Environment Agency, and Manae Kubota from the Economic Planning Agency. Hisako Takahashi was named Justice of the Supreme Court.

The 2000 election returned 7.3 per cent women to the Lower House, while the 2001 election returned 15.4 to the Upper House. Japan appointed a woman to ministerial office for the first time in 1960. Between 1960 and the late 1990s, only sixteen women held cabinet office, none serving for more than a year. In 2001 Prime Minister Yoshio Mori's cabinet included the largest number of women ever: five, although only two of the twenty-eight government committees were chaired by women. These were all older women with fairly traditional political pedigrees; for example, Foreign Minister Makiko Tanaka was the daughter of a former Prime Minister. The women did not have an easy ride, particularly Tanaka, who, although popular with the general public, aroused enmity from male colleagues that spurred a press campaign against her (*Economist* 2001). Prime

Minister Taro Aso's 2004 cabinet includes three women: Yoriko Kawaguchi at Foreign Affairs, Yuriki Koike at the Environment, and Kiyako Ono at Public Safety, Youth, and Food Safety (Japanese Government website).

According to Iwanaga, female politicians in Japan are more likely to focus on child care, education, health care, family and the environment than other political policy areas (Iwanaga 1998: 31). For example, they worked in favour of the 1985 Equal Opportunity Employment Bill, the 1989 Employment Insurance Law, which extended insurance to cover part-time employees, and the 1991 Child Care Leave Bill.

India

India is of course known for the high-profile Gandhi women: Indira and Sonia. In a common pattern, women were to be found in positions of leadership, although not in any significant number among rank-and-file politicians. Article 16(1) of the Indian Constitution guarantees 'equality of opportunity for all citizens in matters relating to employment or appointment to any office under the state' (Jharta 1996: 61). Article 326 emphasizes that elections to the legislative assemblies of states are to be held on the basis of adult enfranchisement.

Women's active participation in politics is considerably less than that of men. In the late 1990s it was still the case in India that fewer women voted than men, a 12 per cent difference, especially apparent in rural areas. None the less, women do vote in huge numbers and take part in social movement-type politics, but they are not conspicuous in positions of power, either locally or nationally (Jharta 1996: 20). Despite women holding several prominent positions in parties, they do not appear to be prominent in party organizations.

None the less, women's political participation in India is greater than that in many other countries, both more and less developed. Almost all the political parties pay special attention to organizing women and selecting them as candidates. This includes regular party forums, cells and front organizations for women. Recently, parties have been taking a stand on women's issues including sati, rape and violence and women have been participating in parties, demonstrating and lobbying (Kaushik 2000: 61).

The number of women in the Lower House, Lok Sabha, has increased, but slowly and not by very much. In 1952 women made up 2.72 per cent of the contestants for the 489 seats in the Lok Sabha and won twenty-three, 4.7 per cent. The number of female contestants has gone up over the years, but so has the number of male contestants, so the percentage of women contesting seats has increased only to 3.74. The percentage of seats won by women had increased to 7.49 in 1991, or thirty-nine out of 521 seats. This was in fact a decrease from the high point of forty-two seats out of 508, or 8.26 per cent, achieved in 1984 and surpassed only in 1999, when 8.8 per cent of MPs elected to the Lower House were women. The pattern is similar in the Upper House, the Rajya Sabha, where the number of women has increased from two in 1952 to nine in 1991 and twenty-five, 10.3 per cent, in 2002.

In the mid-1980s the government drew up a National Perspective Plan which had the goal of a 30 per cent reservation of seats for women in parliament, state legislatures and grass-roots organizations. The government urged parties to take this up, but none came near to 30 per cent in decision-making bodies or candidates. Congress put up 10 per cent women in 1989, the BJP 6.4 per cent, the Communist Party of India (CPI) and the Communist Party of India (Marxist) CPI(M) 5.5 per cent, Janata Dal 3.4 per cent and the JD(S) Jananta Dal (Secular) 2.3 per cent (Jharta 1996: 66). The reservation of seats for women that has been put into practice at local level may push women politicians through the system. Conflict over adoption of a reservation for women in the national parliament continues, as described in chapter 6, but may be getting closer to resolution. The resurgence of grass-roots political movements, like the Chipko movement, the Narmada Bachao Andalan and Arrak Satyagraha, may politicize more women and give them the confidence and contacts to move into formal party politics.

Indira Gandhi became leader of the Congress Party as the daughter of the first Prime Minister, Nehru, backed by the groups that had backed him and with the popular appeal of the family tradition, and became Prime Minister herself. Sonia Gandhi became leader of the Congress Party after the assassination of her husband, Indira Gandhi's son, Rajiv. Sonia was elected to parliament, but her party did not win the 1998 election. Congress did win the 2004 election; however, Sonia declined the position of Prime Minister – thereby achieving the far preferable position of popular quasi-goddess!

The 1998 election, when Sonia took over leadership of the Congress Party and led a high-profile campaign, is also notable for the significance of another powerful woman. The success of the Bharatiya Janata Party (BJP) and its ability to form a government were guaranteed only when Jayalalitha Jayaraman, the female President of Tamil Nadu and leader of a twenty-seven-member group of parties from that state, gave her support (Raj 1998). There have been other prominent women, such as Vijay Lakshmi Pandit, President of the United Nations General Assembly, Ambassador to the USSR and USA, and High Commissioner in London, as well as the first woman minister of the Uttar Pradesh Legislative Assembly, and several women have served as chief ministers at state level. What is referred to as the 'Bibi-Beti-Bahn' syndrome still shapes women's access to positions of political influence. This is the advantage conferred by being the wife, daughter, daughter-in-law or widow of a successful male politician (Jharta 1996: 68).

Despite the three terms served as Prime Minister by Indira Gandhi, there had not been more than one woman at a time in the cabinet until very recently, and in several governments there has been no female cabinet minister (Jharta 1996: 64–6; IPU website). At the end of 2003 there were two women among the twenty-seven members of the cabinet: one had the Health, Family and Parliamentary Affairs portfolio, while the other was Minister without Portfolio. There were also five women Ministers of State who were not in the cabinet. These had responsibility for Power; Human Resources; Petrol and Natural Gas; Parliamentary Affairs, Tourism and Culture; and Water (Indian Parliament website).

Some Other Countries

Despite a history of women's political strength in Nigeria, and the recent phenomenon of Rwanda having more women in parliament than any other country, women's participation in formal politics in African countries has not been high. There are, of course, a number of reasons for this. On the one hand, a range of issues deriving from post-colonialism, development and conflict limit the formal political engagement of both men and women; on the other, cultural, educational and socio-economic factors may constrain women in particular. Having said this, internal and external pressures are having the effect of increasing the numbers of women politically active in the region. South Africa is an interesting case study, although by no means representative.

In the struggle for democracy in South Africa, women's organizations played a key role. Hence, women had a strong claim to inclusion in the resulting government. There is a strong tradition in South Africa of women organizing across party lines in pursuit of gender goals, as with the Federation of South African Women and the Women's National Coalition (WNC) (Goetz 1998). The WNC was created in 1992, with the goal of ensuring that women's demands for inclusion and equity were part of the negotiations for a new South Africa. According to Goetz,

> the interventions of the WNC made the parties involved in the transition aware of an organized women's constituency. Women's interests in gender equity were written into the draft constitution, and women and their concerns became important targets in the election campaign in 1994. Research by the ANC's Election Commission identified women's issues as one of the four major areas, along with education, housing, and jobs, upon which its campaign should concentrate. This made women aware of their potential leverage on the electoral process, enabling some women politicians to campaign on feminist issues. (Goetz 1998: 248)

Before the first democratic elections in South Africa, which took place in 1994, women constituted only 2.7 per cent of all MPs. After the 1999 elections, 29.8 per cent of members of the National Assembly were women, and 31.5 per cent of the Upper House. Further, four of the twenty-five ministers were women, and women chaired ten of the thirty-five committees. The portfolios held by women were not lightweight; they included Minerals and Energy, Public Works, Land Affairs, Health, and Foreign Affairs. The African National Congress (ANC) was established as a radical party, so it is not surprising that women managed to change its charter so that the party is committed to equality.

Uganda presents a very different model of women's inclusion. In 1980 there was only one woman in the Ugandan Parliament. Uganda had failed to achieve its economic potential after independence, and had descended into political corruption, followed by state-sponsored terror. Parties were founded on religious and/or regional lines and had no commitment to gender equality (Pankhurst 2002: 121). In 1981 Yoweri Museveni created the National Resistance Movement to combat corruption. Its ideology included a radical reappraisal of women's roles, and it subsequently attempted to change gender politics. The party opposed discrimination on the grounds of ethnicity, religion, education and sex.

From 1986, with Museveni as President, seats have been reserved for women at all levels of government, and a parallel system of women's committees has ensured women's presence in parliament. Women are also elected to unreserved seats. International organizations have been brought into Uganda to assist in the rebuilding of the economy. As a result, the government has adopted the gender analysis and policies of such organizations. This includes a gendered analysis of the budget. 'The resulting analysis is at the cutting edge of gendered budget analysis internationally and certainly more sophisticated than the mainstream media analysis of British budgets' (Pankhurst 2002: 126).

Museveni, with the support of the Constituent Assembly, suspended multi-party politics in 1995 in an effort to eradicate corruption and sectional conflict. Generally such an act is perceived as an anti-democratic move; however, it has proved advantageous for the inclusion of women in politics. The political parties that continue to operate openly, albeit unofficially, are constituted primarily along religious or ethnic lines, hence their suspension as agents of sectarianism. Elections now operate on a more individual basis, and women activists and legislators have found it easier to build coalitions to promote gender equality (Goetz 1998). As of the 2001 election, there were 24.7 per cent women in the unicameral parliament. This was largely accounted for by the fifty-six seats set aside for District Woman Representatives (Ugandan Government website).

As a region, the Middle East has the lowest levels of women's participation in formal politics. In a small number of countries, neither men nor women vote, and participation in government is not open to all. In Kuwait women are excluded from the vote that men have (although there are efforts to change this). In other countries democracy is weak, and women's achievement of the vote very recent. This, in conjunction with cultural and socio-economic factors, probably accounts for the relatively low numbers of women in political office.

Israel, of course, is unlike other countries in the region. Although party membership is between 40 and 50 per cent women, women are largely absent from the party hierarchies. The Labour Party has a Women's Department and the goal of 20 per cent women in all party institutions. It has 16 per cent women in its National Executive; Likud has 13 per cent on its National Executive (Sharfman 1994: 391). In the first three Knessets (parliaments) after the foundation of the state of Israel, there were 9.1 per cent women. The number fell before it started to slowly increase again, and there is rarely a woman minister (Sharfman 1994: 391). Prior to the 1999 election there had never been more than twelve women among the 120 members of any Knesset. In 1999 sixteen women were elected, 13.3 per cent, and in 2003, 15 per cent (IPU website, 30 October 2003). As in other countries, more women have been elected from left-wing than right-wing parties. Israel has had one woman Prime Minister, Golda Meir, from 1969 to 1974. At the end of 2003 there were two women in the cabinet of twenty-three: Limor Livnat at Education and Yehudith Noat at Environment (Israeli Parliament website).

Lemish and Drep give five factors that may account for the relative absence of women from formal politics. They cite the absence of socialization processes preparing women for public office; the influence of the Israeli electoral system and channels to positions of power; the male dominance of political hierarchies; the nature of Israeli gender roles, in which politics equates to toughness and aggression, while women are expected to be passive and maternal; finally, the heavy burden of politics is thought to be unsuitable for women and their maternal roles (Lemish and Drep 2002: 131).

The emphasis in Israeli politics on conflict, and the escalation of religious sectarianism, appear to disadvantage women here as elsewhere, despite high levels of education and participation in the labour force, including the army.

Conclusion

In both parliaments and cabinets political variables account for much of the disparity in numbers between men and women. In particular we can see that it makes a difference whether women have had the vote since the early or late twentieth century. This is not to dismiss culture: religion, for example, exerts a conservative influence as we see in France, Ireland and the Middle East. However, the examples of India and Uganda, as compared with the USA and France, illuminate the powerful influence of such political factors as party systems, funding regulations, selection mechanisms and quotas.

FURTHER READING

The Inter-Parliamentary Union has been mentioned before. Its publication *Women in Parliaments 1945–1995* is rather out of date, but still of great interest. Researchers tend to write about one country at a time, and there is very little that pulls more than a few countries together. Inglehart and Norris's book *Rising Tide* takes a wider view. The chapters in Bergqvist et al. are good on the Nordic countries, Borrelli is interesting on the US cabinet, Buckley is brilliant on the former Soviet Union, and the chapters in Matland and Montgomery are good on the post-Communist countries. The chapters in Tremblay and Trimble are good on Canada; Boston et al., Deverell et al., and Simms are illuminating on New Zealand and Australia respectively; and those in Poonacha on India. Biographies (and autobiographies) are a good way of getting a real feel of what political life is like – and plenty of politicians write them! Try Pam Corkery's book for the low-down on the Antipodes.

Bergqvist, C. et al. (eds.) 1999: *Equal Democracies? Gender and Politics in the Nordic Countries*. Oslo: Scandinavian University Press.

Borrelli, M. 2000: Gender, Politics and Change in the United States Cabinet: The Madeleine Korbel Albright and Janet Reno Appointments. In S. Tolleson-Rinehart and J. J. Josephson (eds), *Gender and American Politics: Women, Men and the Political Process*. Armonk, NY: M. E. Sharpe, pp. 185–204.

Boston, J., Church, S., Levine, S., McLeay, E. and Roberts, N. 2000: *Left Turn*. Wellington: Victoria University Press.

Buckley, M. 1997: *Post-Soviet Women: From the Baltic to Central Asia*. Cambridge: Cambridge University Press.

Corkery, P. 1999: *Pam's Political Confessions*. Auckland: Hodder Moa Beckett Publishers.

Deverell, K., Huntley, R., Sharpe, P. and Tilly, J. 2000: *Party Girls: Labor Women Now*. Annadale: Pluto Press.

Inglehart, R. and Norris, P. 2003: *Rising Tide: Gender Equality and Cultural Change Around the World*. Cambridge: Cambridge University Press.

IPU 1995: *Women in Parliaments, 1945–1995*. Geneva: IPU.

Matland, R. E. and Montgomery, K. (eds) 2003: *Women's Access to Political Power in Post-Communist Europe*. Oxford: Oxford University Press.

Poonacha, V. (ed.) 1997: *Women, Empowerment and Political Parties*. Research Centre for Women's Studies, SNDT Women's University.

Simms, M. (ed.) 1996: *The Paradox of Politics*. St Leonards: Allen and Unwin.

Tremblay, M. and Trimble, L. 2003: *Women and Electoral Politics in Canada*. Toronto: Oxford University Press.

PART V

Women in Sub-National Government

WOMEN IN STATE AND LOCAL GOVERNMENT

14

Introduction

Part V of *Women in Contemporary Politics* moves away from the nation-state and looks at women's participation in sub-national and local government. This chapter sets out some of the general issues relevant to looking at sub-national government, while the following two chapters look at particular examples. In many parts of the world more women are to be found both in local government and as delegates to international governmental organizations (the subject of Part VI) than in national government (the United Kingdom is a case in point, with higher percentages of women in local and regional government and as Members of the European Parliament). It is often assumed that local government is of more interest to women because the issues dealt with at this level are of more relevance to them: local roads, education and health care, as opposed to national economies and defence. Moreover, it is claimed that women may prefer local office since it is easier to combine with home responsibilities.

However, the evidence at this level is rather patchy because, as Matland and Studlar write, 'Most analyses of representation by gender in democratic polities in recent years have been concerned with central-level legislatures. Although there is an abundant literature on political recruitment and representation by gender for state legislatures in the United States, there is relatively little on sub-central levels for other countries' (Matland and Studlar 1998: 118)

International Co-ordination and Data

In its 1998 report, the International Union of Local Authorities (IULA) claimed that

> local government is the closest and most accessible level of government to women. Local governments traditionally provide services utilised by individual households such as electricity, waste disposal, public transport, water, schools, health clinics and other social services. The decisions of local governments therefore have a direct impact on the private lives of women, because they are traditionally responsible for providing for and caring for the family and the home in most countries. (IULA 1998).

On the other hand, it could be that talented women make do with local office because they are frozen out of national politics, either by exclusion from candidacy or by the nature of central government that makes it impossible for them to combine public and private life!

Sub-national government is a vital political arena, and is often overlooked. Given the glamour of presidential elections and cabinet politics, we often forget that most of the things that affect us on a day-to-day level are decided and implemented locally. Moreover, local politics operates as a training ground for the national arena. De Tocqueville and John Stuart Mill both recognized the importance of local politics as a training ground for citizenship, and it is apparent from looking at any national parliament that many politicians cut their teeth on local issues. In the United Kingdom alone, John Major, Prime Minister for two terms in the 1990s, started as a local councillor in London; David Blunkett, ex-Labour Secretary of State for Education and Employment and Home Secretary, was a councillor and Leader of Sheffield Council; and there are many others.

Local politics may be even more important for women, both as a political domain in its own right and as an entry point into national politics. Many of the new female entrants to the UK Parliament in 1997 had been local councillors. Many had also been involved with the local government women's committees discussed in chapter 15.

Entry of women into local politics appears to be less controversial and more open to lobbying than entry into the national arena. This is perhaps because local authorities have been co-operating internationally for far longer than national governments: the International Union of Local Authorities (IULA) was established in Brussels in 1913. The organization has a world secretariat based in The Hague and seven regional sections around the world. The IULA has broad goals to unite and promote democratic local government worldwide, and numbers among its six main areas of work women in local government. It states: 'women [. . .] must be fully part of the local democratic system and have full access to the decision-making structure. Until the interests of women have been represented at the local level, the system is not fully democratic' (IULA 1998). The IULA sets goals, collects statistics, circulates information, organizes conferences, and provides opportunities for communication between local authorities around the world.

Nation-states appear to have less reluctance to promote women's participation at sub-national levels. For example, Australia, which struggles to elect more women nationally, has a National Framework for Women in Local Government, which is directed at increasing women's participation in local government decision-making. This has been translated into local action plans, such as the Women into Local Government Project in Tasmania, the Hands Up for Women in Council and 50/50 projects in New South Wales, and the Government Two Year Plan for 1999–2001 in Western Australia (Tasmania, New South Wales and Western Australia websites).

Local government (particularly in less developed countries) has become a focus for the attention of international political organizations, including both EU and UN bodies. Interaction between the process of reporting back every five years on progress on the twelve key themes that make up the Platform for Action that emerged from the UN Beijing Conference on Women, and other UN initiatives is resulting in a strong emphasis on promoting women's participation in local politics – for example, the focus of UNHCS (Habitat) on Women in Urban Governance for World Habitat Day in 2000 (UN website).

Local government is considered to be an appropriate level for targeting democratic decentralization initiatives, and the inclusion of women is frequently included as both a goal and a measure of success. For example, as part of its strategy to attract European support, Ghana embarked on initiatives to promote the participation of women in local government. Various European organizations assisted Ghana in its efforts, including the ECDPM, the Danish Support for District Assemblies Project (DSDA II), the Netherlands Development Organization (SNV), the German Development Service, and the British Department for International Development. All of these required gendered data collection consultation and the implementation of gender proposals (Ofei-Aboagye 2000).

Esther Ofei-Aboagye points out that these demands have had a 'spill-over effect [of] increased awareness of gender concerns in district assemblies and communities' (Ofei-Aboagye 2000: 6). Non-governmental organizations follow similar strategies in their aid and assistance programmes in less developed countries, such as Action Aid and Save the Children in Ghana. The example of Ghana illustrates how the activities of international governmental organizations in less developed countries strongly encourage initiatives to promote women's political participation at local level by making this part of the measurement of democratization.

None the less, the Cinderella status of local government is underlined by the lack of information and reliable statistical data on women's participation in local politics (IULA 1998: 17). In the parts of the world where more data are available, women made up some 20 per cent of representatives in local government in Europe in the late 1990s (with considerable variation between countries); 7.5 per cent of mayors and 3.8 per cent of municipal councillors in Latin America in the early 1990s; 21 per cent of local councillors and 14 per cent of mayors in Trinidad and Tobago in the late 1990s; and 17 per cent of mayors and 23 per cent of local councillors in the United States in the early 1990s (IULA 1998). Fewer data are available for Africa, where the IULA estimates women's local representation at less than 5 per cent.

The structure of local politics differs tremendously between countries. The first difference, of course, is that between unitary and federal systems. In a unitary system, like that of the United Kingdom prior to the devolution of Scotland, Wales and (with reservations) Northern Ireland, central government takes all the major decisions, while local government is dominated by central and, despite power struggles, largely implements policies decided and funded centrally. Federal systems, on the other hand, have a clear division of responsibilities between national (federal) government and state government. In the United States, for example, the federal government possesses only such powers as the individual states have ceded, and again there are power struggles, but in this case usually generated by the federal government trying to take on more than the representatives of the states think it should. In federal systems there is also local (sub-state) government at city and county level.

Which powers are exclusive to national government, and which to state or local government, varies, and will have been arrived at through history, culture and the constitution. There are frequently tensions.

Political parties operate at both national and sub-national levels, and introduce a whole other area of potential conflict. Sub-national government and national may, by their nature, conflict over jurisdiction; this is aggravated when parties are vying for power using the two political domains as competing power bases. This happened in the UK in the 1980s, when the Conservative Government was ensconced, apparently irremovably, in Westminster, and the Labour Party held the local authorities in all the major cities and conurbations (see Gyford, Leach and Game 1989).

Conclusion

Sub-national government is an important and under-researched area of politics. The presence and activities of women at this level are particularly poorly recorded and analysed. We do know that women are likely to be more active locally than nationally in both formal and informal politics – and that the two are likely to overlap. Why this is so may not be as obvious as is generally assumed. In many countries women were able to participate in local politics long before they were allowed into the national arena; this may have established a precedent. Many of the issues that directly affect the home and the family are governed locally; this may influence participation. On the other hand, local politics is often of lower status and possesses less power than national politics, leading to less interest on the part of the politically ambitious; this may mean that there is less competition for seats and more willingness to let women in.

FURTHER READING

Handler, J. 2002: *Local Government Today*. Manchester: Manchester University Press.
International Union of Local Authorities 1998: *Women in Local Government*, Sweden: IULA.
Stevens, A. 2002: *Politicos' Guide to Local Government*. London: Politicos.

WOMEN IN LOCAL GOVERNMENT IN THE UNITED KINGDOM 15

Introduction

This chapter looks at the roles of women in local government in the United Kingdom. In the UK, local politics has been open to women's participation for far longer, and to greater effect, than central government (Hollis 1979, 1987). Women had significant access to English local government from 1869, when 'women ratepayers who were widows or spinsters were statutorily included in burgess registers, and so could vote for every type of urban local authority' (Anderson 1991: 684). This extended the common law right that women had always had, as long as they met the general qualification, to vote in parish elections and the various elections based on the vestry, and to hold parish offices. Women made good use of the new right and soon formed between one-eighth and one-quarter of municipal electorates. From 1871 women could hold office on school boards, which were of great importance at the time, and from 1875 they began to make use of the existing possibility of serving as Poor Law guardians.

Women's Early Entry into Local Government

The 1888 Local Government Act created new county councils for which women could vote on the same terms. However, the most significant change occurred in 1894, when the legislation to create parish and district councils included a clause which stipulated that marriage should not debar women – if they qualified on the property grounds – from the right to vote for these councils. Up until then married women, whether propertied or not, had been denied the local vote.

By 1900, 1,589 women held office as elected members of local government in comparison with only seventy-nine in 1880. They pushed for measures including school meals and subsidized school milk, and for equal opportunities for women to be appointed to local authority posts as inspectors, teachers and doctors (Anderson and Zinsser 1990: 684). The proportion of women elected to local government continued to exceed the proportion in the House of Commons after women won equal suffrage at national level, and women councillors tended to pursue similar objectives to their predecessors. According to Coote and Patullo, these ranged 'from investigating child mortality to introducing free school meals, from the improvement of sewage systems to slum clearance, from provision of play spaces and allotments to fighting for good and caring practices in workhouses and orphanages, hospitals and asylums' (Coote and Patullo 1990: 218).

Before getting into the nitty-gritty of representation, this chapter first sets out the rather peculiar structure of local government in England, Scotland, Wales and Northern Ireland. It then goes on to look at the numbers of women elected, who they are, and what they do. We close with a discussion of the women's committees initiative of the 1980s and 1990s.

The System of Local Government in the United Kingdom

In 1999 the UK took the notable step of devolving power to new elected assemblies in Scotland, Northern Ireland and Wales, as well as creating a new elected body in London, the Greater London Authority. This created a new layer of sub-national government in an already complex system. To understand what has happened, and where women have found openings, some background to this labyrinth is required.

The local government system in the UK makes little intuitive sense, despite numerous attempts to reform and rationalize it. The layered structure of local government varies across the country, with little obvious rationale to explain the distribution of powers. Prior to the most recent wave of reforms, which started in the 1980s, there were, subordinate to central government, either one, two or even three layers of elected local representatives, depending on the area. In non-metropolitan areas there were elected assemblies at county and district level, while in metropolitan areas there were elected councils at metropolitan and district level.

The trend of reform in the 1980s and 1990s was away from the eccentricity and multiplicity, and towards having only one level of local government in any area. The initial step was to abolish the metropolitan authorities, thus establishing unitary authorities in the five metropolitan areas. In 1996 the two-layer structure of local government in Scotland and Wales was replaced by unitary authorities. No comparable revolution was achieved in England, and a number of unitary authorities were established within the two-tier system existing outside metropolitan areas.[1] The next set of reforms in 1999 created a new layer of local government, the regional authorities.

With the devolution of Scotland, Wales and Northern Ireland, a new layer of administration, regional government, was brought into being (although this is not operating in Northern Ireland at the time of writing). At the same time, metropolitan government was reintroduced in the London area in the form of a new regional authority:

the London Assembly and a directly elected mayor which together comprise the Greater London Authority (GLA). The UK is now described as an incomplete federation, and there are arguments for the creation of regional assemblies in various parts of England to achieve some degree of homogeneity.

The powers possessed by any level of local government are determined centrally, and any expansionism is curtailed by the imposition of *ultra vires*. The shape of local government is the result of centuries of local innovation modified by intermittent central government intrusion.[2] Local government possesses two functions: those of serving the interests of the local population and of administering the policies of central government. Sometimes local interest and government policy coincide, but problems arise when they do not.

The same parties that dominate national politics dominate local politics (with the regional exceptions of Sinn Féin, Plaid Cymru, and the Unionist and Republican parties in Northern Ireland). This has not always been the case, and some independent candidates and minority parties still get elected locally, but they are very much a minority.[3] This has advantages in terms of organization and resources, but also causes confusion and conflict. Confusion results from the frequent failure of party ideology to shed light upon local issues, and conflict arises when the policy battles of the centre are fought out locally.

Local Government Elections

In addition to the reforms described above, central government has been encouraging local authorities to revise their internal structure. Traditionally, local authorities organize themselves less hierarchically than central government, with a structure of administrative departments each directed by a committee of elected councillors. Government would like local authorities to move away from this model and towards a parliamentary cabinet model, in which cabinet members, rather than committees, have responsibility for particular areas of administration. One of the goals of this change was to encourage more women and members of minority ethnic groups to stand for election to local government. With women making up only some 22 per cent of local government cabinet members, it may be too early to tell whether this model will alter the career patterns of women councillors (or even whether it will replace the tradition), but it is certainly something to be borne in mind.

Across the UK, 25.5 per cent of local councillors were women in 2001, but this varied considerably by area. Generally, more women are elected in the south-east and in metropolitan areas than in rural areas. Wales has a particularly poor showing when it comes to electing women to local as well as central government, with one of the lowest proportions of women of all in the Isle of Anglesey, at 5 per cent. Immediately before the 2003 round of local elections, the Fawcett Society issued a press release predicting that women were likely to remain under-represented in local government, because parties were failing to tackle the barriers that discouraged them from standing.

England is the one area of the UK that now lacks a regional assembly. In 2001, 26.4 per cent of English local councillors were women (see table 15.1). This varied from 51.1 per cent in the Cotswolds to 8.1 per cent in Bolsover. Despite the remarkable 50 per cent women in the Welsh Assembly, the numbers of women in Welsh local government remain

Table 15.1 Women elected to local government in the UK

Region	Year	%
Scotland	1999	22.6
Wales	2001	19.9
England	2001	26.4
Northern Ireland	2001	18.4

Table 15.2 Women elected to Scottish local government, 1999

Party	%
Liberal Democrats	32.3
Scottish Nationalists	24.0
Conservative	23.1
Labour	21.8
Independent	15.7

Source: Breitenbach 2001: 7

low. In 2001 women made up only 19.9 per cent of Welsh local councillors. Further, only 1 per cent of councillors were members of ethnic minorities, while the age profile of councillors was much older than that of the general population. In light of this, the Welsh Assembly and Welsh Local Government Association actively sought out a new generation of councillors who could better represent the population, by holding special events to inform and encourage potential councillors. Perhaps more importantly, many councils have increased the allowances made to councillors in an effort to compensate people for any loss of earnings entailed in being elected.

While England and Wales were an administrative unit until the creation of the Welsh Assembly, Scotland has always possessed a degree of administrative devolution from Westminster. This was an effect of the nature of the union between England and Scotland in 1707, which left Scotland with some institutional autonomy over its legal system, education and the Church. This has meant that an elite group of policy-makers existed in Scotland, independent of the policy elites in London. As Breitenbach points out, this elite has been predominantly male, white and middle class, to the detriment of women's participation in politics and public life in general (Breitenbach 2001: 4). In 1999, 22.6 per cent of the local councillors in Scotland were women, compared to 27 per cent in England and Wales. Although higher than the proportion of female MPs returned to Westminster from Scotland, it was lower than that elected to the new regional assembly.

The parties differed somewhat in their proportions of women councillors. The Liberal Democrats have 32.3 per cent; the Scottish Nationalists, 24 per cent; the Conservatives, 23.1 per cent; Labour, 21.8 per cent; and 15.7 per cent of Independent councillors are women (Scottish Local Government Information Unit: 199) (see table 15.2). It seems odd that the enthusiasm for achieving high numbers of women in the new assembly did not translate into getting more women elected in local government. Breitenbach suggests that the Labour government's programme for modernizing local government, and ongoing debates about the role of local government and its relationship to the community, will ensure that the representativeness of local government – and hence the proportions of women and minorities – becomes a pressing issue (Breitenbach 2001: 7).

Local government in Northern Ireland, like much else in the politics of the region, has suffered from the focus on sectarian conflict. The powers of local authorities are more limited than in the rest of the UK, and have been severely undermined by direct rule from Westminster. Numbers of women elected to local government have been lower here than in the rest of the UK, just as numbers elected to national and regional government are lower. The Peace Process and the creation of the Northern Ireland Legislative Assembly have done little to energize local authorities. The 2001 election returned twenty-two more female councillors than the previous election, increasing the percentage of women from 14.6 to 18.4 – still lower than England, Scotland and even Wales. The highest proportions of women elected were in Newtownabbey, 32 per cent, and North Down and Derry, 33.3 per cent, while Antrim and Ballymoney elected no women at all. The greatest gains were in Belfast, where the number of women increased from seven to twelve, making up 23.6 per cent of the council (M. Ward 2001).

All the major parties in Northern Ireland increased their numbers of female candidates for the election, although the numbers of women elected were only a small increase on the previous election. The SDLP has 24 per cent female councillors, Sinn Féin 13 per cent, the UUP 14.2 per cent, and the DUP 15.2 per cent. The Alliance has 32.5 per cent women councillors – but this amounts to only nine seats, because the party did so poorly – and the NIWC only managed to get one of their candidates elected (M. Ward 2001). Interestingly, the proportions of women among the Unionist parties at this level are noticeably better than in the regional assembly, while that for Sinn Féin is considerably worse. Women's representation is higher in the more industrial east, and lower in the more rural west.

Local Councillors

In recent years the profile of the average local councillor has changed. The traditional, stereotypical councillor was white, male, middle-aged and had come into local politics through local business or the professions.[4] However, observers in the 1970s and 1980s wrote about a new breed of councillor, people who were younger than the stereotypical representative, more likely to be female or non-white, and less likely to come from traditional backgrounds. The new councillor, epitomized in the Labour Party perhaps by Merle Amory, Bernie Grant, Ken Livingstone or Valerie Wise, was more likely to have been in higher education, quite likely to work in one of the public services, and very likely to have an awareness of, if not an actual involvement with, the new social movements that had developed in the 1960s and 1970s.[5]

Who becomes a local councillor?

What does a local councillor look like? In 1997 the Local Government Management Board (LGMB) undertook a national census, the first of such, of local authority coun-

Table 15.3 Women councillors in English and Welsh electoral districts

Type of authority	%
Shire districts	28.9
English unitaries	29.7
Shire counties: England	24.1
Shire counties: Wales	20.4

Source: LGMB 1998: 4

Table 15.4 Employment status of councillors

Employment	Male (%)	Female (%)
Full-time	32.9	20.7
Part-time	5.5	15.6
Retired	35.9	32.3
Caring for family	0.6	12.8

Source: LGMB 1998: 21

cillors in England and Wales. The survey found that 73 per cent of the councillors were male, and 27 per cent female; 97 per cent were white, and 3 per cent from ethnic minorities; 11 per cent were disabled (LGMB 1998). A sample survey in 1993 had shown 25 per cent female councillors, so this shows a slight rise (Young and Rao 1994). Comparing the different authorities, the 1997 survey found that there were more women in shire districts, 28.9 per cent (shire districts are the lower level in non-metropolitan areas), English unitaries, 29.7 per cent (areas where there is only one level of local government, urban), and lower proportions in shire counties, 24.1 per cent in England and 20.4 per cent in Wales, (LGMB 1998: 4) (see table 15.3).

There tended to be fewer women under the age of forty-four than men, and fewer over the age of sixty. Members of ethic minorities, on the other hand, tended to be slightly younger than their white colleagues, with a greater proportion under the age of forty-five. Among ethnic minority councillors, there were similar numbers of black men and women, but far fewer Asian women than men (LGMB 1998: 19). The same pattern is true for disabled councillors. When it comes to caring responsibilities, more male councillors claim to be responsible for both dependent children and adults than female, 35.4 per cent as opposed to 30.7 per cent. Councillors from ethnic minorities have the highest level of responsibility for dependents, at 51.9 per cent, and 31.3 per cent of disabled councillors have caring responsibilities (LGMB 1998: 20).

When we look at the employment status of councillors, differences again appear. While 32.9 per cent of male councillors are in full-time employment, only 20.7 per cent of females are. By contrast, only 5.5 per cent of male councillors are in part-time employment, and 15.6 per cent of females. Some 35.9 per cent of men and 32.3 per cent of women are retired, and 0.6 per cent of men and 12.8 per cent of women are looking after a family (see table 15.4). Comparing white councillors with those from ethnic minorities, while

Table 15.5 Occupational status of councillors

Employment category	Men (%)	Women (%)	Total (%)
Managerial	35.2	24.1	32.5
Professional/ technical	29.1	25.1	28.1
Lecturer, etc.	10.6	17.6	12.3
Administration	9.6	25.6	13.4
Manual or craft	15.5	7.6	13.7

Source: LGMB 1998: 22

29.1 per cent of white councillors are in full-time employment, 41.8 per cent of ethnic minority councillors are. Some 8.3 per cent of white councillors are in part-time employment, and 7.4 per cent of ethnic minority councillors. Some 35.5 per cent of white councillors are retired, compared with 20.4 per cent of ethnic minority councillors, and while 4 per cent of white councillors are looking after a family, 1.9 per cent of ethnic minority councillors are. With regard to disabled councillors, 13.1 per cent are in full-time employment, and 5.4 per cent in part-time employment. Some 44.9 per cent are retired, and 2.8 per cent are looking after a home and family (LGMB 1998: 21).

In terms of how these councillors were employed, the vast majority fell into the categories: managerial and executive (32.5 per cent), professional or technical (28.1 per cent), or lecturer, teacher or researcher (12.3 per cent) (see table 15.5). The main differences between groups were that there were fewer women than men in the managerial and executive category, 24.1 as opposed to 35.2 per cent, and there were more women than men in the administration, clerical and sales category, 25.6 as opposed to 9.6 per cent (LGMB 1998: 22).

What conclusions can we draw from all this data? First, there are far fewer women than men. Women councillors tend to be older than their male counterparts. Although a similar proportion of men and women are employed, far more men than women are in full-time jobs, and far more women than men are in part-time jobs. Perhaps connected to this, women are less likely to be employed in high-status (high-wage) professions, and more likely to be employed in service professions (which probably puts a larger number of them in the public rather than the private sector). Interestingly, more men than women have caring responsibilities, perhaps suggesting that when men are primary carers, they get more help than women in similar positions and are thus enabled to take up other interests.

The proportion of women in local (and regional) government is higher than that in national government; there are many more women politically active in local arenas than national ones. This might be explained by proximity – a woman can join in local politics without acquiring a second home and living part of the week in London – or by the pertinence of the issues – it is argued that the business of local politics is related to the locality, the home, the domestic sphere, and is therefore closer to women than the international political economy of Westminster – or we could argue that since local politics is considered to be of low status and marginal relevance, there is less competition for candidature, and men are somewhat less interested in the posts. Whatever the explanation, it is certainly the case that in the UK, as in most other countries, women have a greater presence in sub-national than national politics.

It is argued that, just as with national politics, the grip of parties and their selection procedures tends to favour men of a certain type (depending on the party) to women and people from minorities (Chapman 1993). Very similar factors come into play in the local arena as in the national, described above, but there are some differences. Many wards (the local government equivalent of constituencies) return more than one councillor (multi-member constituencies). This opens up a space for women and minorities in a way similar to that provided by proportional representation. Further, the new regional assemblies have adopted the Additional Member system, and some parties have used this to include more women. Perhaps most importantly, there is often very little competition for local authority seats.

What do councillors do?

Having considered what local councillors look like, the next thing to ask is 'what do they do?' Rather like members of parliament, local councillors are representatives of their parties, advocates for their constituents, and (sometimes) the voice of particular interests. They debate in the chamber, but, rather more often, they sit on committees. The career of a local councillor is defined by the committees she sits on and, more importantly, chairs.

Looking at positions on local councils, the LGMB study found that 2.1 per cent of men were Leader of the Council, and 1.2 per cent women (see table 15.6). This is a small

Table 15.6 Percentage of male and female councillors achieving key posts on councils

Post	Men (%)	Women (%)
Leader of council	2.1	1.21
Party leader	6.4	4.2
Committee chair	22.5	18.7
Membership of Policy, Finance, Legal or IT Committee	54.2	45.1
Membership of Economic Regeneration Committee	32.3	23.9
Membership of Planning Committee	46.4	42.7
Membership of Equal Opportunities Committee	16.2	22.6
Membership of Housing Committee	34.6	39.2
Membership of Social Services Committee	22.9	30.0

Source: LGMB 1998: 29

percentage difference; but since there are fewer female than male councillors, and since each council can have only one leader at a time, this shows that there are many more male than female leaders, and that women have a much smaller chance of becoming leader.

Some 6.4 per cent of men and 4.2 per cent of women were party leaders (LGMB 1998: 26). Again, since there are fewer women than men, and since a party can have only one leader at a time, this is a much larger difference than it appears to be. Men and women were on very similar numbers of committees, but there was a fair amount of variation in the proportions of men and women on different committees. Some 22.5 per cent of men were committee chairs, as compared to 18.7 per cent of women – a small but noticeable gap. However, it is impossible to know the full meaning of this without knowing which committees are chaired by whom.

More male councillors (54.2 per cent) than female (45.1 per cent) were members of Policy, Finance and Strategy, Legal and Information Technology committees. More male councillors (32.3 per cent) than female (23.9 per cent) were on Economic Regeneration committees, and more men (46.4 per cent) than women (42.7 per cent) were on Planning committees. However, more women (22.6 per cent) than men (16.2 per cent) were on Equal Opportunities committees, more women (39.2 per cent) than men (34.6 per cent) were on Housing committees, and more women (30.0 per cent) than men (22.9 per cent) were on Social Services committees (LGMB 1998: 29).

Bearing in mind the considerably smaller numbers of women than men councillors, this means that there would actually have been very few female leaders of the council, party leaders, committee chairs, or women sitting on important policy and financial committees. Percentages may tell us that men and women, once elected, do fairly similar things, but the election data tell us that 1 per cent of women is only a quarter the size of 1 per cent of men.

The data used here are seven years old at the time of writing. There has been one full election cycle in that time (local elections vary: some areas go to the polls every four years and all councillors are up for election, others put one-third of councillors up for election for each of three years and then take a year off; because of this any analysis of councillors is something of a moving target). The proportions of men and women will have changed slightly as a result of elections, but not radically. Local authorities have been strongly encouraged to change their structure away from the relatively broadly based committee framework, towards a more hierarchical cabinet-led framework that reflects the structure of central government. There is a concern that this change will tend to favour the dominance of a small group of established local politicians, and thus men.

Women's Committees

In the 1980s new women's committees were created in a number of Labour-controlled local authorities in the UK. The committees were committed not only to improving the conditions of women's lives, but also to changing local politics and local government. They were an anomaly within local government, because their brief was not the management of a statutory duty, such as Education or Planning, but the scrutiny of other departments. They were established to monitor policies and practices, and to ensure that women's interests were brought to bear on the conduct of council business.[6] Their commitment to political change entailed introducing new or marginalized issues to the main political agenda, including child care, employment policies, women's access to services, and domestic violence. Their commitment to changing local government entailed engaging with the community, working across departmental boundaries and overcoming unnecessary hierarchies.

In 1981 the Greater London Council (GLC, forerunner of the Greater London Authority created in 1999) established the first women's committee (Webster 1983; Goss 1988). Subsequently, similar committees were formed in London boroughs and around the country, most of which were modelled on the example of the GLC (Watson 1983; Edwards 1988; Coote and Patullo 1990: 231–6). The committees were a formal part of local government and bound by the relevant rules and regulations. The majority were established in urban areas with large and diverse populations. Nothing else in central government or the political parties came close to this as a sign of how seriously women and women's issues were to be addressed.[7]

Eleven committees were recorded in 1983, and by July 1987 there were at least forty-three women's committees (Webster 1983; Edwards 1988; Halford 1989; Cooper 1991; Parkin 1992; Bottomley 1990). At their peak there were around fifty-six committees of varying status that claimed some sort of responsibility for women, in the 514 local authorities in England, Scotland and Wales, or 10.89 per cent.[8]

The goals and strategies of the women's committees were very similar, although the GLC committee was exceptional in terms of resources. The women's committee of the GLC had full standing status, a large support unit of paid staff, a large budget over which it had considerable discretion, and the general support of the leader of the council (Mackintosh and Wainwright 1987: 106). It came into being as the result of pressure from female councillors. Valerie Wise, who was vice-chair of the Industry and Employment Committee, set up a women's advisory group, which developed the idea of a women's committee. As Mackintosh and Wainwright note, the goal was to rewrite the GLC's agenda on employment policy: no small undertaking, but uncontroversial in comparison with the diverse projects which later women's committees and the GLC committee itself were to adopt (Mackintosh and Wainwright 1987: 106).

A commitment to increasing council democracy through the direct involvement of local people in policy-making was put into practice through open committee meetings, public meetings and the inclusion of co-opted members (Webster 1983; Coote and Patullo 1990: 231–51). In addition to councillors, the GLC committee included twenty members from the community, some of whom were elected at public meetings. Eight of these had full voting rights. Six of those with voting rights were elected to represent particular groups of women: women of colour, women with disabilities, and lesbians; the remaining two were selected by the south-east region of the TUC.[9] The twelve non-voting members were there to advise on disability, transport, older women's interests, youth service, media and the arts, peace, employment, health, and violence against women (Loach 1985a).

In their summary of the achievements of the women's committee within the GLC, Mackintosh and Wainwright concluded that

> The traditionally formal and bureaucratic structures of the council have been transformed and at least now the practices and policies of the council are informed by feminism. The GLC has monitored its own recruitment practices and introduced positive action programmes to

promote equal opportunities both among its own employees and the organisations that it funds.

However, these achievements stopped short of radical political change, and 'the actual power relationships within this bastion of left democracy remain unchanged' (Mackintosh and Wainwright 1987: 21). In the committee's defence, it was not in existence for very long, and it was path-breaking: other committees had longer, and benefited from its example.

The committees that drew inspiration from the GLC adopted similar aims and structures. The early journalism made it clear that the succession of women's committees in different areas arose out of each other, particularly influenced by the examples of the GLC and London boroughs (Edwards 1988: 51). While for some authorities the establishment of committees to consider the concerns of specific groups was part of a general approach, in other areas their achievement was the result of a slow struggle for support and funding (Button 1984). Councillors and council officers who were trying to establish committees, or had succeeded in doing so, communicated with each other through both formal and informal channels.

In 1985 a specific co-ordinating body for women's committees was set up: the National Association of Local Government Women's Committees (NALGWC), later the Women's Local Authority Network (WLAN) (Coote and Patullo 1990: 249). This was financed through the affiliation of interested councils. In 1993 NALGWC, based in Manchester, had two full-time employees. It organized regular meetings of delegates from affiliated women's committees around specific issues, held records of the activities of all affiliated women's committees, copies of relevant published articles and unpublished academic research. It also undertook an annual survey of all local authorities to ascertain where women's initiatives were taking place.[10]

Following the model of the GLC committee, the co-option of local women was widely espoused, and a range of consultative procedures introduced. Where funds were available for designated staff, attempts were made to employ women with a pre-existing commitment to women's issues and to initiate flexible working arrangements both amongst staff and between staff and committee members (Parkin 1992; Stone 1988). The committees' brief was, broadly, to further the interests of women in their areas and in the employ of local authorities, taking account of both private and public aspects of their lives.

Although their terms of reference varied, five general aims can be attributed to most of the committees:

* to promote the welfare and interests of women and women's rights;
* to work for the elimination of discrimination against women in legislation, policies and practices;
* to encourage the adoption of positive action to promote real equality of opportunity for women;
* to encourage and support the development of women's groups and organizations;
* to open up council decision-making structures to women in the community, and to make them more accountable to that community. (Webster 1983)

By 1989 women's committees were undergoing various processes of restructuring in response to their own experiences, on the one hand, and council pressures, on the other. For some this entailed no more than reassessing their objectives and operations; for others it meant losing their distinct identity and becoming part of an equal opportunities committee, with a brief to consider a range of forms of disadvantage. The latter course was met with dismay: '[f]eminism, anti-racism, anti-sexism, anti-heterosexism, and anti-ablism are now replaced with "equal opportunities" or as the Leader of one London Labour authority so quaintly put it, "We are bringing everyone up to the starting line"' (Roelofs 1989: 47).

Less drastic restructuring was only a little more welcome. It achieved a wider acceptance for the committees, because it signalled the abandonment of 'silliness' in favour of a practical approach to working within council procedures. John Cunningham, for example, wrote approvingly in the *Guardian* about 'a sort of Mark Two committee [which] is emerging, defensive and chastened' (Roelofs 1989: 47). However, Sarah Roelofs interpreted the changes as entailing a regrettable diminution of the links between committees, the women's movement, and feminist activists in the local community (Roelofs 1989: 47). In another article, Davina Cooper expressed concern that women's equality was being removed from the agenda of local government as suddenly as it had been introduced. Although the numbers of women in positions of power had increased, she worried that the critical mass necessary to ensure that achievements would not be lost had not been reached. She blamed the relative absence of women from positions of power, combined with restrictions on council budgets, for the committees' loss of influence and resources (Cooper 1991).

The loss of women's committees, including their dissolution into equal opportunities committees, suggests that the main body of a number of councils remained unconvinced that the achievement of equal citizenship for women required the creation of special facilities. This may have been due to the feeling that special measures were 'undemocratic', or to suspicions about hidden agendas which privileged particular groups of women (Halford 1992). Certainly, few councils had enough female councillors to make a stand, and budgetary restrictions were a real consideration. It is perhaps unfortunate that the committees were strongly identified with Labour and rarely gained cross-party support. Their identification with Labour – and often with particular sections within Labour – meant that they were vulnerable to conflict between and within parties. However, the national Labour Party must take some responsibility for failing to take adequate interest in the committees.[11]

It is possible that in some cases the goals of the committees had been transmitted to the mainstream departments and the women's committees had fulfilled their function. Despite constraints, closures, amalgamation and restructuring, women's committees have not disappeared, although their numbers continue to diminish. Towards the end of 1995 there were an estimated four full committees and ten women's subcommittees in existence (Labour Research 1995: 15). This estimate did not take account of equal opportunities committees which had a brief for women's issues.

The committees influenced the adoption of consultative mechanisms, public meetings, conferences, advisory forums and surveys, and involved the community more closely in democracy. They were instrumental in the increased provision of child care and training facilities, and in attention to women's safety. The pursuit of improved opportunities for women in employment and better treatment for women as parents and carers, the concern with male violence and commitment to instituting practices influenced by women's experiences, demonstrated the committees' commitment to feminist goals (Stokes 1998).

Issues that had been outside the remit of politics became firmly embedded in local government policies during the period of the committees' existence: not only child care and fair employment measures, but also women's safety, both on the street and in their homes. Women's committees and units took up a range of issues that had not previously been addressed by local government, or not addressed adequately. The committees were also active in establishing new roles for local government: as a central resource for organizing events and collecting and disseminating information; as a facilitator providing services in consultation with the public; and as an initiator experimenting with new ideas in conjunction with the public (Stokes 1998).

Conclusion

Local politics is often considered to be more hospitable to women than national politics. In the UK women have had greater access at the local level for a longer time than at the national level, yet this has translated into only a few extra percentage points in the number of female councillors, as opposed to MPs. Local political culture seems to be an influence, since the percentage of women varies considerably between urban and rural areas and between regions.

As councillors, women are less likely than men to hold senior office; therefore there are many more male than female council leaders and senior officers. We can account for this only in the same terms as for central government: the domination of the political process by parties with conservative (if not sexist) habits (see Jenny Chapman's (1993) research in Strathclyde for some illumination of local processes).

Women's committees were an interesting and innovative attempt to shift both the agenda and practices of local government on to a more woman-friendly and democratic track. Despite their demise, they have been influential both in reshaping practices and by providing a training ground for female politicians.

FURTHER READING

Although generally regarded as the 'Cinderella' of UK political science, the study of local government has been taken up by a number of researchers, who have observed the initiatives being taken by and for women at this level. The history has been well documented by Patricia Hollis. The present situation in Scotland has been followed by a group from Edinburgh University, while Northern Ireland is the subject of researchers from Queens University, Belfast. Wales is less extensively considered, but Paul Chaney is doing a good job. The complexities of England have been addressed by Catherine Bochel, while the story of the women's committees described here has been recounted by Julia Edwards and is included in Lovenduski and Randall's book. The Centre for Advancement of Women in Politics at Queen's University, Belfast runs a website that presents data and research: <www.qub.ac.uk/cawp/>.

The 1980s period of revolution in local government is recounted by John Gyford et al., while such writers as John Stewart give good accounts of the perversity of local government structure. The Local Government Management Board initiates and publishes local government research.

Bochel, C. and Bochel, H. M. 2000: *The Careers of Councillors: Gender, Party and Politics*. London: Ashgate Publishing.

Breitenbach, E., Brown, A., Mackay, F. and Webb, J. (eds) 2001: *The Changing Politics of Gender Equality in Twentieth Century Britain*. London: Palgrave Macmillan.

Chapman, J. 1993: *Politics, Feminism and the Reformation of Gender*. London: Routledge.

Edwards, J. 1988: Local Government Women's Committees. *Critical Social Policy*, 24: 50–64.

Galligan, Y., Ward, R. and Wilford, R. (eds) 1999: *Contesting Politics*. Oxford: Westview Press.

Goss, S. 1984: Women's Initiatives in Local Government. In M. Boddy and C. Fudge (eds), *Local Socialism: Labour Councillors and New Left Alternatives*. London: Macmillan.

Gyford, J., Leach, S. and Game, C. 1989: *The Changing Politics of Local Government*. London: Unwin Hyman.

Hollis, P. 1979: *Women in Public: The Women's Movement 1850–1900*. London: Allen and Unwin.

Hollis, P. 1987: *Ladies Elect: Women in English Local Government 1865–1915*. Oxford: Clarendon Press.

Lovenduski, J. and Randall, V. 1993. *Contemporary Feminist Politics*. Oxford: Oxford University Press.

Stewart, J. and Stoker, G. (eds) 1995: *Local Government in the 1990s*. London: Macmillan.

WOMEN IN SUB-NATIONAL GOVERNMENT OUTSIDE THE UNITED KINGDOM

16

Introduction

This chapter looks at the position of women in sub-national government in a number of different countries. This is a difficult area to write about. In a few countries sub-national government has been studied extensively (although this does not necessarily mean that attention has been paid to women), but in others not much has been written at all. In federal states, state-level government gets attention, but local government tends to get overlooked. In unitary states, interest in local government is dependent on the history of the institutions and their developing practices. Once we start looking around the world at this level, the lack of data on women becomes glaringly obvious (Matland and Studlar 1998). Possibly it is the combination of two themes thought to be of little interest or relevance: local politics and women. International organizations are important both in prompting interest and supporting research, and some of the information here has been pulled from media sources. None the less, it is apparent that women are more visible at the local level, although similar patterns of marginalization and obstruction are present.

The Republic of Ireland

The arguments deployed to explain women's relatively low representation in the Irish parliament (that women are considered to be vote losers, that parties do not select women, the use of the single transferable vote electoral system, the persistence of patriarchy, and the influence of the Catholic Church) also apply at local level, with the additional factor that local government is generally regarded as of little relevance. Symptomatic of this is the regular central government practice of postponing local elections (Galligan and Wilford 1999b: 133). In 1961, 3.2 per cent of councillors were women. This increased to 8.1 per cent in 1985, and 12 per cent in 1991. The 2004 elections to Irish county councils returned 16 per cent women councillors. The elections to borough councils in the same year returned 15 per cent women councillors, while the elections to city councils showed a rather better outcome of 22 per cent women councillors (Centre for the Advancement of Women in Politics website). Galligan and Wilford argue that women candidates are widely believed to be vote losers. As long as political parties are the gatekeepers to candidacy, and they are reluctant to select women, little is likely to change.

There has been legislation attempting to increase the presence of women among state bureaucrats: from 1991 State Boards have been required to have 14 per cent women. The Commission on the Status of Women recommended 40 per cent, and this was implemented by government in 1993. This resulted in an increase of women from 15 per cent in 1992 to 26 per cent in 1996. Looking at the general situation of women in the politics of the Republic, Galligan and Wilford conclude that 'a complex interaction of individuated, situational, and structural variables . . . have the aggregate effect of making the public realm a near-male monopoly' (Galligan and Wilford 1999b: 145).

The Nordic Countries

Around the world it is common to find more women in local than national politics. The Nordic countries buck this trend by returning lower numbers of women in local than in national elections (see table 16.1). Towards the end of the 1990s, Sweden had 42 per cent women in local government and 43 per cent in national; Norway had 34 per cent in local government, and 36 per cent in national; Denmark had 27 per cent in local, and 37 per cent in national; while Finland had 31.4 per cent in local, and 37 per cent in national. It is not at all clear why this is the case, but, even so, the proportion of women in Nordic local government is higher than in other countries. Nordic local government is relatively powerful and autonomous, taking responsibility for a range of welfare services, making it a desirable political location, unlike in the UK, where it is sometimes argued that its relative powerlessness means that men and highly-driven women quickly dismiss local office (Inter-Parliamentary Union website).

Sweden

The breakthrough in Swedish municipal politics came in the 1980s, when women's representation averaged 29 per cent. This increased to 41 per cent by the end of the 1990s (Hedlund and Pehrman 2000).

Table 16.1 Women elected to local government in the Nordic countries

Country	Local (%)	National (%)
Sweden	42.0	43.0
Norway	34.0	36.0
Denmark	27.0	37.0
Finland	31.4	37.0

Even with lower numbers in the 1970s, women politicians had exerted considerable influence, achieving, for example, a high level of publicly provided child care. In her 1980s study, Hedlund found that women municipal politicians differed from their male counterparts in having a stronger orientation towards care and welfare. The women taking part in the research were also found both to introduce new questions and to have a particular attitude to the issues discussed. Their approach to people's needs was characterized by a care-oriented rationality, in which they brought their special experiences of daily-life reality into the decision-making process (Hedlund 1998).

Hedlund argues that women in municipal government in the 1980s exercised relatively little influence on organization or finance, while women regarded themselves as having particular knowledge, and playing an important part as representatives of their constituents, particularly children, young people and the elderly (Hedlund and Pehrman 2000). Swedish local government traditionally worked through committees, which had responsibility for particular policy areas. Women were therefore more likely to be active on welfare-directed committees. Hedlund argues that during the first half of the 1980s one-third of social service committees were chaired by women, and that these women assumed an active role in the extension of child care, as demonstrated by the better child care facilities in municipalities with greater numbers of female representatives.

The increase in numbers of women elected in the 1990s paralleled increased numbers in the local executives, and a change in thinking with regard to local government. Local government was reconceived as more of a business or entrepreneurial enterprise, with politicians expected to behave more like members of a board making economically rational choices, rather than representatives in the traditional sense. In many municipalities statutory committees were abolished, and the purchaser/provider model introduced.

The women who have entered local politics recently are, Freidenvall (2000) argues, somewhat different from their older colleagues. Problems of combining political and private life remain the same, although more of the younger women had professional careers that enabled them to prepare for their political activities rather more easily than their colleagues. Freidenvall found little difference between younger and older women in terms of political interest, but did find that younger men were closer to women in their areas of interest than older men were. So male politicians were found to be changing, perhaps in response to the increasing numbers of women and exposure to their concerns.

A very high proportion of all the politicians surveyed by Freidenvall supported gender parity in local politics. They largely agreed with the four contentions that: local politics should reflect the important groups in society, that women have different life experiences from men, that the forms of work and atmosphere of discussion would improve, and that the political agenda would change if more women were included. The younger men were closer to women in believing that the presence of more women would change the content and process of politics.

In terms of what they do, a high percentage of women politicians agreed that they contributed less than men in formal political meetings (although far fewer younger women agreed with this than older ones), that women presented women's interests better than men, that women introduced different questions on to the political agenda, and that women had a greater interest than men in soft (welfare) political issues.

Freidenvall found that young women had much less contact with women's organizations than did the older women, but they nevertheless still felt it was important to pursue women's interests and to represent women.

Finland

As we have seen, Finland was among the first countries in the world to give women full political rights, and women achieved a political presence in central government remarkably quickly. Universal suffrage at local level was achieved somewhat later, in 1917. In Finland, the municipalities are the main providers of welfare services. The power of local government increased during the 1990s as central control diminished. Local government is an important employer, especially for women. Some 63 per cent of women are active in the labour force (compared to 69 per cent of men), and one-third of these are employed by local government organizations (9 per cent of men) (Pikkala 2000). Local government is also an important recruiting ground for other political offices.

Legislation in 1984 and 1995 specified that a minimum of 40 per cent of both men and women should be present on government committees, advisory boards and other corresponding bodies, and municipal bodies, with the exception of municipal councils. Finnish local government consists of the municipal council, the highest decision-making body; the executive board, responsible for the practical running of the local administration; and the municipal committees. These last work under the municipal board, handling specific policy areas including social and health care, education and cultural affairs, the technical sector (building, planning, etc.) and auditing.

Before the new legislation kicked in, women tended to be concentrated in the less prestigious, less powerful, welfare-focused areas of local government: 25 per cent at the executive level, 30 per cent in the councils, and 35 per cent in the committees. On committees, while the technical service and economic committees in most areas would need to increase the numbers of women to meet the 40 per cent quota, many social and health care committees needed to increase the numbers of men.

The 1996 local elections were the first to take place after the new legislation. Taking account of the 40 per cent quota, parties nominated more female candidates than previously, yet most did not reach the 40 per cent level. According to Pikkala it is unclear whether the insufficient number of female candidates is a consequence of the parties' negative attitude toward women or, as they claim, that women are less willing to stand than men. Despite the effort made and the change in legislation, the increase in the number of women elected to local office in 1996 showed the poorest growth in almost thirty years (from 30 to 31.4 per cent). Despite concerns prior to 1996 about being able to fill the 40 per cent quota of women, Pikkala's investigation after the election shows considerable success. Only 2 per cent of the local government organizations had less than 40 per cent women.

Belgium

Rather like the UK, Belgium has recently created new regional parliaments. The Flemish Parliament held its first elections in 1995, along with its equivalents in Wallonia and Brussels (Celis and Woodward 2000). Of the elected representatives, 17.7 per cent (22 out of 124) were women: considerably more than the 11 per cent in the national House of Representatives. This increased to 18.5 per cent in 1999. Many of the women elected came from political families: 54 per cent of them had at least one politically active family member, as compared to 34 per cent of the men elected. As in the UK, the majority of both men and women were between the ages of forty-six and fifty-five.

In the first legislature women were concentrated in three committees: Welfare, Health and Family; Culture and Sport; and Education and Science Policy. Only two out of the thirteen committees had women as chairs. None the less, Celis and Woodward found that the women in the Flemish Parliament were more active than their male counterparts – as measured by the numbers of initiatives taken.

Celis and Woodward found that the majority of representatives agreed that 'the "woman question" was a question for women' (2000: 13). Women representatives brought new issues to the political agenda, particularly initiatives dealing specifically with women, but also children's rights. Interestingly, they found that women members of the Flemish Parliament were contacted by women's organizations far more than were men: all of them were contacted at least once a month, as compared to 75 per cent of the men contacted once or twice per year. Perhaps this is connected to the fact that the women considered working with local interest groups more important than men did. They tended to see opposition as constructive rather than confrontational, and placed a higher emphasis on an ethical code than the men did.

Russia and Central-Eastern Europe

The number of women in Russian government, national, regional and local, diminished radically after 1990. Although the average figure in 1997 was 9 per cent, this hid considerable variation, with four regional legislatures returning no women, and others returning up to 30 per cent. According to Kochkina (2001), in 1997 women politicians comprised only 2.16 per cent of regional executive bodies, occupying only seven of the 322 policy and leadership posts. No woman was elected President in the seventeen republics, and there were no women among the sixteen chairs of republic governments. Kochkina argues that there is no shortage of qualified women who could take leadership posts. The absence of women is an effect of the centralized control of politics and the unwillingness of the centre to promote women.

By the time Nowacki was writing in 2003, the proportions of women had again decreased, and (where there were women at all) varied from 4.64 per cent in the Central Black Earth region to 9.11 per cent in the Urals and 17.03 per cent in East Siberia. Nowacki found that women were losing ground in regional assemblies, at least in part because political parties were losing ground, since a higher proportion of female than male candidates relied on parties for nomination (other candidates being nominated by voters). She found that women were more likely than men to be nominated by the Communist Party (Nowacki 2003: 184). Like Kochkina, Nowacki found that women were highly educated and achieving professional careers – but she found that they did not number highly in the professions most strongly linked to political success. Most male leaders came from backgrounds in economic and political administration, while the female politicians were emerging from the leadership of schools and hospitals. She found that, as in other countries, female deputies were older than male deputies (although fewer were over age sixty), and that the majority were married with adult children (Nowacki 2003).

Women do rather better in Polish local government. In the local elections of 1998, women constituted 15.98 per cent of the councillors elected. There was considerable variation, however. Provincial parliaments elected the lowest proportion of women, while in town and commune councils the percentages were higher. Among province councillors women made up 10.88 per cent, varying from 4.4 per cent in two of the sixteen provinces to 16 per cent in three others. In seven provinces there was at least one woman on the province board, and in three of these there were women vice-chairs. Women achieved higher representation in urban areas. In province cities the proportion of women ranged from 12 per cent in Bialystok to 30.9 per cent in Bydgoszcz (Participation of Women in Local Government in Poland, 24 May 2002, Oska National Women's Information Centre).

The United States of America

By the start of the twentieth century women had been admitted to the local franchise in all the states of the United States, although each state did so independently. In 1937 an average of three women served on each of the forty-eight state legislatures (Darcy, Welch and Clark 1994: 52). By 1993 this had increased to 21 per cent, but there was considerable variation between states. The year 1992 is referred to as the Year of the Woman: not only were an unprecedented number of women nominated for the federal Congress, but high numbers of women were nominated for posts in state legislatures – some 2,375 – and more were elected than ever before (McGlen et al. 2002: 91). The trend continued, and in 2000 five states elected female governors, rising to eight by 2004. In 2004 there were seventeen female lieutenant-governors, and five attorney generals. Between 1981 and 2001 the percentage of women elected to state legislatures increased from 13 to 22.4 per cent. Across the USA, 25.7 per cent of the state-wide elective positions were held by women. In 2001 there were women mayors in twelve of the largest 100 cities in the USA, and 17.5 per cent of cities with populations of 100,000 or more had a woman mayor. In all, around one-fifth of elected local officials were women (McGlen et al. 2002: 93; <www.gender-gap.com>).

Sue Thomas examined the profiles of women elected to state legislatures in the USA in the 1970s and 1980s, in order to identify any changes taking place. Looking at state legislators in the 1970s she found that they had fewer years in higher education than their male comparators; that they came primarily from low-status, poorly-paid professions; that although the majority of legislators were married, this was more the case for men than women, and that the women had fewer children; that the women who were married with children were likely to be older than their male colleagues; and that they had different prior political experience: women tended to have been on school boards, whereas the men were more likely to have been on a city council (Thomas 1994: 32–3).

By the 1980s the women on state legislatures had more experience of higher education than those ten years earlier, and came from a more diverse range of occupations. A similar proportion of both men and women had prior experience of political office, 40 per cent, and there was no difference in the type of office that had been held. However, the pattern of family status remained broadly similar to that in the 1970s, and the women still had lower incomes than the men. With regard to their attitudes to office, the women legislators saw themselves as harder working but less effective than their male colleagues (Thomas 1994: 34). They claimed that they could ask awkward questions and break the rules, and that they could support community interests. On the other hand, their commitment to constituency issues cost them time, and they claimed a high level of experience of sexism.

How did the men sitting alongside them see things? They saw less evidence of discrimination and sex-stereotyping than the women did, and did not see the harder work that the women claimed to be doing. They thought that the women were less politically astute than themselves, and possessed less relevant training, although they considered that the women had special expertise in dealing with people. Despite these judgements, they attributed discrimination against women to constituent bias rather than to bias on their own part or that of their colleagues (Thomas 1994: 37).

In the 1980s female legislators still felt that politics was a hostile place for women, but argued that they had become better at overcoming the hostility. Some 41 per cent of female state legislators thought that women in their position were more effective than men, but only 6 per cent of men agreed with them (Thomas 1994: 49). In practical terms, there was little difference in the frequency with which male and female legislators spoke on the floor or in committees, or met with lobbyists (Thomas 1994: 53). Women were to be found on a range of committees, and no more likely than men to be on Education, although they were more likely than men to be on Health and Welfare, and less likely to have a business assignment (Thomas 1994: 65).

In the 1980s a gender gap in support for the Equal Rights Amendment, liberal abortion laws, and provision of child care, first identified in the 1970s, continued to exist (Thomas 1994: 64). In addition, fewer women than men supported the building of more nuclear power plants or agreed that the private sector could solve economic problems with minimal government regulation. On the other hand, men had come around to government-sponsored child care, and both men and women supported increased taxation to provide social services to compensate for reduced past funding levels (Thomas 1994: 65).

As Thomas comments, women have integrated, but have they accepted the *status quo*, or are they on their way to making changes?

Canada

Like the Nordic countries, Canada is unusual in electing higher proportions of women to the national parliament than to sub-national assemblies (Studlar and Matland 1996). Percentages of women in the provincial assemblies lagged behind the national until the 1990s. For example, in 1988, while 13.4 per cent of the federal assembly were women, only 11.8 per cent of representatives elected to the provincial assemblies were. By 1993 this had shifted to 18 per cent at federal level and 18.4 per cent at state level. The proportions of women elected in different states varies widely: from 1.9 per cent in New-foundland to 13.0 per cent in British Columbia in 1988, and from 5.8 per cent in New-foundland to 25.3 per cent in British Columbia in 1993.

Studlar and Matland attribute the difference between national and state assemblies to three connected variables. Provincial governments are significant centres of political power in their own right, and are therefore targeted by the politically ambitious, whereas sub-national government in other countries is often seen as a far less desirable or impor-tant destination. Perhaps linked to this, politicians do not move from provincial govern-ment to federal; instead there are two separate career channels. Finally, seats in provincial legislatures have a slower turnover than at federal level. Together, these factors combine to restrict women's opportunities in provincial legislatures in comparison with federal (Studlar and Matland 1996: 275).

As the numbers from Newfoundland and British Columbia suggest, elected members of provincial legislatures are more likely to be female in metropolitan and urban areas than in rural ones. This is particularly the case in districts with no incumbents and where the New Democratic Party (NDP) wins. Where there is a history of women being elected, women tend to continue to be elected. Matland and Studlar (1998) predict that since the election of women first broke through in metropolitan areas and then in urban, it will spread to rural areas, but will take time.

Australia and New Zealand

Australia is a federal nation; therefore it has both state and local government as well as national (federal) government. It has established a formidable framework for the promo-tion of women in sub-national government. The National Framework for Women in Local Government was developed by the Australian Local Government Women's Association (ALGWA) for the Commonwealth Office of the Status of Women, which is in the Depart-ment of the Prime Minister and Cabinet. Developed in collaboration with a wide range of women's organizations from across the country, many of which were already engaged in the promotion of women in local government, the document lays out the issues and dis-cusses strategies. It has been adopted around the country at both state and local level.

Both Western Australia and Victoria had women premiers in the early 1990s: Carmen Lawrence and Joan Kirner. Both headed Labor (ALP) governments. While in Lawrence's Cabinet one-third of the members were women, Kirner appointed less than a quarter – fewer women than in the previous ALP Cabinet. By 1997, ninety-three women had been ministers at state level – two-thirds of them since 1970. The proportion of female Cabinet members at this level had been slightly exceeding the proportion of women in the state parliaments since 1950, and also exceeding the proportion in the federal government (Moon and Fountain 1997). The numbers of female Cabinet members were higher in Western Australia and Victoria than in other states. Queensland, Southern Australia and New South Wales had similar proportions of women, whereas Tasmania had fewer. Moon and Fountain argue that the numbers of women seem to correlate with ALP governments. Even where numbers were increasing, they found that women disproportionately repre-sented 'soft' policy areas.

In 2000 women comprised 23.6 per cent of members of states' Upper Houses, 21.4 per cent of members of Lower Houses, and 22.3 per cent of the members of Cabinets. At the level of local, rather than state, government, 15 per cent of mayors were women, as were 23.3 per cent of elected local councillors (Country Report: Australia). More women were found to be mayors in metropolitan areas than in rural ones.

The Women's Electoral Lobby was founded in 1973 with the goal of promoting women's participation in political parties. The main political parties all have good intentions with regard to getting women elected to local government; the Australian Labor Party has a target of 35 per cent, while the Liberal Party encourages women through the Liberal Women's Forum. The Democrats do best, with women in 40 per cent of decision-making and senior positions.

Australia shares certain characteristics with its near neighbour, New Zealand, but the latter is rather more successful at getting women elected both nationally and locally. In New Zealand there is a Women's Electoral Lobby that encourages women into politics through training, making information available, and fund raising. Women's achievements of office at local level are rather good, with 31.5 per cent of local councillors in 2000 and 26 per cent of mayors. There is broad agreement among political parties on a principle of gender balance. The New Zealand Labour Party has a National Women's Council, a National Women's Organizer, and Women's Organizers at local branches.

India and its Neighbours

Women in India are active in a wide range of political activities, although this does not fully translate into elected office. As Veena Poonacha points out, Indian women are active in peasant, tribal, labour, women's civil rights and environmental movements. They were also active in an anti-alcohol movement in Uttar Pradesh in the late 1990s, in which 'women have attacked liquor shops armed with rods, sticks and brooms' (Poonacha 1997a: 17). Poonacha argues that the anti-alcohol movement has prompted co-operation among women and led to rural women setting up credit co-operatives. These have enabled newly literate women to enter local politics.

The Panchayati Raj Act of April 1993 and the 73rd and 74th amendments to the Constitution pushed through progressive decentralization and devolution of power to local village communities. At this level, 33 per cent of seats are reserved for scheduled castes, 33 per cent for scheduled tribes, and 33 per cent for women. ('Scheduled' here means those groups specified by the government.) While the reservations for castes and tribes can be varied according to local populations, and are time-limited, the reservation for women is fixed and permanent, and is not a barrier to women seeking election to other seats (Poonacha 1997a: 20). As a result of the legislation, around one million women have been elected to panchayats and municipal bodies.

Despite the creation of legal measures to facilitate women's participation, analysts indicate a range of obstacles and problems for women seeking political office. Poonacha points out that government is enthusiastic about passing legislation that appears to favour women, and extends its own powers to punish law-breakers, but is much less keen to implement social legislation that would actually encourage change in gender relations

(Poonacha 1997a: 10). The political changes legislated for villages are being implemented against a background of caste and gender prejudice, in which women who seek office independently are subject to ridicule and informal systems of community control. A common practice is for men to attempt to subvert the reservations by putting forward women from their families for election. Thakkar and Gawankar describe how, having achieved the election of women from their families, men then act for them. The women are not informed of procedures, and may not attend meetings or join in debate. They may be required to sign documents that are sent to them at home without knowing what it is that they are signing. Husbands may accompany or even replace their wives at meetings (Thakkar and Gawankar 1997: 92).

There are problems of caste and tradition. If a woman from a low caste is elected, she may be boycotted; hence, most women who contest elections are from elite families with political connections (Thakkar and Gawankar 1997: 95). Traditionally, women sit on the floor while men sit on chairs, and this causes problems when politicians have chairs! The writers describe one situation where a woman was elected to an office that had a chair reserved for it. Despite resistance from the men, she insisted on sitting on the chair. At the next meeting the chair had disappeared. If a woman decides to run for office independently of family and connections, men may try to obstruct her by misinforming her about procedures; she may find herself the victim of character assassination and even of criminalization (Desai 1997: 52). If a woman insists on acting independently, she may find that the men just leave.

Nevertheless, women are elected to local assemblies, and their presence will have an effect over time. The obstacles that Desai points to – illiteracy, lack of exposure to public proceedings and lack of confidence, as well as fear of retribution for daring to step outside of tradition – will diminish with time and practice (Desai 1997: 52). Desai identifies a clear set of goals pursued by elected women. These include the supply of drinking water, the installation of pumps, the construction of toilets, closing liquor shops, building playgrounds, and the transfer of land rights to women (Desai 1997: 53). These goals are also identified by Bharat Dogra, a journalist who recognized the problems of the reserved seats initiative, but found a number of determined and successful elected women.

He describes how individual women have resisted the corruption that plagues Indian local government, used their budgets carefully, and cleared the debts of their locality. The women he interviewed pursued different goals from the men elected in their areas, particularly combating domestic violence, controlling the sale and consumption of alcohol, safeguarding drinking water, improving sanitation, establishing girls' education, and catering for women's health and maternity.

Women are generally known to have a greater capacity for resolving disputes. When she was chairperson Suriya Begum's door always remained open for many victims of domestic violence. She helped resolve many disputes. Pushpa Rana prevailed upon villagers to first settle all disputes locally and go to the police only if village level efforts failed. The result was that the money people had to spend on paying bribes to the police and middlemen was saved. (Dogra 2001)

Women in Asia achieve rather better representation at local level than at national. In 2001 the Philippines had 16.5 per cent women; Thailand 18.1; China 22.1; Nepal 24.1; Vietnam

Table 16.2 Women elected to local government in Asia, 2001

Country	%
Pakistan	25
Philippines	16.5
Thailand	18.1
China	22.1
Nepal	24.1
Vietnam	26.6
India	33.0
Bangladesh	33.3
Sri Lanka	2.0
Japan	6.2

Source: Drage 2001

26.6; India 33; and Bangladesh 33.3. The last two of these are the result of the imposition of reserved seats. Although not ground-breaking, these results match much of the rest of the world, and show gradual improvement. Sri Lanka at 2 per cent and Japan at 6.2 per cent, on the other hand, are very poor (Drage 2001).

The military government of Pakistan announced plans in 2000 to revise regulations so that local government had greater power. The three levels of local government have reserved seats for women as part of a complex structure of seat reservations for peasants, workers and minorities; so giving more power to local government will give more power to women. However, local elections have been held irregularly for many years, and, despite the efforts of different groups to encourage women's participation, there are no reliable statistics prior to the late 1990s, and recent statistics are patchy. It looks as if about 25 per cent of councillors are women, but this is a rather approximate calculation because of the gaps in the information (Country Report: Pakistan).

The two main political parties in Bangladesh have female leaders (from elite political families), there are thirty reserved seats for women in the national parliament, and one-third of seats in local government are reserved. More than 12,000 women were elected to local government posts in the 1998 elections. Women's active participation is considered to be important, and the political parties have women's wings to encourage this. There is also pressure from non-governmental and women's organizations. Local governments have initiated programmes to encourage women's participation, including micro-credit and training programmes. There are also gender programmes aimed at sensitizing the general population and local government officers to gender issues (Country Report: Bangladesh).

Some Other Countries

The development of international governmental and non-governmental organizations has been influential in increasing the visibility of women and their concerns in less economically developed countries. The gender initiatives of the United Nations, particularly the

Platform for Action deriving from the Beijing Conference, have been important, and so have European Union programmes. Ghana, like other African countries, has been encouraged to embark on democratic decentralization by European assistance programmes promoting development and poverty reduction. Sex equality, including political participation, has been given increasing priority by European donors, since women figure very highly among poor groups in the population.

Women's poverty is associated with their limited access to social services, including education. Ofei-Aboagye argues that provisions made in the process of decentralization, including the use of local languages, should make it easier for women to participate in local politics. Only 3 per cent of elected officials were women in 1994, which increased to 5 per cent in 1998. In 1998 central government directed that 30 per cent of seats in local assemblies should be reserved for women, although this does not appear to have had much effect as yet. Ofei-Aboagye gives the usual range of explanations for the low numbers of women: lack of money for campaigning; time constraints because of having to combine family, economic and political roles; lack of skills; and the fear of male intimidation. She adds that in Ghana politics is seen as both dirty – and thus unsuitable for women – and a male domain. Men are therefore unwilling to have the women of their families involved in politics. The low number of women elected is compounded by the low number of women in the administration of local government (Ofei-Aboagye 2000).

The international organizations involved in Ghana do not just make demands on the local people; they also make suggestions about how women's participation can be increased and organize programmes to that end. Suggestions show considerable creativity – for example, not just supporting the elected women, but also targeting their spouses, collaborating with women in the media to get their support for women politicians, and using existing structures of influence to lobby chiefs and traditional authorities on women's behalf (Ofei-Aboagye 2000: 7).

According to IULA, the Middle East has the lowest representation of women in local government in the world – not surprising, since the representation of women at national level is also very low in the region. Its July 2003 newsletter gives the example of two countries: Jordan and Syria. Both countries appear to have good intentions with regard to the election of women: Jordan has put in place a quota system, and Syria has a National Women's Strategy which aims to increase women's participation to 30 per cent.

Jordan has a mixed system of elected and appointed posts. Although the 2003 elections resulted in the election of only five women councillors in the 554 municipal council seats, each municipality has to appoint one woman member. This resulted in ninety-nine additional women councillors and one woman mayor (*Women in Local Decision-Making Newsletter*, July 2003, IULA). The proportion of women councillors in Syria is low, 6.6 per cent, although the likelihood of a female candidate being elected is quite good: 879 of the 2,000 female candidates were elected in 1999.

Conclusion

As with central government, so with local governments, we see that the Nordic countries have higher levels of representation than elsewhere. As in central government, parties are the key determinant of representation. In the Nordic countries there is broad party consensus around the goal of sex equality, while in Russia this is of little concern. Reserved seats in the local governments of India and Bangladesh have had remarkable effects on the number of women, although it will take time for the political culture to catch up. Communication between local government organizations through the IULA appears to be influential, as are the policies of international political organizations in generating change, especially in less developed countries.

FURTHER READING

The literature here is rather dispersed. International organizations are invaluable sources of data and commentary – here are reports from the United Nations, the Inter-Parliamentary Union and the International Union of Local Authorities. Dominelli and Jonsdottir's article on the creation of the women's list in Iceland tells an interesting story of Icelandic local politics, while Jones and Jonasdottir's collection is one of the few to look at a number of countries. Jharta looks at women at all levels of Indian politics.

Dominelli, L. and Jonsdottir, G. 1988: Feminist Political Organisation in Iceland: Some Reflections on the Experience of Kwenna Frambothid. *Feminist Review*, 28: 36–60.
Drage, J. 2001: *Women in Local Government in Asia and the Pacific: A Comparative Analysis of Thirteen Countries*. UN ESCAP. <http://www.cities-localgovernments.org/101a/upload/docs/womeninurbanlocalgovernment(comparativeanalysis 13countries).pdf>
International Union of Local Authorities 1998: *Women in Local Government*. Sweden: IULA.
Inter-Parliamentary Union 1993: *Women and Political Power*. Geneva: Reports and Documents 19.
Jharta, B. 1996: *Women and Politics in India*. New Delhi: Deep and Deep.
Jones, K. and Jonasdottir, A. (eds) 1985b: *The Political Interests of Gender*. London: Sage.

PART VI

Women in International Governmental Organizations

WOMEN AND THE EUROPEAN UNION

17

Introduction

So far, this book has been about women in elected office. Now that we come to look at the European Union (EU), this takes us to the women elected to the European Parliament (EP). However, the EP is not like the parliaments of nation-states. Members of the European Parliament (MEPs) are elected, and the process of election is one that may be becoming more important in European countries as the role of the Parliament is debated. However, the powers of the EP and its members are rather dwarfed by the powers of the Commission, members of which are appointed. Here, we also take account of bureaucracies and examine policies, although previous sections have not done so. This chapter will describe the structure of the EU before looking at the membership of women in the EP, and the importance of the EU in promoting sex equality. The EU is of growing importance in both Europe and the world. It has five main component parts: the European Parliament, the European Commission, the Council of the European Union (formerly the Council of Ministers), the Court of Justice, and the Court of Auditors.

Structure of the European Union

The number of member states in the EU increased to twenty-five from fifteen in 2004, when ten Central and Eastern European countries joined. Initially established as the European Coal and Steel Community in 1951, what is now the EU has developed over the intervening years through a series of treaties. Most important among these are the Treaty of Rome, 1957, which established the European Economic Community; the Maastricht Treaty on European Union, 1992, which established the European Community and put in place the mechanisms by which this later became the European Union; the Treaty of Amsterdam, 1997, which amended and renumbered the existing treaties; and the Treaty of Nice, 2001, which merged the existing treaties into one consolidated version.

The EU has thus developed into an increasingly encompassing set of economic, social and political agreements, although there is ongoing conflict about what should be its goals and powers. Member states are still more powerful than the Union, as demonstrated by the relative powers of the Council, the Commission, and the European Parliament (see below).

The framework of the EU was established by the Treaty of Rome in 1957. This set out the structure and relationships between the European Parliament, the European Commission, and the Council of Ministers. Although modified by subsequent treaties, the basic structure of the EU and the relationships between the different constituent parts remains the same. The Parliament is the only element that is democratically elected, and therefore representative of the people of Europe in any conventional sense; the Commission is comprised of appointed Commissioners and bureaucrats, while the Council is made up of ministers from the governments of the member states.

The European Parliament (EP)

Unlike a regular parliament, the EP has no legislative power, no ruling party and no formal opposition. Its decisions are made in committees rather than plenary sessions, and tend to be reached through compromise and consensus. It possesses four sets of powers. First is to examine and adopt (or not) European legislation, as recommended by the Commission. The co-decision procedure established by the Amsterdam Treaty sets out the terms of this power, which is shared with the Council. Second is to approve (or not) the EU budget. Third is to exercise democratic control over the other EU institutions, which it does by interviewing and approving new Commissioners, monitoring the procedures of the Commission, monitoring the work of the Council, and setting up committees of enquiry. Part of its democratic function is the power to call for the mass resignation of the Commission. Fourth is to assent (or not) to important international agreements, such as the inclusion of new member states. Generally, its powers are limited to advice and supervision. However, these have developed over time and continue to do so, making the Parliament an increasingly significant political location.

The Parliament is headed by a president and twelve vice-presidents, who direct the activities of the Parliament and supervise the administration. At the end of 2003, 31 per cent of elected Members of the European Parliament were women.

The European Commission (EC)

The European Commission is the real powerhouse of the EU. Here lies the power to initiate and enforce legislation, to oversee expenditure, and to administer the decisions of the Council of the European Union. Its members, Commissioners, are appointed (not elected – appointment may be a reward or a consolation prize given by a national government in recognition of service) by member states for a four-year term. The larger member states have two Commissioners, the smaller have just one. Prior to enlargement in 2004, there were twenty Commissioners, five of whom were women, from Spain, Luxembourg, Germany, Sweden and Greece. The Commission has a staff of 24,000 civil servants.

The Council of the European Union (formerly the Council of Ministers)

This is where decisions are made. The Council passes or rejects legislation generated by the Commission, sometimes in consultation with the EP. The Council is made up of government ministers from the member states. Although when the Council was established, it was assumed that it would comprise the Foreign Ministers from the different countries, in fact different ministers attend, depending on the subject under discussion. There are nine different Council configurations: General Affairs and External Relations; Economic and Financial Affairs; Employment and Social Policy; Health and Consumer Affairs; Competitiveness; Transport, Telecommunications, and Energy; Agriculture and Fisheries; Environment; and Education, Youth, and Culture. These are attended by the specialist minister from each country. In addition to Council meetings, there are meetings of heads of government two or three times a year. The Council of Ministers is supported and assisted by the Committee of Permanent Representatives, a body of civil servants from the member states.

The Council has six areas of responsibility: to pass European laws, often jointly with the EP; to co-ordinate the economic policies of member states; to conclude agreements between the EU and other states or international organizations; to approve the budget jointly with the EP; to develop the EU's common foreign and security policy; and to co-ordinate co-operation between the national courts and police forces on criminal matters.

The number of women in the Council depends on the numbers of women who are heads of government or senior ministers in member states.

European Court of Justice

The European Court of Justice interprets treaties and other EU legislation. It is the final court of appeal with regard to EU law, and its judgements are binding. The court consists of one judge from each member state and five advocates-general. The advocates-general represent the public interest and give their opinion after the case has been heard, but before the judges consider their opinion.

The court has proved important in enforcing equal pay and equal treatment directives on member states.

The European Court of Auditors

This body ensures that EU funds are spent legally, economically, and for the intended purpose.

According to Vallance and Davies (writing before the European Economic Community became the European Union, as a result of the Maastricht Treaty),

> Most MEPs believe that the Parliament should be given legislative power, and indeed will have to be given that power if public confidence in the EEC is to be retained. The Parliament, they argue, is the only democratically elected institution of the EEC and it therefore seems anomalous that the non-elected executive should also be to all intents and purposes the legislature. Others, who are opposed to strengthening the EEC, believe that to give the Parliament legislative power would mean the end of national sovereignty since there would be no argument against its legitimacy on any subject. (Vallance and Davies 1986: 34)

The Parliament is, in fact, gradually accumulating more powers, especially since the Treaty of Amsterdam.

Equality and the European Union

The goal of equality has been explicit in the existence and activities of the EU from its inception: equality between participant nations in order to achieve stability and prosperity. Sex equality within nation-states in pursuit of the same goals was made explicit in Article 119 of the Treaty of Rome (1957), which became Article 141 of the Amsterdam Treaty (1997), and a range of subsequent directives. Directives and rules have been developed to outlaw unequal treatment on the basis of sex, race, religion, sexuality, disability and age. While many of these are aimed at the workplace (along with measures to protect part-time workers and to enhance job security), they do extend to social rights, in terms of welfare benefits, pensions and so on, and tentatively into the political arena. Although there is no binding provision at EU level for the achievement of equal representation, the Council of Europe adopted a recommendation on balanced participation of women in decision-making in 2003. Further, equalities directives have been interpreted to suggest this, and EU institutions have adopted equality in decision-making positions as a goal for the Parliament, committees and the Commission.

The Role of the European Parliament

Although of increasing importance, the Parliament is often overlooked in discussion of what the EU does, since the activities of the Commission and the Council are so much more in the public eye. From the perspective of women and women's issues, the Commission's importance is undeniable: its equality agenda has changed the ground rules of women's employment, welfare entitlement and family life across member states. Women have found employment in the Commission, and mechanisms for women's advancement have been established there. However, women have also made inroads into the less analysed EP.

The EP is not like any other parliament – rather an obvious statement, but one that is of great importance for the presence, politics and policies of women who are or wish to be MEPs. The EU is of increasing importance to the politics and society of member states, and so, therefore, is the role of the EP. Hilary Footitt considers that 'the European Parliament operates within what might be called a narrative of eccentricity. Although often described as important to the overall development of the EU, its importance is understood in undetermined and vague ways. The European Parliament is placed outside "normal" political processes' (Footitt 2002: 30). The European Parliament has been given very little attention in the literature of integration; much more attention has been paid to the role of the Commission.

In part this is because of the peculiarity of the Parliament. It moves between Brussels and Strasbourg, thus lacking a clear geographically situated identity; instead of parties, it has transnational political groups formed on the basis of broad ideological positions; instead of party competition, opposition and confrontation, it exhibits a rather more consensual pursuit of rational solutions to problems; rather than focusing on issues of immediate importance, it focuses on systemic change in relations between itself and other EU institutions. Thus, the EP is generally regarded as 'sui generis, as operating in an entirely different context, and with very different processes from those of national parliaments' (Footitt 2002: 310–31).

Women Members of the European Parliament

The role of MEPs is evolving. MEPs are not yet considered to be anything like as important as representatives in a national assembly, and the decision-making powers of the EP are limited by comparison with the Commission and the Council. However, this is changing as the role of the EU is continually renegotiated.

The workload of an MEP is more structured than that of an MP, but it entails a lot of travel (although, unlike their colleagues in the UK Parliament, representatives are adequately supported by staff and expense accounts). Parliament operates on a four-week rota: two weeks in Strasbourg and two weeks in Brussels. In addition, there are parliamentary (political) group meetings in London and Brussels.

Plenary sessions take place once a month for a week in Strasbourg; committees meet at least once a month in Brussels; each MEP is on at least one committee. Parliamentary groups meet for two or three days in the week before each session in London or Brussels. In addition, MEPs either have other responsibilities in the parliament, or are appointed to one of the many delegations that maintain contact with countries that trade with the EU.

So the life of an MEP encompasses responsibilities and travel between London, Brussels, Strasbourg and her constituency. This suggests the potential for considerable tension between the career and the family and private life of a representative.

The potential of the EP has gained impetus since direct elections were introduced in 1979. As a new political space, without traditions and with no historical role, it might be expected that women (and other often marginalized groups) would find fewer obstacles

Table 17.1 Women in the European Parliament, 1999

Country	% women
Finland	43.8
France	42.5
Sweden	40.9
Belgium	40.0
Germany	38.4
Austria	38.1
Denmark	37.5
Netherlands	35.5
Ireland	33.3
Luxembourg	33.3
Spain	31.3
United Kingdom	24.1
Portugal	24.0
Greece	16.0
Italy	11.5
Total	31.0

Source: IPU website, June 2004

to office here than in the parliaments of member states. For women from most countries this has proved true.

The number of women in the EP has been growing gradually since its creation. Between 1952 and 1958 the Common Assembly included one woman among seventy-eight representatives (1.3 per cent). This increased to 3 per cent in the period 1958–1972 and to 5.5 per cent in 1978. Once direct elections had been introduced, the numbers of women leapt to 16.8 per cent in 1979, 25 per cent in 1994, and 31 per cent in 1999 (Norris 1997b: 211; IPU website). Although this is a steady improvement, it is uneven, and the average is considerably smaller than the percentage of women from the most egalitarian countries. The countries achieving the most equal representation have little room for improvement; this means that improvement has to come from the lowest-achieving countries that are most resistant to change. Norris argues that 'based on trends since the first direct elections, we can estimate that women will achieve parity in the European Parliament in the year 2044' (Norris 1997b: 211).

To illustrate the differences, in 1999 Finland elected the highest percentage of women, 43.8, and Italy the lowest, 11.5 (see table 17.1). The proportion of women elected in any country tends to reflect that in the national parliament, with the Nordic countries returning the highest proportions of women and southern European countries the lowest. The proportion elected to the EP tends to be slightly higher than that elected to the home parliament. The UK, for example, returned 24.1 per cent women to the EP in 1999, in comparison with 20 per cent in the UK Parliament at the time (although in the UK the difference may be exaggerated by the use of PR for EU elections as against FPP for national).

Looking more closely at representation, the UK had eighty-seven seats in the 1999 Parliament (see table 17.2). These seats were shared between ten parties. The Conservative

Table 17.2 Women from the UK in the European Parliament

Party	Number of men	Number of women	Total	% women
Conservative	33	3	36	8
Labour	18	11	29	38
Liberal Democrat	5	5	10	50
UKIP	3	0	3	0
SNP	2	0	2	0
Plaid Cymru	1	1	2	50
Green	0	2	2	100
SDLP	1	0	1	0
DUP	1	0	1	0
UUP	1	0	1	0
Total	65	22	87	25

Source: Fawcett Society website

Party had the largest share at thirty-six seats, of which only 8 per cent were held by women (reflecting the representation of Conservative women in the UK Parliament). Labour had the next largest block of seats at twenty-nine, 38 per cent of which were held by women. The Liberal Democrats had ten seats, half of which were held by women, the result of the Liberal Democrats alternating men and women (zipping) on their party list. The Green Party had only two seats, both of which were held by women, giving them a startling 100 per cent, while Plaid Cymru, with one of its two seats occupied by a woman, achieved 50 per cent. Other parties had three or fewer seats and no women (Fawcett Society website).

Accounting for the higher numbers of women in the EP

As the example of the UK demonstrates, higher proportions of women are elected to the EP in parties that are more to the left of the political spectrum. When they did their research in 1986, Vallance and Davies found that the highest proportion of women was to be found in the Rainbow Group of Ecology and Green parties (25 per cent) and the lowest in the European Right (5 per cent), with the liberal and socialist groups having around 20 per cent (Vallance and Davies 1986: 60). This trend has continued, and in the 1999 Parliament the highest percentages of women were to be found in the Green and European Free Alliance Group, 43.5, and the Socialists, 37.6.

Vallance and Davies give a number of reasons that may account for the relatively high number of women in the European Parliament (compared with national parliaments). First, since it does not legislate, and the party groupings are multiple and loosely aligned, there is little debate and almost no confrontation. Instead, the Parliament is run largely through committees, and the processes tend to involve clause-by-clause study of proposals. Once a proposal gets to the floor of the Parliament, most of the differences of opinion have already been dealt with. It may be that this way of working is more hospitable to women, or perhaps less challenging for men (Vallance and Davies 1986: 8).

Second, Vallance and Davies suggest that the nature and image of the EP itself makes it more accessible to women: 'the rather ambiguous status of European politics in general and of its Parliament in particular. To many people it seemed – and still does – a somewhat remote institution with undefined powers and little importance. The European Parliament, after all, does not legislate. Its relationship to the Commission and the Council of Ministers is confused for most people' (Vallance and Davies 1986: 9). Here the suggestion is that there is less competition for a place in an assembly that does not carry obvious access to status and power. If men are less intent on achieving positions that carry little public recognition, status or opportunity for advancement, women may have greater room to manoeuvre.

Their third suggestion is along the same lines. Since this was a new parliament, all the important politicians were already busy doing politics in their own countries. All the political parties of the member states, except for the British Labour Party, allow dual mandate – that is, membership of both the national and the European parliaments – but the pressure of doing both jobs is prohibitive. Selection for candidacy of the European Parliament is seen as something of a consolation prize, so women who wanted to go there faced little competition, and women who had been unsuccessful in selection for national candidacy might see this as a viable alternative to banging their heads against the brick walls of party intransigence! At the same time, the prejudice against women of selectors was presumably mitigated by their belief that these were not important posts.

Fourth, and also related to the newness of the parliament, it had no long-established traditions of male presence or masculine culture, or of excluding women. It was not built on the model of a men's club (Vallance and Davies 1986: 10).

Fifth is the newness of the electoral system. Prior to 1979, MEPs were chosen delegates from their home government. When elections were introduced in 1979, there were no incumbents for women to challenge, and parties had to find a large number of candidates in a short space of time, when most of the proven political players were already engaged in the national game, thus opening up a space for women. Moreover, an electoral system had to be agreed. Since most of the countries operated some form of proportional representation, this was the obvious way to go – despite the protests of UK parties. As discussed in previous chapters, PR is generally seen as providing more access to women than first-past-the-post, so the eventual adoption of PR for the election of UK and French MEPs was a bonus for women of those countries.

Finally, Vallance and Davies suggest that the organization and resources of the EP make it a comfortable place to work for both men and women. Moreover, it conducts its business according to a planned, predictable timetable. These characteristics may make it particularly hospitable to women, who may have less experience, money and time than men, and therefore appreciate having facilities provided and a timetable that allows them to plan their family responsibilities (Vallance and Davies 1986: 14).

Who are the women who become MEPs?

Analysing the women who became MEPs, Vallance and Davies found that their early careers were very similar to those of national MPs: they had started with voluntary party work at the constituency level and moved on to involvement in national politics (Vallance and Davies 1986: 39). Many MEPs had previous experience in national politics before entering the EP, whereas others, some 20 per cent, had gone into local government from party work before entering the EP. A small number, 5 per cent, had been employed by the EEC before entering the Parliament, while 4 per cent had been civil servants in their home countries, and 3 per cent had been employed by trades unions (Vallance and Davies 1986: 41).

Most women MEPs were graduates, 62 per cent. There was a high number of former teachers or academics, 23 per cent; of journalists, 15 per cent; and of lawyers, 10 per cent. Only 4 per cent of female MEPs regarded themselves as businesswomen (Vallance and Davies 1986: 42).

The EP has had only one woman as President, Simone Veil (1979–81). Vallance and Davies found that women received rather less than their fair share of places on EP delegations to other countries (1986: 62). There is at least one woman on each committee, although women tend to be found more on 'soft' committees: those dealing with social issues such as Social Affairs (23 per cent in 1986), Environment (26 per cent in 1986) and Youth (16 per cent in 1986), although they have become more of a presence on 'harder' committees such as Transport (1 per cent) and Economy (14 per cent). At the time of the research, six of the seventeen committees were chaired by women. These included External Economic Relations, Legal Affairs, and Development and Co-operation, as well as Women's Rights and Youth.

Sex Equality Bodies

In order to ascertain and pursue sex equality and women's interests, specialist bodies have been created in both the EP and the Commission. The first parliamentary body with special responsibility for women was an ad hoc committee created in 1979 to prepare for a parliamentary debate on the situation of women in Europe. Of the thirty-five members of the committee, twenty-five were women. The resulting report was presented to parliament in 1981, and many of its recommendations were incorporated into the New Community Action Programme for Equal Opportunities 1982–5, issued by the Commission. Among other things, the committee recommended the establishment of a permanent committee on the situation of women. This became the eighteen-member Committee of Enquiry into the Situation of Women in Europe. In 1984 the Committee of Enquiry became the Committee on Women's Rights.

The European Commission is where legislation is initiated and implemented; therefore the positioning of an equal opportunities body within the Commission is vital. The Equal Opportunities Unit was created within the Directorate-General for Employment, Industrial Relations and Social Affairs in 1976. It has responsibility for ensuring that member states comply with the Directives on equal treatment and equal opportunities, and for encouraging the integration of women into the labour market. It is also responsible for implementation of the Community Framework Strategy on gender equality (see below). There is also the Commissioners' Group on Equality, comprising the President of the

Commission and three Commissioners. This group has a duty to oversee equal opportunities between men and women within the Commission, and to monitor mainstreaming of gender perspectives into all services and policies (European Women's Lobby website).

Within the Council the equalities body is the Advisory Committee on Equal Opportunities between Women and Men, established in 1981. This is composed of expert ministerial representatives from the member states, and works closely with the Equal Opportunities Unit. It meets regularly to give opinions to the European Commission on major new policies that have implications for women.

Thus, equality issues are explicitly included in EU business by the creation of specific institutions. According to Footitt, 'some of the major work on women in Europe has concerned the equality agenda of the EU, with scholars suggesting that the EU – a legal structure of integration – has been a particularly propitious site for the development of women's rights and for the production of legal texts on equal rights/treatment for women'. (Footitt 2002: 25). There are ongoing debates about the best way to achieve equality. One key issue is whether specialist units are the way forward or 'mainstreaming'. Mainstreaming has become the dominant theme since 1995 – of which, more below.

Sex Equality Legislation and Directives

Catherine Hoskyns, who has written extensively on the EU, analyses its policy agenda and its ambivalences: on the one hand, it provides binding rules and offers opportunities for different systems of law to interact; on the other, the rules are hard to apply, and provide only limited solutions to the needs of particular groups of women (Hoskyns 1996a: 13). Hoskyns suggests that the EU has proved to be a site in which women's rights can develop because of its complexity. Although women and gender issues are not central to EU concerns, there are spaces into which they have crept. In this analysis, 'women are located at the edges and borders of the EU, working hard at infiltrating their concerns out to the rest of the institutional space' (Footitt 2002: 26).

The founding treaty of the EU, the Treaty of Rome (1957), included Article 119, which outlawed discrimination in rates of pay between men and women in all member states. This was weakly implemented, and adopted less than enthusiastically by member states – for example, it was not until 1974 that the UK implemented sex discrimination legislation. Attitudes within both the EU and member states have gradually hardened. From 1974 it has been accepted that Article 119 should not be narrowly interpreted to apply only to economic issues, but rather should be taken to have broad social implications (Vallance and Davies 1986: 75). When the Treaty of Amsterdam came into force in 1999, Article 119 became Article 141, consolidating previous case law of the European Court of Justice on equal pay, and adding a reference to work of equal value, a new legal basis for the development of equal opportunity legislation for men and women in employment, and a provision that allows member states to implement positive discrimination measures (European Women's Lobby website).

Since the Treaty of Rome, a number of Directives (European legislative acts) have been issued that have had considerable impact on women's rights in member states (see table

Table 17.3 EU Directives

Year	Directive	Subject of Directive
1975	75/117/EEC	Equal pay
1976	76/207/EEC	Equal treatment
1978	79/7/EEC	Equal welfare
1986	86/378/EEC	Equality in private sector
1986	86/613/EEC	Equality for the self-employed
1992	92/85/EEC	Protection of pregnant women
1996	96/34/EEC	Parental leave
1998	97/80/EEC	Indirect discrimination
2000	2000/443/EC	Race/ethnicity
2000	2000/78/EC	Religion/belief/ age/sexual orientation
2002		Sexual harassment

Source: European Women's Lobby website

17.3). The 1975 Directive on Equal Pay (75/117/EEC) closed loopholes in equal pay leg-islation throughout Europe by asserting the principle of equal pay for work of equal value. This was augmented by the 1976 Equal Treatment Directive (76/207/EEC), which states that equal treatment means more than the absence of discrimination, thus enabling affirmative action. These were followed by the 1978 Directive (79/7/EEC) that covered equality in social security and access to welfare benefits such as invalidity, old age, unem-ployment and sickness. These three directives are key, not only to women's equality and welfare in the EU, but also to the expanding role of the EU from the economies into the societies of the member states.

The next tranche of legislation took place from 1986. The first of these Directives extended the scope of the 1978 Directive to cover much of the private sector (86/378/EEC). The next extended the principle of equal treatment to the self-employed, including those in agriculture, and the protection of pregnant women and mothers (86/613/EEC). This was followed in 1992 by a further Directive aimed at protecting preg-nant women from hazardous working conditions (92/85/EEC), and another in 1996 secur-ing parental leave (96/34/EEC). In 1998 a Directive addressed cases of sex discrimination and the problem of the burden of proof resting with the complainant (usually an indi-vidual coming up against an organization). The Directive shifts the burden of proof some-what, enabling member states in certain circumstances to require the defending party to prove that they have not violated the principle of equal treatment. This Directive also establishes the definition of indirect discrimination for the first time (97/80/EC) (European Women's Lobby website).

Two Directives in 2000 attempted to further implement the general principles of equality contained in Article 141. The first of these implemented equal treatment irrespective of racial or ethnic origin (2000/443/EC), and the second prohibited discrimination in employment on the basis of racial or ethnic origin, religion or belief, age, or sexual orientation (2000/78/EC). Further, in 2002 the 1976 Directive was amended to define sexual harassment and recognize it as a form of sexual discrimination. It also includes increased employment safeguards for parental leave.

Taken together, these Directives, supported by the European Court of Justice and by the European Charter of Fundamental Rights, constitute a strong framework for the achievement of equality between men and women. Their primary focus is on the workplace, in terms of equal pay, equal treatment and opposition to discrimination. But this has been extended to include those elements of the broader society that impact on employment: welfare benefits, pensions, consideration of pregnancy and parental responsibilities. Member states are obliged to conform to the Directives, and can be taken to the European Court if they do not do so; but how they choose to conform is not prescribed.

The broader employment and social strategies of the EU have implications for women, such as the protection extended to part-time workers and measures that give workers greater job security. It has also legislated and created programmes to combat human trafficking, particularly relevant to women who are trafficked not just as labour but also for sexual exploitation.

Action Programmes

The Equal Opportunities Unit, working with the Advisory Committee, has developed a series of Medium Term Community Action Programmes, to support the implementation of EU equalities Directives. The first Community Action Programme on the Promotion of Equal Opportunities for Women and Men (1982–5) attempted to achieve equality and equal treatment by using positive action to strengthen individual rights. This was done through the enactment of law and the creation of networks of independent experts across the member states to support the programme (Rees 1998: 60). The second programme (1986–90) followed the strategy of the first, did more to establish networks, and prompted actions directed at particular target groups, such as single parents. It revolved around seven key themes: law, education and training, employment, new technologies, social security, family responsibilities and consciousness-raising.

The third programme (1991–5) was aimed at promoting social and economic equality through entrenching equalities policies in all the policies of the EU and member states, and the fourth (1996–2000) aimed to 'promote the integration of the equal opportunities agenda into the preparation, implementation and monitoring of all EU and Member State activities, while being mindful of the sensitives of culture within Member States' (Rees 1998: 66). With each programme the commitment of the EU to sex equality both deepened and widened. Although equality in the labour market is still key, awareness that this cannot be achieved without wider social and political change has shaped the newer, more extensive strategies.

Mainstreaming

The third and fourth action programmes were influenced by the growing commitment to mainstreaming as the key equality strategy in the global policy community. Main-streaming is an approach to promoting equality based on the argument that equalities policy and procedures should not be separate from other policy areas, but should be inte-grated across the policy agenda. This is underpinned by the contention that all good policy is policy that takes account of equal opportunity and access. The rise of main-streaming to a position of dominance has been contested. Enthusiasts have suggested that all policies, activities and specialists should be mainstreamed, and that specialist com-mittees, departments and units should be disbanded. This argument is based on the premiss that specialist groupings lead to ghettoization and relieve everyone else of respon-sibility for equality. Opponents of mainstreaming have argued that without specialist groups expertise would be lost, and the result of everyone having responsibility would be that no one took responsibility. The outcome that seems to have emerged is something of a middle way, with some specialist units continuing to exist in parallel with broad main-streaming policies and initiatives.

Conclusion

The EU is still a new and evolving political initiative. Its ambition and scope are unique, but there is a lot of disagreement between and within the governments and populations of member states about what it should be and do. Its extensive equalities agenda has been contentious, with governments like that of the UK resisting the potential costs of imple-mentation. Differences between the member states over equality are very real and lead to tensions: the pro-active Nordic approach is in radical contrast to those of the far more traditional cultures of Greece and even France.

The policies are forward-looking, and there is considerable impetus behind them, even if they are not central to the goals of the organization. Similarly, women's participation in the parliament has been greater than in the government of many member states, and this becomes more significant as the role of the parliament increases. The number of women participating in the Council depends on the number of women who are Heads of State, Heads of Government, or Ministers in the relevant areas in member states. Given the percentage of women in the Cabinets of the member states, we can expect that the number of women in Council will usually be quite low, although on the increase.

FURTHER READING

There is a tendency for people writing about the EU to adopt the language of the EU – which does not make for easy reading! Catherine Hoskyns has researched and written extensively in this area, while remaining readable. The Lovenduski and Stephenson text is invaluable as a guide to the literature, and Theresa Rees focuses on the specific issue of mainstreaming. The EU publishes a lot about itself, both on the internet and on paper.

Footitt, H. 2002: *Women, Europe and the New Language of Politics*. London: Continuum.
Hoskyns, C. 1996: *Integrating Gender*. London: Verso.
Lovenduski, J. and Stephenson, S. 1999: *Women in Decision-Making: Report on Existing Research in the EU*. Brussels: EC, Employment and Social Affairs.
Rees, T. 1998: *Mainstreaming Equality in the European Union*. London: Routledge.

WOMEN AND THE UNITED NATIONS

18

Introduction

The United Nations (UN) was created in the aftermath of the Second World War as a replacement for the League of Nations and in order to encourage and support the 'peoples of the world to live peacefully in a democratic world community' (Open Letter, 12 February 1946, A.PV.29 United Nations). Over the years it has increased in size, so that now almost all the countries in the world are members. The UN is served by appointed delegates from member nations rather than elected representatives, and these seldom appear as individuals or personalities: they are delegated by their home countries to act on instruction. In response to the particular nature of the General Assembly, although we look briefly at the numbers of women included in it, this chapter takes account of bureaucracies and examines policies, unlike previous chapters. Here we shall look briefly at the structure of the UN before considering the role of women in the General Assembly, the sex equality organizations within the UN, the creation and implementation of the International Convention on the Elimination of All Forms of Discrimination against Women, and the organization of international conferences on women.

The Structure of the UN

The UN attempts to bind nations to international agreements, to maintain international order, keep the peace and foster development, but its powers are limited in relation to the autonomy of the member states.

The main representative body of the UN is the General Assembly, in which all member states have a seat. The General Assembly meets every year from September to January in plenary session. It also convenes special sessions every few years on general topics. Its main power lies in control of the finances for UN programmes; it can pass resolutions on particular issues, but these are not binding. Most of the work of the UN is conducted through committees. The president and twenty-one vice-presidents make up the General Committee, and there are six other key committees: Disarmament and International Security; Economic and Financial; Social, Humanitarian and Cultural; Special Political and Decolonization; Financial and Budgetary; and Legal. The General Assembly also co-ordinates the programmes undertaken by such specialist agencies as the World Health Organization (WHO), the United Nations Children's Fund (UNICEF), the United Nations Educational, Scientific, and Cultural Organization (UNESCO), and the United Nations Higher Commission for Refugees (UNHCR), through its Economic and Social Council (ECOSOC).

The other central UN Bodies are the Security Council, the World Court (formerly the International Court of Justice) and the Secretariat. The Security Council is responsible for maintaining world peace and restoring it when it breaks down. It has five permanent and ten non-permanent members, who rotate on the Council for two years at a time. Substantive decisions require nine votes of the fifteen, but each permanent member has a veto. Decisions made here are binding on member states, and the Security Council has considerable power to define the existence and nature of a threat, to structure a response, and to enforce its decision through mandatory Directives to UN members.

The World Court is the judicial arm of the UN, and consists of a panel of fifteen judges elected for nine-year terms by a majority of the members of both the Security Council and the General Assembly. It can act only when states in dispute refer their problem to the Court, and only about one-third of member states recognize the Court's jurisdiction.

The Secretariat is the executive branch of the UN. The Secretary-General of the Secretariat is the nearest thing there is to a president of the world (with a far higher public profile than the President of the General Assembly). This is the bureaucracy for the administration of UN policy and programmes.

UN activities in pursuit of peace and stability have multiplied and diversified over the years. Encouragement of development and democracy have always been key targets, on the assumption that prosperity and democratic equality are antithetical to conflict. Equality between men and women has proved to be important under both headings. In terms of development, it has become clear that women's roles in less developed countries are vital to the subsistence, health, education and thus development of any community. In terms of democracy, women's absence from public decision-making is generally agreed to signal a democratic deficit (UN website).

Sex Equality and the UN

The founding delegates to the first session of the United Nations included a number of women who were already successful and powerful in their own countries. These women ensured that sex equality was included in the founding documents of the organization.

Hence, Article 8 of the UN Charter specifies that men and women are eligible to partic-ipate equally in any capacity in any of the institutions of the UN, and Article 55c asserts that human rights are universal, without distinction of race, sex, language or religion. Two other provisions of the Charter have proved important for women: first, its mandate to promote economic and social development, which has led to the creation of bodies which have funded and supported programmes beneficial to women; and second, Article 71, which created the framework within which non-governmental organizations can acquire consultative status with the UN. This has given a range of women's organizations access to the UN, and has enabled them to inform and shape policy right from the begin-ning. The provisions in the Charter led to the creation of the Commission on the Status of Women (CSW); the CSW then had input to the Universal Declaration of Human Rights. As a result, the Declaration refers to 'human beings', 'everyone' and 'no one', rather than 'men' (UN website).

The UN pursues sex equality in a number of different ways: first, through the creation of UN institutions and agreements directed at equality, particularly the Commission on the Status of Women (CSW), the Department for the Advancement of Women (DAW), and the Convention on the Elimination of All Forms of Discrimination against Women (CEDAW); second, through the policies that underpin its various initiatives around the world, especially, but not exclusively, in less developed countries; and third, through the organization of a series of international conferences on women, especially the Beijing Conference in 1995. A twelve-point Programme for Action emerged from Beijing, to which all participating states were signatories. Signatory states report back every five years on their progress on the twelve points. Beijing + 5 took place in 2000, and Beijing + 10 is in preparation for 2005.

Women in the General Assembly

The first thing to say about women at the United Nations is that it is extremely difficult to find out the proportion of women among delegates to the General Assembly. At the first session of the UN, women were included in eleven of the fifty-one delegations, of whom five were delegates. Together, these women formulated an Open Letter to the Women of the World, which was presented to the General Assembly by Eleanor Roosevelt, representing the USA. The letter announced that '[i]n view of the variety of tasks which women performed so notably and valiantly during the war, we are gratified that seventeen women representatives and advisers, representatives of eleven Member States, are taking part at the beginning of this new phase of International Development' (Open Letter, 12 February 1946, A.PV.29 United Nations). Her optimism was to prove premature.

In 1950 the then Secretary-General reported to the Commission on the Status of Women that at the fourth regular session of the United Nations there were eighty-eight women representatives, alternates and advisers from fifty-nine member states. These were four representatives, from Canada, Chile, India and the United States; nine women alter-nates, two from Sweden and one each from Belgium, Denmark, Mexico, the Netherlands, Norway, the United Kingdom and the Republic of Ireland; eleven women advisers, two each from Australia, Iraq, and the Netherlands, one each from China, France, Israel, the Philippines and Poland.

At this point there had been no woman President, vice-president or chair of any one of the key United Nations Committees; there had been only one vice-chair and one rapporteur on any of the seven main committees. Of the other committees and commissions, none had numbered more than one woman member, and most had numbered none. (Report of the Secretary-General to the CSW on the participation of women in the work of the UN, 16 March 1950, E.CN.6/132).

In 1977 the then Secretary-General again reported on women in the General Assembly (there do not appear to have been any reports in between). Reporting on numbers as of 1974, by this time 7.6 per cent of the delegates from member states were women, as compared to 2.5 per cent in 1948. There was little difference between advanced industrial states and others, or between original and new Members of the United Nations. Only two women had ever held the Presidency: Mrs Vijay Lakshmi Pandit, Member of Parliament and Chairman of the Delegation of India at the 1953 session, and Miss Angie Brooks, Assistant Secretary of State, Liberia, at the 1969 session.

Of the seven main committees, only two had ever had a woman chair. Only the third committee, which deals with humanitarian and cultural questions, had achieved several female chairs and a significant – more than 20 per cent – female membership. Only one woman and two alternates had ever sat on the Security Council; the Economic and Social Council had included 7.3 per cent women overall. However, since there had been 17 per cent in its 52nd session but only 13 per cent in its 54th, an upward trend could not be guaranteed. The Trusteeship Council had included 6.9 per cent women overall, while the International Council of Justice had never included a woman (United Nations 1977).

In a 1989 report the Secretary-General stated that out of 1,689 representatives for 159 delegations, only 337 were women – 20 per cent. Fifty-seven delegations (30 per cent) listed no women, and there were considerable regional differences. While Latin American and Caribbean delegations included 39 per cent women, Western European delegations included 26 per cent, delegations from Africa and the Pacific included 12 per cent women, and Eastern European delegations only 4 per cent (Report of the Secretary-General to the CSW on the first review and appraisal of the implementation of the Nairobi Forward Thinking Strategies, E.CN.6/1990; 5.22.11.1989).

Sex Equality Institutions within the UN

The Commission on the Status of Women (CSW)

The Commission on the Status of Women (CSW) was created right at the start of the UN. Initially it was a Sub-Commission of the Commission on Human Rights, and its first task, in 1946, was to complete a comparative study on the status of women and report to ECOSOC. It reported back in 1947, at which point, in response to pressure from its members, it became an autonomous Commission directly answerable to ECOSOC. It was chaired by Bodily Begtrup, President of the Danish Council of Women, and members included women who had been active in the founding of the UN. As an independent

Commission, CSW was able to set its own agenda and to make proposals directly to ECOSOC.

The CSW had few resources and only a small staff in the Section on the Status of Women within the Secretariat; however, it made up for this with the enthusiasm and commitment of its members. Initially these were experts who headed national women's organizations, like Bodily Begtrup, or held distinguished posts. More recently, they have been drawn from government ministries. At its first session, CSW stated its intention to prepare recommendations and reports for ECOSOC on the promotion of women's participation in political, economic, civil and educational fields, and to make recommendations on urgent problems requiring immediate attention in the field of women's rights (E/RES/2/11, 21 June 1946).

Galey (1995) divides the activities of the CSW into three phases. In the early years of its existence it focused on defining a women's agenda, paying particular attention to legal rights and their role in development. This led to the proposal and adoption of two important Conventions. The Convention on the Political Rights of Women, which asserts the right of women to vote, stand for election, and hold office on equal terms with men, was adopted by the General Assembly in 1952 (UN Treaty Series vol. 193, no. 2613 p. 135). The Convention on the Elimination of All Forms of Discrimination Against Women (CEDAW) was adopted by the UN in 1979, and ratified by most countries by 1996 (see below).

In the second phase it focused on International Women's Day and Year (1975), and facilitated the merging of the women's agenda with the larger UN agenda. During this period the programme of the CSW broadened to include assisting in the implementation of the World Plan of Action, creation of the Voluntary Fund for the Decade for Women (which later became UNIFEM), the establishment of the International Research and Training Institute for the Advancement of Women (INSTRAW), the Programme for the Second Half of the UN Decade for Women, and the implementation of the Nairobi forward-looking strategies for the advancement of women.

In 1987 the mandate of the CSW was considerably expanded by ECOSOC to include advocating equality, development and peace; monitoring the implementation of international agreements for the advancement of women; and reviewing and appraising progress at national, regional and international levels (E/RES/1987/24). This led in the third phase, in which the CSW has transformed its approach into a complex agenda to influence governments and institutions in order to advance women's status (Galey 1995: 15).

Throughout, its endeavours have been encouraged by pressure from, and collaboration with, a range of women's non-governmental organizations that used Article 71 to achieve consultative status. Results of this include the Conventions mentioned above and four world conferences on women, in Mexico City (1975), Copenhagen (1980), Nairobi (1985) and Beijing (1995), for which the CSW acted as the preparatory Commission. These conferences initiated the practice, since adopted by world conferences on other issues, of involving large numbers of NGOs in the process and conference.

The Department for the Advancement of Women (DAW)

The Department for the Advancement of Women (DAW) was established in 1946 as the Section on the Status of Women, in the Human Rights Division of the Department of

Social Affairs, as the administrative body parallel to the CSW. In 1972 it was upgraded to the Branch for the Promotion of Equality for Men and Women, under the Centre for Social Development and Humanitarian Affairs of the UN Office in Vienna. In 1978 it was renamed the Branch for the Advancement of Women, and in 1993 it moved to New York, where it was part of the Department of Policy Co-ordination and Sustainable Development, which became the Department of Economic and Social Affairs in 1996. The present Director of DAW is Carolyn Hannan, of Sweden (<http://www.un.org/womenwatch/daw>).

The brief of DAW is to work for the equality of men and women, and for the improved status of women. It promotes the equality of women in both industrialized and less developed countries, including their access to government and human rights. It undertakes research and develops policies. It works to enhance communication between all participants in policy-making. It was active in the organization of the four world conferences on women, and has ongoing responsibility for the implementation of the Platform for Action that came out of the Beijing conference. It also supports the work of the CEDAW Committee.

Alongside the CSW, DAW is important internationally in making links between NGOs and encouraging their goals. It is in large part a result of the international conferences that there is an international agenda, and that women around the world collaborate, despite their considerable differences.

The Convention on the Elimination of All Forms of Discrimination against Women (CEDAW)

Despite the assertion of sex equality in the UN Charter and the Declaration of Human Rights, it was apparent right from the start that women and men were not equal around the world. In 1963 twenty-two countries introduced a resolution to the General Assembly calling for a declaration on eliminating discrimination against women to be drafted. The resolution concluded with reports on the world social situation that emphasized factors affecting women, and presented a range of agenda items relevant to women (Fraser 1995: 78).

Governments, UN specialist agencies and non-governmental organizations were invited to comment on the resolution, and the resulting ideas were pulled together by the CSW, which in 1965 created a committee to draft a declaration on the elimination of discrimination against women (Fraser 1995: 79). In 1967 the declaration, consisting of a preamble and eleven articles, was completed and adopted by the General Assembly. It was then proposed that the declaration should become a Convention, which has stronger force. The Convention was drafted from the declaration, and eventually adopted by the General Assembly in 1979 (Fraser 1995: 84). In 1981 it had been ratified by twenty nations, and therefore came into force. More governments sign up to the Convention all the time, and as of September 2003 there were ninety-eight signatories. Exceptions are interesting and depressing. Only two of the permanent members of the Security Council have signed: the USA, the UK and China have not.

The Convention adopts a broad definition of discrimination: 'any distinction, exclusion or restriction made on the basis of sex which has the effect or purpose of impairing or nullifying the recognition or exercise by women, irrespective of their marital status, on the basis of equality of men and women, of human rights and fundamental freedoms in the political, economic, social, cultural, civil, or any other field' (<http://www.un.org/womenwatch/daw>).

States that agree to the Convention and sign up commit themselves to abolishing any discriminatory laws on their statute books, and making equality part of their legal system. This entails setting up such institutions as are necessary to protect women from discrimination, and to eliminate discrimination throughout the society. The Convention applies to public life as well as education, health and the economy. It targets citizenship, cultural practices and reproductive issues. Signatory states are bound to put the provisions of the Convention into practice, and to report back on their progress. The Committee on CEDAW monitors the implementation of the Convention, with the support of DAW.

CEDAW provides a focus for the activities of the CSW and DAW. Since it should be incorporated into all UN policy, it gives a common thread of equality to development, democratic and peace-keeping initiatives around the world, as well as constituting a platform from which such initiatives can be challenged for failure to eliminate discrimination! Further, it is a tool for equalities bodies within signatory states and for international non-governmental organizations.

International Conferences

The first international conference on women organized by the UN was held in Mexico City in 1975 to mark the start of International Women's Year. The conference adopted a Plan of Action aimed at improving the status of women, and the Women's Year was extended into a Decade for Women, 1976–85. This was of particular importance for women in less developed countries, since it required governments to assess the roles of women in development. Women's officers were established within development agencies with responsibility for ensuring that policies and their implementation took account of women (Steans 1998: 147). Halfway through the Decade, a second conference was held in Copenhagen, in 1980. However, by the end of the Decade, research strongly suggested that the status of women had actually declined. Although the Plan of Action cannot be blamed for this – various countries failed to implement the recommendations, and the long-term effects of previous policies cannot be ignored – criticisms did lead to a change of direction (Steans 1998: 148).

One aspect of this change was to consider the relationship between women, development and the environment and to develop policy that addressed all three. A second aspect was to shift the approach from the establishment of women's officers and organizations to mainstreaming. The Third UN Conference on Women, held in Nairobi in 1985, introduced mainstreaming and produced the document, *Forward-Looking Strategies for the Advancement of Women to the Year 2000* (FLSAW). The strategies developed in the document focused on women's interests in health, employment, family life, political life and the promotion of their human rights. The mainstreaming approach pushed for the consideration of women's input and interests in all policy areas (Steans 1998: 151).

The Fourth UN Conference on Women, held in Beijing in 1995, was the largest and most high-profile of the conferences. With a huge parallel conference of NGOs running alongside the main conference, it attracted a larger number of journalists than ever before. The conference took place in the shadow of disappointment with progress made under FLSAW. In its place a Platform for Action emerged that, while echoing many of FLSAW's themes and goals, made explicit links between women's empowerment, equality, human rights and access to reproductive health care, and put in place a procedure for monitoring progress. The Platform for Action contains twelve critical areas of concern: Women and Poverty, Education and Training of Women, Women and Health, Violence against Women, Women and Armed Conflict, Women and the Economy, Women in Power and Decision-Making, Institutional Mechanisms for the Advancement of Women, Human Rights of Women, Women and the Media, Women and the Environment, and the Girl Child. Progress by each signatory state in each of these areas was reported back at Beijing + 5, and will be reported again at Beijing + 10.

Women as Employees of the UN

The UN demonstrated a concern for women right from the start in Article 8 of its Constitution, but this was more with regard to its policies than its own employment or representative practices. In 1954 Dag Hammarskjøld, then Secretary-General, assured the Commission on the Status of Women that under his administration there would be no discrimination against women, with particular reference to the employment of women in the Secretariat. Unfortunately, that same year the CSW was told that it would no longer be given statistics of women in the Secretariat.

In 1970 the CSW expressed the hope that the UN would set an example of opportunities for women at senior levels, and requested the Secretary-General to include data on women in his reports to the General Assembly on the composition of the Secretariat. This was not acted on until 1974. By this time 19.4 per cent of the staff at the headquarters of the UN were women, and 17 per cent in the whole system. In general services, the majority of employees, 51 per cent, were women (United Nations 1977).

Since 1974 the statistics have been routinely included in the Secretary-General's reports to the fifth committee on the composition of the Secretariat, and a number of other measures have been taken to improve the situation of women (Report of the Committee on the Elimination of All Forms of Discrimination against Women (CEDAW) on progress achieved in the Implementation of the Convention paras 46–7; CEDAW/C/1995/7; 14 November 1994).

Since 1985 the General Assembly has set goals for increasing women's representation among the professional staff. The first was to achieve 30 per cent by 1990, which was actually achieved by 1991. The Commission on the Status of Women demonstrated a concern to see more women in all UN bodies and appointed to policy-making positions in the Secretariat. Reporting in 1994, the CSW recorded that it had acquired statistics and made recommendations, which for the most part had not been followed up. In

December 1998 the goal of 50: 50 by 2000 was set. This has not been achieved. Women represented 39 per cent of professional staff as of November 1999; this comprised 48 per cent of junior professional staff, but only 21 per cent of senior management. Of twenty-one Under Secretary-Generals, only two were women.

In specialized agencies the proportions were lower. In 1998 only 32 per cent of professional staff and 16 per cent of managers were women. The numbers were highest when organizations were headed by women: in UNICEF, 48 per cent of staff and 39 per cent of senior managers; in UNFPA, 47 per cent of staff and 39 per cent of senior managers; in the World Food Programme, 40 per cent of staff and 22 per cent of senior managers; in UNHCR, 38 per cent of staff and 14 per cent of senior managers. Other agencies with relatively high proportions of women are UNDP, with 38 per cent of staff and 21 per cent of senior managers, and UNESCO, with 39 per cent of staff and 20 per cent of senior management. The best representation of women of all was in the Pan American Health Organization and the Joint UN Programme on HIV/AIDS, where 50 per cent of the senior managers were women. Data for 2000 on UNFPA puts women at 50 per cent of total staff and 60 per cent of senior managers.

Conclusion

Despite setbacks in its peace-keeping role, the UN remains the only organization with authority and resources adequate to the pursuit of an international policy agenda. Since its creation, it has been a focus of attention for women with a sex equality agenda. This agenda has been developed in terms of human and civil rights. It is not an easy task. Cultural and economic differences mean that the content of an equality agenda differs around the world and is prone to conflict. Different perceptions of gender and women's roles, compounded by mistrust of post-colonial agendas and Western domination, cause disputes about appropriate goals and strategies. However, CEDAW, the conferences, the CSW and DAW, provide invaluable forums for debate of these issues. There is an international dialogue going on through these organizations and the NGOs that the UN has encouraged, which provides an alternative perspective on the world from that offered by the Security Council and the World Trade Organization.

FURTHER READING

The UN publishes a huge amount of material. There are numerous publications detailing its efforts to address gender in the world, but very little on addressing gender within its own ranks. Winslow's collection of essays attempts to address this. Jill Steans is good on the role of the UN with regard to women and the conferences.

Steans, J. 1998: *Gender and International Relations*. Cambridge: Polity.
Winslow, A. (ed.) 1995: *Women, Politics and the United Nations*. Westport, CT: Greenwood Press.

CONCLUSION

This book has had a dual purpose: as well as describing where women can be found in contemporary politics and what they are doing, it has attempted to understand the factors that have enabled and handicapped them. As chapter 4 has shown, from at least the eighteenth century social justice has been interpreted as meaning that the law should not differentiate between people on the ground of their sex any more than any other characteristic. This has entailed extending the franchise to women, as well as to working people and immigrants. Equal treatment was taken further in the twentieth century, when the implementation of the law was considered in its widest context. This meant taking on issues of discrimination in the formulation and execution of the law, and then addressing the gendered assumptions of the societies from which the laws emerged.

This book has focused on the period from the 1970s to the present, during which it has become clear that social justice was being interpreted in a number of countries to include women's active participation in politics. The demand for women's increased participation has been justified on two broad grounds: first, equality of opportunity, and second, that women have a particular contribution to make to politics. The first ground relies on arguments about using the best talents in the society, and preventing discrimination from getting in the way of people fulfilling their ambitions, that are generally acceptable to people of an egalitarian bent, and can be used with respect to all sorts of groups of people in a society (religious, ethnic, language, etc.).

The second is a more feminist ground, and relies on the contention that women are different from men. This need not be an essentialist argument about sex/gender. It may say no more than that at a particular time and place men and women have different experiences of life as a result of laws and customs. Those experiences mean that men and women understand the world differently, live in the world differently, and value things differently. As a result, they will come to politics with different priorities, different goals and different ways of going about things. These differences may be extreme or quite minor, depending on the circumstances and the individual politician.

It is clear from all the material we have looked at here that women entering politics around the world have not had an easy or comfortable time. Long-standing assumptions about gender roles in the private and public spheres have spilled over into the treatment of elected women by fellow politicians and the media. It has often been assumed that they are women before they are politicians – sometimes to the effect that they should behave better than men, sometimes with the expectation that they will behave worse. Women have withstood barracking in the House and ridicule (or occasionally beatification – the example of Mo Mowlam in the UK springs to mind) in the Press. The general public, at least in the United Kingdom, has a very limited sense of who female politicians are and what they do. A common response to my writing this book has been the assumption that I am writing about Margaret Thatcher and Condoleezza Rice, or perhaps the only two female Italian politicians anyone has heard of: the porn star and Mussolini's grand-daughter!

The numbers of women in elected office are growing almost daily. My research has entailed regular monitoring of the Inter-Parliamentary Union's table of parliaments around the world, and I have watched the percentages steadily increase and the different countries shift their positions. In the past few years the achievement of office by women in less developed countries has been the most remarkable change. This bears witness to the efforts of campaigners to get women elected, of international governmental organizations to make the position of women a marker of democracy, and of women themselves. This book has focused on the position and prevalence of women in office: investigating how many women there are and attempting to explain it. It has not looked in any detail at equalities legislation or what the United Nations calls institutional mechanisms for the advancement of women – there are plenty of other books that do this very well.

From an equal opportunities standpoint, we are clearly making some headway: more of the women who want to get elected are getting there. It is difficult: the obstacles of electoral systems, party tradition, incumbency, and both overt and covert discrimination persist, but these are gradually being recognized and compensated for. From a democratic standpoint, the picture is more complex. More women are being elected, but does this of itself constitute democracy? If the women are all from elite groups, if they can only operate in politics along party lines determined by senior men, has democracy been improved? Where women are elected in larger numbers, we can see the beginning of diversification, both in the backgrounds of the women concerned and in their policy priorities, but again, this is a slow process. Third-wave feminism is a project that is still in the making. We don't know what the outcome will be; we can't predict what a parliament will look like or act like once sex parity has become thoroughly established. We can, perhaps, echo Susan Moller Okin's optimistic guess: that a parliament which includes a hefty proportion of people (men and women) who have hands-on experience of taking care of another human being might make some different choices from those we are used to.

> For those who believe there is some genuine difference in the experience of males and females, the justification of balanced representation is self-evident. For those who do not consider that there are differences of substance, the proposal should present no real problems since the gender make-up of Parliament should make no difference for better or worse. (Lindsay 2001: 176)

NOTES

Introduction

1 The notable exception to this is the Nordic countries, especially Norway, where legislation has ensured balanced representation of men and women on all public boards and commissions since the early 1980s.

2 See the introduction to Githens et al., *Different Roles, Different Voices* for a brief discussion of the emergence of feminist political research.

3 See e.g. Lynne E. Ford, *Women and Politics: The Pursuit of Equality*, for a discussion of the USA; Nikki Craske, *Women and Politics in Latin America*; Sarah Childs, *New Labour's Women MPs: Women Representing Women*; Christine Bergqvist et al., *Equal Democracies?* for the Nordic countries.

4 E.g. Anne Phillips, *Which Equalities Matter?*; H. Mirza, *Black British Feminism*; Patricia Hill Collins, *Fighting Words: Black Women and the Search for Justice*; Judith Butler, *Bodies that Matter: On the Discursive Limits of Sex*; Jean Bethke Elshtain, *Public Man, Private Woman*.

Chapter 1 Feminist Theory and Women's Political Activism

1 The name most associated with a narrow view of democracy, selecting a government through competitive elections, is that of J. A. Schumpeter in his book *Capitalism, Socialism and Democracy*; Robert Dahl is most strongly associated with pluralism and particularly polyarchy, although he has shifted his position slightly over the years to take on criticisms of pure pluralism.

2 See e.g. the extensive writing of Alain Touraine, including *The Voice and the Eye: An Analysis of Social Movements* (Cambridge: Cambridge University Press, 1981); and

Ronald Inglehart, including 'Culture Shift', in *Advanced Industrial Society* (Princeton: Princeton University Press, 1990).

3 A. Phillips, *Engendering Democracy* (1991); S. Mendus, 'Losing the Faith: Feminism and Democracy' (1992); C. Pateman, *The Sexual Contract*.

4 This problem is raised by Sheila Rowbotham (1986), Carole Pateman (1992), Susan Mendus (1992), and Anne Phillips (1991, 1992).

5 Some feminist writers, notably Ruddick (1990), Dinnerstein (1987) and Elshtain (1981), maintain that women have a radically different approach to life and politics, which would alter the nature of politics if practised; this is encapsulated by the short-hand 'an ethic of care', or 'maternal thinking'. The extent to which this depends upon something essential to the nature of women or upon the ways in which women's experiences differ from men's is not clear; nor is it entirely clear whether men could practise maternal thinking if equipped with appropriate training and experience. The position which I am adopting here is not a strong one about women's nature, but a rather weak one emphasizing women's particular experiences. The same point is applicable to any group which has specific experiences which are connected to group identity and are different from the norm.

6 I. M. Young (1990) and Phillips (1995) write about the possibilities of group-based politics, while Ruddick (1990), Elshtain (1981) and Dinnerstein (1987) develop theories of maternal thinking. The latter used families and friendships as models for an alternative politics.

7 e.g. Burnheim (1985); Bobbio (1989); Phillips (1992); Fishkin (1991); Sunstein (1991).

8 Darcy, Welch and Clark (1994) summarize reasons given for why there should be more women in elected office: 'ideological advantage', pressing policies to which women have more commitment than men, particularly feminist goals; 'women's expertise', taking advantage of the knowledge and insight into some matters which women possess and men do not; 'societal benefits', society benefits from competition for office, which is constrained if half the population is not competing; 'legitimising the system' – in order to truly represent the population, a legislature should include the various elements of the society (pp. 15–18).

9 It has been pointed out to me that African Americans are, in fact, remarkably cohesive in their voting for the Democratic candidate in almost every partisan election. But the point being made here is one of identity, and I think my point (at any rate a tentative one) holds when levels of voter registration and turn-out are considered.

10 Historically, women have been assumed to possess concerns which were different from, but complementary to, those of men. According to such as Rousseau, Wollstonecraft, John Stuart Mill and Harriet Taylor, these exerted a 'civilizing' influence upon men and were to the benefit of the community. The strongest conception of women's interests comes from radical and eco-feminists, who have taken strong positions on women in relation to peace, the environment, violence and pornography. The assumption that women share a set of material goals which can be asserted politically underpins the creation of women's parties and the study of 'gender gaps' in political affiliation and behaviour: Anna Jonasdottir argues that 'men and women are beginning to constitute themselves as two basic societal corporations' (Jonasdottir 1985: 53). Jones and Jonasdottir (1985a) claim that feminists identify a range of women's interests, but '[t]raditional concepts of interest do not seem adequate to define the political and moral values that women strive to achieve in having their interests represented'.

Chapter 6 Quotas for Women in Parties and Parliaments

1 Joni Lovenduski refers to the first of these as rhetorical strategies and positive action, and to the second as positive discrimination (Lovenduski 1993: 8).
2 For an extended discussion of differences between the Nordic countries, see Bergqvist et al. 1999.
3 The quotas referred to here are candidate quotas, designed for elections and the system of representative democracy. Most parties in the Nordic countries operate internal quota systems for party offices, with the exception of Denmark, where all quotas were banned in 1996 (Christensen 1999: 80).

Chapter 7 Political Parties: Background Information

1 Uganda, theoretically, has had a no-party system since President Museveni suspended multi-party politics in 1995. Museveni's National Resistance Movement is a party, but people can stand for election without belonging to it and without having to join it on election. The parties continue to mobilize freely, although unofficially. State Socialist, or Communist, countries usually only had or have one party – the Communist Party – but other countries are in effect one-party states, such as Zimbabwe. Two-party systems are rarely just that. The UK has a multiplicity of parties, although two of them dominate at any one time, and even the USA has a number of small parties in addition to the big two. On the other hand, multi-party systems may be less multiple than they appear to be if parties, in effect, organize in ideological or strategic blocs.

Chapter 8 Women in Political Parties in the United Kingdom

1 The shrinking support for the Labour Party was analysed in the context of the 1983 election by Heath, Jowell and Curtice, who in their book *How Britain Votes* (Oxford: Pergamon Press, 1985), p. 171, concluded that it was a result of the diminishing proportion of the population employed in the industries which had formed the traditional base of the party's support. This was contrary to the theory of class dealignment proposed by D. Butler and D. Stokes, *Political Change in Britain: The Evolution of Political Choice*, 2nd edn (London, Macmillan, 1974), and at variance with Ivor Crewe's argument that Labour's policies failed to reflect working-class interests in 'The Labour Party and the Electorate', in J. Kavanagh (ed.), *The Politics of the Labour Party* (London: Allen and Unwin, 1982), pp. 9–50. This is discussed by Sue Goss in *Local Labour and Local Government* (Edinburgh: Edinburgh University Press, 1988), pp. 135–55.

Chapter 15 Women in Local Government in the United Kingdom

1 For a discussion of the recent history of local government see Gyford, Leach and Game 1989.

2 This has increased exponentially in recent years: according to John Stewart and Gerry Stoker, 'some forty Acts dealing with local government were passed between 1979 and 1987' (Stewart and Stoker 1995: 2).

3 An interesting measure of partisanship is the presence of 'Independent' councillors: in the 1985 local elections, 'just over eighty Independent councillors were returned out of a total of over 3000' (Gyford, Leach and Game 1989: 27).

4 Gyford, Leach and Game discuss changes in the profile of local councillors between the report of the Maud Committee in 1964 and that of the Widdecombe Committee in 1986 (1989: 44–54).

5 Gyford, Leach and Game discuss whether these councillors were typical, or prominent because they were atypical, and conclude that they were both! Changes have occurred, but gradually, and in terms of representation, councillors continued to 'mismatch' their electorates (1989: 46–8).

6 See e.g. S. Button's (1984) commentary on the shape and goals of women's committees and her account of the foundation of the Haringey women's panel and forum.

7 At the time when women's committees were being established, the Women's Action Committee was set up in the Labour Party, and women's sections were started around the country (Perrigo 1986; Parker 1981). Nevertheless, women's committees were both novel and potentially powerful because of their links with organized women outside any political party and because of their brief to monitor the activities of other local authority committees and departments.

8 Marilyn Taylor of the National Association of Local Government Women's Committees (now renamed the Local Government Women's Network) (private letter) estimated that women's committees peaked in the late 1980s at about fifty. What actually constituted a women's committee presented some difficulty. In some areas subcommittees were given more power than in others, and an equalities committee in one area might concentrate on women's issues while that in another might prioritize race or disability. Further, a non-committee-level women's working group might, by virtue of the people involved and support within the council, exert considerable pressure.

9 Co-optees were able to vote until debarred by the 1989 Local Government and Housing Act. This was the result of a recommendation of the Widdecombe Committee, which reported in 1986 (Gyford, Leach and Game 1989: 296).

10 In 1992, for example, NALGWC organized conferences around the following: Housing Policy: Focusing on Women (January), Violence against Women: Challenges for the 90s (April), Violence against Women in the Home: Challenges for the 90s (June), and Child Care Strategies (October).

11 Beatrix Campbell blames the indifference of the Parliamentary Labour Party and the statist focus of labourism for betraying the local democratic initiatives spearheaded by women and minorities. Along the same lines, a worker from the Labour Party's head office at Walworth Road told me that, in her opinion, women's committees happened despite the party rather than because of it.

REFERENCES

Abdela, L. 1989: *Women with X Appeal*. London: Macdonald and Co. Publishers.

Abrar, S., Lovenduski, J. and Margetts, M. 1998: Sexing London: The Gender Mix of Urban Policy Actors. *International Political Science Review*, 19 (2): 147–71.

ACT 2000: *Values not Politics*. Wellington: ACT.

Adell Cook, E., Thomas, S. and Wilcox, C. (eds) 1994: *The Year of the Woman*. Boulder, Co: Westview.

Adell Cook, E. 1998: Voter Reaction to Women Candidates. In S. Thomas and C. Wilcox (eds), *Women and Elective Office: Past, Present and Future*, Oxford: Oxford University Press, pp. 71–95.

Alexander, W. 2000: Women and the Scottish Parliament. In A. Coote (ed.), *New Gender Agenda*, London: IPPR, pp. 81–8.

Anderson, B. S. and Zinsser, J. P. 1990: *A History of their Own: Women in Europe from Prehistory to the Present*, vol. 2. Harmondsworth: Penguin.

Appleton, A. and Mazur, A. 1993: Transformation or Modernisation: The Rhetoric and Reality of Gender and Party Politics in France. In J. Lovenduski and P. Norris, *Gender and Party Politics*, London: Sage, pp. 86–112.

Arora, R. 2003: No More Discussion on the Women's Reservation Bill, say Activists. <http://www.infochangeindia.org/features122.jsp>

Atkinson, N. 2003: *Adventures in Democracy: A History of the Vote in New Zealand*. Dunedin: University of Chicago Press.

Australian Parliament website. <http//www.aph.gov.au>

Australian Women's Party website. <http://www.isis.aust.com/awp/aboutus.htm>

Banaszak, L., Beckwith, K. and Rucht, D. (eds) 2003: *Women's Movements Facing the Reconfigured State*. Cambridge: Cambridge University Press.

Banks, O. 1986: *Faces of Feminism*. Oxford: Basil Blackwell.

Barber, E. S. and Natason, B. O. One Hundred Years toward Suffrage. <http://memory.loc.gov/ammem/vfwtl.html>

Barrett, M. and Phillips, A. 1992: *Destabilizing Theory*. Cambridge: Polity.

Baskevin, S. 1991: Women's Participation in Political Parties. In K. Megyery (ed.), *Women in Canadian Politics*, Toronto: Dundurn Press, pp. 61–80.

Beckwith, K. 2003: The Gendering Ways of States: Women's Representation and State Reconfiguration in France, Great Britain and the United States. In L. Banaszak, K. Beckwith and D. Rucht, *Women's Movements Facing the Reconfigured State*, Cambridge: Cambridge University Press, pp. 169–202.

Bergqvist, C. et al. (eds) 1999: *Equal Democracies? Gender and Politics in the Nordic Countries*. Oslo: Scandinavian University Press.

Birch, S. 2003: Women and Political Representation in Contemporary Ukraine. In R. E. Matland and K. Montgomery (eds), *Women's Access to Political Power in Post-Communist Europe*, Oxford: Oxford University Press, pp. 130–52.

Bird, K. 2003: Who are the Women? Where are the Women? And What Difference Can They Make? Effects of Gender Party in French Municipal Elections. *French Politics*, 1: 5–38.

Bobbio, N. 1989: *Democracy and Dictatorship*. Cambridge: Polity.

Bochel, C. and Bochel, H. M. 2000: *The Careers of Councillors: Gender, Party and Politics*. London: Ashgate Publishing.

Bochel, C. and Briggs, J. 2000: Do Women Make a Difference? *Politics*, 20 (2): 63–8.

Bochel, C. and Denver, D. 1983: Candidate Selection in the Labour Party: What the Selectors Seek. *British Journal of Political Science*, 13: 45–69.

Bock, G. and James, S. (eds) 1992: *Beyond Equality and Difference*. London: Routledge.

Boddy, M. and Fudge, C. (eds) 1984: *Local Socialism: Labour Councillors and New Left Alternatives*. London: Macmillian.

Bokhari, F. 2001: For Pakistan's Women, Election Quotas are a Start. *Christian Science Monitor*, 93 (130): 7.

Borrelli, M. 2000: Gender, Politics and Change in the United States Cabinet: The Madeleine Korbel Albright and Janet Reno Appointments. In S. Tolleson-Rinehart and J. J. Josephson (eds), *Gender and American Politics: Women, Men and the Political Process*, Armonk, NY: M. E. Sharpe, pp. 185–204.

Boston, J., Church, S., Levine, S., McLeay, E. and Roberts, N. 2000: *Left Turn*. Wellington: Victoria University Press.

Boston, J., Church, S., Levine, S., McLeay, E. and Roberts, N. 2003: *New Zealand Votes: The General Election of 2002*. Wellington: Victoria University Press.

Boston, J., Levine, S., McLeay, E. and Roberts, N. 1996: *New Zealand under MMP*. Auckland: Auckland University Press.

Bottomley, P. M. 1990: The Political Interactions of Women's Initiatives in Local Government. Dept. of Urban Planning, School of the Environment, Leeds Polytechnic.

Breitenbach, E. 2001: Women in Scotland and Constitutional Change. <http:// www.sociology.ed.ac.uk/TeachingandLearning/Honours/Honours%20course%20handouts%20etc/Scotland%20sssc/Breitenbach_Femecosse_English.pdf>

Breitenbach, E. and Mackay, F. (eds) 2001a: *Women and Contemporary Scottish Politics*. Edinburgh: Polygon.

Breitenbach, E. and Mackay, F. 2001b: Introduction, in E. Breitenbach and F. Mackay (eds), *Women and Contemporary Scottish Politics*, Edinburgh: Polygon, pp. 1–20.

Broad, C. and Kirner, J. 1996: Australian Parties Confronting the Changing Social and Political Environment. In M. Simms (eds), *The Paradox of Parties*, St Leonards: Allen and Unwin, pp. 79–86.

Brown, A. 1999: Taking their Place in the House: Women and the Scottish Parliament. *Scottish Affairs*, no. 28: 44–50.

Brown, A. 2001a: Deepening Democracy: Women in the Scottish Parliament. In E. Breitenbach and F. Mackay (eds), *Women and Contemporary Scottish Politics*, Edinburgh: Polygon, pp. 213–29.

Brown, A. 2001b: Taking their Place in the New House: Women and the New Scottish Parliament. In E. Breitenbach and F. Mackay (eds), *Women and Contemporary Scottish Politics*, Edinburgh: Polygon, pp. 241–53.

Brown, A. 2001c: Women and Politics in Scotland. In E. Breitenbach and F. Mackay (eds), *Women and Contemporary Scottish Politics*, Edinburgh Polygon, pp. 197–212.

Brown, A. and Galligan Y. 1995: Views from the Periphery: Changing the Political Agenda for Women in the Republic of Ireland and in Scotland. *West European Politics*, 16(2): 165–89.

Brown, A., Donoghy, T. B., Mackay, F. and Meehan, E. 2002: Women and Constitutional Change in Scotland and Northern Ireland. *Parliamentary Affairs*, 55 (1): 71–84.

Brown, A., McCrone, D. and Paterson, L. 1998: *Politics and Society in Scotland*. London: Macmillan.

Bruegel, I. 1994: Municipal Feminism: Relating Gender and Class to Hierarchies, Markets and Networks. Paper presented to the ESRC Women and Welfare Seminar, London.

Bryson, V. 1999: *Feminist Debates: Issues of Theory and Political Practice*. Basingstoke: Macmillan Press Ltd.

Brzinski, J. B. 2003: Women's Representation in Germany. In R. E. Matland and K. Montgomery (eds), *Women's Access to Political Power in Post-Communist Europe*, Oxford: Oxford University Press, pp. 63–80.

Buckley, M. 1997a: Adaptation of the Soviet Women's Committee: Deputies' Voices from 'Women of Russia'. In M. Buckley (ed.), *Post-Soviet Women: From the Baltic to Central Asia*, Cambridge: Cambridge University Press, pp. 157–85.

Buckley, M. (ed.) 1997b: *Post-Soviet Women: From the Baltic to Central Asia*. Cambridge: Cambridge University Press.

Burnheim, J. 1985: *Is Democracy Possible?* Cambridge: Polity.

Burns, N., Lehman Schlozman, K. and Verba, S. 2001: *The Private Roots of Public Action*. Cambridge, MA: Harvard University Press.

Burrell, B. C. 1994: *A Women's Place is in the House*. Ann Arbor: University of Michigan Press.

Burrell, B. 1998: Campaign Finance: Women's Experience in the Modern Era. In C. Thomas and C. Wilcox (eds), *Women and Elective Office*, New York: Oxford University Press, pp. 26–37.

Busby, N. and McLeod, C. 2002: Maintaining a Balance: The Retention of Women MPs in Scotland. *Parliamentary Affairs*, 55 (1): 30–42.

Bussemaker, J. and Voet, R. (eds) 1998: *Gender, Participation and Citizenship in the Netherlands*. Aldershot: Ashgate.

Butler, D. and Stokes, D. 1974: *Political Change in Britain: The Evolution of Political Choice*, 2nd edn. London: Macmillan.

Butler, J. 1993: *Bodies that Matter: On the Discursive Limits of Sex*. London: Routledge.

Button, S. 1984: Women's Committees: A Study of Gender and Local Government Policy Formation, Working Paper 45. University of Bristol School for Advanced Urban Studies.

Buxton, F. 2001: *Equal Balance: Electing More Women MPs for the Conservative Party*. London: Bow Group.

Campbell, B. 1987: Labour's Left Councils: Charge of the Light Brigade. *Marxism Today* (February): 10–13.

Campbell, R. 2004: Gender, Ideology and Issue Preference: Is There such a Thing as a Political Women's Interest in Britain? *British Journal of Politics and International Relations*, 6 (1): 20–44.

Canadian Government website. <http://www.parl.gc.ca/english/cabinet/secmin.htm>

Caress, S. M. 1999: The Influence of Term Limits on the Electoral Success of Women. *Women and Politics*, 20 (3): 45–63.

Caul, M. 2001: Political Parties and the Adoption of Candidate Gender Quotas: A Cross-National Analysis. *Journal of Politics*, 63 (4): 1214–29.

Celis, K. and Woodward, A. 2000: Gendering the New Political Culture? Women in the First Flemish Parliament. Working paper for the European Consortium of Political Research, Joint Sessions April 2000 Copenhagen. Workshop 16: Gender and Local Governance: Structural and Institutional Changes in the Nineties.

Centre for Advancement of Women in Politics, Queens University, Belfast website. <http://www.qub.ac.uk/cawp/>

Centre for Europe's Children 1999: *The Monee Report*. Innocenti Research Centre, UNICEF.

Chaddock, G. R. 1997: Quotas Boost Women Pols. *Christian Science Monitor*, 89 (118): 1.

Chandler, J. 2002: *Local Government Today*. Manchester: Manchester University Press.

Chaney, P. 2002: Women and the Post-Devolution Equality Agenda in Wales. Paper presented to the Gender Research Forum, Women and Equality Unit, Cabinet Office.

Chaney, C. and Sinclair, B. 1994: Women and the 1992 House Elections. In E. Adell Cook, S. Thomas and C. Wilcox (eds), *The Year of the Woman*, Boulder: Westview, pp. 123–40.

Chant, S. and Craske, K. 2003: *Gender in Latin America*. London: Latin American Bureau.

Chapman, J. 1993: *Politics, Feminism and the Reformation of Gender*. London: Routledge.

Childs, S. 2001: In Their Own Words: New Labour Women and the Substantive Representation of Women. *British Journal of Politics and International Relations*, 3 (2): 173–90.

Childs, S. 2002a: Hitting the Target: Are Labour Women MPs 'acting for women'? *Parliamentary Affairs*, 55 (1): 14–53.

Childs, S. 2002b: The Sex Discrimination (Election Candidates): Act 2002 and its Implications. *Representation*, 39 (2): 8–13.

Childs, S. 2004a: A Feminized Style of Politics? Women MPs in the House of Commons. *British Journal of Politics and International Relations*, 6 (1): 3–19.

Childs, S. 2004b: *New Labour's Women MPs: Women Representing Women*. London: Routledge.

Christensen, A. 1999: Women in the Political Parties. In C. Bergqvist et al. (eds), *Equal Democracies? Gender and Politics in the Nordic Countries*, Oslo: Scandinavian University Press, pp. 65–87.

Christian Science Monitor 1997: Socialist Win Means 'Vive L'Egalité!'. Vol. 89, issue 134, p. 1.

Christy, C. A. 1987: *Sex Differences in Political Participation*. New York: Praeger.

Clements, B. Evans 1997: *Bolshevik Women*. Cambridge: Cambridge University Press.

Cohen, D. 1997: New Zealand Politics: A Woman's Place. *Christian Science Monitor*, 89 (241): 1.

Cohen, D. 2000: New Zealand's 'New-Girl Network' at the Top. *Christian Science Monitor*, 92 (201): 7.

Collins, P. H. 1998: *Fighting Words: Black Women and the Search for Justice*. Minneapolis: University of Minnesota Press.

Conover, P. J. and Gray, V. 1983: *Feminism and the New Right: Conflict over the American Family*. New York: Praeger.

Conservative Party website. <http://www.tory.org.uk>

Conway, M. M. 2000: Gender and Political Participation. In S. Tolleson-Rinehart and J. J. Josephson, (eds), *Gender and American Politics: Women, Men and the Political Process*, Armonk, NY: M. E. Sharpe, pp. 74–88.

Coole, D. 1988: *Women in Political Theory*. Brighton: Harvester.

Cooper, D. 1991: After the Boom, the Doom and Gloom? *Everywoman* (April): 16–17.

Coote, A. (ed.) 2000: *New Gender Agenda*. London: IPPR.

Coote, A. and Patullo, P. 1990: *Power and Prejudice: Women and Politics*. London: Weidenfeld and Nicolson.

Corkery, P. 1999: *Pam's Political Confessions*. Auckland: Hodder Moa Beckett Publishers.

Corrin, C. 2002: Developing Democracy in Kosova: From Grass-Roots to Government. *Parliamentary Affairs*, 55 (1): 99–108.

Country Report: Australia. <http://www.cities-localgovernments.org/iula/upload/ stateofwomeninurbanlocalgovernment(australia).pdf>

Country Report: Bangladesh. <http://www.cities-localgovernments.org/iula/upload/ stateofwomeninurbanlocalgovernment(bangladesh).pdf>

Country Report: Germany. <http://www.cities-localgovernments.org/iula/upload/ stateofwomeninurbanlocalgovernment(germany).pdf>

Country Report: India. <http://www.cities-localgovernments.org/iula/upload/ stateofwomeninurbanlocalgovernment(india).pdf>

Country Report: Pakistan. <http://www.cities-localgovernments.org/iula/upload/ Stateofwomeninurbanlocalgovernment(pakistan).pdf>

Cowley, P. and Childs, S. 2003: Too Spineless to Rebel? New Labour's Women MPs. *British Journal of Political Science*, 33: 34–65.

Craske, N. 1999: *Women and Politics in Latin America*. Cambridge: Polity.

Craske, N. 2003: Gender, Politics and Legislation. In S. Chant and K. Craske, *Gender in Latin America*, London: Latin American Bureau, pp. 19–45.

Craske, N. and Moyneux, M. (eds) 2002: *Gender, the Politics of Rights and Democracy in Latin America*. Basingstoke: Palgrave.

Crewe, I. 1982: The Labour Party and the Electorate. In J. Kavanagh (ed.), *The Politics of the Labour Party*, London: Allen and Unwin, pp. 9–50.

Dahlerup, D. 1998: Using Quotas to Increase Women's Political Participation. In A. Karam et al. (eds), *Women in Parliament: Beyond Numbers*, Stockholm, International Institute for Democracy and Electoral Assistance (IDEA), pp. 91–106.

Darcy, R. and Nixon, D. L. 1997: Women in the 1946 and 1993 Japanese House of Representatives Elections: The Role of the Election System. *Journal of North-East Asian Studies*, 15 (1): 3–20.

Darcy, R., Welch, S. and Clark, J. 1994: *Women, Elections and Representation*. Lincoln: University of Nebraska Press.

Davis, R. H. 1997: *Women and Power in Parliamentary Democracies*. Lincoln and London: University of Nebraska Press.

Delli Carpini, M. X. and Keeter S. 2000: Gender and Political Knowledge. In S. Tolleson-Rinehart and J. J. Josephson (eds), *Gender and American Politics: Women, Men and the Political Process*, Armonk, NY: M. E. Sharpe, pp. 21–52.

Desai, N. 1997: Negotiating Political Space: Indian Women's Movement and Political Participation. In V. Poonacha (ed.), *Women, Empowerment and Political Parties*, Research Centre for Women's Studies, SNDT Women's University, pp. 46–60.

De Vaus, D. and McAllister, I. 1989: The Changing Politics of Women: Gender and Political Alignment in 11 Nations. *European Journal of Political Research*, 17: 241–62.

Deverall, K., Huntley, R., Sharpe, P. and Tilly, J. 2000: *Party Girls: Labor Women Now*. Annadale: Pluto Press.

Diamond, I. and Hartsock, N. 1975: Beyond Interests: A Comment on Virginia Sapiro's Research Frontier Essay. *American Political Science Review*, 75: 717–21.

Dietz, M. 1985: Citizenship with a Feminist Face: The Problem with Maternal Thinking. *Political Theory*, 13 (1): 19–37.

Dinnerstein, D. 1987: *The Rocking of the Cradle and the Ruling of the World*. London: Women's Press.

Dodson, D. and Carroll, S. J. 1991: *Reshaping the Agenda: Women in State Legislatures*. New Brunswick, NY: CAWP, Rutgers University.

Dogra, B. 2001: Women Justify Reservation Policy in Panchayats. <http://www.goodnewsindia.com/Pages/content/transitions/panwomen.html>

Dominelli, L. and Jonsdottir, G. 1988: Feminist Political Organisation in Iceland: Some Reflections on the Experience of Kwenna Frambothid. *Feminist Review*, 28: 36–60.

Drage, J. 2001: *Women in Local Government in Asia and the Pacific: A Comparative Analysis of Thirteen Countries*. UN ESCAP. <http://www.cities-localgovernments.org/iula/upload/docs/stateofwomeninurbanlocalgovernment(comparativeanalysis13countries).pdf>

Duerst-Lahti, G. 1998: The Bottleneck: Women Becoming Candidates. In S. Thomas and C. Wilcox (eds), *Women and Elective Office: Past, Present and Future*, Oxford: Oxford University Press, 15–24.

Duverger, M. 1955: *The Political Role of Women*. Paris: UNESCO.

Economic Commission for Europe 2000: *Women and Men in Europe and North America*. New York: United Nations Census Bureau.

Economist 1999: The French Gaullist's New Lady. Vol. 353, issue 8149, p. 45.

Economist 2001: Will the Lady Go? Vol. 361, issue 8247, pp. 40–1.

Edwards, J. 1988: Local Government Women's Committees. *Critical Social Policy*, 24: 50–64.

Edwards, J. and McAllister, L. 2002: One Step Forward and Two Steps Back? Women in the Two Main Political Parties in Wales. *Parliamentary Affairs*, 55 (1): 154–66.

Eisenstein, H. 1990: Femocrats, Official Feminism and the Uses of Power. In S. Watson (ed.), *Playing the State*, London: Verso, pp. 87–104.

Eldergill, A. 1984: *Women's Lot: Political Purdah and the Labour Party*. London: Institute of Workers' Control.

Electoral Commission 2004: *Gender and Political Participation*. London: Electoral Commission.

Elgie, R. and Griggs, S. 2000: *French Politics*. London: Routledge.

Elman, R. A. (ed.) 1996: *Sexual Politics and the EU*. Providence, RI: Berg Hahn.

Else-Mitchell, R. 2000: Women on the Political Pedestal: Beyond the Golden Girl Syndrome. In K. Deverall, R. Huntley, P. Sharpe and J. Tilly (eds), *Party, Girls: Labor Women Now*, Annadale: Pluto Press, pp. 10–19.

Elshtain, J. Bethke 1981: *Public Man, Private Woman: Women in Social and Political Thought*. Oxford: Martin Robertson.

Equal Opportunities Commission 1988: *Local Authority Equal Opportunity Policies: Report of a Survey by the Equal Opportunities Commission*. Manchester: EOC.

Esaiasson, P. and Heidar, K. (eds) 2000: *Beyond Westminster and Congress: The Nordic Experience*. Columbus: Ohio State University Press.

European Women's Lobby website. <http://www.womenlobby.org>

Evans, R. 1977: *The Feminists*. London: Croom Helm.

Fawcett Society website. <www.fawcettsociety.org.uk>

Fawcett Society 2003a: Conservative Candidates – where are the Women? <http://www.fawcettsociety.org.uk>

Fawcett Society 2003b: Experiences of Labour Party Women in Parliamentary Selections: Internal Findings. <http://www.fawcettsociety.org.uk>

Fawcett Society 2003c: Experiences of Liberal Democrat Women in Parliamentary Selections: Internal Findings. <http://www.fawcettsociety.org.uk>

Feldman, L. 2003: Election Coverage of Women: More on Personality, Less on Issues. <http://www.csmonitor.com/atcsmonitor/specials/women/politics/politics102599.html>

Firestone, S. 1979: *The Dialectic of Sex*: The Case for Feminist Revolution. London: Women's Press.

Fishkin, J. 1991: *Deliberation and Democracy: New Directions for Democratic Reform*. New Haven: Yale University Press.

Flannelly, K. 2002: Voting for Female Candidates: Effects of Voters' Age, Ethnicity and Gender. *Journal of Social Psychology*, 142 (3): 397–401.

Flanz, G. H. 1983: *Comparative Women's Rights and Political Participation in Europe*. Dobbs Ferry, NY: Transnational Publishers Inc.

Foerstel, K. and Foerstel, H. N. 1996: *Climbing the Hill: Gender Conflict in Congress*. London: Praeger.

Footitt, H. 2002: *Women, Europe and the New Language of Politics*. London: Continuum.

Ford, L. E. 2002: *Women and Politics: The Pursuit of Equality*. Boston: Houghton Mifflin.

Fox, R. 1997: *Gender Dynamics in Congressional Elections*. Thousand Oaks, CA: Sage.

Fox, R. 2000: Gender and Congressional Elections. In S. Tolleson-Rinehart and J. J. Josephson (eds), *Gender and American Politics: Women, Men and the Political Process*. Armonk: M. E. Sharpe, pp. 227–56.

Fraser, A. S. 1995: The Convention on the Elimination of All Forms of Discrimination Against Women (The Women's Convention). In A. Winslow (ed.), *Women, Politics and the United Nations*, Westport, CT: Greenwood Press, pp. 77–94.

Freeman, J. 1982: *The Tyranny of Structurelessness*. London: Dark Star.

Freidenvall, L. 2000: The Meaning of Gender for Local Politicians from a Generational Perspective. Paper from the Gender and Local Governance Panel, European Consortium for Political Research, Copenhagen.

French Government website. <http://<www.assemblee-nat.fr./english/index.asp>

Galey, M. E. 1995: Women Find a Place. In A. Winslow (ed.), *Women, Politics and the United Nations*, Westport, CT: Greenwood Press, pp. 11–27.

Galligan, Y. and Wilford, R. 1999a: Gender and Party Politics in the Republic of Ireland. In Y. Galligan, R. Ward and R. Wilford (eds), *Contesting Politics*, Oxford: Westview Press, pp. 149–68.

Galligan, Y. and Wilford, R. 1999b: Women's Political Representation in Ireland. In Y. Galligan, R. Ward and R. Wilford (eds), *Contesting Politics*, Oxford: Westview Press, pp. 130–48.

Galligan, Y., Ward, R. and Wilford, R. (eds) 1999: *Contesting Politics*. Oxford: Westview Press.

Galloway, K. and Robertson, J. 2001: A Woman's Claim of Right in Scotland. In E. Breitenbach and F. Mackay (eds), *Women and Contemporary Scottish Politics*. Edinburgh: Polygon.

Gardiner, J. and Ferguson, C. 1996: Women and the National Party of Australia. In M. Simms (ed.), *The Paradox of Parties*, St Leonards: Allen and Unwin, pp. 87–93.

German Government website. <http://www.bundesregierung.de>

Gidengil, E. 1996: Gender Attitudes toward Quotas for Women Candidates in Canada. *Women and Politics*, 16 (4): 21–44.

Gidengil, A., Blais, A., Nadeu, R. and Nevitte, N. 2003: Women to the Left? Gender Difference in Political Beliefs and Policy Preference. In M. Tremblay and L. Trimble (eds), *Women and Electoral Politics in Canada*, Ontario: Oxford University Press, pp. 140–56:

Gilligan, C. 1982: *In a Different Voice*. Cambridge, MA: Harvard University Press.

Githens, M. 1983: The Elusive Paradigm: Gender, Politics and Political Behaviour: The State of the Art. In A. W. Fenifer (ed.), *Political Science: The State of the Art*, American Political Association, pp. 471–99.

Githens, M., Norris, P. and Lovenduski, J. (eds) 1994: *Different Roles, Different Voices*. New York: Harper Collins.

Goetz, A. M. 1996: Women Development Agents in Bangladesh. In S. Rai and G. Lievesly (eds), *Women and the State*, London: Taylor and Francis, pp. 123–35.

Goetz, A. M. 1998: Women in Politics and Gender Equity in Policy: South Africa and Uganda. *Review of African Political Economy*, 25 (76): 241–63.

Goot, M. and Reid, E. 1984: Women: If Not Apolitical, Then Conservative. In J. Siltanen and M. Stanworth (eds), *Women and the Public Sphere*, London: Hutchinson, pp. 122–36 (originally published 1975).

Goss, S. 1984: Women's Initiatives in Local Government. In M. Boddy and C. Fudge (eds), *Local Socialism: Labour Councillors and New Left Alternatives*. London: Macmillan.

Goss, S. 1988: *Local Labour and Local Government*. Edinburgh: Edinburgh University Press.

Gray, T. 2003: Electoral Gender Quotas: Lessons from Argentina and Chile. *Bulletin of Latin American Research*, 22 (1): 52–78.

Green, P. 1985: *Retrieving Democracy: In Search of Civic Equality*. London: Methuen.

Greenleft: New women's party a blow to ALP. <http://www.greenleft.org.au/back/1995/200/200p12.htm>

Grey, S. 2002: Does Size Matter? Critical Mass and New Zealand's Women MPs. *Parliamentary Affairs*, 55 (1): 19–29.

Gyford, J., Leach, S. and Game, C. 1989: *The Changing Politics of Local Government.* London: Unwin Hyman.

Ha'aretz, English edition 18 Dec. 2003: 'Women in the Knesset.' <http://www.haaretz.com/hasen/pages/ShartElection.jhtml?itemNo=244696&contrassI>

Haase-Dubosc, D. 1999: Sexual Difference and Politics in France Today. *Feminist Studies*, 25 (1): 183–211.

Halford, S. 1987: Women's Initiatives in Local Government: Tokenism or Power? Working paper 58, Urban and Regional Studies, University of Sussex.

Halford, S. 1989: Local Authority Women's Initiatives 1982–1988. Working Paper 69, Urban and Regional Studies, University of Sussex.

Halford, S. 1992: Feminist Change in a Patriarchal Organisation: The Experience of Women's Initiatives in Local Government and Implications for Feminist Perspectives on State Institutions. In M. Savage and A. Witz (eds), *Gender and Bureaucracy*, Oxford: Basil Blackwell, pp. 155–85.

Handler, J. 2002: *Local Government Today*. Manchester: Manchester University Press.

Harris, S. 2000: Following the Leaders. In J. Boston, S. Church, S. Levine, E. McLeay and N. Roberts (eds), *Left Turn*, Wellington: Victoria University Press, pp. 77–88.

Hayes, B. C. and McAllister, I. 1997: Gender, Party Leader, and Election Outcomes in Australia, Britain and the United States. *Comparative Political Studies*, 30 (1): 3–27.

Heath, A., Jowell, R. and Curtice, J. 1985: *How Britain Votes*. Oxford: Pergamon Press.

Hedlund, G. 1985: Wameris Interests in Local Politics. In K. Jones and A. Jonsdottir (eds), *The Political Interests of Gender*, London: Sage, pp. 79–105.

Hedlund, G. 1998: Gender, Power and Organisational Changes in Swedish Local Politics. Paper presented at Aarhus.

Hedlund, G. and Pehrman, K. 2000: Gender, Power and Organisation in Local Politics. Paper presented in the Gender and Local Politics or Governance: Structural and Institutional Changes in the 90s, panel. European Consortium for Political Research, Copenhagen.

Hellenic Women's Political Party 1998: <http://kommaellinidgynaikon.tripod.com/english/righten.html>

Henderson, A, Kernot, C. and Delahunty, M. 2000: In the Party: We Want You as a New Recruit! In K. Deverell, R. Huntley, P. Sharpe and J. Tilly (eds), *Party Girls: Labor Women Now*. Annadale: Pluto Press.

Hesli, V. L., Ha-Lyong, J., Reisinger, W. M. and Miller, A. H. 2001: The Gender Divide in Russian Politics: Attitudinal and Behaviourial Considerations. *Women and Politics*, 22 (2): 41–77.

Heywood, A. 2004: *Politics*. London: Palgrave Macmillan.

Hollis, P. 1979: *Women in Public: The Women's Movement 1850–1900*. London: Allen and Unwin.

Hollis, P. 1987: *Ladies Elect: Women in English Local Government 1865–1915*. Oxford: Clarendon Press.

Hoskyns, C. 1994: Gender Issues in International Relations: The Case of the European Community. *Review of International Studies*, 20: 225–39.

Hoskyns, C. 1996a: The EU and the Women Within. In R. A. Elman (ed.), *Sexual Politics and the EU*, Providence, RI:Berg Hahn, pp. 13-22.

Hoskyns, C. 1996b: *Integrating Gender*. London: Verso.

Hoskyns, C. 2001: Gender Politics in the EU: The Context for Job Training. In A. G. Mazur (ed.), *State Feminism, Women's Movements, and Job Training*, New York: Routledge, pp. 31–48.

Htun, M. and Jones, M. 2002: Engendering the Right to Participate in Decision-Making: Electoral Quotas and Women's Leadership in Latin America. In N. Craske and M. Molyneux (eds), *Gender, the Politics of Rights and Democracy in Latin America*, Basingstoke: Palgrave, pp. 432–56.

Huddy, L. and Terkildsen, N. 1993a: The Consequences of Gender Stereotypes for Women Candidates at Different Levels and Types of Office. *Political Research Quarterly*, 46 (3): 503–25.

Huddy, L. and Terkildsen, N. 1993b: Gender Stereotypes and the Perception of Male/Female Candidates. *American Journal of Political Science*, 37 (1): 119–47.

Huntley, R. 2000: Party Culture, Popular Images. In K. Deverall, R. Huntley, P. Sharpe and J. Tilly (eds), *Party Girls: Labor Women Now*, Annadale: Pluto Press, pp. 2–9.

Indian Parliament website: <http://164.100.24.208/1s/1smember/mindetail.sp?minType=ca>

Inglehart, M. L. 1981: Political Interest in West European Women. *Comparative Political Studies*, 14 (3): 299–326.

Inglehart, R. and Norris, P. 2003: *Rising Tide: Gender Equality and Cultural Change around the World*. Cambridge: Cambridge University Press.

International Institute for Democracy and Electoral Assistance (IDEA) 2003: Women in Politics Beyond Numbers: Women in Parliament Beyond Numbers. <http://www.idea int/women/parl htm>

International Union of Local Authorities 1998: *Women in Local Government*, Sweden: IULA.

International Union of Local Authorities 2003: Women in Local Decision-making Newsletter, July 2003. <http://www.iula-int.org/iula/upload/template/templatedocs/iulanewsletter wldmoctober 2003(eng)2.doc>

Inter-Parliamentary Union 1992: *Women and Political Power*. Geneva: Reports and Documents 19.

Inter-Parliamentary Union 1995: *Women in Parliaments, 1945–1995*. Geneva: Reports and Documents 23.

Inter-Parliamentary Union 1997: *Men and Women in Politics: Democracy Still in the making*. Geneva: Reports and Documents 100.

Inter-Parliamentary Union website. <http://www.ipu.org/wmn-e/world.htm>

Irish Government website. <www.ivlgov.ie>

Ishiyama, J. 2003: Women's Parties in Post-Communist Politics. *East European Politics*, 17 (2): 266–304.

Israeli Parliament website: <http://www.knesset.gov.il/mk/eng/mkindex_current_eng.asp?view=4>

Iwanaga, K. 1998: *Women in Japanese Politics*. Occasional Paper 37. Stockholm: Stockholm University, Centre for Pacific Asia Studies.

Jaggar, A. and Young, I. M. (eds) 1999: *The Blackwell Companion to Feminist Philosophy*. Oxford: Basil Blackwell.

Japanese Government website. <http://Kantei.go.JP>

Jenson, J. and Valiente, C. 2003: Comparing Two Movements for Gender Parity. In L. Banaszak, K. Beckwith and D. Rucht (eds), *Women's Movements Facing the Reconfigured State*, Cambridge: Cambridge University Press, pp. 69–93.

Jharta, B. 1996: *Women and Politics in India*. New Delhi: Deep and Deep.

Johnson, C. 1996: Gendered Transitions in Eastern Europe, *Feminist Review*, 52: 102–18.

Jonsdottir, A. 1985: On the Concept of Interests, Women's Interests and the Limitations of Interest Theory. In K. Jones and A. Jonsdottir (eds), *The Political Interests of Gender*, London: Sage, pp. 33–65.

Jones, K. and Jonsdottir, A. 1985a: Gender as an Analytic Category. In K. Jones and A. Jonsdottir (eds), *The Political Interests of Gender*. London: Sage, pp. 1–10.

Jones, K. and Jonsdottir, A. (eds) 1985b: *The Political Interests of Gender*. London: Sage.

Jones, M. 1998: Gender Quotas, Electoral Laws, and the Election of Women: Lessons from the Argentine Provinces. *Comparative Political Studies*, 31 (1): 3–21.

Jones, R. and Trystan, D. 2001: Wales. In P. Norris (ed.), *Britain Votes 2001*, Oxford: Oxford University Press.

Kahn, K. F. 1996: *The Political Consequences of Being a Woman*. New York: Columbia University Press.

Kampworth, K. 1998: Feminism, Anti-feminism, and Electoral Politics in Postwar Nicaragua and El Salvador. *Political Science Quarterly*, 113 (2): 259–80.

Kanter, R. Moss 1977: *Men and Women of the Corporation*. New York: Basic Books.

Karvonen, L. and Selle, P. (eds) 1995: *Women in Nordic Politics: Closing the Gap*. Aldershot: Dartmouth.

Kaushik, S. 2000: Women and Political Parties. In N. Sinha (ed.), *Women in Indian Politics*, New Delhi: Gyam Press, pp. 53–68.

Kavanagh J. (ed.) 1982: *The Politics of the Labour Party*. London: Allen and Unwin.

Keane, J. 1988: *Democracy and Civil Society*. London: Verso.

Kenworthy, L. and Malami, M. 1999: Gender Inequality in Political Representation: A Worldwide Comparative Analysis. *Social Forces*, 78 (1): 235–69.

Koch, J. 1997: Candidate Gender and Women's Psychological Engagement in Politics. *American Politics Quarterly*, 25 (1): 118–34.

Kochkina, E. V. 2001: Women in Russian Government Bodies. *Russian Social Science Review*, 42 (2): 44–60.

Kolinsky, E. 1993: Party Change and Women's Representation in Germany. In J. Lovenduski and P. Norris (eds), *Gender and Party Politics*, London: Sage, pp. 113–46.

Kostadinova, T. 2003: Women's Legislative Representation in Post-Communist Bulgaria. In R. E. Matland and K. Montgomery (eds), *Women's Access to Political Power in Post-Communist Europe*, Oxford: Oxford University Press, pp. 304–20.

Kuzio, T. 2002a: Gender Issues Hijacked by 'Party of Power' in Ukraine's Election Campaign. 26 Feb. <http://www.rferl.org/newsline/2002/02/5-NOT/not-260202.asp>

Kuzio, T. 2002b: Women's Parties Seek to Rally Voters. *Ukrainian Weekly*, 70 (8) 24 Feb. <http://www.ukrweekly.com/Archive/2002/080208.shtml>

Labour Party 1994: Quotas for Women in the Labour Party: Briefing for MPs from Clare Short, Shadow Minister for Women. London: The Labour Party.

Labour Party 1995a: Fair Shares: Getting More Women into Local Government. London: The Labour Party.

Labour Party 1995b: Implementing Quotas for Women in Local Government: A Labour Party Consultation Paper. London: The Labour Party.

Labour Research 1995: March, p. 15.

Leblanc, R. N. 1999: *Bicycle Citizens*. Berkeley: University of California Press.

Leijenaar, M. 1998: Political Empowerment of Women in the Netherlands. In J. Bussemaker and R. Voet (eds), *Gender, Participation and Citizenship in the Netherlands*. Aldershot: Ashgate, pp. 91–107.

Lemish, D. and Drep, G. 2002: 'All the time his wife': Portrayals of First Ladies in the Israeli Press. *Parliamentary Affairs*, 55 (1): 129–42.

Levy, C. 2001: A Woman's Place? The Future Scottish Parliament. In E. Breitenbach and F. Mackay (eds.), *Women and Contemporary Scottish Politics*. Edinburgh: Polygon, pp. 183–6.

Liberal Democrats 1993: *Women*. Consultation Paper number 8. Dorchester: Liberal Democrat Publications.

Liberal Democrats 1995: *Equal Citizens*. Liberal Democrat Policy Paper.

Liddle, J. and Michielsens, E. 2000: Gender, Class and Political Power in Britain. In S. M. Rai (ed.), *International Perspectives on Gender and Democratisation*. Basingstoke: Macmillan, pp. 127–50.

Lindsay, I. 2001: Constitutional Change and the Gender Deficit. In E. Breitenbach and F. Mackay (eds), *Women and Contemporary Scottish Politics*, Edinburgh: Polygon, pp. 171–93.

Lister, R. 1995: Dilemmas in Engendering Citizenship. *Economy and Society*, 24 (1): 1–39.

Lister, R. 1997: *Citizenship: Feminist Perspectives*. Basingstoke: Macmillan Press Ltd.

Loach, L. 1985a: Local Government: What Have Women Got to Lose? *Spare Rib*, 151: 19–21.

Loach, L. 1985b: The Pains of Women in Labour. *Spare Rib*, 159: 18.

Local Government Management Board 1998: *First National Census: Survey of Local Authority Councillors in England and Wales in 1997*. London: Local Government Management Board.

Lovenduski, J. (ed.) 1988: *Women and European Politics: Contemporary Feminism and Public Policy*. Brighton: Wheatsheaf.

Lovenduski, J. 1993: Introduction: The Dynamics of Gender and Party. In J. Lovenduski and P. Norris (eds), *Gender and Party Politics*, London: Sage, pp. 8–11.

Lovenduski, J. 1996: Sex, Gender and British Politics. *Parliamentary Affairs*, 49 (1): 1–16.

Lovenduski, J. 1997: Gender Politics: A Breakthrough for Women? *Parliamentary Affairs*, 50 (4): 708–19.

Lovenduski, J. (ed.) 2000: *Feminism and Politics*. Aldershot: Ashgate-Dartmouth.

Lovenduski, J. 2001: Women and Politics. In P. Norris (ed.), *Britain Votes 2001*, Oxford: Oxford University Press, pp. 179–94.

Lovenduski, J. 2004: *Feminising Politics*. Cambridge: Polity.

Lovenduski, J. and Norris, P. (eds) 1993: *Gender and Party Politics*. London: Sage Publications.

Lovenduski, J. and Norris, P. 2003. Westminster Women: The Politics of Presence. *Political Studies*, 51 (1): 84–102.

Lovenduski, J. and Randall, V. 1993. *Contemporary Feminist Politics*. Oxford: Oxford University Press.

Lovenduski, J. and Stephenson, S. 1999: *Women in Decision-making: Report on Existing Research in the EU*. Brussels: EC, Employment and Social Affairs.

Lovenduski, J., Norris, P. and Burns, C. 1994: The Party and Women. In A. Seldon and S. Ball (eds), *Conservative Century*, Oxford: Oxford University Press, pp. 611–35.

McDiven, C. 1996: The Liberal Party and Women. In M. Simms (ed.), *The Paradox of Parties*. St Leonards: Allen and Unwin, pp. 94–9.

McDougall, L. 1998: *Westminster Women*. London: Vintage.

McGlen, N., O'Connor, K., van Assendelft, L. and Gunther, W. 2002: *Women, Politics and American Society*. New York: Longman.

MacIvor, H. 1996: *Women and Politics in Canada*. Ontario: Broadview Press.

MacIvor, H. 2003: Women and the Canadian Electoral System. In M. Tremblay and L. Trimble (eds), *Women and Electoral Politics in Canada*, Toronto: Oxford University Press, pp. 22–36.

Mackay, F. 2001: *Love and Politics*. London: Continuum.

Mackay, F. 2004: Gender and Political Representation in the UK: The State of the Discipline. *British Journal of Politics and International Relations*, 6 (1): 99–120.

Mackintosh, M. and Wainwright, H. 1987: *A Taste of Power*. London: Verso.

McLeay, E. 1995: *The Cabinet and Political Power in New Zealand*. Toronto: Oxford University Press.

McLeay, E. 2000: The New Parliament. In J. Boston, S. Church, S. Levine, E. McLeay and N. Roberts, *Left Turn*, Wellington: Victoria University Press, pp. 203–16.

McLeay, E. 2003: Representation, Selection and Election: The 2002 Parliament. In J. Boston, S. Church, S. Levine, E. McLeay and N. Roberts, *New Zealand Votes: the General Election of 2002*, Wellington: Victoria University Press, pp. 283–308.

McRobbie, A. 1997: Feminism and the Third Way. *Feminist Review*, 64: 97–113.

McSmith, A. 2003: Revolt over All-Women Short List Threatens Bevan's Seat. *Independent on Sunday*, p. 10. 14.12.2003

Maguire, G. E. 1998: *Conservative Women: A History of Women and the Conservative Party, 1874–1997*. Basingstoke: Macmillan.

Mansbridge, J. 1999: Should Blacks Represent Blacks and Women Represent Women? A Contingent 'Yes'. *Journal of Politics*, 61 (3): 628–58.

Matland, R. E. and Montgomery, K. (eds) 2003: *Women's Access to Political Power in Post-Communist Europe*. Oxford: Oxford University Press.

Matland, R. E. and Studlar, D. T. 1996: The Contagion of Women Candidates in Single-Member District and Proportional Representation Electoral Systems: Canada and Norway. *Journal of Politics*, 58 (3): 707–33.

Matland, R. E. and Studlar, D. T. 1998: Gender and the Electoral Opportunity Structure in the Canadian Provinces. *Political Research Quarterly*, 51, (1): 117–40.

Matland, R. E. and Studlar, D. T. 2004: Determinants of Legislative Turnover: A Cross-National Analysis. *British Journal of Political Science*, 34 (1): 87–113.

Matland, R. E. and Taylor, M. M. 1997: Electoral System Effects on Women's Representation: Theoretical Arguments and Evidence from Costa Rica. *Comparative Political Studies*, 30 (20): 186–210.

Mazur, A. G. 1995: *Gender Bias and the State*. Pittsburgh: University of Pittsburgh Press.

Mazur, A. G. (ed.) 2001: *State Feminism, Women's Movements, and Job Training*. New York: Routledge.

Mazur, A. G. 2002: *Theorising Feminist Policy*. Oxford: Oxford University Press.

Megyery, K. (ed.) 1991: *Women in Canadian Politics*. Toronto: Dundurn Press.

Mendus, S. 1992: Losing the Faith: Feminism and Democracy. In J. Dunn (ed.), *Democracy the Unfinished Journey*, Oxford: Oxford University Press, pp. 207–20.

Miller, R. Lee, Wilford, R. and Donoghue, F. 1996: *Women and Political Participation in Northern Ireland*. Aldershot: Avebury.

Mindanews 2003: Gabriela Women's Party convened in Davao. <http://www.mindanews.com/2003/04/13nws-women.html>

Mirza, H. 1997: *Black British Feminism*. London: Routledge.

Mitchell, J. 1975: *Women and Equality*. Capetown: University of Cape Town Press.

Mitchell, J. 1976: The Rights and Wrongs of Women. In J. Mitchell and A. Oakley (eds), *The Rights and Wrongs of Women*, Harmondsworth: Penguin, pp. 304–78.

Mitchell, J. 1984: *Women: The Longest Revolution*. London: Virago.

Mitchell, J. and Oakley, A. (eds) 1976: *The Rights and Wrongs of Women*. Harmondsworth: Penguin.

Mitchell, J. and Oakley, A. (eds) 1986: *What is Feminism?* Oxford: Basil Blackwell.

Montane, M. 2000: More Women Politicians but not so Many Women Leaders? The Double-Level Gender Gap in French Local Politics. ECPR, Copenhagen, Gender and local politics or governance: structural and institutional changes in the 90s panel.

Moon, J. and Fountain, I. 1997: Keeping the Gates? Women as Ministers in Australia, 1970–96. *Australian Journal of Political Science*, 32 (3): 455–67.

Moser, R. G. 2003: Electoral Systems and Women's Representation: The Strange Case of Russia. In R. E. Matland and K. Montgomery (eds.), *Women's Access to Political Power in Post-Communist Europe*, Oxford: Oxford University Press, pp. 153–72.

Motion, J. 1999: Politics as Destiny, Duty and Devotion. *Political Communication*, 16 (1): 61–77.

Mowlem, M. 2003: *Momentum: The Struggle for Peace, Politics and the People*. London: Coronet.

Mueller, C. M. (ed.) 1985: *The Politics of the Gender Gap*. London: Sage.

Myakayaka-Manzini, M. 2003: Women Empowered: Women in Parliament in South Africa. <http://www.idea.int/women/parl/studies5a.htm>

Nairn, T. 2001: Gender Goes to the Top of the Agenda. In E. Breitenbach and F. Mackay (eds), *Women and Contemporary Scottish Politics*, Edinburgh: Polygon, pp. 195–6.

Nelson, B. and Chowdhury, N. (eds) 1994: *Women and Politics Worldwide*. Newhaven and London: Yale University Press.

New South Wales Parliament website. <http://www.parliament.NSW.gov.av>

New Zealand Government website. <www.dpme.govt.nz>

Nicholson, E. 1996: *Secret Society: Inside – and Outside – the Conservative Party*. London: Indigo.

Niven, D. 1998: Party Elites and Women Candidates: The Shape of Bias. *Women and Politics*, 19 (2): 57–80.

Norris, P. 1985: The Gender Gap: A Cross-National Trend? In C. M. Mueller (ed.), *The Politics of the Gender Gap*, London: Sage, pp. 217–36.

Norris, P. 1987: *Politics and Sexual Equality*. Boulder, CO: Lynne Rienner Publishers Inc.

Norris, P. 1996a: Gender Realignment in Comparative Perspective. In M. Simms (ed.), *The Paradox of Parties*, St Leonards: Allen and Unwin, pp. 109–29.

Norris, P. 1996b: Mobilising the 'Women's Vote': The Gender-Generation Gap in Voting Behaviour. *Parliamentary Affairs*, 49 (2): 333–42.

Norris, P. 1997a: Anatomy of a Labour Landslide. In P. Norris and N. T. Gavin (eds), *Britain Votes 1997*, Oxford: Oxford University Press, pp. 1–24.

Norris, P. 1997b: Conclusions: Comparing Passages to Powers. In P. Norris (ed.), *Passages to Power*, Cambridge: Cambridge University Press, pp. 209–31.

Norris, P. (ed.) 1997c: *Passages to Power*. Cambridge: Cambridge University Press.

Norris, P. 1997d: Theories of Recruitment. In P. Norris (ed.), *Passages to Power*, Cambridge: Cambridge University Press, pp. 1–14.

Norris, P. (ed.) 1998: *Elections and Voting Behaviour*. Aldershot: Dartmouth.

Norris, P. 2001: *Britain Votes 2001*. Oxford: Oxford University Press.

Norris, P. and Gavin, N. T. (eds) 1997: *Britain Votes 1997*. Oxford: Oxford University Press.

Norris P. and Lovenduski, J. 1993: If Only More Candidates Came Forward: Supply-Side Explanations of Candidate Selection in Britain. *British Journal of Political Science*, 23 (3): 373–418.

Norris, P. and Lovenduski, J. 1995: *Political Recruitment: Gender, Race and Class in the British Parliament*. Cambridge: Cambridge University Press.

Nowacki, D. 2003: Women in Russian Regional Associations. In R. E. Matland and K. Montgomery (eds), *Women's Access to Political Power in Post-Communist Europe*, Oxford: Oxford University Press, pp. 173–95.

Oakley, A. and Mitchell, J. (eds) 1997: *Who's Afraid of Feminism?* London: Hamish Hamilton.

Ofei-Aboagye, E. 2000: Promoting the Participation of Women in Local Governance and Development: The Case of Ghana. ECDPM Discussion Paper 18. Maastricht: ECDPM.

Okin, S. M. 1980: *Women in Western Political Thought*. London: Virago.

Ośka: National Women's Information Centre. Participation of women in local government in Poland. <http://www.oska.org.pl.English/womeninpoland/local/html>, accessed 24 May 2002.

Outshoorn, J. 1998: Furthering the 'Cause': Femocrat Strategies in National Government. In J. Bussemaker and R. Voet (eds), *Gender, Participation and Citizenship in the Netherlands*, Aldershot: Ashgate, pp. 108–21.

Pankhurst, D. 2002: Women and Politics in Africa: The case of Uganda. *Parliamentary Affairs*, 55 (1): 119–28.

Parker, J. 1981: Labour Women – the Battle for a Political Voice. *Spare Rib*, 109: 31.

Parkin, D. 1992: Women's Units at a Time of Change. Occasional Paper No. 5. Work and Gender Research Unit, Bradford University.

Parry, G., Moyser, G. and Day, N. 1991: *Political Participation and Democracy in Britain*. Cambridge: Cambridge University Press.

Pateman, C. 1970: *Participation and Democratic Theory*. Cambridge: Cambridge University Press.

Pateman, C. 1988: *The Sexual Contract*. Cambridge: Polity.

Pateman, C. 1992: *The Disorder of Women*. Cambridge: Polity.

Perkins, A. 2004: *The Authorised Biography of Barbara Castle*. London: Pan.

Perrigo, S. 1986: Socialist Feminism and the Labour Party: Some Experiences from Leeds. *Feminist Review*, 23: 101–8.

Phillips, A. 1987: *Divided Loyalties: Dilemmas of Sex and Class*. London: Virago.

Phillips, A. 1991: *Engendering Democracy*. Cambridge: Polity.

Phillips, A. 1992: Universal Pretensions in Political Thought. In M. Barrett and A. Phillips (eds), *Destabilizing Theory: Contemporary Feminist Debates*, Cambridge: Polity, pp. 511–19.

Phillips, A. 1993: *Democracy and Difference*. Cambridge: Polity.

Phillips, A. 1995: *The Politics of Presence*. Oxford: Oxford University Press.

Phillips, A. (ed.) 1998: *Feminism and Politics*. Oxford: Oxford University Press.

Phillips, A. 1999: Democracy. In A. Jaggar and I. M. Young (eds), *The Blackwell Companion to Feminist Philosophy*, Oxford: Basil Blackwell, pp. 511–19.

Phillips, A. 1999: *Which Equalities Matter?* Cambridge: Polity.

Phomphipak, V. and Henk, S. Women's Party takes Single-Minded Approach to Winning. <http://www.ijf-cij.org/folder_file_for_cambodia/9.htm>, Retrieved 18 Dec. 2003.

Pikkala, S. 2000: Representation of Women in Finnish Local Government: Effects of the 1995 Gender Quota Legislation. Paper presented in the Gender and Local Politics or Governance: Structural and Institutional Changes in the 1990s panel, European Consortium for Political Research, Copenhagen.

Pitkin, H. 1972: *The Concept of Representation*. Berkeley: University of California Press.

Poonacha, V. 1997a: From the Fringes to the Centre. In V. Poonacha (ed.), *Women, Empowerment and Political Parties*, Research Centre for Women's Studies, SNDT Women's University, pp. 1–33.

Poonacha, V. (ed.) 1997b: *Women, Empowerment and Political Parties*. Research Centre for Women's Studies, SNDT Women's University.

Pringle, R. and Watson, S. 1992: Women's Interests and the Post-Structuralist State. In M. Barrett and A. Phillips (eds), *Destabilizing Theory*, Cambridge: Polity, pp. 53–73.

Puwar, N. 2004: Thinking About Making a Difference. *British Journal of Politics and International Relations*, 6 (1): 3–19.

Raaum, N. C. 1999: Women in Parliamentary Politics: Historical Lines of Development. In Bergqvist et al. (eds), *Equal Democracies*, Oslo: Scandinavian University Press, pp. 27–47.

Radice, L. 1985: *Winning Women's Votes*. London: Fabian Society, no. 507, Blackrose Press.

Rai, S. 1996: Women and the State in the Third World: Some Issues for Debate. In S. Rai and G. Lievesly (eds), *Women and the State*, London: Taylor and Francis, pp. 17–26.

Rai, S. M. (ed.) 2000: *International Perspectives on Gender and Democratisation*. Basingstoke: Macmillan.

Rai, S. and Lievesly, G. (eds) 1996: *Women and the State*. London: Taylor and Francis.

Rai, S. M. and Sharma, K. 2000: Democratising the Indian Parliament: The 'Reservations for Women' Debate. In S. M. Rai (ed.), *International Perspectives on Gender and Democratisation*, Basingstoke: Macmillan, pp. 151–63.

Raj, R. D. 1998: Women Leaders Pave the Way for New Government. <http://www.oneworld.org/ips2/mar98/15_30_054.html>

Ramchander, M. and Lakshmi, K. 1993: *Women and Politics: A Study in Political Participation*. Hyderabad: Booklinks.

Rees, T. 1998: *Mainstreaming Equality in the European Union*. London: Routledge.

Reynolds, A. 1999: Women in the Legislatures and Executives of the World: Knocking at the Highest Glass Ceiling. *World Politics*, 51: 547–72.

Rhode, D. 1989: *Justice and Gender: Sex Discrimination and the Law*. New Haven: Yale University Press.

Rhode, D. 1990: *Theoretical Perspectives as Sexual Difference*. New Haven: Yale University Press.

Rhode, D. 1992: The Politics of Paradigms: Gender Difference and Gender Disadvantage. In G. Bock and S. James (eds), *Beyond Equality and Difference*, London: Routledge.

Roelofs, S. 1989: In and Against the State. *Spare Rib*, 200 (March): 47.

Rose, R. (ed.) 2000: *International Encyclopedia of Elections*. London: Macmillan.

Rowbotham, S. 1986: Feminism and Democracy. In D. Held (ed.), *New Forms of Democracy*, London: Sage.

Rowbotham, S. 1992: *Women in Movement*. London: Routledge.

Rowbotham, S. 1997: *The Century of Women*. London: Penguin.

Ruddick, S. 1990: *Maternal Thinking: Towards a Politics of Peace*. London: Women's Press.

Rueschemeyer, M. 2003: Women in Politics in East Germay. In R. E. Matland and K. Montgomery (eds), *Women's Access to Political Power in Post-Communist Europe*, Oxford: Oxford University Press, pp. 231–49.

Russell, M. 2000a: *Women's Representation in UK Politics*. London: The Constitution Unit, University College London.

Russell, M. 2000b: *Women's Representation in UK Politics: What Can be Done within the Law?* London: The Constitution Unit, University College.

Salmenniemi, S. 2003: Democracy without Women? Russian Parliamentary Elections and Gender Equality. <http://www.balticdata.info/russia_elections_suvi.htm>

Sapiro, V. 1975: Research Frontier Essay: When are Interests Interesting? *American Political Science Review*, 75: 701–16.

Sassoon, A. Showstack 1987: *Women and the State*. London: Routledge.

Savage, M. and Witz, A. (eds) 1992: *Gender and Bureaucracy*. Oxford: Basil Blackwell.

Sawer, M. 2002: The Representation of Women in Australia: Meaning and Make-Believe. *Parliamentary Affairs*, 55 (1): 5–18.

Schumpeter, J. A. 1966: *Capitalism, Socialism and Democracy*. London: Unwin University Books.

Scottish Local Government Unit 1999: The 1999 Scottish Elections. *SLGIU Bulletin*, 113 (May/June).

Scottish Parliament website. <http://www.scottish.parliament.uk/msps/ministers220503.htm>

Seldon, A. 2001: *The Blair Effect*. London: Little, Brown.

Seldon, A. and Ball, S. 1994: *Conservative Century*. Oxford: Oxford University Press.

Selzer, R. A., Newman, J. and Leighton, M. V. 1997: *Sex as a Political Variable*. Boulder, CO: Lynne Reiner.

Shanley, M. Lydon and Narayan, U. 1997: *Reconstructing Political Theory: Feminist Perspectives*. Cambridge: Polity.

Sharfman, D. 1994: Women and Politics in Israel. In B. Nelson and N. Chowdhury (eds), *Women and Politics Worldwide*, New Haven and London: Yale University Press, pp. 380–95.

Sillaste, G. G. 1995: Sociogender Relations in the Period of Social Transformation in Russia. *Russian Social Science Review*, 36 (4): 66–79.

Siltanen, J. and Stanworth, M. (eds) 1984: *Women and the Public Sphere*. London: Hutchinson.

Simms, M. (ed.) 1996: *The Paradox of Politics*. St Leonards: Allen and Unwin.

Simon-Peirano, D. 2000: Report from France. Women in Decision-making. European Database. <http://www.db-decision.de/CoRe/France.htm>

Sinha, N. 2000: *Women in Indian Politics*. New Delhi: Gyan Press.

Skjeie, H. 1991: The Rhetoric of Difference: On Women's Inclusion into Political Elites. *Politics and Society*, 19: 233–63.

Skjeie, H. 1992: Den politiske betydningen av kjonn. En studie av norsk topp-politikk. Rapport nr. 11. Oslo: Hovedoppgave i statsvitenskap.

Skjeie, H. 1993: Ending the Male Political Hegemony: The Norwegian Experience. In J. Lovenduski and P. Norris (eds), *Gender and Party Politics*, London: Sage, pp. 231–62.

Social Statistics and Indicators 2000: *The World's Women*. New York: United Nations.

Squires, J. 1996: Quotas for Women: Fair Representation? *Parliamentary Affairs*, 49 (1): 71–88.

Squires, J. and Wickham-Jones, M. 2001: *Women in Parliament: A Comparative Analysis*. Manchester: Equal Opportunities Commission.

Stark, A. 1997: Combating the Backlash: How Swedish Women Won the War. In A. Oakley and J. Mitchell (eds), *Who's Afraid of Feminism?* London: Hamish Hamilton, pp. 224–41.

Steans, J. 1998: *Gender and International Relations*. Cambridge: Polity.

Stephenson, M. 1998: *The Glass Trap Door*. London: Fawcett.

Stephenson, M. 2001: *Fawcett Survey of Women MPs*. London: Fawcett.

Stevens, A. 2002: *Politicos' Guide to Local Government*. London: Politicos.

Stewart, J. 1995: A Future for Local Government as Community Government. In J. Stewart and G. Stoker (eds), *Local Government in the 1990s*, London: Macmillan, pp. 249–68.

Stewart, J. and Stoker, G. (eds) 1995: *Local Government in the 1990s*. London: Macmillan.

Stokes, W. 1998: Feminist Democracy: The Case for Women's Committees. *Contemporary Politics*, 4 (1): 23–37.

Stone, I. 1988: Equal Opportunities in Local Authorities – Developing Effective Strategies for the Implementation of Policies for Women. Equal Opportunities Commission Research Series, HMSO.

Studlar, D. T. and McAllister, I. 1998: Candidate Gender and Voting in the 1997 British General Election: Did Labour Quotas Matter? *Journal of Legislative Studies*, 4 (3): 72–91.

Studlar, D. T. and Matland, R. E. 1996: The Dynamics of Women's Representation in the Canadian Provinces: 1975–1994. *Canadian Journal of Political Science*, 29 (2): 269–93.

Studlar, D. T., McAllister, I. and Hayes, B. C. 1998: Explaining the Gender Gap in Voting: A Cross-National Analysis. *Social Science Quarterly*, 79 (4): 779–98.

Styrkarsdottir, A. 1999: Women's Lists in Iceland – A Response to Political Lethargy. In C. Bergqvist et al. (eds), *Equal Democracies? Gender and Politics in the Nordic Countries*, Oslo: Scandinavian University Press, pp. 88–96.

Sundberg, J. 1995: Women in Scandinavian party organisations. In L. Karvonen and P. Selle (eds), *Women in Nordic Politics: Closing the Gap*, Aldershot: Dartmouth, pp. 813–14.

Sunstein, C. 1991: Preferences and Politics. *Philosophy and Public Affairs*, 20 (1): 3–34.

Swarup, H. L., Sinha, N., Ghosh, C. and Rajput, P. 1994: Women's Political Engagement in India. In B. Nelson and N. Chowdhury, *Women and Politics Worldwide*, New Haven and London: Yale University Press, pp. 361–79.

Tasmanian Parliament website. <http://www.parliament.tas.gov.au>

Thakkar, U. and Gawankar, R. 1997: Reservation and the Empowerment of Women: The Emerging Issues. In V. Poonacha (ed.), *Women, Empowerment and Political Parties*, Research Centre for Women's Studies, SNDT Women's University, pp. 87–100.

Thatcher, M. 1995: *The Downing Street Years*. London: HarperCollins.

Thomas, S. 1994: *How Women Legislate*. Oxford: Oxford University Press.

Thomas, S. and Wilcox, C. 1998: *Women and Elective Office: Past, Present and Future*. Oxford: Oxford University Press.

Thompson, J. A. and Moncrief, G. F. 1993: The Implications of Term Limits for Women and Minorities: Some Evidence from the States. *Social Science Quarterly*, 74 (2): 320–2.

Tolleson-Rinehart, S. and Josephson, J. J. (eds) 2000: *Gender and American Politics: Women, Men and the Political Process*. Armonk, NY: M. E. Sharpe.

Tremblay, M. 1998: Do Female MPs Substantively Represent Women? A Study of Legislative Behaviour in Canada's 35th Parliament. *Canadian Journal of Political Science*, 31 (3): 435–65.

Tremblay, M. 2003: Women's Representational Role in Australia and Canada: The Impact of Political Context. *Australian Journal of Political Science*, 38 (2): 215–38.

Tremblay, M. and Trimble, L. 2003: *Women and Electoral Politics in Canada*. Toronto: Oxford University Press.

Tronto, J. C. 1987: Beyond Gender Difference to a Theory of Care. *Signs*, 12: 644–63.

Turquet, L. 2003a: *Women's Votes and the Conservative Party 2003*. London: Fawcett Society.

Turquet, L. 2003b: *Women's Votes and the Liberal Democrats 2003*. London: Fawcett Society.

Ugandan Government website: <http://www.parliament.go.ug/index_composition.htm>

United Nations 1977: *Women in the United Nations*. New York: United Nations.

United Nations website. <http://www.UN.ORG>

United States Government website. <www.firstgov.gov>

Vallance, E. and Davies, E. 1986: *Women of Europe: Women MEPs and Equality Policy*. Cambridge: Cambridge University Press.

Voet, R. 1998: Citizenship and Female Participation. In J. Bussemaker and R. Voet, *Gender, Participation and Citizenship in the Netherlands*, Aldershot: Ashgate, pp. 11–24.

Wangerud, L. 2000: Representing Women. In P. Esaiasson and K. Heidar (eds), *Beyond Westminster and Congress: The Nordic Experience*, Columbus: Ohio State University Press.

Ward, L. 2000: Learning from the 'Babe' Experience: How the Finest Hour Became a Fiasco. In A. Coote (ed.), *New Gender Agenda*, London: IPPR, pp. 23–32.

Ward, M. 2001: Women and the Local Government Elections 2001. Constitutionalism and Governance in Transition, University of Ulster Transitional Justice Seminar Series, Waterfront Hall, 2 November 2001 (unpublished paper).

Ward, M. 2002: Gender in Transition? Social and Political Transformation in Northern Ireland. Paper presented to the Gender Research Forum, Women's and Equality Unit, Cabinet Office.

Ward, R. 2002: Invisible Women: The Political Roles of Unionist and Loyalist Women in Contemporary Northern Ireland. *Parliamentary Affairs*, 55 (2): 167–78.

Waring, M., Greenwood, G. and Pintat, C. 2000: *Politics: Women's Insights.* Inter-Parliamentary Union. <http://www.IPU.ORG/spl3-e/hr04/womensinsight.pdf>

Watson, J. 1983: Take Over Town Hall. *Spare Rib*, 129: 18.

Watson, P. and Anand, V. 1984: *Women and Politics.* London: The Committee for Socialist Renewal.

Watson, S. (ed.) 1990: *Playing the State.* London: Verso.

Webb, P. 2002: *Political Parties in Advanced Industrial Democracies.* Oxford: Oxford University Press.

Webster, B. 1983: Women's Committees. *Local Government Policy Making*, November, pp. 27–34.

Welch, S. 1977: Women as Political Animals? A Test of Some Explanations for Male–Female Political Participation Differences. *American Journal of Political Science*, 4: 711–30.

Welsh Assembly website. <http://wales.gov.uk/organicabinet/content/members/cabinet-members-e.htm>

Western Australia website. <http://www.parliament.WA.gov.AU>

Wilcox, C., Stark, B. and Thomas, S. 2003: Popular Support for Electing Women in Eastern Europe. In R. E. Matland and K. Montgomery (eds), *Women's Access to Political Power in Post-Communist Europe*, Oxford: Oxford University Press, pp. 43–62.

Wilford, R. and Galligan, Y. 2000: Gender and Party Politics in Northern Ireland. In Y. Galligan, R. Ward and R. Wilford (eds), *Contesting Politics*, Oxford, Westview Press, pp. 169–80.

Wilkinson, H. 1994: *No Turning Back, Generations and the Genderquake.* London: Demos.

Winslow, A. (ed.) 1995: *Women, Politics and the United Nations.* Westport, CT: Greenwood Press.

Women's International Network News 1994a: France: Women Absent from Political Office. 20 (1): 65–70.

Women's International Network News 1994b: Japan: Political Participation by Women Still Limited. 20 (3): 57–63.

Women's International Network News 1997: Japan: Only 23 Women Elected to Parliament. 23 (1): 58–9.

Women's International Network News 2000: Japan: Women Win 35 Seats in General Election and Two Governors. 26 (4): 53–6.

World Campaign for Human Rights 1995: *Discrimination Against Women: The Convention and the Committee.* Geneva: United Nations.

Young, H. 1993: *One of Us.* London: Pan.

Young, I. M. 1990: *Justice and the Politics of Difference.* Princeton: Princeton University Press.

Young, K. and Rao, N. 1994: *Coming to Terms with Change: The Local Government Councillor in 1993.* London: Joseph Rowntree Foundation and LGC Communications.

Young, L. 2000: *Feminists and Party Politics.* Vancouver: University of British Columbia Press.

INDEX

activism, political: gender differences in, 51–4
Adams, Abigail, 49
Additional Member system (UK), *see under* proportional representation
Aelvoet, Magda, 137
Africa: enfranchisement of women in, 40; political participation of women in, 169
African Americans: as Democrat voters, 235 n. 9; as interest group, 19
African National Congress (ANC; South Africa): women and, 170
Akamatsu, Ryoko, 167
Albright, Madeleine, 163
Alexander, Wendy, 150, 151
Algeria, 6
all-women short lists, 7, 61, 66, 72, 85, 102, 108, 109
Alliance (APNI; Northern Ireland), 8, 84, 109, 110, 154
Alliance 90/Green Party, *see* Green Party, in Germany
Alliot-Marie, Michele, 142, 160
American Equal Rights Association (AERA), 49
American Woman Suffrage Association (AWSA), 49
Amory, Merle, 183
Amos, Baroness, 150
Andorra: elects same proportion of women as USA, 163
Angiolini, Elish, 151
Anthony, Susan B., 49, 50
anti-slavery movement: and women's suffrage, 49
Arab countries: enfranchisement of women in, 40–1; exclusion of women from public life

in, 41, 142, 171; women in local government in, 204
Argentina: quotas in, 89; women politicians in, 31, 64; women's party in, 130
Armstrong, Hilary, 150
Asia: enfranchisement of women in, 40; women in local government in, 202–3, table 16.2
Aso, Taro, 168
Astell, Mary: and women's rights, 14
Athens Charter, 86
Aubry, Martine, 160
Aurat Foundation (Pakistan), 91
Australia, 6, 8; enfranchisement of women in, 40; 'mateship' culture of, 124, 126; political system of, 166; support for left by women voters in, 56; women in cabinet of, 166; women ignored in political literature of, 123–4; women in local government in, 176–7, 200–1; women in parliament of, 22, 166; women Senators in, 31
Australian Labor Party (ALP), 124–5, 166, 200; quotas in, 124–5, 126, 137
Australian Liberal Party: women's organizations in, 125–6
Australian Women's Party (AWP), 136, 137, 166

Baillie, Jackie, 151
Bangladesh: quotas (reserved seats) in, 91, 205; women in local government in, 203
Banotti, Mary, 114, 115
Beckett, Margaret, 100, 148, 149, 150, 155
Begtrup, Bodily, 226, 227
Beijing Conference, 225, 230

Free Democratic Party (FDP; Germany), 119, 120
Freeman, Jo, 18
Front National (FN; France), 117

Gandhi, Indira, 141, 168, 169
Gandhi, Sonia, 168, 169
gender: and equality, 1–2; ignored in Northern Ireland, 35, 109–10; and representation, 18, 233, *see also* representation, of women
'gender dealignment', 56
gender gap: in voting patterns, 56, 57, 68; and women's interests, 235 n. 10
gender-neutrality, 17
Georgiana, duchess of Devonshire, 95
Germany: electoral system in, 161; influence of Greens in, 88–9; political parties in, 89, 119; quotas in, 78, 88–9; voting patterns in, 119; women in cabinet in, 161; women MPs in, 4, 161; women's political participation in, 118–20
Ghana: democratic decentralization in, 204; women in local government in, 177
Gilligan, Carol, 22
Githens, Marianne, 51, 52
Godman, Trish, 151
Gorman, Theresa, 64
government, local, *see* local government
government, regional, *see* local government
government, sub-national, *see* local government
Grant, Bernie, 183
Greater London Authority (GLA), 146, 180, 180–1
Greater London Council (GLC): women's committee of, 188–9
Greece: women's party in, 136
Green Party: in Germany, 88, 119, 120, 137, 161; in France, 137; in Ireland, 115; in UK, 100, 106, 111; UK women MEPs from, 85, 215; and women's parties, 136, 137
Grey, Sandra, 34
Guarnieri, Albina, 165

Hammerskjøld, Dag, 230
Harman, Harriet, 102, 148, 149, 150, 155
Harney, Mary, 115, 158
Hart, Edwina, 152
Hewitt, Patricia, 149, 150, 155
Hironaka, Wakako, 167
House of Representatives (US): elections for, 62
Howard, Michael, 104
Howard Davis, Rebecca, 143–4
Hume, John
Hutt, Jane, 84, 152

Iceland: enfranchisement of women in, 48; no quotas in, 87, 88; women in cabinet in, 159; women MPs in, 158; women and political parties in, 96; women's political parties in, 30, 33, 88, 98, 137
IGOs, 9; *see* European Union; United Nations
India, 6; enfranchisement of women in, 51; equality legislation in, 168, 201–2; reserved seats (quotas) for women in, 78, 90–1, 168–9, 201, 205; women candidates in, 169; women in local government in, 27–8, 201–2; women MPs in, 168; women voters in, 168
inequality, gender: supply/demand-side explanations of, 2
interests: gender-specific, 20, 26, 144, 235 n. 10; versus perspectives, 20; political, 18–19, 20
International Union of Local Authorities (IULA): and inclusion of women, 176, 205
Ireland, Republic of, 8; change and tradition in, 115, 158; local government in, 193–4; voting system in, 158; women in Dáil of, 157–8; women and political parties in, 96, 113–15, 158, 194
Irish Labour Party: gender quotas in, 115; women candidates from, 157
Israel: cultural factors and women's political participation in, 171; quotas in, 89–90; women MPs in, 171; women's lists in, 136
Italy: quotas in, 89; women MEPs from, 214; women politicians in, 233

Jamieson, Cathy, 151
Japan: women and political parties in, 96; women's electoral fortunes in, 71–2, 167
Jay, Baroness, 149
Jayaraman, Jayalalitha, 169
Jewett, Pauline, 165
Jospin, Lionel, 160
Jowell, Tessa, 149, 150
Juppe, Alain, 160
justice: and discrimination, 22, 232

Kanter, Elisabeth Moss, 23
Kawaguchi, Yoriko, 168
Kelly, Petra, 120
Kernot, Cheryl, 124
Kirner, Joan, 200
Kochkina, Elena, 162
Koike, Yuriki, 168
Kolinsky, Eva, 88
Kollontai, Alexandra, 49
Kubota, Manae, 167
Kuchma, Liudmyla, 135
Kuhn, Fritz, 120
Kunast, Renate, 161
Kuzio, Taras, 135